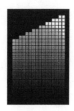

Knowledge and Strategy

Resources for the Knowledge-Based Economy

KNOWLEDGE AND STRATEGY
Michael H. Zack

KNOWLEDGE AND SPECIAL LIBRARIES
James M. Matarazzo and Suzanne D. Connolly

RISE OF THE KNOWLEDGE WORKER
James W. Cortada

THE ECONOMIC IMPACT OF KNOWLEDGE
Dale Neef, G. Anthony Siesfeld, and Jacquelyn Cefola

THE KNOWLEDGE ECONOMY
Dale Neef

KNOWLEDGE IN ORGANIZATIONS
Laurence Prusak

KNOWLEDGE MANAGEMENT AND ORGANIZATIONAL DESIGN
Paul S. Myers

KNOWLEDGE MANAGEMENT TOOLS
Rudy L. Ruggles III

Knowledge and Strategy

Edited by
Michael H. Zack

BUTTERWORTH
HEINEMANN

Boston   Oxford   Auckland   Johannesburg   Melbourne   New Delhi

Butterworth-Heinemann supports the efforts of the American Forests and the Global Releaf program in its campaign for the betterment of trees, forests, and our environment.

Library of Congress Cataloging-in-Publication Data

Knowledge and strategy / edited by Michael H. Zack.
    p. cm.
  Includes bibliographical references and index.
  ISBN 0-7506-7088-6 (alk. paper)
   1. Knowledge management. 2. Information technology. 3. Strategic
  planning. 4. Organization. I. Zack, Michael H.
  HD30.2.K636   1999
  658.4'012—dc21

                                99-18731
                                    CIP

British Library Cataloguing-in-Publication Data
A catalogue record for this book is available from the British Library.

The publisher offers special discounts on bulk orders of this book.
For information, please contact:
Manager of Special Sales
Butterworth–Heinemann
225 Wildwood Avenue
Woburn, MA 01801–2041
Tel: 781-904-2500
Fax: 781-904-2620

For information on all Butterworth–Heinemann publications available, contact our World Wide Web home page at: http://www.bh.com

10 9 8 7 6 5 4 3 2 1

Printed in the United States of America

Contents

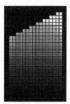

Introduction

KNOWLEDGE AND STRATEGY

The concept of treating organizational knowledge as a valuable strategic asset has become quite popular recently. Organizations are being advised by management theorists and consultants alike that to remain competitive, they must efficiently and effectively create, capture, harvest, share, and apply their organization's knowledge and expertise. Further, they must have the dynamic capability to bring that knowledge to bear rapidly on problems and opportunities as they emerge.

Knowledge management efforts have been primarily focused on developing new applications of information technology, supplemented to a lesser degree with implementing new organizational forms. The link between knowledge and business strategy has essentially been ignored. Thus knowledge management has, *de facto,* become an issue of information technology first, followed by organizational behavior as a distant second, with business strategy not even in the running. Although the discussions about knowledge often start at a more strategic level, they quickly move to issues of application design, knowledge repository architecture, search engines, and the like. The tangible easily drives out the ethereal. Using knowledge to create strategic advantage and business value makes intuitive sense, but the strategic issues quickly become dominated by the latest technology.

This situation is reminiscent of information technology in the 1970s, when the unguided assumption also was that automation was good business. Information technology (IT) implemented without some guiding context, however, did not provide the level of value that was expected. This productivity paradox has been widely reported. However, by the 1980s, the notion of tying information technology to the firm's business strategy was coming into vogue, with promises of significantly greater return for the IT dollar. And today this approach has become the mantra of most MIS directors, CIOs, and even a few CEOs.

But as Santayana said, "Those who cannot remember the past are condemned to repeat it." So why have we forgotten? What is different about using information technology for managing knowledge? For one, knowledge management technologies are relatively more exciting. They've captured our attention like children in a video arcade, and we can't wait to get them up and running. All it takes is a glitzy demonstration of an intranet to the senior executives. Who would not get more excited by multimedia groupware or the World Wide Web than by a cost accounting system? But perhaps more importantly, we had access to economic and strategic models such as the "five forces" model developed by Michael Porter, that helped us to link the use of the more traditional applications of information technology to business strategy. They provided a strategic rationale for investing in the technology and guidance as to the applications that would yield the greatest strategic impact. Those models were appropriate for evaluating the transaction processing systems representing the infrastructure underlying Porter's "value system" and, to a lesser degree, to the control systems such as those used in TQM, customer service, and quick response programs. But those economic models were not intended to guide strategic decisions regarding the dynamic creation and application of knowledge.

We are missing the strategic perspective on knowledge management. We do not have well-developed strategic models today that help us to link knowledge-oriented technologies and organizational forms to business strategy. We need a pragmatic, yet theoretically sound model of what I call *knowledge strategy*. Knowledge strategy is a natural extension of the historical development of business strategy in general, and what we know about strategic management sets the foundation for its development.

BUSINESS STRATEGY

Raise the issue of business strategy with anyone exposed to a formal business education and the first thing that typically comes to mind is "SWOT." SWOT stand for strengths, weaknesses, opportunities, and threats. It is a framework for strategic planning made popular by Ken Andrews of the Harvard Business School in the mid-1960s, and has since influenced both practice and research in the field of strategic management. Performing a SWOT analysis involves describing and analyzing a firm's internal capabilities—its strengths and weaknesses—relative to the external opportunities and threats of the competitive marketplace. Organizations are advised to take strategic actions to preserve or sustain strengths, offset weaknesses, avert or mitigate threats, and capitalize on opportunities. Strategy can be seen as the balancing act performed by the firm as it straddles the high wire strung between the external environment (opportunities and threats) and the internal capabilities of the firm (strengths and weaknesses).

Application of the SWOT framework has been dominated during the last 20 years by Michael Porter's "five forces" model. This model focuses on the external side of the strategic balancing act, helping firms to understand those forces in an industry that give rise to opportunities and threats. The five forces that impinge on a firm's ability to earn profits in an industry and therefore determine the attractiveness of participating in that industry are (1) the bargaining power of customers, (2) the bargaining power of suppliers, (3) the threat of new entrants, (4) the threat of substitute products, and (5) the strength and nature of traditional rivalry among firms in the industry. Industries structured so as to enable firms to dictate terms to its suppliers and customers and to provide barriers to new entrants and substitute products are seen as favorable. Strategy becomes a matter of choosing an appropriate industry and positioning the firm in that industry according to a generic strategy of either low cost or product differentiation.

While enjoying much popularity, in no small part because it was perhaps the first attempt to apply solid economic thinking to strategic management in a practical and understandable way, the five forces model has come under some criticism of late. The economic theory behind the Porter model was developed to help formulate federal antitrust policy. The theory was initially focused on understanding how the structure of a particular industry might enable collusion and monopoly profits to be earned by firms in that industry. The model therefore is more concerned with the profitability of industries rather than firms. The assumption is that firms, *per se*, do not matter with regard to profit performance. It is the overall pattern of relationships among firms in the industry, not the firms themselves, that makes the difference. If the industry as a whole is structured properly (i.e., with sufficient barriers and other impediments to competition), then all firms should realize excess returns.

Although the theory behind the Porter model had little to say about what any particular firm should do, the model has been applied for years to strategic planning for individual firms within an industry. One criticism is that it does not help particular firms to identify and leverage unique and therefore sustainable advantages. However, perhaps the most important criticism comes from studies showing that characteristics of particular firms within an industry *can* make a difference in terms of profit performance. To address this criticism and to put balance back into the original notion of business strategy, recent work in the area of strategic management and economic theory has begun to focus on the internal side of the equation—the firm's capabilities. A review of any recent management periodical demonstrates how firms are being exhorted to compete based on their unique or distinctive capabilities, competences, and resources. This new perspective is referred to as the *resource-based view* of the firm.

Strategic management models, including Porter's, traditionally have defined the firm's strategy in terms of its product/market positioning—the products it makes and the markets it serves. The resource-based approach, however, prescribes that firms position themselves strategically based on their *resources and capabilities* rather than on the products and services derived from those capabilities. Resources and capabilities, especially organizational skills and practices learned over time, can become highly unique to a particular firm and hard to imitate by others. Competitive advantage based on resources and capabilities therefore is potentially much more sustainable than that based on product and market positioning. The firm's resources and capabilities can be thought of as a platform from which the firm derives various products for various markets. Leveraging the firm's capabilities across markets and products, rather than targeting specific products for specific markets, becomes the strategic driver. Products and markets may come and go, but the firm's capabilities are more enduring. Therefore, creating strategy based on unique resources and capabilities provides a more long-term view of strategy than the traditional approach, and one more robust in today's uncertain and dynamic competitive environment.

TOWARD A MODEL OF KNOWLEDGE STRATEGY

Today, *knowledge* is being considered the most important strategic resource, and the ability to create and apply it the most important capability for building and sustaining competitive advantage. Intuitively, it makes sense that the firm that knows more about its customers, products, technologies, markets, and their linkages should perform better. Resource-based theories of the firm offer the promise of a solid intellectual foundation for validating these (to a large extent unsupported) claims made for knowledge by the popular press. This view is leading to a further development in resource-based economic theory called the *knowledge-based view* of the firm. The firm is seen primarily as a vehicle for creating, integrating, storing, and applying knowledge.

In the past, knowledge has been treated like air. It is ubiquitous, invisible, taken for granted, and never explicitly valued or managed. However, in today's dynamic global economy, none of the old rules apply. Today's firms must explicitly address a range of decisions regarding the creation, development, and maintenance of their knowledge resources and capabilities. The problem is that there is yet little solid guidance for the practicing manager. Although much is beginning to be written about processes and infrastructures for sharing and codifying knowledge (especially using new forms of information technology such as electronic mail, groupware, and the World Wide Web), little is being done from a *strategic* perspective regarding key knowledge resource decisions.

Firms embracing the knowledge-based view of the world have many difficult questions to answer in formulating their *knowledge strategy*. If we update the original model of strategy to reflect today's knowledge-intensive environment, then knowledge strategy becomes the way in which the firm balances its *knowledge* resources and *knowledge processing* capabilities with the knowledge required to create its products for its markets in a manner superior to its competitors. In essence, firms need to perform a *knowledge-based* SWOT analysis.

Identifying which knowledge is a unique and valuable resource, which knowledge processes represent unique and valuable capabilities, and how those resources and capabilities support the firm's product and market positions are the essential elements of a knowledge strategy. The firm must identify what is has to "know" for a given product/market position. Every firm requires some level of knowledge about its technology, markets, products, customers, and industry merely to participate and hold its own in its industry. The strategic choices that companies make regarding these factors directly influence what the firm and its members must know to effectively compete. Strategic choices such as whether to provide products or services, engage in manufacturing or assembly, and compete through low cost or differentiation have a profound influence on the knowledge, skills, and core competencies required to compete and excel in an industry. These choices all set the stage for the development of future knowledge through the processes of learning and innovation.

Conversely, the firm, given what it knows, must identify the best product and market opportunities for exploiting that knowledge. The creation of unique, strategic knowledge takes time, forcing the firm to balance short- and long-term strategic resource decisions. The firm therefore must determine whether its efforts are best focused on knowledge creation, exploitation, or both, and then balance its knowledge processing resources and efforts accordingly.

Knowledge and learning go hand in hand. Defending and growing a given knowledge position is most effectively accomplished by continual organizational learning. The ability of an organization to learn, accumulate knowledge from its experiences, and reapply that knowledge is itself a skill or competence that, beyond the core competencies directly related to delivering its product or service, may provide strategic advantage.

The firm must determine those properties of knowledge and the processes for its creation, transfer, and utilization that provide a competitive advantage yet are not easily imitated by other firms. All signs point to the value of tacit, situated, collective knowledge built from practical experience and embedded in the routines and memories of the organization's members as being the highest value and hardest to imitate form of knowledge. However, growing a knowledge-based firm requires sharing that knowledge among members of the organization, and that often requires its articulation and codification. This presents a paradox: On the one hand, knowledge must be made explicit and transferable to share it among the firm. Yet, once made explicit, it is subject to being appropriated by other firms, reducing or eliminating its competitive value.

Looking externally to its competitors, the firm must assess the knowledge resources and capabilities required by its industry merely to "play the game," those required to be competitive, and those required to be uniquely innovative. In addition to assessing its capabilities to produce the products it sells to the markets it serves, the firm must evaluate its capabilities relative to its competitors. For example, if the firm intends to be a unique innovator, is its knowledge position appropriate to that role and superior to its competition? Does the firm have all of the knowledge it needs to compete in those markets or is some form of strategic alliance required to complement its knowledge resources? Is it vulnerable in some markets or products due to knowledge resources that lag its competitors?

These questions and others need to be rigorously and systematically addressed to turn today's knowledge management movement into a theory of knowledge strategy and an enduring way to do business in the 21st century. If knowledge management is to take hold rather than become merely a passing fad, it will have to be solidly linked the creation of economic value and competitive advantage. This can be accomplished by grounding knowledge management within the context of business strategy. Today we are just beginning this quest.

Although much work remains to be done to directly and systematically examine the link between strategy, knowledge, and performance in business organizations, many things have been written that do address the issue and hence form a useful place to begin the discussion. The articles in this book offer some of the intellectual foundation for developing the concept of knowledge strategy. They address several themes and perspectives.

The articles in Part One provide background on the resource-based view of the firm. Grant, Collis, and Montgomery provide highly readable overviews of the theory and its relationship to competing on capabilities. The article by Prahalad and Hamel provides interesting real-world examples.

The articles in Part Two use the resource-based view as a jumping-off point to explicitly consider knowledge as a key strategic resource. This part leads with an excerpt from a book by Edith Penrose, who is credited with originating the resource- and knowledge-based theories of the firm, proposing that competitive advantage comes from combining resources with the unique knowledge of the firm. An article by Paul Romer, a leading contemporary economist whose work builds on that of Penrose, discusses the role of knowledge in today's economy. The works by Teece *et al.*, Spender, and Grant elaborate on the theme of knowledge as a strategic resource and capability.

The articles in Part Three examine characteristics of knowledge that enable it to function as a strategic resource and the implications for its management. Winter develops a taxonomy of knowledge and identifies strategic implications. Hall provides a useful framework for classifying intangible assets in general. Liebeskind raises strategic issues that must be addressed in managing knowledge assets.

The articles in Part Four explicitly relate knowledge and strategy. Saint-Onge makes the case in highly pragmatic terms that strategy drives knowledge and knowledge influences the capability to execute strategy. Bierly and Chakrabarti identify several important dimensions of a firm's knowledge strategy and use that to define four strategy archetypes. Boisot discusses the strategic issues around protecting versus diffusing a firm's knowledge. The article by Quinn *et al.* provides valuable guidance on managing knowledge to create competitive advantage.

Part One
The Resource-Based View of the Firm

1

The Resource-Based Theory of Competitive Advantage: Implications for Strategy Formulation

Robert M. Grant

Strategy has been defined as "the match an organization makes between its internal resources and skills . . . and the opportunities and risks created by its external environment."[1] *During the 1980s, the principal developments in strategy analysis focussed upon the link between strategy and* the external environment. Prominent examples of this focus are Michael Porter's analysis of industry structure and competitive positioning and the empirical studies undertaken by the PIMS project.[2] By contrast, the link between strategy and the firm's resources and skills has suffered comparative neglect. Most research into the strategic implications of the firm's internal environment has been concerned with issues of strategy implementation and analysis of the organizational processes through which strategies emerge.[3]

Recently there has been a resurgence of interest in the role of the firm's resources as the foundation for firm strategy. This interest reflects dissatisfaction with the static, equilibrium framework of industrial organization economics that has dominated much contemporary thinking about business strategy and has renewed interest in older theories of profit and competition associated with the writings of David Ricardo, Joseph Schumpeter, and Edith Penrose.[4] Advances have occurred on several fronts. At the corporate strategy level, theoretical interest in economies of scope and transaction costs have focussed attention on the role of corporate resources in determining the industrial and geographical boundaries of the firm's activities.[5] At the business strategy level, explorations of

From *California Management Review*, Vol. 33, No. 3, Spring 1991, pp. 114–135. Copyright © 1991, by The Regents of the University of California. Reprinted by permission of The Regents.

the relationships between resources, competition, and profitability include the analysis of competitive imitation,[6] the appropriability of returns to innovations,[7] the role of imperfect information in creating profitability differences between competing firms,[8] and the means by which the process of resource accumulation can sustain competitive advantage.[9]

Together, these contributions amount to what has been termed "the resource-based view of the firm." As yet, however, the implications of this "resource-based theory" for strategic management are unclear for two reasons. First, the various contributions lack a single integrating framework. Second, little effort has been made to develop the practical implications of this theory. The purpose of this article is to make progress on both these fronts by proposing a framework for a resource-based approach to strategy formulation which integrates a number of the key themes arising from this stream of literature. The organizing framework for the article is a five-stage procedure for strategy formulation: analyzing the firm's resource base; appraising the firm's capabilities; analyzing the profit-earning potential of firm's resources and capabilities; selecting a strategy; and extending and upgrading the firm's pool of resources and capabilities. Figure 1.1 outlines this framework.

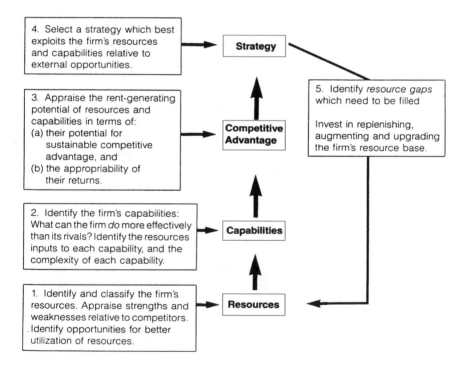

FIGURE 1.1 A Resource-Based Approach to Strategy Analysis: A Practical Framework

RESOURCES AND CAPABILITIES AS THE FOUNDATION FOR STRATEGY

The case for making the resources and capabilities of the firm the foundation for its long-term strategy rests upon two premises: first, internal resources and capabilities provide the basic direction for a firm's strategy, second, resources and capabilities are the primary source of profit for the firm.

Resources and Capabilities as a Source of Direction

The starting point for the formulation of strategy must be some statement of the firm's identity and purpose—conventionally this takes the form of a mission statement which answers the question: "What is our business?" Typically the definition of the business is in terms of the served market of the firm: e.g., "Who are our customers?" and "Which of their needs are we seeking to serve?" But in a world where customer preferences are volatile, the identity of customers is changing, and the technologies for serving customer requirements are continually evolving, an externally focused orientation does not provide a secure foundation for formulating long-term strategy. When the external environment is in a state of flux, the firm's own resources and capabilities may be a much more stable basis on which to define its identity. Hence, a definition of a business in terms of what it is capable of doing may offer a more durable basis for strategy than a definition based upon the needs which the business seeks to satisfy.

Theodore Levitt's solution to the problem of external change was that companies should define their served markets broadly rather than narrowly: railroads should have perceived themselves to be in the transportation business, not the railroad business. But such broadening of the target market is of little value if the company cannot easily develop the capabilities required for serving customer requirements across a wide front. Was it feasible for the railroads to have developed successful trucking, airline, and car rental businesses? Perhaps the resources and capabilities of the railroad companies were better suited to real estate development, or the building and managing of oil and gas pipelines. Evidence suggests that serving broadly defined customer needs is a difficult task. The attempts by Merrill Lynch, American Express, Sears, Citicorp, and, most recently, Prudential-Bache to "serve the full range of our customers' financial needs" created serious management problems. Allegis Corporation's goal of "serving the needs of the traveler" through combining United Airlines, Hertz car rental, and Westin Hotels was a costly failure. By contrast, several companies whose strategies have been based upon developing and exploiting clearly defined internal capabilities have been adept at adjusting to and exploiting external change. Honda's focus upon the technical excellence of 4-cycle engines carried it successfully from motorcycles to automobiles to a broad range of gasoline-engine products. 3M Corporation's expertise in applying adhesive and coating technologies to new product development has permitted profitable growth over an ever-widening product range.

Resources as the Basis for Corporate Profitability

A firm's ability to earn a rate of profit in excess of its cost of capital depends upon two factors: the attractiveness of the industry in which it is located, and its establishment of competitive advantage over rivals. Industrial organization economics emphasizes industry attractiveness as the primary basis for superior profitability, the implication being that strategic management is concerned primarily with seeking favorable industry environments, locating attractive segments and strategic groups within industries, and moderating competitive pressures by influencing industry structure and competitors' behavior. Yet empirical investigation has failed to support the link between industry structure and profitability. Most studies show that differences in profitability within industries are much more important than differences between industries.[10] The reasons are not difficult to find: international competition, technological change, and diversification by firms across industry boundaries have meant that industries which were once cozy havens for making easy profits are now subject to vigorous competition.

The finding that competitive advantage rather than external environments is the primary source of inter-firm profit differentials between firms focuses attention upon the sources of competitive advantage. Although the competitive strategy literature has tended to emphasize issues of strategic positioning in terms of the choice between cost and differentiation advantage, and between broad and narrow market scope, fundamental to these choices is the resource position of the firm. For example, the ability to establish a cost advantage requires possession of scale-efficient plants, superior process technology, ownership of low-cost sources of raw materials, or access to low-wage labor. Similarly, differentiation advantage is conferred by brand reputation, proprietary technology, or an extensive sales and service network.

This may be summed up as follows: business strategy should be viewed less as a quest for monopoly rents (the returns to market power) and more as a quest for Ricardian rents (the returns to the resources which confer competitive advantage over and above the real costs of these resources). Once these resources depreciate, become obsolescent, or are replicated by other firms, so the rents they generate tend to disappear.[11]

We can go further. A closer look at market power and the monopoly rent it offers, suggests that it too has its basis in the resources of firms. The fundamental prerequisite for market power is the presence of barriers to entry.[12] Barriers to entry are based upon scale economies, patents, experience advantages, brand reputation, or some other resource which incumbent firms possess but which entrants can acquire only slowly or at disproportionate expense. Other structural sources of market power are similarly based upon firms' resources: monopolistic price-setting power depends upon market share which is a consequence of cost efficiency, financial strength, or some other resource. The resources which confer market power may be owned individually by firms, others may be owned jointly. An industry standard (which raises costs of entry), or a cartel, is a resource which is owned collectively by the industry members.[13] Figure 1.2 summarizes the relationships between resources and profitability.

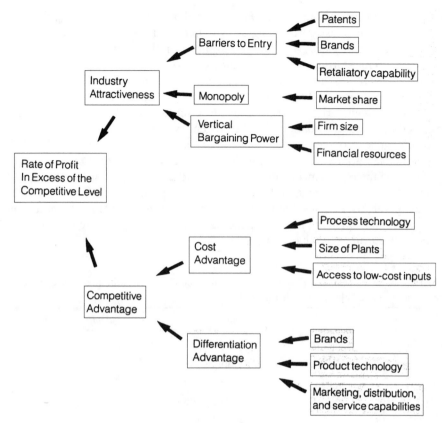

FIGURE 1.2 Resources as the Basis for Profitability

TAKING STOCK OF THE FIRM'S RESOURCES

There is a key distinction between resources and capabilities. Resources are inputs into the production process—they are the basic units of analysis. The individual resources of the firm include items of capital equipment, skills of individual employees, patents, brand names, finance, and so on.

But, on their own, few resources are productive. Productive activity requires the cooperation and coordination of teams of resources. A capability is the capacity for a team of resources to perform some task or activity. While resources are the source of a firm's capabilities, capabilities are the main source of its competitive advantage.

Identifying Resources

A major handicap in identifying and appraising a firm's resources is that management information systems typically provide only a fragmented and incomplete picture of the firm's resource base. Financial balance sheets are notoriously inadequate because they disregard intangible resources and people-based skills—probably the most strategically important resources of the firm.[14] Classification can provide a useful starting point. Six major categories of resource have been suggested: financial resources, physical resources, human resources, technological resources, reputation, and organizational resources.[15] The reluctance of accountants to extend the boundaries of corporate balance sheets beyond tangible assets partly reflects difficulties of valuation. The heterogeneity and imperfect transferability of most intangible resources precludes the use of market prices. One approach to valuing intangible resources is to take the difference between the stock market value of the firm and the replacement value of its tangible assets.[16] On a similar basis, valuation ratios provide some indication of the importance of firms' intangible resources. Table 1.1 shows that the highest valuation ratios are found among companies with valuable patents and technology assets (notably drug companies) and brand-rich consumer-product companies.

TABLE 1.1 Twenty Companies Among the U.S. Top 100 Companies with the Highest Ratios of Stock Price to Book Value on March 16, 1990

Company	Industry	Valuation Ratio
Coca Cola	Beverages	8.77
Microsoft	Computer software	8.67
Merck	Pharmaceuticals	8.39
American Home Products	Pharmaceuticals	8.00
Wal Mart Stores	Retailing	7.51
Limited	Retailing	6.65
Warner Lambert	Pharmaceuticals	6.34
Waste Management	Pollution Control	6.18
Marrion Merrell Dow	Pharmaceuticals	6.10
McCaw Cellular Communications	Telecom Equipment	5.90
Bristol Myers Squibb	Pharmaceuticals	5.48
Toys R Us	Retailing	5.27
Abbot Laboratories	Pharmaceuticals	5.26
Walt Disney	Entertainment	4.90
Johnson & Johnson	Health care products	4.85
MCI Communications	Telecommunications	4.80
Eli Lilly	Pharmaceuticals	4.70
Kellogg	Food products	4.58
H.J. Heinz	Food products	4.38
Pepsico	Beverages	4.33

Source: The 1990 Business Week Top 1000

The primary task of a resource-based approach to strategy formulation is maximizing rents over time. For this purpose we need to investigate the relationship between resources and organizational capabilities. However, there are also direct links between resources and profitability which raise issues for the strategic management of resources:

- *What opportunities exist for economizing on the use of resources?* The ability to maximize productivity is particularly important in the case of tangible resources such as plant and machinery, finance, and people. It may involve using fewer resources to support the same level of business, or using the existing resources to support a larger volume of business. The success of aggressive acquirers, such as ConAgra in the U.S. and Hanson in Britain, is based upon expertise in rigorously pruning the financial, physical, and human assets needed to support the volume of business in acquired companies.
- *What are the possibilities for using existing assets more intensely and in more profitable employment?* A large proportion of corporate acquisitions are motivated by the belief that the resources of the acquired company can be put to more profitable use. The returns from transferring existing assets into more productive employment can be substantial. The remarkable turnaround in the performance of the Walt Disney Company between 1985 and 1987 owed much to the vigorous exploitation of Disney's considerable and unique assets: accelerated development of Disney's vast landholdings (for residential development as well as entertainment purposes), exploitation of Disney's huge film library through cable TV, videos, and syndication; fuller utilization of Disney's studios through the formation of Touchstone Films; increased marketing to improve capacity utilization at Disney theme parks.

IDENTIFYING AND APPRAISING CAPABILITIES

The capabilities of a firm are what it can do as a result of teams of resources working together. A firm's capabilities can be identified and appraised using a standard functional classification of the firm's activities.

For example, Snow and Hrebimak examined capabilities (in their terminology, "distinctive competencies") in relation to ten functional areas.[17] For most firms, however, the most important capabilities are likely to be those which arise from an integration of individual functional capabilities. For example, McDonald's possesses outstanding functional capabilities within product development, market research, human resource management, financial control, and operations management. However, critical to McDonald's success is the integration of these functional capabilities to create McDonald's remarkable consistency of products and services in thousands of restaurants spread across most of the globe. Hamel and Prahalad use the term "core competencies" to describe these central, strategic capabilities. They are "the collective learning in the organization, especially how to coordinate diverse production skills and integrate multiple streams of technology."[18] Examples of core competencies include:

- NEC's integration of computer and telecommunications technology
- Philips' optical-media expertise

- Casio's harmonization of know-how in miniaturization, microprocessor design, material science, and ultra thin precision casting
- Canon's integration of optical, microelectronic, and precision-mechanical technologies which forms the basis of its success in cameras, copiers, and facsimile machines
- Black and Decker's competence in the design and manufacture of small electric motors

A key problem in appraising capabilities is maintaining objectivity. Howard Stevenson observed a wide variation in senior managers' perceptions of their organizations' distinctive competencies.[19] Organizations frequently fall victim to past glories, hopes for the future, and wishful thinking. Among the failed industrial companies of both America and Britain are many which believed themselves world leaders with superior products and customer loyalty. During the 1960s, the CEOs of both Harley Davidson and BSA-Triumph scorned the idea that Honda threatened their supremacy in the market for "serious motorcycles."[20] The failure of the U.S. steel companies to respond to increasing import competition during the 1970s was similarly founded upon misplaced confidence in their quality and technological leadership.[21]

The critical task is to assess capabilities relative to those of competitors. In the same way that national prosperity is enhanced through specialization on the basis of comparative advantages, so for the firm, a successful strategy is one which exploits relative strengths. Federal Express's primary capabilities are those which permit it to operate a national delivery system that can guarantee next day delivery; for the British retailer Marks and Spencer, it is the ability to manage supplier relations to ensure a high and consistent level of product quality; for General Electric, it is a system of corporate management that reconciles control, coordination, flexibility, and innovation in one of the world's largest and most diversified corporations. Conversely, failure is often due to strategies which extend the firm's activities beyond the scope of its capabilities.

Capabilities as Organizational Routines

Creating capabilities is not simply a matter of assembling a team of resources: capabilities involve complex patterns of coordination between people and between people and other resources. Perfecting such coordination requires learning through repetition. To understand the anatomy of a firm's capabilities, Nelson and Winter's concept of "organizational routine" is illuminating. Organizational routines are regular and predictable patterns of activity which are made up of a sequence of coordinated actions by individuals. A capability is, in essence, a routine, or a number of interacting routines. The organization itself is a huge network of routines. These include the sequence of routines which govern the passage of raw material and components through the production process, and top management routines which include routines for monitoring business unit performance, for capital budgeting, and for strategy formulation.

The concept of organizational routines offers illuminating insights into the relationships between resources, capabilities, and competitive advantage:

- *The relationship between resources and capabilities.* There is no predetermined functional relationship between the resources of a firm and its capabilities. The types, the amounts, and the qualities of the resources available to the firm have an important bearing on what the firm can do since they place constraints upon the range of organizational routines that can be performed and the standard to which they are performed. However, a key ingredient in the relationship between resources and capabilities is the ability of an organization to achieve cooperation and coordination within teams. This requires that an organization motivate and socialize its members in a manner conducive to the development of smooth-functioning routines. The organization's style, values, traditions, and leadership are critical encouragements to the cooperation and commitment of its members. These can be viewed as intangible resources which are common ingredients of the whole range of a corporation's organizational routines.

- *The trade-off between efficiency and flexibility.* Routines are to the organization what skills are to the individual. Just as the individual's skills are carried out semi-automatically, without conscious coordination, so organizational routines involve a large component of tacit knowledge, which implies limits on the extent to which the organization's capabilities can be articulated. Just as individual skills become rusty when not exercised, so it is difficult for organizations to retain coordinated responses to contingencies that arise only rarely. Hence there may be a trade-off between efficiency and flexibility. A limited repertoire of routines can be performed highly efficiently with near-perfect coordination—all in the absence of significant intervention by top management. The same organization may find it extremely difficult to respond to novel situations.

- *Economies of experience.* Just as individual skills are acquired through practice over time, so the skills of an organization are developed and sustained only through experience. The advantage of an established firm over a newcomer is primarily in the organizational routines that it has perfected over time. The Boston Consulting Group's "experience curve" represents a naive, yet valuable attempt to relate the experience of the firm to its performance. However, in industries where technological change is rapid, new firms may possess an advantage over established firms through their potential for faster learning of new routines because they are less committed to old routines.

- *The complexity of capabilities.* Organizational capabilities differ in their complexity. Some capabilities may derive from the contribution of a single resource. Du Pont's successful development of several cardiovascular drugs during the late 1980s owed much to the research leadership of its leading pharmacologist Pieter Timmermans.[22] Drexel Burnham Lambert's capability in junk bond underwriting during the 1980s resided almost entirely in the skills of Michael Millken. Other routines require highly complex interactions involving the cooperation of many different resources. Walt Disney's "imagineering" capability involves the integration of ideas, skills, and knowledge drawn from movie making, engineering, psychology, and a wide variety of technical disciplines. As we shall see, complexity is particularly relevant to the sustainability of competitive advantage.

EVALUATING THE RENT-EARNING
POTENTIAL: SUSTAINABILITY

The returns to a firm's resources and capabilities depend upon two key factors: first, the sustainability of the competitive advantage which resources and capabilities confer upon the firm; and, second, the ability of the firm to appropriate the rents earned from its resources and capabilities.

Over the long-term, competitive advantage and the returns associated with it are eroded both through the depreciation of the advantaged firm's resources and capabilities and through imitation by rivals. The speed of erosion depends critically upon the characteristics of the resources and capabilities. Consider markets where competitive advantage is unsustainable: in "efficient" markets (most closely approximated by the markets for securities, commodities, and foreign exchange) competitive advantage is absent; market prices reflect all available information, prices adjust instantaneously to new information, and traders can only expect normal returns.

The absence of competitive advantage is a consequence of the resources required to compete in these markets. To trade in financial markets, the basic requirements are finance and information. If both are available on equal terms to all participants, competitive advantage cannot exist. Even if privileged information is assumed to exist ("weakly efficient" markets), competitive advantage is not sustainable. Once a trader acts upon privileged information, transactions volume and price movements signal insider activity, and other traders are likely to rush in seeking a piece of the action.

The essential difference between industrial markets and financial markets lies in the resource requirements of each. In industrial markets, resources are specialized, immobile, and long-lasting. As a result, according to Richard Caves, a key feature of industrial markets is the existence of "committed competition-rivalrous moves among incumbent producers that involve resource commitments that are irrevocable for non-trivial periods of time."[23] The difficulties involved in acquiring the resources required to compete and the need to commit resources long before a competitive move can be initiated also implies that competitive advantage is much more sustainable than it is in financial markets. Resource-based approaches to the theory of competitive advantage point towards four characteristics of resources and capabilities which are likely to be particularly important determinants of the sustainability of competitive advantage: durability, transparency, transferability, and replicability.

Durability

In the absence of competition, the longevity of a firm's competitive advantage depends upon the rate at which the underlying resources and capabilities depreciate or become obsolete. The durability of resources varies considerably: the increasing pace of technological change is shortening the useful life-spans of most capital equipment and technological resources. On the other hand, reputation (both brand and corporate) appears to depreciate relatively slowly, and these assets can normally be maintained by modest rates of replacement investment. Many of the consumer brands which command the strongest loyalties today (e.g., Heinz sauces, Kellogg's cereals, Campbell's soup, Hoover vacuum cleaners) have been market leaders for close to a century. Corporate reputation displays similar longevity: the reputations of GE, IBM, Du Pont, and Proctor and Gamble as well-managed, socially responsible, financially sound companies which produce reliable products and treat their employees well has been established over several decades. While increasing environmental turbulence shortens the life spans of many resources, it is possible that it may have the effect of bolstering brand and corporate reputations.

Firm capabilities have the potential to be more durable than the resources upon which they are based because of the firm's ability to maintain capabilities through replacing individual resources (including people) as they wear out or move on. Rolls Royce's capability in the craft-based manufacture of luxury cars and 3M's capability in new product introduction have been maintained over several generations of employees. Such longevity depends critically upon the management of these capabilities to ensure their maintenance and renewal. One of the most important roles that organizational culture plays in sustaining competitive advantage may be through its maintenance support for capabilities through the socialization of new employees.[24]

Transparency

The firm's ability to sustain its competitive advantage over time depends upon the speed with which other firms can imitate its strategy. Imitation requires that a competitor overcomes two problems. First is the information problem: What is the competitive advantage of the successful rival, and how is it being achieved? Second is the strategy duplication problem: How can the would-be competitor amass the resources and capabilities required to imitate the successful strategy of the rival? The information problem is a consequence of imperfect information on two sets of relationships. If a firm wishes to imitate the strategy of a rival, it must first establish the capabilities which underlie the rival's competitive advantage, and then it must determine what resources are required to replicate these capabilities. I refer to this as the "transparency" of competitive advantage. With regard to the first transparency problem, a competitive advantage which is the consequence of superior capability in relation to a single performance variable is more easy to identify and comprehend than a competitive advantage that involves multiple capabilities conferring superior performance across several variables. Cray Research's success in the computer industry rests primarily upon its technological capability in relation to large, ultra-powerful computers. IBM's superior performance is multidimensional and is more difficult to understand. It is extremely difficult to distinguish and appraise the relative contributions to IBM's success of research capability, scale economies in product development and manufacturing, self-sufficiency through backward integration, and superior customer service through excellence in sales, service, and technical support.

With regard to the second transparency problem, a capability which requires a complex pattern of coordination between large numbers of diverse resources is more difficult to comprehend than a capability which rests upon the exploitation of a single dominant resource. For example, Federal Express's next-day delivery capability requires close cooperation between numerous employees, aircraft, delivery vans, computerized tracking facilities, and automated sorting equipment, all coordinated into a single system. By contrast, Atlantic Richfield's low-cost position in the supply of gasoline to the California market rests simply on its access to Alaskan crude oil. Imperfect transparency is the basis for Lippman and Rumble's theory of "uncertain imitability": the greater the uncertainty within a market over how successful companies "do it," the more inhibited are potential entrants, and the higher the level of profit that established firms can maintain within that market.[25]

Transferability

Once the established firm or potential entrant has established the sources of the superior performance, imitation then requires amassing the resources and capabilities necessary for a competitive challenge. The primary source of resources and capabilities is likely to be the markets for these inputs. If firms can acquire (on similar terms) the resources required for imitating the competitive advantage of a successful rival, then that rival's competitive advantage will be short lived. As we have seen, in financial markets the easy access by traders to finance and information causes competitive advantage to be fleeting. However, most resources and capabilities are not freely transferable between firms; hence, would-be competitors are unable to acquire (on equal terms) the resources needed to replicate the competitive advantage of an incumbent firm. Imperfections in transferability arise from several sources:

- *Geographical immobility*. The costs of relocating large items of capital equipment and highly specialized employees puts firms which are acquiring these resources at a disadvantage to firms which already possess them.
- *Imperfect information*. Assessing the value of a resource is made difficult by the heterogeneity of resources (particularly human resources) and by imperfect knowledge of the potential productivity of individual resources.[26] The established firm's ability to build up information over time about the productivity of its resources gives it superior knowledge to that of any prospective purchaser of the resources in question.[27] The resulting imperfection of the markets for productive resources can then result in resources being either underpriced or overpriced, thus giving rise to differences in profitability between firms.[28]
- *Firm-specific resources*. Apart from the transactions costs arising from immobility and imperfect information, the value of a resource may fall on transfer due to a decline in its productivity. To the extent that brand reputation is associated with the company which created the brand reputation, a change in ownership of the brand name erodes its value, Once Rover, MG, Triumph, and Jaguar were

merged into British Leyland, the values of these brands in differentiating auto-mobiles declined substantially. Employees can suffer a similar decline in productivity in the process of inter-firm transfer. To the extent that an employee's productivity is influenced by situational and motivational factors, then it is unreasonable to expect that a highly successful employee in one company can replicate his/her performance when hired away by another company. Some resources may be almost entirely firm specific—corporate reputation can only be transferred by acquiring the company as a whole, and even then the reputation of the acquired company normally depreciates during the change in ownership.[29]

- *The immobility of capabilities.* Capabilities, because they require interactive teams of resources, are far more immobile than individual resources—they require the transfer of the whole team. Such transfers can occur (e.g., the defection of 16 of First Boston's mergers and acquisitions staff to Wasserstein, Perella and Company).[30] However. even if the resources that constitute the team are transferred, the nature of organizational routines—in particular, the role of tacit knowledge and unconscious coordination—makes the recreation of capabilities within a new corporate environment uncertain.

Replicability

Imperfect transferability of resources and capabilities limits the ability of a firm to buy in the means to imitate success. The second route by which a firm can acquire a resource or capability is by internal investment. Some resources and capabilities can be easily imitated through replication. In retailing, competitive advantages which derive from electronic point-of-sale systems, retailer charge cards, and extended hours of opening can be copied fairly easily by competitors. In financial services, new product innovations (such as interest rate swaps, stripped bonds, money market accounts, and the like) are notorious for their easy imitation by competitors.

Much less easily replicable are capabilities based upon highly complex organizational routines. IBM's ability to motivate its people and Nucor's outstanding efficiency and flexibility in steel manufacture are combinations of complex routines that are based upon tacit rather than codified knowledge and are fused into the respective corporate cultures. Some capabilities appear simple but prove exceptionally difficult to replicate. Two of the simplest and best-known Japanese manufacturing practices are just-in-time scheduling and quality circles. Despite the fact that neither require sophisticated knowledge or complex operating systems, the cooperation and attitudinal changes required for their effective operation are such that few American and European firms have introduced either with the same degree of success as Japanese companies. If apparently simple practices such as these are deceptively difficult to imitate, it is easy to see how firms that develop highly complex capabilities can maintain their competitive advantage over very long periods of time. Xerox's commitment to customer service is a capability that is not located in any particular department, but it permeates the whole corporation and is built into the fabric and culture of the corporation.

Even where replication is possible, the dynamics of stock-flow relationships may still offer an advantage to incumbent firms. Competitive advantage depends upon the stock of resources and capabilities that a firm possesses. Dierickx and Cool show that firms which possess the initial stocks of the resources required for competitive advantage may be able to sustain their advantages over time.[31] Among the stock-flow relationships they identify as sustaining advantage are: "asset mass efficiencies"—the initial amount of the resource which the firm possesses influences the pace at which the resource can be accumulated; and "time compression diseconomies"—firms which rapidly accumulate a resource incur disproportionate costs ("crash programs" of R&D and "blitz" advertising campaigns tend to be less productive than similar expenditures made over a longer period).

Evaluating Rent-Earning Potential: Appropriability

The returns to a firm from its resources and capabilities depend not only on sustaining its competitive position over time, but also on the firm's ability to appropriate these returns. The issue of appropriability concerns the allocation of rents where property rights are not fully defined. Once we go beyond the financial and physical assets valued in a company's balance sheet, ownership becomes ambiguous. The firm owns intangible assets such as patents, copyrights, brand names, and trade secrets, but the scope of property rights may lack precise definition. In the case of employee skills, two major problems arise: the lack of clear distinction between the technology of the firm and the human capital of the individual; and the limited control which employment contracts offer over the services provided by employees. Employee mobility means that it is risky for a firm's strategy to be dependent upon the specific skills of a few key employees. Also, such employees can bargain with the firm to appropriate the major part of their contribution to value added.

The degree of control exercised by a firm and the balance of power between the firm and an individual employee depends crucially on the relationship between the individual's skills and organizational routines. The more deeply embedded are organizational routines within groups of individuals and the more are they supported by the contributions of other resources, then the greater is the control that the firm's management can exercise. The ability of IBM to utilize its advanced semiconductor research as an instrument of competitive advantage depends, in part, upon the extent to which the research capability is a team asset rather than a reflection of the contribution of brilliant individuals. A firm's dependence upon skills possessed by highly trained and highly mobile key employees is particularly important in the case of professional service companies where employee skills are the overwhelmingly important resource.[32] Many of the problems that have arisen in acquisitions of human-capital-intensive companies arise from conflicts over property rights between the acquiring company and employees of the acquired company. An interesting example is the protracted dispute which followed the acquisition of the New York advertising agency Lord, Geller, Fredrico, Einstein by WPP Group in 1988. Most of the senior executives of the acquired company left to form a new advertising agency taking several former clients with them.[33] Similar conflicts have arisen over technology ownership in high-tech start-ups founded by former employees of established companies.[34]

Where ownership is ambiguous, relative bargaining power is the primary determinant of the allocation of the rents between the firm and its employees. If the individual employee's contribution to productivity is clearly identifiable, if the employee is mobile, and the employee's skills offer similar productivity to other firms, then the employee is well placed to bargain for that contribution. If the increased gate receipts of the L.A. Kings ice hockey team can be attributed primarily to the presence of Wayne Gretzky on the team and if Gretzky can offer a similar performance enhancement to other teams, then he is in a strong position to appropriate (as salary and bonuses) most of the increased contribution. The less identifiable is the individual's contribution, and the more firm-specific are the skills being applied, the greater is the proportion of the return which accrues to the firm. Declining profitability among investment banks encouraged several to reassert their bargaining power vis-a-vis their individual stars and in-house gurus by engineering a transfer of reputation from these key employees to the company as a whole. At Citibank, Salomon Brothers, Merrill Lynch, and First Boston, this resulted in bitter conflicts between top management and some senior employees.[35]

FORMULATING STRATEGY

Although the foregoing discussion of the links between resources, capabilities, and profitability has been strongly theoretical in nature, the implications for strategy formulation are straightforward. The analysis of the rent-generating potential of resources and capabilities concludes that the firm's most important resources and capabilities are those which are durable, difficult to identify and understand, imperfectly transferable, not easily replicated, and in which the firm possesses clear ownership and control. These are the firm's "crown jewels" and need to be protected; and they play a pivotal role in the competitive strategy which the firm pursues. The essence of strategy formulation, then, is to design a strategy that makes the most effective use of these core resources and capabilities. Consider, for example, the remarkable turnaround of Harley-Davidson between 1984 and 1988. Fundamental was top management's recognition that the company's sole durable, non-transferable, irreplicable asset was the Harley-Davidson image and the loyalty that accompanied that image. In virtually every other area of competitive performance—production costs, quality, product and process technology, and global market scope—Harley was greatly inferior to its Japanese rivals. Harley's only opportunity for survival was to pursue a strategy founded upon Harley's image advantage, while simultaneously minimizing Harley's disadvantages in other capabilities. Harley-Davidson's new models introduced during this period were all based around traditional design features, while Harley's marketing strategy involved extending the appeal of the Harley image of individuality and toughness from its traditional customer group to more affluent professional types. Protection of the Harley-Davidson name by means of tougher controls over dealers was matched by wider exploitation of the Harley name through extensive licensing. While radical improvements in manufacturing efficiency and quality were essential components of the turnaround strategy, it was the enhancing and broadening of Harley's market appeal which was the primary driver of Harley's rise from 27 to 44 percent of the U.S. heavyweight motorcycle market between 1984 and 1988, accompanied by an increase in net income from $6.5 million to $29.8 million.

Conversely, a failure to recognize and exploit the strategic importance of durable, untransferable, and irreplicable resources almost inevitably has dire consequences. The troubles of BankAmerica Corporation during the mid-1980s can be attributed to a strategy that became increasingly dissociated from the bank's most important assets: its reputation and market position in retail banking in the Western United States. The disastrous outcome of U.S. Air Group's acquisition of the Californian carrier, PSA, is similarly attributable to U.S. Air's disregard for PSA's most important asset—its reputation in the Californian market for a friendly, laid-back style of service.

Designing strategy around the most critically important resources and capabilities may imply that the firm limits its strategic scope to those activities where it possesses a clear competitive advantage. The principal capabilities of Lotus, the specialist manufacturer of sports cars, are in design and engineering development; it lacked both the manufacturing capabilities or the sales volume to compete effectively in the world's auto market. Lotus's turnaround during the 1980s followed its decision to specialize upon design and development consulting for other auto manufacturers, and to limit its own manufacturing primarily to formula one racing cars.

The ability of a firm's resources and capabilities to support a sustainable competitive advantage is essential to the time frame of a firm's strategic planning process. If a company's resources and capabilities lack durability or are easily transferred or replicated, then the company must either adopt a strategy of short-term harvesting or it must invest in developing new sources of competitive advantage. These considerations are critical for small technological start-ups where the speed of technological change may mean that innovations offer only temporary competitive advantage. The company must seek either to exploit its initial innovation before it is challenged by stronger, established rivals or other start-ups, or it must establish the technological capability for a continuing stream of innovations. A fundamental flaw in EMI's exploitation of its invention of the CT scanner was a strategy that failed to exploit EMI's five-year technical lead in the development and marketing of the X-ray scanner and failed to establish the breadth of technological and manufacturing capability required to establish a fully fledged medical electronics business.

Where a company's resources and capabilities are easily transferable or replicable, sustaining a competitive advantage is only feasible if the company's market is unattractively small or if it can obscure the existence of its competitive advantage. Filofax, the long-established British manufacturer of personal organizers, was able to dominate the market for its products so long as that market remained small. The boom in demand for Filofaxes during the mid-1980s was, paradoxically, a disaster for the company. Filofax's product was easily imitated and yuppie-driven demand growth spawned a host of imitators. By 1989, the company was suffering falling sales and mounting losses.[36] In industries where competitive advantages based upon differentiation and innovation can be imitated (such as financial services, retailing, fashion clothing, and toys), firms have a brief window of opportunity during which to exploit their advantage before imitators erode it away. Under such circumstances, firms must be concerned not with sustaining the existing advantages, but with creating the flexibility and responsiveness to that which permits them to create new advantages at a faster rate than the old advantages are being eroded by competition.

Transferability and replicability of resources and capabilities is also a key issue in the strategic management of joint ventures. Studies of the international joint ventures point to the transferability of each party's capabilities as a critical determinant of the allocation of benefits from the venture. For example, Western companies' strengths in distribution channels and product technology have been easily exploited by Japanese joint venture partners, while Japanese manufacturing excellence and new product development capabilities have proved exceptionally difficult for Western companies to learn.[37]

IDENTIFYING RESOURCE GAPS AND DEVELOPING THE RESOURCE BASE

The analysis so far has regarded the firm's resource base as predetermined, with the primary task of organizational strategy being the deployment of these resources so as to maximize rents over time. However, a resource based approach to strategy is concerned not only with the deployment of existing resources, but also with the development of the firm's resource base. This includes replacement investment to maintain the firm's stock of resources and to augment resources in order to buttress and extend positions of competitive advantage as well as broaden the firm's strategic opportunity set. This task is known in the strategy literature as filling "resource gaps."[38]

Sustaining advantage in the face of competition and evolving customer requirements also requires that firms constantly develop their resources bases. Such "upgrading" of competitive advantage occupies a central position in Michael Porter's analysis of the competitive advantage of nations.[39] Porter's analysis of the ability of firms and nations to establish and maintain international competitive success depends critically upon the ability to continually innovate and to shift the basis of competitive advantage from "basic" to "advanced" factors of production. An important feature of these "advanced" factors of production is that they offer a more sustainable competitive advantage because they are more specialized (therefore less mobile through market transfer) and less easy to replicate.

Commitment to upgrading the firm's pool of resources and capabilities requires strategic direction in terms of the capabilities that will form the basis of the firm's future competitive advantage. Thus, Prahalad and Hamel's notion of "core competencies" is less an identification of a company's current capabilities than a commitment to a path of future development. For example, NEC's strategic focus on computing and communications in the mid-1970s was not so much a statement of the core strengths of the company as it was a long-term commitment to a particular path of technological development.

Harmonizing the exploitation of existing resources with the development of the resources and capabilities for competitive advantage in the future is a subtle task. To the extent that capabilities are learned and perfected through repetition, capabilities develop automatically through the pursuit of a particular strategy. The essential task, then, is to ensure that strategy constantly pushes slightly beyond the limits of the firms capabilities at any point of time. This ensures not only the perfection of capabilities required by the current strategy, but also the development of the capabilities required to meet the challenges of the future. The idea that, through pursuing its present strategy, a firm develops the expertise required for its future strategy is referred to by Hiroyuki Itami as "dynamic resource fit":

> Effective strategy in the present builds invisible assets, and the expanded stock enables the firm to plan its future strategy to be carried out. And the future strategy must make effective use of the resources that have been amassed.[40]

Matsushita is a notable exponent of this principle of parallel and sequential development of strategy and capabilities. For example, in developing production in a foreign country, Matsushita typically began with the production of simple products, such as batteries, then moved on to the production of products requiring greater manufacturing and marketing sophistication:

> In every country batteries are a necessity, so they sell well. As long as we bring a few advanced automated pieces of equipment for the processes vital to final product quality, even unskilled labor can produce good products. As they work on this rather simple product, the workers get trained, and this increased skill level then permits us to gradually expand production to items with increasingly higher technology level, first radios, then televisions.[41]

The development of capabilities which can then be used as the basis for broadening a firm's product range is a common feature of successful strategies of related diversification. Sequential product addition to accompany the development of technological, manufacturing, and marketing expertise was a feature of Honda's diversification from motorcycles to cars, generators, lawnmowers, and boat engines; and of 3M's expansion from abrasives to adhesives, video tape, and computer disks.

In order both to fully exploit a firm's existing stock of resources, and to develop competitive advantages for the future, the external acquisition of complementary resources may be necessary. Consider the Walt Disney Company's turnaround between 1984 and 1988. In order for the new management to exploit more effectively Disney's vast, under-utilized stock of unique resources, new resources were required. Achieving better utilization of Disney's film studios and expertise in animation required the acquisition of creative talent in the form of directors, actors, scriptwriters, and cartoonists. Putting Disney's vast real estate holdings to work was assisted by the acquisition of the property development expertise of the Arvida Corporation. Building a new marketing team was instrumental in increasing capacity utilization at Disneyland and Disney World.

CONCLUSION

The resources and capabilities of a firm are the central considerations in formulating its strategy: they are the primary constants upon which a firm can establish its identity and frame its strategy, and they are the primary sources of the firm's profitability. The key to a resource-based approach to strategy formulation is understanding the relationships between resources, capabilities, competitive advantage, and profitability—in particular, an understanding of the mechanisms through which competitive advantage can be sustained over time. This requires the design of strategies which exploit to maximum effect each firm's unique characteristics.

REFERENCES

1. Charles W. Hofer and Dan Schendel, *Strategy Formulation: Analytic Concepts* (St. Paul, MN: West, 1978), p. 12.
2. Robert D. Buzzell and Bradley T. Gale, *The PIMS Principles: Linking Strategy to Performance* (New York, NY: Free Press, 1987).
3. See, for example, Henry Mintzberg, "Of Strategies, Deliberate and Emergent," *Strategic Management Journal*, 6 (1985): 257–272; Andrew M. Pettigrew, "Strategy Formulation as a Political Process," *International Studies of Management and Organization*, 7 (1977): 78–87; J.B. Quinn, *Strategies for Change: Logical Incrementalism* (Homewood, IL: Irwin, 1980).
4. David Ricardo, *Principles of Political Economy and Taxation* (London: G. Bell, 1891); Joseph A. Schumpeter, *The Theory of Economic Development* (Cambridge, MA: Harvard University Press, 1934); Edith Penrose, *The Theory of the Growth of the Firm* (New York, NY: John Wiley and Sons, 1959).
5. David J. Teece, "Economics of Scope and the Scope of the Enterprise," Journal of *Economic Behavior and Organization*, 1 (1980): 223–247; S. Chatterjee and B. Wernerfelt, "The Link between Resources and Types of Diversification: Theory and Evidence," *Strategic Management Journal*, 12 (1991): 33–48.
6. R.P. Rumelt, "Towards a Strategic Theory of the Finn," in R.B. Lamb, ed., *Competitive Strategic Management* (Englewood Cliffs, NJ: Prentice Hall, 1984); S.A. Lippman and R.P. Rumelt, "Uncertain Imitability: An Analysis of Interfirm Differences in Efficiency under Competition," *Bell Journal of Economics*, 23 (1982):

418–438; Richard Reed and R.J. DeFillippi, "Causal Ambiguity, Barriers to Imitation, and Sustainable Competitive Advantage," *Academy of Management Review*, 15 (January 1990): 88–102.

7. David J. Teece, "Capturing Value from Technological Innovation: Integration, Strategic Partnering, and Licensing Decisions," *Interfaces*, 18/3 (1988): 46–61.

8. Jay B. Barney, "Strategic Factor Markets: Expectations, Luck and Business Strategy," *Management Science*, 32/10 (October 1986): 1231–1241.

9. Ingemar Dierickx and Karel Cool, "Asset Stock Accumulation and the Sustainability of Competitive Advantage," *Management Science*, 35/12 (December 1989): 1504–1513.

10. R. Schmalensee, "Industrial Economics: An Overview," *Economic Journal*, 98 (1988): 643–681; R.D. Buzzell and B.T. Gale, *The PIMS Principles* (New York, NY: Free Press, 1987).

11. Because of the ambiguity associated with accounting definitions of profit, the academic literature increasingly uses the term "rent" to refer to "economic profit." "Rent" is the surplus of revenue over the "real" or "opportunity" cost of the resources used in generating that revenue. The "real" or "opportunity" cost of a resource is the revenue it can generate when put to an alternative use in the firm or the price which it can be sold for.

12. W.J. Baumol, J.C. Panzer, and R.D. Willig, *Contestable Markets and the Theory of Industrial Structure* (New York, NY: Harcourt Brace Jovanovitch, 1982).

13. In economist's jargon, such jointly owned resources are "public goods"—their benefits can be extended to additional firms at negligible marginal cost.

14. Hiroyuki Itami [*Mobilizing Invisible Assets* (Cambridge, MA: Harvard University Press, 1986)] refers to these as "invisible assets."

15. Based upon Hofer and Schendel, op. cit., pp. 145–148.

16. See, for example, Iain Cockburn and Zvi Griliches, "Industry Effects and the Appropriability Measures in the Stock Market's Valuation of R&D and Patents," *American Economic Review*, 78 (1988): 419–423.

17. General management, financial management, marketing and selling, market research, product R&D, engineering, production, distribution, legal affairs, and personnel. See Charles C. Snow and Lawrence G. Hrebiniak, "Strategy, Distinctive Competence, and Organizational Performance," *Administrative Science Quarterly*, 25 (1980): 317–336.

18. C.K Prahalad and Gary Hamel, "The Core Competence of the Corporation," *Harvard Business Review* (May/June 1990), pp. 79–91.

19. Howard H. Stevenson, "Defining Corporate Strengths and Weaknesses," *Sloan Management Review* (Spring 1976), pp. 51–68.

20. Richard T. Pascale, "Honda (A)," *Harvard Business School*, Case no. 9–384–049, 1983.

21. Paul R. Lawrence and Davis Dyer, *Renewing American Industry* (New York, NY: Free Press, 1983), pp. 60–83.

22. "Du Pont's "Drug Hunter" Stalks His Next Big Trophy," *Business Week*, November 27, 1989, pp. 174–182.

23. Richard E. Caves, "Economic Analysis and the Quest for Competitive Advantage," *American Economic Review*, 74 (1984): 127–128.

24. Jay B. Barney, "Organizational Culture: Can It Be a Source of Sustained Competitive Advantage?" *Academy of Management Review,* 11 (1986): 656–665.

25. Lippman and Rumelt, op. cit.

26. This information problem is a consequence of the fact that resources work together in teams and their individual productivity is not observable. See A.A. Alchian and H. Demsetz, "Production, Information Costs, and Economic Organization," *American Economic Review,* 62 (1972): 777–795.

27. Such asymmetric information gives rise to a "lemons" problem. See G. Akerlof, "The Market for Lemons: Qualitative Uncertainty and the Market Mechanism," *Quarterly Journal of Economics,* 84 (1970): 488–500.

28. Barney, op. cit.

29. The definition of resource specificity in this article corresponds to the definition of "specific assets" by Richard Caves ["International Corporations: The Industrial Economics of Foreign Investment," *Economica,* 38 (1971): 1–271; it differs from that used by O.E. Williamson [*The Economic Institutions of Capitalism* (New York, NY: Free Press, 1985), pp. 52–561. Williamson refers to assets which are specific to particular transactions rather than to particular firms.

30. "Catch a Falling Star," *The Economist,* April 23, 1988, pp. 88–90.

31. Dierickx and Cool, op. cit.

32. The key advantage of partnerships as an organizational form for such businesses is in averting conflict over control and rent allocation between employees and owners.

33. 'Ad World Is Abuzz as Top Brass Leaves Lord Geller Agency," *Wall Street Journal,* March 23, 1988, p. A1.

34. Charles Ferguson ["From the People Who Brought You Voodoo Economics," *Harvard Business Review* (May/June 1988), pp. 55–63] has claimed that these start-ups involve the individual exploitation of technical knowledge which rightfully belongs to the former employers of these new entrepreneurs.

35. "The Decline of the Superstar," *Business Week,* August 17, 1987, pp. 90–96.

36. "Faded Fad," *The Economist,* September 30, 1989, p. 68.

37. Gary Hamel, Yves Doz, and C.K. Prahalad, "Collaborate with Your Competitors— and Win," *Harvard Business Review* (January/February 1989), pp. 133–139.

38. Stevenson (1985), op. cit.

39. Michael E. Porter, *The Competitive Advantage of Nations* (New York, NY: Free Press, 1990).

40. Itami, op. cit., p. 125.

41. Arataroh Takahashi, *What I Learned from Konosuke Matsushita* (Tokyo: Jitsugyo no Nihonsha, 1980) [in Japanese]. Quoted by Itami, op. cit., p. 25.

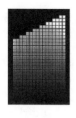

2

Competing on Resources: Strategy in the 1990s

David J. Collis and Cynthia A. Montgomery

How do you create and sustain a profitable strategy?

As recently as ten years ago, we thought we knew most of what we needed to know about strategy. Portfolio planning, the experience curve, PIMS, Porter's five forces—tools like these brought rigor and legitimacy to strategy at both the business-unit and the corporate level. Leading companies, such as General Electric, built large staffs that reflected growing confidence in the value of strategic planning. Strategy consulting boutiques expanded rapidly and achieved widespread recognition. How different the landscape looks today. The armies of planners have all but disappeared, swept away by the turbulence of the past decade. On multiple fronts, strategy has come under fire.

At the business-unit level, the pace of global competition and technological change has left managers struggling to keep up. As markets move faster and faster, managers complain that strategic planning is too static and too slow. Strategy has also become deeply problematic at the corporate level. In the 1980s, it turned out that corporations were often destroying value by owning the very divisions that had seemed to fit so nicely in their growth/share matrices. Threatened by smaller, less hierarchical competitors, many corporate stalwarts either suffered devastating setbacks (IBM, Digital, General Motors, and Westinghouse) or underwent dramatic transformation programs and internal

David J. Collis is an associate professor of business administration and Cynthia A. Montgomery is a professor of business administration at the Harvard Business School in Boston, Massachusetts. Their research focuses on corporate strategy and the competitiveness of diversified companies.

reorganizations (GE and ABB). By the late 1980s, large multibusiness corporations were struggling to justify their existence.

Not surprisingly, waves of new approaches to strategy were proposed to address these multiple assaults on the premises of strategic planning. Many focused inward. The lessons from Tom Peters and Bob Waterman's "excellent" companies led the way, closely followed by total quality management as strategy, reengineering, core competence, competing on capabilities, and the learning organization. Each approach made its contribution in turn, yet how any of them built on or refuted the previously accepted wisdom was unclear. The result: Each compounded the confusion about strategy that now besets managers.

A framework that has the potential to cut through much of this confusion is now emerging from the strategy field. The approach is grounded in economics, and it explains how a company's resources drive its performance in a dynamic competitive environment. Hence the umbrella term academics use to describe this work: the *resource-based view of the firm* (RBV).[1] The RBV combines the *internal* analysis of phenomena within companies (a preoccupation of many management gurus since the mid-1980s) with the *external* analysis of the industry and the competitive environment (the central focus of earlier strategy approaches). Thus the resource-based view builds on, but does not replace, the two previous broad approaches to strategy by *combining* internal and external perspectives.[2] It derives its strength from its ability to explain in clear managerial terms why some competitors are more profitable than others, how to put the idea of core competence into practice, and how to develop diversification strategies that make sense. The resource-based view, therefore, will be as powerful and as important to strategy in the 1990s as industry analysis was in the 1980s. (See the insert "A Brief History of Strategy.")

The RBV sees companies as very different collections of physical and intangible assets and capabilities. No two companies are alike because no two companies have had the same set of experiences, acquired the same assets and skills, or built the same organizational cultures. These assets and capabilities determine how efficiently and effectively a company performs its functional activities. Following this logic, a company will be positioned to succeed if it has the best and most appropriate stocks of resources for its business and strategy.

Valuable resources can take a variety of forms, including some overlooked by the narrower conceptions of core competence and capabilities. They can be *physical,* like the wire into your house. Potentially, both the telephone and cable companies are in a very strong position to succeed in the brave new world of interactive multimedia because they own the on-ramp to the information superhighway. Or valuable resources may be *intangible,* such as brand names or technological know-how. The Walt Disney Company, for example, holds a unique consumer franchise that makes Disney a success in a slew of businesses, from soft toys to theme parks to videos. Similarly, Sharp Corporation's knowledge of flat-panel display technology has enabled it to dominate the $7 billion worldwide liquid-crystal-display (LCD) business. Or the valuable resource may be an *organizational capability* embedded in a company's routines, processes, and culture. Take, for example, the skills of the Japanese automobile companies—first in low-cost, lean manufacturing; next in high-quality production; and then in fast product development. These capabilities, built up over time, transform otherwise pedestrian or commodity inputs into superior products and make the companies that have developed them successful in the global market.

Competitive advantage, whatever its source, ultimately can be attributed to the ownership of a valuable resource that enables the company to perform activities better or more cheaply than competitors. Marks & Spencer, for example, possesses a range of resources that demonstrably yield it a competitive advantage in British retailing. (See the exhibit "How Marks & Spencer's Resources Give It Competitive Advantage.") This is true both at the single-business level and at the corporate level, where the valuable resources might reside in a particular function, such as corporate research and development, or in an asset, such as corpo-

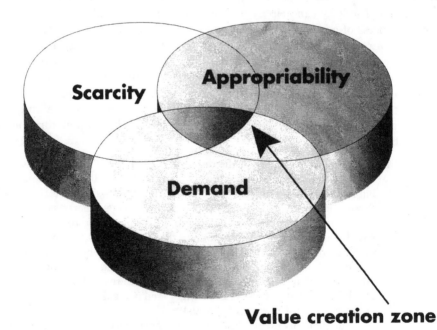

The dynamic interplay of three fundamental market forces determines the value of a resource or a capability.

FIGURE 2.1 What Makes a Resource Valuable?

rate brand identity. Superior performance will therefore be based on developing a *competitively distinct* set of resources and deploying them in a well-conceived strategy.

COMPETITIVELY VALUABLE RESOURCES

Resources cannot be evaluated in isolation, because their value is determined in the interplay with market forces. A resource that is valuable in a particular industry or at a particular time might fail to have the same value in a different industry or chronological context. For example, despite several attempts to brand lobsters, so far no one has been successful in doing so. A brand name was once very important in the personal computer industry, but it no longer is, as IBM has discovered at great cost. Thus the RBV inextricably links a company's internal capabilities (what it does well) and its external industry environment (what the market demands and what competitors offer). Described that way, competing on resources sounds simple. In practice, however, managers often have a hard time identifying and evaluating their companies' resources objectively. The RBV can help by bringing discipline to the often fuzzy and subjective process of assessing valuable resources.

For a resource to qualify as the basis for an effective strategy, it must pass a number of external market tests of its value. Some are so straightforward that most managers grasp them intuitively or even unconsciously. For instance, a valuable resource must contribute to the production of something customers want at a price they are willing to pay. Other tests are more subtle and, as a result, are commonly misunderstood or misapplied. These often turn out to cause strategies to misfire.

1. **The test of inimitability: Is the resource hard to copy?** Inimitability is at the heart of value creation because it limits competition. If a resource is inimitable, then any profit stream it generates is more likely to be sustainable. Possessing a resource that competitors easily can copy generates only temporary value. But because managers fail to apply this test rigorously, they try to base long-term strategies on resources that are imitable. IBP the first meat-packing company in the United States to modernize, built a set of assets (automated plants located in cattle-rearing states) and capabilities (low-cost "disassembly" of beef) that enabled it to earn returns of 1.3% in the 1970s. By the late 1980s, however, ConAgra and Cargill had replicated these resources, and IBP's returns fell to 0.4%.

    Inimitability doesn't last forever. Competitors eventually will find ways to copy most valuable resources. But managers can forestall them—and sustain profits for a while—by building their strategies around resources that have at least one of the following four characteristics:

    The first is *physical uniqueness,* which almost by definition cannot be copied. A wonderful real estate location, mineral rights, or Merck & Company's pharmaceutical patents simply cannot be imitated. Although managers may be tempted to think that many of their resources fall into this category, on close inspection, few do.

A greater number of resources cannot be imitated because of what economists call *path dependency.* Simply put, these resources are unique and, therefore, scarce because of all that has happened along the path taken in their accumulation. As a result, competitors cannot go out and buy these resources instantaneously. Instead, they must be built over time in ways that are difficult to accelerate.[3]

The Gerber Products Company brand name for baby food, for example, is potentially imitable. Recreating Gerber's brand loyalty, however, would take a very long time. **Banking on the durability of most core competencies is risky. They have limited lives and will earn only temporary profits.** Even if a competitor spent hundreds of millions of dollars promoting its baby food, it could not buy the trust that consumers associate with Gerber. That sort of brand connotation can be built only by marketing the product steadily for years, as Gerber has done. Similarly, crash R&D programs usually cannot replicate a successful technology when research findings cumulate. Having many researchers working in parallel cannot speed the process, because bottlenecks have to be solved sequentially. All this builds protection for the original resource.

The third source of inimitability is *causal ambiguity.* Would-be competitors are thwarted because it is impossible to disentangle either what the valuable resource is or how to re-create it. What *really* is the cause of Rubbermaid's continued success in plastic products? We can draw up lists of possible reasons. We can try, as any number of competitors have, to identify its recipe for innovation. But, in the final analysis, we cannot duplicate Rubbermaid's success.

Causally ambiguous resources are often organizational capabilities. These exist in a complex web of social interactions and may even depend critically on particular individuals. As Continental and United try to mimic Southwest's successful low-cost strategy, what will be most difficult for them to copy is not the planes, the routes, or the fast gate turnaround. All of those are readily observable and, in principle, easily duplicated. However, it will be difficult to reproduce Southwest's culture of fun, family, frugality, and focus because no one can quite specify exactly what it is or how it arose.

The final source of inimitability, *economic deterrence,* occurs when a company preempts a competitor by making a sizable investment in an asset. The competitor could replicate the resource but, because of limited market potential, chooses not to. This is most likely when strategies are built around large capital investments that are both scale sensitive and specific to a given market. For example, the minimum efficient scale for float-glass plants is so large that many markets can support only one such facility. Because such assets cannot be redeployed, they represent a credible commitment to stay and fight it out with competitors who try to replicate the investment. Faced with such a threat, potential imitators may choose not to duplicate the resource when the market is too small to support two players the size of the incumbent profitably. That is exactly what is now occurring in Eastern Europe. As companies rush to modernize, the first to build a float-glass facility in a country is likely to go unchallenged by competitors.

A Brief History of Strategy

The field of strategy has largely been shaped around a framework first conceived by Kenneth R. Andrews in his classic book *The Concept of Corporate Strategy* (Richard D. Irwin, 1971). Andrews defined strategy as the match between what a company can do (organizational strengths and weaknesses) within the universe of what it might do (environmental opportunities and threats).

Although the power of Andrew's framework was recognized from the start, managers were given few insights about how to assess either side of the equation systematically. The first important breakthrough came in Michael E. Porter's book *Competitive Strategy: Techniques for Analyzing Industries and Competitors* (Free Press, 1980). Porter's work built on the structure-conduct-performance paradigm of industrial-organization economics. The essence of the model is that the structure of an industry determines the state of competition within that industry and sets the context for companies' conduct—that is, their strategy. Most important, structural forces (which Porter called the five forces) determine the average profitability of the industry and have a correspondingly strong impact on the profitability of individual corporate strategies.

This analysis put the spotlight on choosing the "right industries" and, within them, the most attractive competitive positions. Although the model did not ignore the characteristics of individual companies, the emphasis was clearly on phenomena at the industry level.

With the appearance of the concepts of core competence and competing on capabilities, the pendulum swung dramatically in the other direction, moving from outside to inside the company. These approaches emphasized the importance both of the skills and collective learning embedded in an organization and of management's ability to marshal them. This view assumed that the roots of competitive advantage were inside the organization and that the adoption of new strategies was constrained by the current level of the company's resources. The external environment received little, if any, attention, and what we had learned about industries and competitive analysis seemed to disappear from our collective psyche.

The emerging resource-based view of the firm helps to bridge these seemingly disparate approaches and to fulfill the promise of Andrew's framework. Like the capabilities approaches, the resource-based view acknowledges the importance of company specific resources and competencies, yet it does so in the context of the competitive environment. The resource-based view shares another important characteristic with industry analysis: It, too, relies on economic reasoning. It sees capabilities and resources as the heart of a company's competitive position, subject to the interplay of three fundamental market forces: demand (does it meet customers' needs, and is it competitively superior?, scarcity (is it imitable or substitutable, and is it durable?), and appropriability (who owns the profits?). The five tests described in the article translate these general economic requirements into specific, actionable terms.

2. **The test of durability: How quickly does this resource depreciate?** The longer lasting a resource is, the more valuable it will be. Like inimitability, this test asks whether the resource can sustain competitive advantage over time. While some industries are stable for years, managers today recognize that most are so dynamic that the value of resources depreciates quickly. Disney's brand name survived almost two decades of benign neglect between Walt Disney's death and the installation of Michael D. Eisner and his management team. In contrast, technological know-how in a fast-moving industry is a rapidly wasting asset, as the list of different companies that have dominated successive generations of semiconductor memories illustrates. Economist Joseph A. Schumpeter first recognized this phenomenon in the 1930s. He described waves of innovation that allow early movers to dominate the market and earn substantial profits. However, their valuable resources are soon imitated or surpassed by the next great innovation, and their superior profits turn out to be transitory. Schumpeter's description of major companies and whole industries blown away in a gale of "creative destruction" captures the pressure many managers feel today. Banking on the durability of most core competencies is risky. Most resources have a limited life and will earn only temporary profits.

3. **The test of appropriability: Who captures the value that the resource creates?** Not all profits from a resource automatically flow to the company that "owns" the resource. In fact, the value is always subject to bargaining among a host of players, including customers, distributors, suppliers, and employees. What has happened to leveraged buyout firms is revealing. A critical resource of LBO firms was the network of contacts and relationships in the investment banking community. However, this resource often resided in the individuals doing the deals, not in the LBO firms as a whole. These individuals could—and often did—depart to set up their own LBO funds or move to another firm where they could reap a greater share of the profits that their resource generated. Basing a strategy on resources that are not inextricably bound to the company can make profits hard to capture.

4. **The test of substitutability: Can a unique resource be trumped by a different resource?** Since Michael E. Porter's introduction of the five-forces framework, every strategist has been on the lookout for the potential impact of substitute products. The steel industry, for example, has lost a major market in beer cans to aluminum makers in the past 20 years. The resource-based view pushes this critical question down a level to the resources that underpin a company's ability to deliver a good or service. Consider the following example. In the early 1980s, People Express Airlines challenged the major airlines with a low-price strategy. Founder Donald C. Burr pursued this strategy by developing a unique no-frills approach and an infrastructure to deliver low-cost flights. Although the major airlines were unable to replicate this approach, they nevertheless were able to retaliate using a *different* resource to offer consumers equivalent low-cost fares—their computer reservation systems and yield-management skills. This substitution eventually drove People Express into bankruptcy and out of the industry.

5. **The test of competitive superiority: Whose resource is really better?** Perhaps the greatest mistake managers make when evaluating their companies' resources is that they do not assess them relative to competitors'. Core com-

petence has too often become a "feel good" exercise that no one fails. Every company can identify one activity that it does relatively better than other activities and claim that as its core competence. Unfortunately, core competence should not be an internal assessment of which activity, of all its activities, the company performs best. It should be a harsh external assessment of what it does better than competitors, for which the term *distinctive competence* is more appropriate. How many consumer packaged-goods companies assert that their core competence is consumer marketing skills? They may indeed all be good at that activity, but a corporate strategy built on such a core competence will rapidly run into trouble because other competitors with better skills will be pursuing the same strategy.

The way to avoid the vacuousness of generic statements of core competence is to disaggregate the corporation's resources. The category *consumer marketing skills,* for example, is too broad. But it can be divided into subcategories such as effective brand management, which in turn can be divided into skills such as product-line extensions, cost effective couponing, and so on. Only by looking at this level of specificity can we understand the sources of a company's uniqueness and measure by analyzing the data whether it is competitively superior on those dimensions. Can anyone evaluate whether Kraft General Foods' or Unilever's consumer marketing skills are better? No. But we can demonstrate quantitatively which is more successful at launching product-line extensions.

Disaggregation is important not only for identifying truly distinctive resources but also for deriving actionable implications. How many companies have developed a statement of their core competencies and then have struggled to know what to do with it? One manufacturer of medical-diagnostics test equipment, for example, defined one of its core competencies as instrumentation. But this intuitively obvious definition was too broad to be actionable. By pushing to deeper levels of disaggregation, the company came to a powerful insight. In fact, its strength in instrumentation was mainly attributable to its competitive superiority in designing the interface between its machines and the people who use them. As a result, the company decided to reinforce its valuable capability by hiring ergonomists, and it expanded into doctors' offices, a fast-growing segment of its market. There, the company's resources created a real competitive advantage, in part because its equipment can be operated by office personnel rather than only by technicians.

Although disaggregation is the key to identifying competitively superior resources, sometimes the valuable resource is a combination of skills, none of which is superior by itself but which, when combined, make a better package. Honeywell's industrial automation systems are successful in the marketplace—a measure that the company is good at something. Yet each individual component and software program might not be the best available. Competitive superiority lies either in the weighted average (the company does not rank first in any resource, but it is still better on average than any competitor) or in its system-integration capability.

The lesson for managers is that conclusions about critical resources should be based on objective data from the market. In our experience, managers often

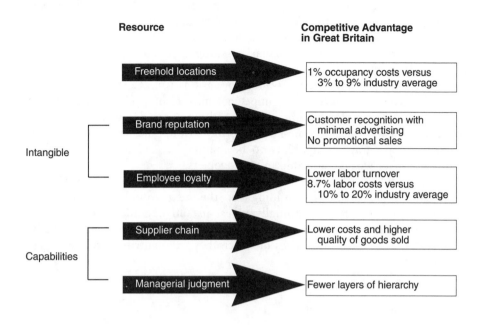

FIGURE 2.2 How Marks & Spencer's Resources Give It Competitive Advantage

treat core competence as an exercise in intuition and skip the thorough research and detailed analysis needed to get the right answer.

STRATEGIC IMPLICATIONS

Managers should build their strategies on resources that meet the five tests outlined above. The best of these resources are often intangible, not physical, hence the emphasis in recent approaches on the softer aspects of corporate assets—the culture, the technology, and the transformational leader. The tests capture how market forces determine the value of resources. They force managers to look inward and outward at the same time.

However, most companies are not ideally positioned with competitively valuable resources. More likely, they have a mixed bag of resources—some good, some mediocre, and some outright liabilities, such as IBM's monolithic mainframe culture. The harsh truth is that most companies' resources do not pass the objective application of the market tests.

Even those companies that are fortunate enough to have unusual assets or capabilities are not home free. Valuable resources must still be joined with other resources and embedded in a set of functional policies and activities that distinguish the company's position in the market—after all, competitors can have core competencies, too.

Strategy requires managers to look forward as well. Companies fortunate enough to have a truly distinctive competence must also be wise enough to realize that its value is eroded by time and competition. Consider what happened to Xerox. During what has become known as its "lost decade," the 1970s, Xerox believed its reprographic capability to be inimitable. And while Xerox slept, Canon took over world leadership in photocopiers.

In a world of continuous change, companies need to maintain pressure constantly at the frontiers—building for the next round of competition. Managers must therefore continually invest in and upgrade their resources, however good those resources are today, and leverage them with effective strategies into attractive industries in which they can contribute to a competitive advantage.

Investing in Resources

Because all resources depreciate, an effective corporate strategy requires continual investment in order to maintain and build valuable resources. One of Eisner's first actions as CEO at Disney was to revive the company's commitment to animation. He invested $50 million in *Who Framed Roger Rabbit?* to create the company's first animated feature-film hit in many years and quadrupled its output of animated feature films—bringing out successive hits, such as *Beauty and the Beast, Aladdin,* and *The Lion King.*

Similarly, Marks & Spencer has periodically reexamined its position in its only business—retailing—and has made major investments to stay competitive. In the early 1980s, the British company spent billions on store renovation, opened new edge-of-town locations, and updated its procurement and distribution systems. In contrast, the U.S. retailer Sears, Roebuck and Company diversified into insurance, real estate, and stock brokerages, while failing to keep up with the shift in retailing to new mall locations and specialty stores.

The mandate to reinvest in strategic resources may seem obvious. The great contribution of the core competence notion is its recognition that, in corporations with a traditional divisional structure, investment in the corporation's resources often takes a backseat to optimizing current divisional profitability. Core competence, therefore, identifies the critical role that the corporate office has to play as the guardian of what are, in essence, the crown jewels of the corporation. In some instances, such guardianship might even require explicitly establishing a corporate officer in charge of nurturing the critical resources. Cooper Industries, a diversified manufacturer, established a manufacturing services group to disseminate the best manufacturing practices throughout the company. The group helped "Cooperize" acquired companies, rationalizing and improving their production facilities. The head of the services group, Joseph R. Coppola, was of a caliber to be hired away as CEO of Giddings & Lewis, the largest U.S. machine tool manufacturer. Similarly, many professional service firms, such as Coopers & Lybrand, have a senior partner in charge of their critical capabilities—client-relationship management, staff training, and intellectual development. Valuable corporate resources are often supradivisional, and, unless someone is managing them on that basis, divisions will underinvest in them or free ride on them.

At the same time, investing in core competencies without examining the competitive dynamics that determine industry attractiveness is dangerous. By ignoring the marketplace, managers risk investing heavily in resources that will yield low returns. Masco Corporation did exactly that. It built a competence in metalworking and diversified into tightly related industries. Unfortunately, the returns from this strategy were lower than the company had expected. Why? A straightforward five-forces analysis would have revealed that the structure of the industries Masco entered was poor—buyers were price sensitive with limited switching costs, entry barriers were low, and suppliers were powerful. Despite Masco's metalworking expertise, its industry context prevented it from achieving exceptional returns until it developed the skills that enabled it to enter more attractive industries.

Similarly, if competitors are ignored, the profits that could result from a successful resource-based strategy will dissipate in the struggle to acquire those resources. Consider the value of the cable wire into your house as a source of competitive advantage in the multimedia industry. Companies such as Time Warner have been forced by competitors, who can also see the value of that wire, to bid billions of dollars to acquire control of even modest cable systems. As a result, they may never realize substantial returns on their investment. This is true not only for resources acquired on the market but also for those core competencies that many competitors are simultaneously trying to develop internally.

Upgrading Resources

What if a company has no unusually valuable resources? Unfortunately, that is a common experience when resources are evaluated against the standard of competitive superiority. Or what if a company's valuable resources have been imitated or substituted by competitors? Or perhaps its resources, like Masco's, are valuable only in industries so structurally unattractive that, regardless of how efficiently it operates, its financial returns will never be stellar. In these cases—indeed, in nearly all cases—companies must continually upgrade the number and quality of their resources and associated competitive positions in order to hold off the almost inevitable decay in their value.

Upgrading resources means moving beyond what the company is already good at, which can be accomplished in a number of ways. The first is by adding new resources, the way Intel Corporation added a brand name, IntelInside, to its technological resource base. The second is by upgrading to

What Ever Happened to the Dogs and Cash Cows?

In the late 1960s and early 1970s, the wisdom of the day was that companies could transfer the competitive advantage of professional management across a broad range of businesses. Many companies responded to the perceived opportunity: Armed with decentralized structures and limited, but tight, financial controls, they diversified into a number of related and unrelated businesses, mostly through acquisition. In time, such conglomerates came to resemble miniature economies in their own right. There appeared to be no compelling limits to the scope of corporations.

As the first oil crisis hit in 1973, corporate managers faced deteriorating performance and had little advice on how to act. Into this vacuum came the Boston Consulting Group and portfolio management. In BCG's now famous growth/share matrix, corporate management was finally given a tool with which to reassert control over its many divisions.

This simple matrix allowed managers to classify each division, since renamed a strategic business unit, into a quadrant based on the growth of its industry, and the relative strength of the unit's competitive position.

There was a prescribed strategy for each position in the matrix: sustain the cash-generating cows, divest or harvest the dogs, take cash from the cows and invest in question marks in order to make them stars, and increase the market share of the stars until their industry growth slowed and they became the next generation of cash cows. Such simple prescriptions gave corporate management both a sense of what their strategy should accomplish—a balanced portfolio of businesses—and a way to control and allocate resources to their divisions.

The problem with the portfolio matrix was that it did not address how value was being created across the divisions, which could be as diverse as semiconductors and hammers. The only relationship between them was cash. As we have come to learn, the relatedness of businesses is at the heart of value creation in diversified companies.

The portfolio matrix also suffered from its assumption that corporations had to be self-sufficient in capital. That implied that they should find a use for all internally generated cash and that they could not raise additional funds from the capital market. The capital markets of the 1980s demonstrated the fallacy of such assumptions.

In addition, the growth/share matrix failed to compare the competitive advantage a business received from being owned by a particular company with the costs of owning it. In the 1980s, many companies built enormous corporate infrastructures that created only small gains at the business-unit level. During the same period, the market for corporate control heated up, focusing attention on value for shareholders. Many companies with supposedly model portfolios were accordingly dissolved.

alternative resources that are threatening the company's current capabilities. AT&T is trying to build capabilities in multimedia now that its physical infrastructure—the network—is no longer unique or as critical as it once was. Finally, a company can upgrade its resources in order to move into a structurally more attractive industry, the way Nucor Corporation, a U.S. steel company, has made the transition from competitive, low-margin, downstream businesses, such as steel joists, into more differentiated, upstream businesses, such as thin-slab cast-steel sheets.

Perhaps the most successful examples of upgrading resources are in companies that have added new competencies sequentially, often over extended periods of time. Sharp provides a wonderful illustration of how to exploit a virtuous circle of sequentially upgrading technologies and products, what the Japanese call "seeds and needs." In the late 1950s, Sharp was an assembler of televisions and radios, seemingly condemned to the second rank of Japanese consumer electronics companies. To break out of that position, founder Tokiji Hayakawa, who had always stressed the importance of innovation, created a corporate R&D facility. When the Japanese Ministry of International Trade and Industry blocked Sharp from designing computers, the company used its limited technology to produce the world's first digital calculator in 1964. To strengthen its position in this business, Sharp backward integrated into manufacturing its own specialized semiconductors and made a strong commitment to the new liquid-crystal-display technology. Sharp's bet on LCD technology paid off and enabled it to develop a number of new products, such as the Wizard electronic organizer. Over time, the superiority of its display technology gave Sharp a competitive advantage in businesses it had previously struggled in, such as camcorders. Its breakthrough product, Viewcam, captured 20% of the Japanese market within six months of release in 1992.

At each stage, Sharp took on a new challenge, whether to develop or improve a technology or to enter or attack a market. Success in each endeavor improved the company's resources in technology, distribution, and organizational capability. It also opened new avenues for expansion. Today, Sharp is the dominant player in the LCD market and a force in consumer electronics.

Cooper provides another example. Challenged to justify its plan to acquire Champion Spark Plug Company in 1989, when fuel injection was replacing spark plugs, Cooper reasoned that it had the resources to help Champion improve its position, as it had done many times before with products such as Crescent wrenches, Nicholson files, and Gardner-Denver mining equipment. But what really swung the decision, according to Cooper chairman and CEO Robert Cizik, was the recognition that Cooper lacked a critical skill it needed for the future—the ability to manage international manufacturing. With its numerous overseas plants, Champion offered Cooper the opportunity to acquire global management capabilities. The Champion acquisition, in Cizik's view, was a way to upgrade Cooper's resources. Indeed, a review of the company's history shows that Cooper has deliberately sought to improve its capabilities gradually by periodically taking on challenges it knows will have a high degree of difficulty for the organization.

Leveraging Resources

Corporate strategies must strive to leverage resources into all the markets in which those resources contribute to competitive advantage or to compete in new markets that improve the corporate resources. Or, preferably, both, as with Cooper's acquisition of Champion. Failure to do so, as occurred with Disney following the death of its founder, leads a company to be undervalued. Eisner's management team, which extended the scope of Disney's activities into hotels, retailing, and publishing, was installed in response to a hostile-takeover threat triggered by the underutilization of the company's valuable resources.

Good corporate strategy, then, requires continual reassessment of the company's scope. The question strategists must ask is, How far can the company's valuable resource be extended across markets? The answer will vary widely because resources differ greatly in their specificity, from highly fungible resources (such as cash, many kinds of machinery, and general management skills) to much more specialized resources (such as expertise in narrow scientific disciplines and secret product formulas). Specialized resources often play a critical role in securing competitive advantage, but, because they are so specific, they lose value quickly when they are moved away from their original settings. Shell Oil Company's brand name, for example, will not transfer well outside autos and energy, however valuable it is within those fields. Highly fungible resources, on the other hand, transfer well across a wide range of markets but rarely constitute the key source of competitive advantage.

The RBV helps us understand why the track record of corporate diversification has been so poor and identifies three common and costly strategic errors companies make when they try to grow by leveraging resources. First, managers tend to overestimate the transferability of specific assets and capabilities. The irony is that because valuable resources are hard to imitate, the company itself may find it difficult to replicate them in new markets. Despite its great success in Great Britain, Marks & Spencer has failed repeatedly in attempts to leverage its resources in the North American market—a classic example of misjudging the important role that context plays in competitive advantage. In this case, the concepts of path dependency and causal ambiguity are both at work. Marks & Spencer's success is rooted in its 100-year reputation for excellence in Great Britain and in the skills and relationships that enable it to manage its domestic supply chain effectively. Just as British competitors have been unable to duplicate this set of advantages, Marks & Spencer itself struggles to do so when it tries to enter a new market against established competitors.

Second, managers overestimate their ability to compete in highly profitable industries. Such industries are often attractive precisely because entry barriers limit the number of competitors. Entry barriers are really resource barriers: The reason competitors find it so hard to enter the business is that accumulating the necessary resources is difficult. If it could be done easily, competitors would flock to the opportunity, driving down average returns. Many managers fail to see the connection between company-level resources and industry-level profits and convince themselves that they can vault the entry barrier, without considering which factors will ultimately determine success in the industry. Philip Morris Companies' entry into soft drinks, for example, foundered on the difficulties it faced managing the franchise distribution network. After years of poor performance in that business, it gave up and divested 7-Up.

The third common diversification mistake is to assume that leveraging generic resources, such as lean manufacturing, will be a major source of competitive advantage in a new market—regardless of the specific competitive dynamics of that market. Chrysler Corporation seems to have learned this lesson. Expecting that its skills in design and manufacturing would ensure success in the aerospace industry, Chrysler acquired Gulfstream Aerospace Corporation—only to divest it five years later in order to concentrate on its core businesses.

Despite the common pitfalls, the rewards for companies that leverage their resources appropriately, as Disney has, are high. Newell Company is another stunning example of a company that has built a set of capabilities and used them to secure commanding positions for products in a wide range of industries. Newell was a modest manufacturer of drapery hardware in 1967, when a new CEO, Daniel C. Ferguson, articulated its strategy: The company would specialize in high-volume production of a variety of household and office staple goods that would be sold through mass merchandisers. The company made a series of acquisitions, each of which benefited from Newell's capabilities—its focused control systems; its computer links with mass discounters, which facilitate paperless invoicing and automatic inventory restocking; and its expertise in the "good-better-best" merchandising of basic products, in which retailers typically choose to carry only one brand, with several quality and price levels. In turn, each acquisition gave Newell yet another opportunity to strengthen its capabilities. Today, Newell holds leading market positions in drapery hardware, cookware, glassware, paintbrushes, and office products and maintains an impressive 15% earnings growth annually. What differentiates this diversified company from a host of others is how it has been able to use its corporate resources to establish and maintain competitive advantage at the business-unit level.

However, even Newell benefits from the attractiveness of the markets in which it competes. All its products are infrequently purchased, low-cost items. Most consumers will not spend time comparison shopping for six glasses, nor do they have a sense of the market price. Do you know if $3.99 is too much to pay for a brass curtain rod? Thus Newell's resources are all the more valuable for being deployed in an attractive industry context.

Whether a company is building a strategy based on core competencies, is developing a learning organization, or is in the middle of a transformation process, those concepts can all be interpreted as a mandate to build a unique set of resources and capabilities. However, this must be done with a sharp eye on the dynamic industry context and competitive situation, rigorously applying market tests to those resources. Strategy that blends two powerful sets of insights about capabilities and competition represents an enduring logic that transcends management fads.

That this approach pays off is demonstrated by the impressive performance of companies such as Newell, Cooper, Disney, and Sharp. Although these companies may not have set out explicitly to craft resource-based strategies, they nonetheless capture the power of this logic and the returns that come to those who do.

REFERENCES

1. A number of insightful articles have been written on the resource-based view, including: Birger Wernerfelt, "A Resource-Based view of the Firm," *Strategic Management Journal*, September-October 1984, p. 171; J.B. Barney, "Strategic Factor Markets: Expectations, Luck and Business Strategy," *Management Science*, October 1986, p. 1,231. Richard P. Rumelt, "Theory, Strategy, and Entrepreneurship," in *The Competitive Challenge: Strategies for Industrial Innovation and Renewal*, ed. David J. Teece (Cambridge, Mass.: Ballinger, 1987), p. 1371 Ingemar Dierickx and Karel Cool, "Asset Stock Accumulation and Sustainability of Competitive Advantage," *Management Science*, December 1989, p. 1,504; Kathleen R. Conner, "A Historical Comparison of Resource-Based Theory and Five Schools of Thought Within Industrial Organization Economics: Do We Have New Theory of the Firm?" *Journal of Management*, March 1991, p. 121; Raphael Amit and Paul J.H. Schoemaker, "Strategic Assets and Organizational Rent," *Strategic Management Journal*, January 1993, p. 33; and Margaret A. Peteraf, "The Cornerstones of Competitive Advantage: A Resource-Based View," *Strategic Management Journal*, March 1993, p. 179.

2. To date, the most attention paid to the integration of the two perspectives has been by Michael E. Porter in *Competitive Advantage: Creating and Sustaining Superior Performance* (New York: Free Press, 1985) and, in the dynamic context, in his article "Towards a Dynamic Theory of Strategy," *Strategic Management Journal*, Winter 1991, p. 95.

3. These ideas were first discussed in two articles published in *Management Science*: Ingemar Dierickx and Karel Cool, "Asset Stock Accumulation and Sustainability of Competitive Advantage," December 1989, p. 1,504; and J.B. Barney, "Asset Stocks and Sustained Competitive Advantage," December 1989, p. 1,512.

3

The Core Competence of the Corporation

C. K. Prahalad and Gary Hamel

The most powerful way to prevail in global competition is still invisible to many companies. During the 1980s, top executives were judged on their ability to restructure, declutter, and delayer their corporations. In the 1990s, they'll be judged on their ability to identify, cultivate, and exploit the core competencies that make growth possible—indeed, they'll have to rethink the concept of the corporation itself.

Consider the last ten years of GTE and NEC. In the early 1980s, GTE was well positioned to become a major player in the evolving information technology industry. It was active in telecommunications. Its operations spanned a variety of businesses including telephones, switching and transmission systems, digital PABX, semiconductors, packet switching, satellites, defense systems, and lighting products. And GTE's Entertainment Products Group, which produced Sylvania color TVs, had a position in related display technologies. In 1980, GTE's sales were $9.98 billion, and net cash flow was $1.73 billion. NEC, in contrast, was much smaller at $3.8 billion in sales. It had a comparable technological base and computer businesses, but it had no experience as an operating telecommunications company.

Yet look at the positions of GTE and NEC in 1988. GTE's 1988 sales were $16.46 billion, and NEC's sales were considerably higher at $21.89 billion. GTE has, in effect, become a telephone operating company with a position in defense and lighting products. GTE's other businesses are small in global terms. GTE has

Reprinted by permission of *Harvard Business Review,* May–June 1990, pp. 79–91. Copyright (1990 by the President and Fellows of Harvard Business College, all rights reserved.

C. K. Prahalad is professor of corporate strategy and international business at the University of Michigan. Gary Hamel is lecturer in business policy and management at the London Business School. Their most recent Harvard Business Review article, "Strategic Intent" (May–June 1989), won the 1989 McKinsey Award for excellence. This article is based on research funded by the Gatsby Charitable Foundation.

divested Sylvania TV and Telenet, put switching, transmission, and digital PABX into joint ventures, and closed down semiconductors. As a result, the international position of GTE has eroded. Non-U.S. revenue as a percent of total revenue dropped from 20% to 15% between 1980 and 1988.

NEC has emerged as the world leader in semiconductors and as a first-tier player in telecommunications products and computers. It has consolidated its position in mainframe computers. It has moved beyond public switching and transmission to include such lifestyle products as mobile telephones, facsimile machines, and laptop computers—bridging the gap between telecommunications and office automation. NEC is the only company in the world to be in the top five in revenue in telecommunications, semiconductors, and mainframes. Why did these two companies, starting with comparable business portfolios, perform so differently? Largely because NEC conceived of itself in terms of "core competencies"; and GTE did not.

RETHINKING THE CORPORATION

Once, the diversified corporation could simply point its business units at particular end product markets and admonish them to become world leaders. But with market boundaries changing ever more quickly, targets are elusive and capture is at best temporary. A few companies have proven themselves adept at inventing new markets, quickly entering emerging markets, and dramatically shifting patterns of customer choice in established markets. These are the ones to emulate. The critical task for management is to create an organization capable of infusing products with irresistible functionality or, better yet, creating products that customers need but have not yet even imagined.

This is a deceptively difficult task. Ultimately it requires radical change in the management of major companies. It means, first of all, that top managements of Western companies must assume responsibility for competitive decline. Everyone knows about high interest rates, Japanese protectionism, outdated antitrust laws, obstreperous unions, and impatient investors. What is harder to see, or harder to acknowledge, is how little added momentum companies actually get from political or macroeconomic "relief." Both the theory and practice of Western management have created a drag on our forward motion. It is the principles of management that are in need of reform.

NEC versus GTE, again, is instinctive and only one of many such comparative cases we analyzed to understand the changing basis for global leadership. Early in the 1970s, NEC articulated a strategic intent to exploit the convergence of computing and communications, what it called "C&C."[1] Success, top management reckoned, would hinge on acquiring competencies, particularly in semiconductors. Management adopted an appropriate "strategic architecture," summarized by C&C, and then communicated its intent to the whole organization and the outside world during the mid-1970s.

[1] For a fuller discussion, see our article, "Strategic Intent" *HBR*, May–June 1989, p. 63.

NEC constituted a "C&C Committee" of top managers to oversee the development of core products and core competencies. NEC put in place coordination groups and committees that cut across the interests of individual businesses. Consistent with its strategic architecture, NEC shifted enormous resources to strengthen its position in components and central processors. By using collaborative arrangements to multiply internal resources, NEC was able to accumulate a broad array of core competencies.

NEC carefully identified three interrelated streams of technological and market evolution. Top management determined that computing would evolve from large mainframes to distributed processing, components from simple ICs to VLSI, and communications from mechanical cross-bar exchange to complex digital systems we now call ISDN. As things evolved further, NEC reasoned, the computing, communications, and components businesses would so overlap that it would be very hard to distinguish among them, and that there would be enormous opportunities for any company that had built the competencies needed to serve all three markets.

NEC top management determined that semiconductors would be the company's most important "core product." It entered into myriad strategic alliances—over 100 as of 1987—aimed at building competencies rapidly and at low cost. In mainframe computers, its most noted relationship was with Honeywell and Bull. Almost all the collaborative arrangements in the semiconductor-component field were oriented toward technology access. As they entered collaborative arrangements, NEC's operating managers understood the rationale for these alliances and the goal of internalizing partner skills. NEC's director of research summed up its competence acquisition during the 1970s and 1980s this way: "From an investment standpoint, it was much quicker and cheaper to use foreign technology. There wasn't a need for us to develop new ideas."

No such clarity of strategic intent and strategic architecture appeared to exist at GTE. Although senior executives discussed the implications of the evolving information technology industry, no commonly accepted view of which competencies would be required to compete in that industry were communicated widely. While significant staff work was done to identify key technologies, senior line managers continued to act as if they were managing independent business units. Decentralization made it difficult to focus on core competencies. Instead, individual businesses became increasingly dependent on outsiders for critical skills, and collaboration became a route to staged exits. Today with a new management team in place, GTE has repositioned itself to apply its competencies to emerging markets in telecommunications services.

THE ROOTS OF COMPETITIVE ADVANTAGE

The distinction we observed in the way NEC and GTE conceived of themselves—a portfolio of competencies versus a portfolio of businesses—was repeated across many industries. From 1980 to 1988, Canon grew by 264%,

Honda by 200%. Compare that with Xerox and Chrysler. And if Western managers were once anxious about the low cost and high quality of Japanese imports, they are now overwhelmed by the pace at which Japanese rivals are inventing new markets, creating new products, and enhancing them. Canon has given us personal copiers, Honda has moved from motorcycles to four-wheel off-road buggies. Sony developed the 8mm camcorder, Yamaha, the digital piano. Komatsu developed an underwater remote-controlled bulldozer, while Casio's latest gambit is a small-screen color LCD television. Who would have anticipated the evolution of these vanguard markets?

In more established markets, the Japanese challenge has been just as disquieting. Japanese companies are generating a blizzard of features and functional enhancements that bring technological sophistication to everyday products. Japanese car producers have been pioneering four-wheel steering, four-valve-per-cylinder engines, in-car navigation systems, and sophisticated electronic engine-management systems. On the strength of its product features, Canon is now a player in facsimile transmission machines, desktop laser printers, even semiconductor manufacturing equipment.

In the short run, a company's competitiveness derives from the price/performance attributes of current products. But the survivors of the first wave of global competition, Western and Japanese alike, are all converging on similar and formidable standards for product cost and quality—minimum hurdles for continued competition, but less and less important as sources of differential advantage. In the long run, competitiveness derives from an ability to build, at lower cost and more speedily than competitors, the core competencies that spawn unanticipated products. The real sources of advantage are to be found in management's ability to consolidate corporatewide technologies and production skills into competencies that empower individual businesses to adapt quickly to changing opportunities.

Senior executives who claim that they cannot build core competencies either because they feel the autonomy of business units is sacrosanct or because their feet are held to the quarterly budget fire should think again. The problem in many Western companies is not that their senior executives are any less capable than those in Japan nor that Japanese companies possess greater technical capabilities. Instead, it is their adherence to a concept of the corporation that unnecessarily limits the ability of individual businesses to fully exploit the deep reservoir of technological capability that many American and European companies possess.

The diversified corporation is a large tree. The trunk and major limbs are core products, the smaller branches are business units; the leaves, flowers, and fruit are end products. The root system that provides nourishment, sustenance, and stability is the core competence. You can miss the strength of competitors by looking only at their end products, in the same way you miss the strength of a tree if you look only at its leaves. (See the chart "Competencies: The Roots of Competitiveness.")

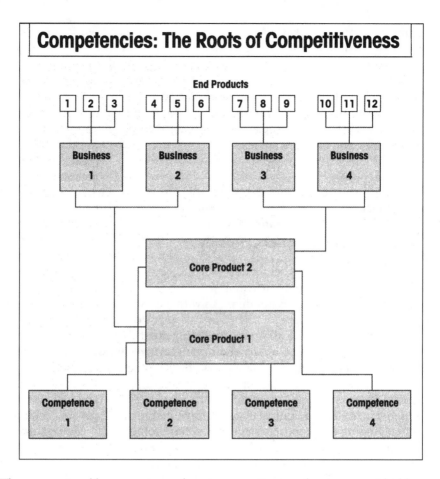

The corporation, like a tree, grows from its roots. Core products are nourished by competencies and engender business units, whose fruit are end products.

FIGURE 3.1 Competencies: The Roots of Competitiveness

Core competencies are the collective learning in the organization, especially how to coordinate diverse production skills and integrate multiple streams of technologies. Consider Sony's capacity to miniaturize or Philips's optical-media expertise. The theoretical knowledge to put a radio on a chip does not in itself assure a company the skill to produce a miniature radio no bigger than a business card. To bring off this feat, Casio must harmonize know-how in miniaturization, microprocessor design, material science, and ultrathin precision casing—the same skills it applies in its miniature card calculators, pocket TVs, and digital watches.

Unlike physical assets, competencies do not deteriorate as they are applied and shared. They grow. If core competence is about harmonizing streams of technology, it is also about the organization of work and the delivery of value. Among Sony's competencies is miniaturization. To bring miniaturization to its products, Sony must ensure that technologists, engineers, and marketers have a shared understanding of customer needs and of technological possibilities. The force of core competence is felt as decisively in services as in manufacturing. Citicorp was ahead of others investing in an operating system that allowed it to participate in world markets 24 hours a day. Its competence in systems has provided the company the means to differentiate itself from many financial service institutions.

Core competence is communication, involvement, and a deep commitment to working across organizational boundaries. It involves many levels of people and all functions. World-class research in, for example, lasers or ceramics can take place in corporate laboratories without having an impact on any of the businesses of the company The skills that together constitute core competence must coalesce around individuals whose efforts are not so narrowly focused that they cannot recognize the opportunities for blending their functional expertise with those of others in new and interesting ways.

Core competence does not diminish with use. Unlike physical assets, which do deteriorate over time, competencies are enhanced as they are applied and shared. But competencies still need to be nurtured and protected; knowledge fades if it is not used. Competencies are the glue that binds existing businesses. They are also the engine for new business development. Patterns of diversification and market entry may be guided by them, not just by the attractiveness of markets.

Consider SM's competence with sticky tape. In dreaming up businesses as diverse as "Post-it" notes, magnetic tape, photographic film, pressure-sensitive tapes, and coated abrasives, the company has brought to bear widely shared competencies in substrates, coatings, and adhesives and devised various ways to combine them. Indeed, SM has invested consistently in them. What seems to be an extremely diversified portfolio of businesses belies a few shared core competencies.

In contrast, there are major companies that have had the potential to build core competencies but failed to do so because top management was unable to conceive of the company as anything other than a collection of discrete businesses. GE sold much of its consumer electronics business to Thomson of France, arguing that it was becoming increasingly difficult to maintain its competitiveness in this sector. That was undoubtedly so, but it is ironic that it sold several key businesses to competitors who were already competence leaders—Black & Decker in small electrical motors, and Thomson, which was eager to build its competence in microelectronics and had learned from the Japanese that a position in consumer electronics was vital to this challenge.

Management trapped in the strategic business unit (SBU) mind-set almost inevitably finds its individual businesses dependent on external sources for critical components, such as motors or compressors. But these are not just components. They are core products that contribute to the competitiveness of a wide range of end products. They are the physical embodiments of core competencies.

HOW NOT TO THINK OF COMPETENCE

Since companies are in a race to build the competencies that determine global leadership, successful companies have stopped imagining themselves as bundles of businesses making products. Canon, Honda, Casio, or NEC may seem to preside over portfolios of businesses unrelated in terms of customers, distribution channels, and merchandising strategy. Indeed, they have portfolios that may seem idiosyncratic at times: NEC is the only global company to be among leaders in computing, telecommunications, and semiconductors *and* to have a thriving consumer electronics business.

But looks are deceiving. In NEC, digital technology, especially VLSI and systems integration skills, is fundamental. In the core competencies underlying them, disparate businesses become coherent. It is Honda's core competence in engines and power trains that gives it a distinctive advantage in car, motorcycle, lawn mower, and generator businesses. Canon's core competencies in optics, imaging, and microprocessor controls have enabled it to enter, even dominate, markets as seemingly diverse as copiers, laser printers, cameras, and image scanners. Philips worked for more than 15 years to perfect its optical-media (laser disc) competence, as did JVC in building a leading position in video recording. Other examples of core competencies might include mechantronics (the ability to marry mechanical and electronic engineering), video displays, bioengineering, and microelectronics. In the early stages of its competence building, Philips could not have imagined all the products that would be spawned by its optical-media competence, nor could JVC have anticipated miniature camcorders when it first began exploring videotape technologies.

Unlike the battle for global brand dominance, which is visible in the world's broadcast and print media and is aimed at building global "share of mind," the battle to build world-class competencies is invisible to people who aren't deliberately looking for it. Top management often tracks the cost and quality of competitors' products, yet how many managers untangle the web of alliances their Japanese competitors have contracted to acquire competencies at low cost? In how many Western boardrooms is there an explicit, shared understanding of the competencies the company must build for world leadership? Indeed, how many senior executives discuss the crucial distinction between competitive strategy at the level of a business and competitive strategy at the level of an entire company?

Let us be clear. Cultivating core competence does *not* mean outspending rivals on research and development. In 1983, when Canon surpassed Xerox in worldwide unit market share in the copier business, its R&D budget in reprographics was but a small fraction of Xerox's. Over the past 20 years, NEC has spent less on R&D as a percentage of sales than almost all of its American and European competitors.

Nor does core competence mean shared costs, as when two or more SBUs use a common facility—a plant, service facility or sales force—or share a common component. The gains of sharing may be substantial, but the search for shared costs is typically a post hoc effort to rationalize production across existing businesses, not a premeditated effort to build the competencies out of which the businesses themselves grow.

Building core competencies is more ambitious and different than integrating vertically moreover. Managers deciding whether to make or buy will start with end products and look upstream to the efficiencies of the supply chain and downstream toward distribution and customers. They do not take inventory of skills and look forward to applying them in nontraditional ways. (Of course, decisions about competencies do provide a logic for vertical integration. Canon is not particularly integrated in its copier business, except in those aspects of the vertical chain that support the competencies it regards as critical.)

IDENTIFYING CORE COMPETENCIES— AND LOSING THEM

At least three tests can be applied to identify core competencies in a company. First, a core competence provides potential access to a wide variety of markets. Competence in display systems, for example, enables a company to participate in such diverse businesses as calculators, miniature TV sets, monitors for laptop computers, and automotive dashboards -which is why Casio's entry into the handheld TV market was predictable. Second, a core competence should make a significant contribution to the perceived customer benefits of the end product. Clearly Honda's engine expertise fills this bill.

Finally, a core competence should be difficult for competitors to imitate. And it *will* be difficult if it is a complex harmonization of individual technologies and production skills. A rival might acquire some of the technologies that comprise the core competence, but it will find it more difficult to duplicate the more or less comprehensive pattern of internal coordination and learning. JVC's decision in the early 1960s to pursue the development of a videotape competence passed the three tests outlined here. RCA's decision in the late 1970s to develop a stylus-based video turntable system did not.

Few companies are likely to build world leadership in more than five or six fundamental competencies. A company that compiles a list of 20 to 30 capabilities has probably not produced a list of core competencies. Still, it is probably a good discipline to generate a list of this sort and to see aggregate capabilities as building blocks. This tends to prompt the search for licensing deals and alliances through which the company may acquire, at low cost, the missing pieces.

Most Western companies hardly think about competitiveness in these terms at all. It is time to take a tough-minded look at the risks they are running. Companies that judge competitiveness, their own and their competitors', primarily in terms of the price/performance of end products are courting the erosion of core competencies—or making too little effort to enhance them. The embedded skills that give rise to the next generation of competitive products cannot be "rented in" by outsourcing and OEM-supply relationships. In our view, too many companies have unwittingly surrendered core competencies when they cut internal investment in what they mistakenly thought were just "cost centers" in favor of outside suppliers.

Consider Chrysler. Unlike Honda, it has tended to view engines and power trains as simply one more component. Chrysler is becoming increasingly dependent on Mitsubishi and Hyundai: between 1985 and 1987, the number of outsourced engines went from 252,000 to 382,000. It is difficult to imagine Honda yielding manufacturing responsibility, much less design, of so critical a part of a car's function to an outside company—which is why Honda has made such an enormous commitment to Formula One auto racing. Honda has been able to pool its engine-related technologies; it has parlayed these into a corporatewide competency from which it develops world-beating products, despite R&D budgets smaller than those of GM and Toyota.

Of course, it is perfectly possible for a company to have a competitive product line up but be a laggard in developing core competencies—at least for a while. If a company wanted to enter the copier business today it would find a dozen Japanese companies more than willing to supply copiers on the basis of an OEM private label. But when fundamental technologies changed or if its supplier decided to enter the market directly and become a competitor, that company's product line, along with all of its investments in marketing and distribution, could be vulnerable. Outsourcing can provide a shortcut to a more competitive product, but it typically contributes little to building the people-embodied skills that are needed to sustain product leadership.

Nor is it possible for a company to have an intelligent alliance or sourcing strategy if it has not made a choice about where it will build competence leadership. Clearly Japanese companies have benefited from alliances. They've used them to learn from Western partners who were not fully committed to preserving core competencies of their own. As we've argued in these pages before, learning within an alliance takes a positive commitment of resources—travel, a pool of dedicated people, test-bed facilities, time to internalize and test what has been learned.[2] A company may not make this effort if it doesn't have clear goals for competence building.

Another way of losing is forgoing opportunities to establish competencies that are evolving in existing businesses. In the 1970s and 1980s, many American and European companies—like GE, Motorola, GTE, Thorn, and GEC—chose to exit the color television business, which they regarded as mature. If by "mature" they meant that they had run out of new product ideas at precisely the moment global rivals had targeted the TV business for entry, then yes, the industry was mature. But it certainly wasn't mature in the sense that all opportunities to enhance and apply video-based competencies had been exhausted.

In ridding themselves of their television businesses, these companies failed to distinguish between divesting the business and destroying their video media-

---

[2] "Collaborate with Your Competitors and Win," HBR January–February 1989, p. 133, with Yves L. Dot.

based competencies. They not only got out of the TV business but they also closed the door on a whole stream of future opportunities reliant on video-based competencies. The television industry considered by many U.S. companies in the 1970s to be unattractive, is today the focus of a fierce public policy debate about the inability of U.S. corporations to benefit from the $20-billion-a-year opportunity that HDTV will represent in the mid- to late 1990s. Ironically the U.S. government is being asked to fund a massive research project—in effect, to compensate U.S. companies for their failure to preserve critical core competencies when they had the chance.

In contrast, one can see a company like Sony reducing its emphasis on VCRs (where it has not been very successful and where Korean companies now threaten), without reducing its commitment to video-related competencies. Sony's Betamax led to a debacle. But it emerged with its videotape recording competencies intact and is currently challenging Matsushita in the 8mm camcorder market.

There are two clear lessons here. First, the costs of losing a core competence can be only partly calculated in advance. The baby may be thrown out with the bath water in divestment decisions. Second, since core competencies are built through a process of continuous improvement and enhancement that may span a decade or longer, a company that has failed to invest in core competence building will find it very difficult to enter an emerging market, unless, of course, it will be content simply to serve as a distribution channel.

American semiconductor companies like Motorola learned this painful lesson when they elected to forgo direct participation in the 256k generation of DRAM chips. Having skipped this round, Motorola, like most of its American competitors, needed a large infusion of technical help from Japanese partners to rejoin the battle in the 1-megabyte generation. When it comes to core competencies, it is difficult to get off the train, walk to the next station, and then reboard.

FROM CORE COMPETENCIES TO CORE PRODUCTS

The tangible link between identified core competencies and end products is what we call the core products—the physical embodiments of one or more core competencies. Honda's engines, for example, are core products, linchpins between design and development skills that ultimately lead to a proliferation of end products. Core products are the components or subassemblies that actually contribute to the value of the end products. Thinking in terms of core products forces a company to distinguish between the brand share it achieves in end product markets (for example, 40% of the U.S. refrigerator market) and the manufacturing share it achieves in any particular core product (for example, 5% of the world share of compressor output).

Canon is reputed to have an 84% world manufacturing share in desktop laser printer "engines," even though its brand share in the laser printer business is minuscule. Similarly Matsushita has a world manufacturing share of about 45% in key VCR components, far in excess of its brand share (Panasonic, JVC, and others) of 20%. And Matsushita has a commanding core product share in compressors worldwide, estimated at 40%, even though its brand share in both the air-conditioning and refrigerator businesses is quite small.

It is essential to make this distinction between core competencies, core products, and end products because global competition is played out by different rules and for different stakes at each level. To build or defend leadership over the long term, a corporation will probably be a winner at each level. At the level of core competence, the goal is to build world leadership in the design and development of a particular class of product functionality—be it compact data storage and retrieval, as with Philips's optical-media competence, or compactness and ease of use, as with Sony's micromotors and microprocessor controls.

To sustain leadership in their chosen core competence areas, these companies *seek to maximize their world manufacturing share in core products*. The manufacture of core products for a wide variety of external (and internal) customers yields the revenue and market feedback that, at least partly determines the pace at which core competencies can be enhanced and extended. This thinking was behind JVC's decision in the mid-1970s to establish VCR supply relationships with leading national consumer electronics companies in Europe and the United States. In supplying Thomson, Thorn, and Telefunken (all independent companies at that time) as well as U.S. partners, JVC was able to gain the cash and the diversity of market experience that ultimately enabled it to outpace Philips and Sony (Philips developed videotape competencies in parallel with JVC, but it failed to build a worldwide network of OEM relationships that would have allowed it to accelerate the refinement of its videotape competence through the sale of core products.)

JVC's success has not been lost on Korean companies like Goldstar, Sam Sung, Kia, and Daewoo, who are building core product leadership in areas as diverse as displays, semiconductors, and automotive engines through their OEM-supply contracts with Western companies. Their avowed goal is to capture investment initiative away from potential competitors, often U.S. companies. In doing so, they accelerate their competence-building efforts while "hollowing out" their competitors. By focusing on competence and embedding it in core products, Asian competitors have built up advantages in component markets first and have then leveraged off their superior products to move downstream to build brand share. And they are not likely to remain the low-cost suppliers forever. As their reputation for brand leadership is consolidated, they may well gain price leadership. Honda has proven this with its Acura line, and other Japanese car makers are following suit.

Control over core products is critical for other reasons. A dominant position in core products allows a company to shape the evolution of applications and end markets. Such compact audio disc-related core products as data drives and lasers have enabled Sony and Philips to influence the evolution of the computer-peripheral business in optical-media storage. As a company multiplies the number of application arenas for its core products, it can consistently reduce the

Two Concepts of the Corporation: SBU or Core Competence

	SBU	*Core Competence*
Basis for competition	Competitiveness of today's products	Interfirm competition to build competencies
Corporate structure	Portfolio of businesses related in product-market terms	Portfolio of competencies, core products, and businesses
Status of the business unit	Autonomy is sacrosanct; the SBU "owns" all resources other than cash	SBU is a potential reservoir of core competencies
Resource allocation	Discrete businesses are the unit of analysis; capital is allocated business by business	Businesses and competencies are the unit of analysis: top management allocates capital and talent
Value added of top management	Optimizing corporate returns through capital allocation trade-offs among businesses	Enunciating strategic architecture and building competencies to secure the future

BOX 3.1 Two Concepts of the Corporation: SBU or Core Competence

cost, time, and risk in new product development. In short, well-targeted core products can lead to economies of scale *and* scope.

THE TYRANNY OF THE SBU

The new terms of competitive engagement cannot be understood using analytical tools devised to manage the diversified corporation of 20 years ago, when competition was primarily domestic (GE versus Westinghouse, General Motors versus Ford) and all the key players were speaking the language of the same business schools and consultancies. Old prescriptions have potentially toxic side effects. The need for new principles is most obvious in companies organized exclusively according to the logic of SBUs. The implications of the two alternates of the corporation are summarized in "Two Concepts of the Corporation: SBU or Core Competence."

Obviously diversified corporations have a portfolio of products and a portfolio of businesses. But we believe in a view of the company as a portfolio of competencies as well. U.S. companies do not lack the technical resources to build competencies, but their top management often lacks the vision to build them and the administrative means for assembling resources spread across multiple businesses. A shift in commitment will inevitably influence patterns of diversification, skill deployment, resource allocation priorities, and approaches to alliances and outsourcing.

We have described the three different planes on which battles for global leadership are waged: core competence, core products, and end products. A corporation has to know whether it is winning or losing on each plane. By sheer weight of investment, a company might be able to beat its rivals to blue-sky technologies yet still lose the race to build core competence leadership. If a company is winning the race to build core competencies (as opposed to building leadership in a few technologies), it will almost certainly outpace rivals in new business development. If a company is winning the race to capture world manufacturing share in core products, it will probably outpace rivals in improving product features and the price/performance ratio.

Determining whether one is winning or losing end product battles is more difficult because measures of product market share do not necessarily reflect various companies' underlying competitiveness. Indeed, companies that attempt to build market share by relying on the competitiveness of others, rather than investing in core competencies and world core-product leadership, may be treading on quicksand. In the race for global brand dominance, companies like 3M, Black & Decker, Canon, Honda, NEC, and Citicorp have built global brand umbrellas by proliferating products out of their core competencies. This has allowed their individual businesses to build image, customer loyalty and access to distribution channels.

When you think about this reconceptualization of the corporation, the primacy of the SBU—an organizational dogma for a generation—is now clearly an anachronism. Where the SBU is an article of faith, resistance to the seductions of decentralization can seem heretical. In many companies, the SBU prism means that only one plane of the global competitive battle, the battle to put competitive products on the shelf *today*, is visible to top management. What are the costs of this distortion?

Underinvestment in Developing Core Competencies and Core Products

When the organization is conceived of as a multiplicity of SBUs, no single business may feel responsible for maintaining a viable position in core products nor be able to justify the investment required to build world leadership in some core competence. In the absence of a more comprehensive view imposed by corporate management, SBU managers will tend to underinvest. Recently companies such as Kodak and Philips have recognized this as a potential problem and have begun searching for new organizational forms that will allow them to develop and manufacture core products for both internal and external customers.

SBU managers have traditionally conceived of competitors in the same way they've seen themselves. On the whole, they've failed to note the emphasis Asian competitors were placing on building leadership in core products or to understand the critical linkage between world manufacturing leadership and the ability to sustain development pace in core competence. They've failed to pursue OEM-supply opportunities or to look across their various product divisions in an attempt to identify opportunities for coordinated initiatives.

Imprisoned Resources

As an SBU evolves, it often develops unique competencies. Typically the people who embody this competence are seen as the sole property of the business in which they grew up. The manager of another SBU who asks to borrow talented people is likely to get a cold rebuff. SBU managers are not only unwilling to lend their competence carriers but they may actually hide talent to prevent its redeployment in the pursuit of new opportunities. This may be compared to residents of an underdeveloped country hiding most of their cash under their mattresses. The benefits of competencies, like the benefits of the money supply depend on the velocity of their circulation as well as on the size of the stock the company holds.

Western companies have traditionally had an advantage in the stock of skills they possess. But have they been able to reconfigure them quickly to respond to new opportunities?

Canon, NEC, and Honda have had a lesser stock of the people and technologies that compose core competencies but could move them much quicker from one business unit to another. Corporate R&D spending at Canon is not fully indicative of the size of Canon's core competence stock and tells the casual observer nothing about the velocity with which Canon is able to move core competencies to exploit opportunities.

When competencies become imprisoned, the people who carry the competencies do not get assigned to the most exciting opportunities, and their skills begin to atrophy. Only by fully leveraging core competencies can small companies like Canon afford to compete with industry giants like Xerox. How strange that SBU managers, who are perfectly willing to compete for cash in the capital budgeting process, are unwilling to compete for people—the company's most precious asset. We find it ironic that top management devotes so much attention to the capital budgeting process yet typically has no comparable mechanism for allocating the human skills that embody core competencies. Top managers are seldom able to look four or five levels down into the organization, identify the people who embody critical competencies, and move them across organizational boundaries.

Bounded Innovation

If core competencies are not recognized, individual SBUs will pursue only those innovation opportunities that are close at hand—marginal product-line

Vickers Learns the Value of Strategic Architecture

The idea that top management should develop a corporate strategy for acquiring and deploying core competencies is relatively new in most U.S. companies. There are a few exceptions. An early convert was Trinova (previously Libbey Owens Ford), a Toledo-based corporation, which enjoys a worldwide position in power and motion controls and engineered plastics. One of its major divisions is Vickers, a premier supplier of hydraulics components like valves, pumps, actuators, and filtration devices to aerospace, marine, defense, automotive, earth-moving, and industrial markets.

Vickers saw the potential for a transformation of its traditional business with the application of electronics disciplines in combination with its traditional technologies. The goal was "to ensure that change in technology does not displace Vickers from its customers." This, to be sure, was initially a defensive move: Vickers recognized that unless it acquired new skills, it could not protect existing markets or capitalize on new growth opportunities. Managers at Vickers attempted to conceptualize the likely evolution of (a) technologies relevant to the power and motion control business, (b) functionalities that would satisfy emerging customer needs, and (c) new competencies needed to creatively manage the marriage of technology and customer needs.

Despite pressure for short-term earnings, top management looked to a 10- to 15-year time horizon in developing a map of emerging customer needs, changing technologies, and the core competencies that would be necessary to bridge the gap between the two. Its slogan was "Into the 21st Century." (A simplified version of the overall architecture developed is shown here.)

Vickers is currently in fluid-power components. The architecture identifies two additional competencies, electric-power components and electronic controls. A systems integration capability that would unite hardware, software, and service was also targeted for development.

The strategic architecture, as illustrated by the Vickers example, is not a forecast of specific products or specific technologies but a broad map of the evolving linkages between customer functionality requirements, potential technologies, and core competencies. It assumes that products and systems cannot be defined with certainty for the future but that preempting competitors in the development of new markets requires an early start to building core competencies. The strategic architecture developed by Vickers, while describing the future in competence terms, also provides the basis for making "here and now" decisions about product priorities, acquisitions, alliances, and recruitment.

Since 1986, Vickers has made more than ten clearly targeted acquisitions, each one focused on a specific component or technology gap identified in the overall architecture. The architecture is also the basis for internal development of new competencies. Vickers has undertaken, in parallel, a reorganization to enable the integration of electronics and electrical capabilities with mechanical-based competencies. We believe that it will take another two to three years before Vickers reaps the total benefits from developing the strategic architecture, communicating it widely to all its employees, customers, and investors, and building administrative systems consistent with the architecture.

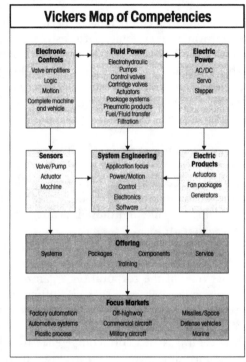

Vickers Map of Competencies

Electronic Controls	**Fluid Power**	**Electric Power**
Valve amplifiers	Electrohydraulic	AC/DC
Logic	Pumps	Servo
Motion	Control valves	Stepper
Complete machine and vehicle	Cartridge valves	
	Actuators	
	Package systems	
	Pneumatic products	
	Fuel/Fluid transfer	
	Filtration	

Sensors	**System Engineering**	**Electric Products**
Valve/Pump	Application focus	Actuators
Actuator	Power/Motion	Fan packages
Machine	Control	Generators
	Electronics	
	Software	

Offering			
Systems	Packages	Components	Service
	Training		

Focus Markets		
Factory automation	Off-highway	Missiles/Space
Automotive systems	Commercial aircraft	Defense vehicles
Plastic process	Military aircraft	Marine

BOX 3.2 Vickers Learns the Value of Strategic Architecture

extensions or geographic expansions. Hybrid opportunities like fax machines, laptop computers, hand-held televisions, or portable music keyboards will emerge only when managers take off their SBU blinkers. Remember, Canon appeared to be in the camera business at the time it was preparing to become a world leader in copiers. Conceiving of the corporation in terms of core competencies widens the domain of innovation.

DEVELOPING STRATEGIC ARCHITECTURE

The fragmentation of core competencies becomes inevitable when a diversified company's information systems, patterns of communication, career paths, managerial rewards, and processes of strategy development do not transcend SBU lines. We believe that senior management should spend a significant amount of its time developing a corporatewide strategic architecture that establishes objectives for competence building. A strategic architecture is a road map of the future that identifies which core competencies to build and their constituent technologies.

By providing an impetus for learning from alliances and a focus for internal development efforts, a strategic architecture like NEC's C&C can dramatically reduce the investment needed to secure future market leadership. How can a company make partnerships intelligently without a clear understanding of the core competencies it is trying to build and those it is attempting to prevent from being unintentionally transferred?

Of course, all of this begs the question of what a strategic architecture should look like. The answer will be different for every company. But it is helpful to think again of that tree, of the corporation organized around core products and, ultimately, core competencies. To sink sufficiently strong roots, a company must answer some fundamental questions: How long could we preserve our competitiveness in this business if we did not control this particular core competence? How central is this core competence to perceived customer benefits? What future opportunities would be foreclosed if we were to lose this particular competence?

The architecture provides a logic for product and market diversification, moreover. An SBU manager would be asked: Does the new market opportunity add to the overall goal of becoming the best player in the world? Does it exploit or add to the core competence? At Vickers, for example, diversification options have been judged in the context of becoming the best power and motion control company in the world (see the insert "Vickers Learns the Value of Strategic Architecture").

The strategic architecture should make resource allocation priorities transparent to the entire organization. It provides a template for allocation decisions by top management. It helps lower level managers understand the logic of allocation priorities and disciplines senior management to maintain consistency. In short, it yields a definition of the company and the markets it serves. 3M, Vickers, NEC, Canon, and Honda all qualify on this score. Honda *knew* it was exploiting what it had learned from motorcycles—how to make high-revving, smooth-running, lightweight engines—when it entered the car business. The task of creating a strategic architecture forces the organization to identify and commit to the technical and production linkages across SBUs that will provide a distinct competitive advantage.

It is consistency of resource allocation and the development of an administrative infrastructure appropriate to it that breathes life into a strategic architecture and creates a managerial culture, teamwork, a capacity to change, and a willingness to share resources, to protect proprietary skills, and to think long term. That is also the reason the specific architecture cannot be copied easily or overnight by competitors. Strategic architecture is a tool for communicating with customers and other external constituents. It reveals the broad direction without giving away every step.

REDEPLOYING TO EXPLOIT COMPETENCIES

If the company's core competencies are its critical resource and if top management must ensure that competence carriers are not held hostage by some particular business, then it follows that SBUs should bid for core competencies in the same way they bid for capital. We've made this point glancingly. It is important enough to consider more deeply.

Once top management (with the help of divisional and SBU managers) has identified overarching competencies, it must ask businesses to identify the projects and people closely connected with them. Corporate officers should direct an audit of the location, number, and quality of the people who embody competence.

This sends an important signal to middle managers: core competencies are *corporate* resources and may be reallocated by corporate management. An individual business doesn't own anybody. SBUs are entitled to the services of individual employees so long as SBU management can demonstrate that the opportunity it is pursuing yields the highest possible pay-off on the investment in their skills.

This message is further underlined if each year in the strategic planning or budgeting process unit managers must justify their hold on the people who carry the company's core competencies.

Elements of Canon's core competence in optics are spread across businesses as diverse as cameras, copiers, and semiconductor lithographic equipment and are shown in "Core Competencies at Canon." When Canon identified an opportunity in digital laser printers, it gave SBU managers the right to raid other SBUs to pull together the required pool of talent. When Canon's reprographics products division undertook to develop microprocessor-controlled copiers, it turned to the photo products group, which had developed the world's first microprocessor-controlled camera.

Also, reward systems that focus only on product-line results and career paths that seldom cross SBU boundaries engender patterns of behavior among unit managers that are destructively competitive. At NEC, divisional managers come together to identify next-generation competencies. Together they decide how much investment needs to be made to build up each future competency and

---

Core Competencies at Canon

	Precision Mechanics	Fine Optics	Micro-electronics
Basic camera	■	□	
Compact fashion camera	■	□	
Electronic camera	■	□	
EOS autofocus camera	■	□	■
Video still camera	■	□	■
Laser beam printer	■	□	■
Color video printer	■		■
Bubble jet printer	■		■
Basic fax	■		■
Laser fax	■		■
Calculator			■
Plain paper copier	■	□	■
Battery PPC	■	□	■
Color copier	■	□	■
Laser copier	■	□	■
Color laser copier	■	□	■
NAVI	■	□	■
Still video system	■	□	■
Laser imager	■	□	■
Cell analyzer	■	□	■
Mask aligners	■		■
Stepper aligners	■		■
Excimer laser aligners	■	□	■

Every Canon product is the result of at least one core competency.

BOX 3.3 Core Competencies at Canon

the contribution in capital and staff support that each division will need to make. There is also a sense of equitable exchange. One division may make a dispro-portionate contribution or may benefit less from the progress made, but such short-term inequalities will balance out over the long term.

Incidentally the positive contribution of the SBU manager should be made visible across the company. An SBU manager is unlikely to surrender key people if only the other business (or the general manager of that business who may be a competitor for promotion) is going to benefit from the redeployment. Cooperative SBU managers should be celebrated as team players. Where priorities are clear, transfers are less likely to be seen as idiosyncratic and politically motivated.

Transfers for the sake of building core competence must be recorded and appreciated in the corporate memory. It is reasonable to expect a business that has surrendered core skills on behalf of corporate opportunities in other areas to lose, for a time, some of its competitiveness. If these losses in performance bring immediate censure, SBUs will be unlikely to assent to skills transfers next time.

Finally there are ways to wean key employees off the idea that they belong in perpetuity to any particular business. Early in their careers, people may be exposed to a variety of businesses through a carefully planned rotation program. At Canon, critical people move regularly between the camera business and the copier business and between the copier business and the professional optical-products business. In mid-career, periodic assignments to cross-divisional project teams may be necessary both for diffusing core competencies and for loosening the bonds that might tie an individual to one business even when brighter opportunities beckon elsewhere. Those who embody critical core competencies should know that their careers are tracked and guided by corporate human resource professionals. In the early 1980s at Canon, all engineers under 30 were invited to apply for membership on a seven-person committee that was to spend two years plotting Canon's future direction, including its strategic architecture.

Competence carriers should be regularly brought together from across the corporation to trade notes and ideas. The goal is to build a strong feeling of community among these people. To a great extent, their loyalty should be to the integrity of the core competence area they represent and not just to particular businesses. In traveling regularly, talking frequently to customers, and meeting with peers, competence carriers may be encouraged to discover new market opportunities.

Core competencies are the wellspring of new business development. They should constitute the focus for strategy at the corporate level. Managers have to win manufacturing leadership in core products and capture global share through brand-building programs aimed at exploiting economics of scope. Only if the company is conceived of as a hierarchy of core competencies, core products, and market-focused business units will it be fit to fight.

Nor can top management be just another layer of accounting consolidation, which it often is in a regime of radical decentralization. Top management must add value by enunciating the strategic architecture that guides the competence acquisition process. We believe an obsession with competence building will characterize the global winners of the 1990s. With the decade underway the time for rethinking the concept of the corporation is already overdue.

Part Two
The Resource-Based
View of Knowledge

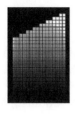

4

Excerpt from *The Theory of the Growth of the Firm*

Edith T. Penrose

THE CONTINUING AVAILABILITY OF UNUSED PRODUCTIVE SERVICES

Resources were defined in Chapter II of *The Theory and the Growth of the Firm* to include the physical things a firm buys, leases, or produces for its own use, and the people hired on terms that make them effectively part of the firm. Services, on the other hand, are the contributions these resources can make to the productive operations of the firm. A resource, then, can be viewed as a bundle of possible services.

The fact that most resources can provide a variety of different services is of great importance for the productive opportunity of a firm. It is the heterogeneity, and not the homogeneity, of the productive services available or potentially available from its resources that gives each firm its unique character. Not only can the personnel of a firm render a heterogeneous variety of unique services, but also the material resources of the firm can be used in different ways, which means that they can provide different kinds of services. This kind of heterogeneity in the services available from the material resources with which a firm works permits the same resources to be used in different ways and for different purposes if the people who work with them get different ideas about how they can be used. In other words there is an interaction between the two kinds of resources of a firm—its personnel and material resources—which affects the productive services available from each.

Interaction between Material and Human Resources

For physical resources the range of services *inherent* in any given resource depends on the physical characteristics of the resource, and it is probably safe to assume that at any given time the known productive services inherent in a resource do not exhaust the full potential of the resource. In other words, it is likely that increases in knowledge can always increase the range or amount of services available from any resource. Of the services available, only a few can be profitably used by a given Firm at a given time. Some of the services may be alternative uses of the resource—if used for one purpose the resource cannot be used for another; some of them may be suitable only for products which the Firm, because of cost and demand conditions, cannot profitably produce under the circumstances; some of them may be useful only in combination with other types of services which the Firm cannot obtain at the time.

The possibilities of using services change with changes in knowledge. More services become available, previously unused services become employed and employed services become unused as knowledge increases about the physical characteristics of resources, about ways of using them, or about products it would be profitable to use them for. Consequently, there is a close connection between the type of knowledge possessed by the personnel of the firm and the services obtainable from its material resources.

That the knowledge possessed by a firm's personnel tends to increase automatically with experience means, therefore, that the available productive services from a firm's resources will also tend to change. In addition, there is likely to be an increase in what, for want of a better term, I have in Chapter IV called 'objective' (or transmissible) knowledge. 'Objective' knowledge does not automatically increase in the same sense that the experience of a firm's personnel will automatically accumulate as the Firm operates. The search for 'objective' knowledge is, in a way, deliberate and voluntary, but at the same time it is so much a part of the normal operations assay thinking of businessmen that it cannot safely be left outside our system of explanation. Economists have, of course, always recognized the dominant role that increasing knowledge plays in economic processes but have, for the most part, found the whole subject of knowledge too slippery to handle with even a moderate degree of precision, and have made little attempt to analyze the effect of changes in the traditional economic variables upon changes in knowledge.[1] We cannot afford to avoid such an analysis here because not only are the significance of resources to a firm and the productive services they can yield, functions of knowledge, but—and this is the crucial fact—*entrepreneurs are fully aware of this*. Surely extensive questionnaires are

---

[1]The argument that the patent system stimulates invention implies that increased knowledge is a function of prospective profits. The economics of the argument have never been developed with any rigor but it remains one of the few economic 'models' in which knowledge becomes a function of an economic variable. See E. T. Penrose, *Economics of the International Patent System* (Baltimore: Johns Hopkins Press, 1951), pp. 34 ff.

not required to convince us that able businessmen are well aware that the more they can learn about the resources with which they are working and about their business the greater will be their prospects of successful action.

A firm is basically a collection of resources. Consequently, if we can assume that businessmen believe there is more to know about the resources they are working with than they do know at any given time, and that more knowledge would be liked to improve the efficiency and profitability of their firm, then unknown and unused productive services immediately become of considerable importance, not only because the belief that they exist acts as an incentive to acquire new knowledge, but also because they shape the scope and direction of the search for knowledge. If there are circumstances in which a businessman acquainted with the properties of the resources at his disposal (including his own abilities) says to himself regarding a particular resource, 'there ought to be some way in which I can use that', and subsequently proceeds to explore the possibilities of using it, then we can fairly conclude that he believes there are productive services inherent in that resource about which at best he knows little or nothing. The effort to discover more about the productive services of a resource may take the form of research into its characteristics or of research into ways of combining its known characteristics with those of other resources.

If ways of using resources which are not profitable at a given time may nevertheless influence the behavior of firms, we are justified in adopting a concept of 'economic resources' that is wider than the concept traditionally used in economic analysis. Resources or services without value are 'free' goods and are universally excluded from any 'productive' classification because they have no 'causal relation to conduct'.[2] It is the traditional view that 'superabundant elements in production' should be taken 'absolutely for granted' and ignored. 'Only the " possibility" of a situation arising in which a thing would not be superabundant can give it significance or lead to its being consciously considered in any way'.[3] Under the assumptions of the familiar equilibrium analysis, and for the purposes for which it is used, this procedure is undoubtedly correct. From the point of view of the present analysis the fact that there are ways of using free goods in production—air is the classic example—has considerable significance for the conduct of the firm. Some materials required in some types of production are in fact obtained from the air. If we assume that the state of the arts is not fixed and, in particular, that knowledge acquired by one Firm is not immediately available to all firms, then the fact that a good, is freely available may encourage innovations which use its services in production. The free resource may never become a valuable good in the economic sense, but it may still powerfully influence economic conduct, partly because the services it can render are not free in the same sense that the resource is free.

---

[2] Frank H. Knight, *Risk, Uncertainty, and Profit* (Boston: Houghton Mifflin, 1921), p. 61.
[3] Ibid., p. 97.

THE CREATION OF NEW PRODUCTIVE SERVICES

The import of the above argument is, essentially, that both an automatic increase in knowledge and an incentive to search for new knowledge are, as it were, 'built into' the very nature of firms possessing entrepreneurial resources of even average initiative. Physically describable resources are purchased in the market for their known services; but as soon as they become part of a firm the range of services they are capable of yielding starts to change. The services that resources will yield depend on the capacities of the men using them, but the development of the capacities of men is partly shaped by the resources men deal with. The two together create the special productive opportunity of a particular firm. The full potentialities for growth provided by this reciprocal change will not necessarily be realized by any given firm, but in so far as they are realized, growth will take place which cannot be satisfactorily explained with reference only to changes in the *environment* of the firm.

The process is one by which new productive services are continually becoming available to a firm, and the new services are not just those of its managerial and other personnel, but also of the physical resources with which a firm works. If these services can profitably be used only in expansion, the Firm will have an incentive to expand. Again, it is clear that a firm may be unable to take advantage of all the opportunities that are created by the new services available to it, since the amount of expansion it can plan is limited. But for the enterprising firm, even in the absence of changes in the external world, there is a continuous impelling pressure to expand, arising from the continuous opening up of new areas of profitable expansion.

To be sure, experience of the external world is part of the experience of a firm's personnel. We have concentrated on experience and increasing knowledge of the productive possibilities inherent in the resources of the firm; we should not ignore the effect of increased experience and knowledge of the external world and the effect of changes in the external world. Clearly external changes may also become part of a firm's stock of knowledge, and consequently they may change the significance of resources to the firm. Knowledge of markets, of technology being developed by other firms, and of the tastes and attitudes of consumers, are of particular importance. Moreover, many developments in technological knowledge become available to firms not simply as new knowledge, but physically embodied in the form of the capital equipment they buy.[4]

Many changes in the external world are appropriately treated as environmental changes affecting the rate of growth of firms through their effect on entrepreneurial expectations about productive possibilities. I have placed the emphasis on the significance of the resources with which a firm works and on

---

[4]A study of the significance of the fact that new technology becomes embodied physically in capital equipment has been made by W. E. G. Salter in a monograph to be published by the Cambridge Institute of Applied Economics.

the development of the experience and knowledge of a firm's personnel because these are the factors that will to a large extent determine the response of the firm to changes in the external work and also determine what it 'sees' in the external world. This is particularly evident when we recognize that changes in the knowledge possessed by the managerial personnel of a firm will not only change the productive services of other resources, but will also change the 'demand conditions' as seen by the firm.

5

Beyond the Knowledge Worker

Paul M. Romer

A new metaphor for business activities is necessary to understand the growing demand for knowledge. The concept of software holds the key, writes Paul Romer.

On a spring night in 1983, a chemist employed by the Cetus Corporation had a wonderful insight. While working on a narrow problem, Kary Mullis stumbled onto the principles of the polymerase chain reaction (PCR). The story behind this discovery is exciting because the stakes involved turned out to be so high. Mullis won a Nobel Prize. Molecular biologists were given a powerful research tool. Doctors got new diagnostic tests. Police investigators could begin to lift DNA "fingerprints" from small and badly degraded biological samples. Discoveries this dramatic are rare, but the underlying elements in the story have broad relevance. They illustrate an important aspect of economic activity that often goes unnoticed in discussions of what it is that managers do.

The activities of a business are typically understood by using the factory as a metaphor. The three basic inputs are assumed to be capital equipment, workers and raw materials. Workers are further subdivided into production and non-production workers. In this image, production workers do the actual work in the factory, aided by equipment. The instructions they follow are taken as given. One imagines that at some time in the past, an engineer trained in the principles of time-and-motion studies was called in to divide tasks between workers and specify actions. This implies that non-production workers such as managers are there merely to see that the production workers follow their instructions. In academic discussions, this image of management is formalised in terms of a "principal-agent" problem. The manager is the principal who must supervise the activities of hired agents who might shirk. Popularly, this image is summarised by the view that what supervisors do is "kick butt and take names."

From "Beyond the Knowledge Worker," *World Link,* January/February 1995.

But the factory never gave a complete picture of economic activity. Its description of non-production workers as regrettable overhead does not give a complete picture of production within manufacturing and is even more misleading in other sectors of the economy. Non-production workers do other tasks that are more important than seeing that production workers stay on the job. These other tasks are becoming ever more important in economic activity. In all sectors—even in manufacturing—the ratio of non-production to production workers has been increasing. Both the number of non-production workers and their wages have been growing over time, so some underlying factor must be increasing the demand for whatever it is that non-production workers like Kary Mullis do. The key to understanding the changes that are taking place in the economy is to develop an abstract image of what that is.

THE GROWING DEMAND FOR KNOWLEDGE

Years ago, Peter Drucker pointed to a distinction that is more useful than the familiar one of production versus non-production workers or workers versus supervisors. Some people, including most production workers, work with physical objects. Others work with intangibles. He called them knowledge workers. This is a start, for Mullis and people like him certainly produce knowledge. It remains for us to understand where the growing demand for knowledge is coming from.

According to recent debate the increase in demand is linked to the imminent arrival of the so-called information superhighway. In this analysis, production workers produce objects that get delivered to consumers on trucks; knowledge workers produce information that gets delivered to its consumers on a wire or through the air. The idea that knowledge workers are really just high-tech inputs into the entertainment industry fits with this industry's exaggerated sense of self-importance. However, the total output from all of the industries that could conceivably send their products over a wire still account for a small fraction of economic output. Relatively few knowledge workers produce information that a consumer will enjoy watching, hearing or reading. Mullis certainly was not one of them.

Some people have made the more useful observation that the knowledge workers employed by the entertainment industry produce the software that runs on hardware systems such as home video players or cable networks. This points to a different and more fruitful way to understanding economic activity, one based on desktop computing.

The computing metaphor replaces the traditional categories of inputs (capital, raw materials, production and non-production workers) with three broad classes of inputs: hardware, software and wetware. Hardware includes all the physical objects used in production—capital equipment, computers, structures, raw materials, infrastructure and so on. Wetware captures what economists call human capital and what philosophers and cognitive scientists sometimes call tacit knowledge. It includes all the things stored in the "wet" computer of a person's human brain.

Software includes all the knowledge that has been codified and can be transmitted to others: literal computer code, blueprints, mechanical drawings, operating instructions for machines, scientific principles, folk wisdom, films, books, musical recordings, the routines followed in a firm, the literal and figurative recipes we use, even the language we speak. It can be stored as text or drawings on paper, as images on film, or as a string of bits on a computer disk or a laser disk. Once the first copy of a piece of software has been produced, it can be reproduced, communicated and used simultaneously by an arbitrarily large number of people.

In the most general sense, what knowledge workers such as Mullis do is produce software. As the entertainment enthusiasts have noted, software can be used with hardware and wetware to please a consumer. Watching a video at home requires a video cassette recorder (the hardware), the software stored on the tape, and at least a bit of wetware—the knowledge of how to operate the VCR or at least where to find the operating instructions for it. A skier uses ski equipment (hardware), an innate sense of balance and learned physical responses (wetware) and instructions spoken to her by her instructor (software).

The problem with most discussions of the information superhighway is that they neglect the important role that software plays as an intermediate input in production. In the desktop environment from which the computer metaphor springs, a writer uses her skills (wetware), a word processing package (software) and a personal computer (hardware) to produce a document. This document could be a book that someone reads for pleasure, but it could also be an analysis of sales in the last quarter or a memo describing new repair procedures for service personnel.

Software has always contributed to production, even in the days before digital electronics brought it dramatically to the foreground. For example, in the textile factories of the last century, software for guiding the actions of a power loom was stored on wooden cards with holes punched in them. More broadly, workers followed explicit instructions that they learned from managers, teachers and colleagues.

Software is just as important in production that takes place outside the factory. In the last 100 years, for example, some improvements in agricultural productivity can be traced to new inputs such as tractors and chemical fertilisers produced in factories according to better software instructions. Other improvements can be traced to improved instructions about how to manage a farm. In the last century, these instructions have been developed through agricultural research and disseminated by agricultural extension services. But ever since the neolithic revolution, people have been accumulating software about how to grow crops and manage domesticated animals. It accumulated through trial and error and spread through face-to-face contact.

Because of software's unique capacity for simultaneous use by an arbitrarily large number of people, an innovation in software can have an impact that is felt on a massive scale. Some of the most important transitions in human history arose from the discovery of new methods for copying, storing and transmitting software. Examples include the introduction of written language, printing with moveable type, telecommunications and digital information processing. Many other revolutions were triggered by the discovery of new instructions for working with raw materials. Discoveries of this type include cereal cultivation methods; recipes for making iron, bronze, gunpowder and steel; techniques for making complicated mechanical goods from interchangeable parts; or methods for converting mechanical energy into electrical energy and back.

CREATING A NEW SET OF INSTRUCTIONS

The polymerase chain reaction that Mullis discovered is a set of instructions for working with biological materials. The instructions themselves are remarkably simple: put a small quantity of DNA, perhaps even a single molecule, into a test tube. Add some reagents. Repeatedly heat and cool the tube. The result is astonishing. With each cycle of heating and cooling, the number of identical copies of the DNA molecule will double (see Box).

One of the remarkable facts about the discovery of this technique is that all of the steps needed to make it work had existed for 15 years before Mullis put them together in just the right sequence. For years, scientists had been using the basic techniques to make single copies of sections of DNA. No one realised how this process could be repeated over and over, or if they did they failed to understand the implications of repeated doubling. After the first cycle one molecule will be copied, leaving two identical molecules. After the next cycles there will be two, four, eight, 16 and so on.

Even after Mullis had done his first experiment and shown that his idea would work, many scientists did not appreciate its significance. In the first few cycles of the reaction, the increase in the quantity of DNA does not seem very impressive but it soon begins to grow dramatically. After 10 cycles, the quantity of DNA has increased by a factor of 2 times itself 10 times, which is roughly equal to 1,000. After 20 cycles it has grown by 2 times itself 20 times, which is about 1 million. After 30 cycles the factor is 1 billion.

Humans have difficulty understanding how quickly the numbers grow in a sequence based on repeated multiplication—including Mullis himself who first conceived of PCR while driving his car. Once he saw its implications he tried to calculate these expansion factors in his head. Because they seemed too big to be believed, he pulled over to the side of the road to check his multiplication.

While driving that night, Mullis created something very valuable—a list of instructions that he could write down on paper which others could follow. Because it could be codified and transmitted to others, this software was soon being used by thousands of biologists all over the world. But the kind of production in which he was engaged was not the kind suggested by the factory metaphor. The company he worked for was a pharmaceutical firm, not a software firm, and Mullis was clearly not a production worker. He did not tend a vat that was brewing a batch of drug or feed a machine that stamped out pills. He was not even one of the people who were discovering and testing the software (the chemical formulae for new drugs) that production workers on a production line would use. That is, he did not synthesise test quantities of a new drug or supervise clinical testing of its effects.

What Mullis did was write software that other people could use when they tried to create software that production workers would ultimately use. At a software company like Microsoft, the analogous activity would be to write software-based programming tools that the people who write the code for software applications could use. In the end, production workers would then use this code to make the good that Microsoft actually sells. They would repeatedly copy it onto floppy disks and put the disks in a box together with a manual.

Most of the goods that consumers value are physical objects, not intangibles. The most important use for software is therefore as an input in the production of valuable objects. Software is something that managers must manage, just as they manage the wetware of their workers and the hardware of their factories. Sometimes they buy it. Sometimes they coordinate the internal production of it. Sometimes they create it themselves.

At the deepest level, the most misleading aspect of the factory model of economic activity is the suggestion that all of the instructions—all of the software—in any production activity can be discovered and perfected in the beginning. The same power of multiplication that makes PCR valuable means that there will always be room for refinement in our software.

To see just how much scope there is for the discovery of new software, think first of literal software stored on a computer disk. Each position or bit in a long string of digits can take on two values: 0 or 1. If the disk had room for just two bits, then it can hold $2 \times 2 = 4$ different computer programs: {0,0}, {0,1}, {1,0} and {1,1} If the computer has room for 10 bits it can store 2 times itself 10 times or 1,024 different programs. The possibilities here grow just as the DNA grows in PCR. Twenty bits can store about 1 million different sequences of zeros and ones, 30 bits about 1 billion and so on.

A typical computer hard disk has room for millions of bits, so the number of possible computer programs (that is, different bit strings) that could be installed on a desktop computer is too large to comprehend. For example, the number of distinct software programs (sequences of zeros and ones) that can be put on a one-gigabyte hard disk is roughly one followed by 2.7 billion zeros. This number of possible bit strings is very large relative to the physical quantities in our universe. A rough guess is that the total number of seconds that have elapsed since the big bang created the universe is about 1 followed by 17 zeros. Another rough guess is that the total number of atoms in the universe is equal to about 1 followed by 100 zeros.

The number of possibilities can be very large, even for very simple hardware systems. Suppose that a worker must assemble 20 numbered parts to make a final good. The software for this system is merely a description of the sequence the worker should use for assembling the parts. The worker could start with part number one, go on to connect part number two, then part number three and so on, proceeding in sequence. Or she could start with part number 13, connect part number 11, then part number 17 and so on. The number of different assembly sequences is equal to about 1 followed by 18 zeros, more than the number of seconds since the Big Bang.

In any actual assembly operations that can involve thousands of parts, there are many assembly sequences that have never been tried. Many of them will be much worse than the sequence currently being used. But almost surely there are others that would generate important efficiency gains. The best managers understand this potential for improvement and encourage workers on the assembly line to consider alternative assembly sequences, to experiment and to communicate their successes to others. In effect, they have made their production workers into knowledge workers as well.

Computers illustrate the potential and the peril that lies in the search for better software. The overwhelming majority of randomly generated bit strings that could be stored on a disk will generate useless garbage when the computer first starts up. Very similar pieces of software can have very different values. A carefully crafted piece of software can do wonderful things, but if even one bit in the program is changed its functionality can be destroyed.

The complexity of separating good from bad in unexplored software territory tends to encourage many managers to leave well enough alone. They do not encourage experimentation and they sometimes fail to pursue promising paths if they lead into unfamiliar terrain. But the big gains for society and big profits for firms will come from innovations in software. This is the lesson that has emerged so clearly from the experience of the computer industry. Firms like Microsoft and Intel earn the bulk of profits in their industries because they control the best software.

THE BEST MANAGERS FOSTER
SOFTWARE INNOVATION

Contrast their experience with that of photographic film giant Kodak, which tried to enter the business of making and selling floppy disks. No matter how talented its marketers, strategic planners and production workers, there was no way for Kodak to make money in this rapidly growing market because it did not control any proprietary software that it could use over and over again. The situation had been very different in its core area of photography, where Kodak's software for making colour film had been protected by patents.

The point is equally true in other areas. For example WalMart is the most successful retail chain in the world because it has the best software for running a discount retail store and it uses that software over and over again in stores throughout North America and perhaps eventually in the rest of the world.

So the best managers at the best companies foster software innovation at all levels, from the assembly line to the research lab. They understand the problems and develop testing systems that keep the downside risks under control. And when they see software that is new and better, they make sure that gets used over and over again and that their firm gets a small share of the benefits each time it is used.

Soon after Mullis made his discovery, PCR was recognised as a research tool, a diagnostic tool and a forensic tool. But it was not a pharmaceutical product and Cetus was in the pharmaceutical business. As in most start-up firms, financial and scientific resources were scarce and senior managers did not want to divert them to an area that was outside Cetus's core business. Fortunately for the shareholders of Cetus, there was one inspired manager who saw the potential and protected Mullis and his discovery. He created joint ventures with outside partners to develop PCR-based products. Ultimately, his efforts led to the sale of Cetus's rights in PCR to Hoffman-La Roche for $300 million. Had it not been for this manager, PCR might have been just another story of how a major technological breakthrough was neglected by the company that sponsored the original research and ended up being commercialised by some other firm.

The firms controlled by managers who understand what is at stake are being transformed to take advantage of the potential for discovering valuable kinds of software. At these firms, a relatively small fraction of the workforce is engaged in pure production, copying floppy disks or loading boxes of pills onto trucks. Most workers are knowledge workers engaged in discovering, testing and refining software. These are the activities that will lead to the biggest gains for business and for society as a whole. But the firms controlled by managers who do not understand the deeper issues will end up like Kodak, living off of slowly eroding profits from an earlier generation of software, wondering why the distinctive black and yellow packaging that seemed to work so well in the film business did not lead to profits in the computer industry.

HOW THE POLYMERASE CHAIN REACTION WORKS

The polymerase chain reaction can produce billions of copies of the DNA molecule that stores all of our genetic information because these molecules are like little zippers. They are double strands, zipped together. In the heating phase of PCR, the two strands become unzipped. If the solution containing these separated strands is cooled under the right conditions, each strand will reconstruct its mate, leaving two molecules that are identical to the original.

For each single strand to be able to reconstruct its mate, the solution in which these single strands are floating must contain free-floating links with hooks that can be used to make the missing side of the zipper. They are the raw materials for this reaction. The solution must also contain an enzyme called polymerase that helps free-floating zipper links connect up with single strands. These free links stick tightly to each other when they are inserted in adjacent open spots on the single strand. As these links accumulate and stick to each other, they form the missing strand that is zipped up with one of the single strands from the original molecule. Because adjacent links stick tightly to each other, this zipped pair of strands will melt into two single strands when the solution is heated again. With each cycle of heating and cooling, the number of copies doubles.

The important feature of this process is that it preserves the information coded in the DNA molecule. In real zippers, all links are the same. In a DNA molecule, each link has a letter or its mirror image stamped on it, and the hook from a link with a particular letter will only fit the hook from another link that has the mirror image of that letter.

The free floating links in the solution used in PCR have letters and their mirror images on them. One of these links will fall into place in the strand that is being made only if its letter is the mirror image of the letter on the opposing link in the single strand. In this way, the new strand has a mirror image of the entire message on the original single strand.

There is one other feature that makes the process very versatile. Molecules called primers can limit the copying to a short stretch of the long message coded in DNA. The situation for a molecular biologist is like that of a spy who knows that there was a paragraph in a vital document that started with "sometimes a . . ." and ends with ". . . originally planned". The spy knows the document has been mixed with millions of other documents and refuse at the local dump. The goal is to read the paragraph.

For a biologist, the problem is to read one short stretch of the code in a DNA molecule that has about 3 billion links with letters on them. The extra spy's documents are like the extraneous regions of DNA. The other refuse is like the other molecules that are mixed together with the DNA.

If the spy had a PCR-like technique, he could create primers that start copying whenever they find "sometimes a" and stop when the process reaches "originally planned". He could add blank paper and ink and mix them into the dump with a catalyst (the polymerase), and then go through cycles of heating and cooling. After as few as 30 cycles, the number of copies will be in the billions. The dump will consist almost entirely of copies of the sought-after paragraph.

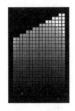

6
Dynamic Capabilities and Strategic Management

David J. Teece, Gary Pisano, and Amy Shuen

The dynamic capabilities framework analyzes the sources and methods of wealth creation and capture by private enterprise firms operating in environments of rapid technological change. The competitive advantage of firms is seen as resting on distinctive processes (ways of coordinating and combining), shaped by the firm's (specific) asset positions (such as the firm's portfolio of difficult-to-trade knowledge assets and complementary assets), and the evolution path(s) it has adopted or inherited. The importance of path dependencies is amplified where conditions of increasing returns exist. Whether and how a firm's competitive advantage is eroded depends on the stability of market demand, and the ease of replicability (expanding internally) and imitability (replication by competitors). If correct, the framework suggests that private wealth creation in regimes of rapid technological change depends in large measure on honing internal technological, organizational, and managerial processes inside the firm. In short, identifying new opportunities and organizing effectively and efficiently to embrace them are generally more fundamental to private wealth creation than is strategizing, if by strategizing one means engaging in business conduct that keeps competitors off balance, raises rival's costs, and excludes new entrants. (1997 by John Wiley & Sons, Ltd.)

From Strategic Management Journal, Vol. 18, No. 7, 1997, pp. 509–533. Reproduced by permission of John Wiley and Sons Ltd.

David J. Teece, Haas School of Business, University of California, Berkeley, California, USA; Gary Pisano, Graduate School of Business Administration, Harvard University, Boston, Massachusetts, USA; and Amy Shuen, School of Business, San Jose State University, San Jose, California, USA.

INTRODUCTION

The fundamental question in the field of strategic management is how firms achieve and sustain competitive advantage.[1] We confront this question here by developing the dynamic capabilities approach, which endeavors to analyze the sources of wealth creation and capture by firms. The development of this framework flows from a recognition by the authors that strategic theory is replete with analyses of firm-level strategies for sustaining and safeguarding extant competitive advantage, but has performed less well with respect to assisting in the understanding of how and why certain firms build competitive advantage in regimes of rapid change. Our approach is especially relevant in a Schumpeterian world of innovation-based competition, price/performance rivalry, increasing returns, and the 'creative destruction' of existing competences. The approach endeavors to explain firm-level success and failure. We are interested in both building a better theory of firm performance, as well as informing managerial practice.

In order to position our analysis in a manner that displays similarities and differences with existing approaches, we begin by briefly reviewing accepted frameworks for strategic management. We endeavor to expose implicit assumptions, and identify competitive circumstances where each paradigm might display some relative advantage as both a useful descriptive and normative theory of competitive strategy. While numerous theories have been advanced over the past two decades about the sources of competitive advantage, many cluster around just a few loosely structured frameworks or paradigms. In this paper we attempt to identify three existing paradigms and describe aspects of an emerging new paradigm that we label dynamic capabilities.

The dominant paradigm in the field during the 1980s was the competitive forces approach developed by Porter (1980). This approach, rooted in the structure-conduct-performance paradigm of industrial organization (Mason, 1949; Bain, 1959), emphasizes the actions a firm can take to create defensible positions against competitive forces. A second approach, referred to as a strategic conflict approach (e.g., Shapiro, 1989), is closely related to the first in its focus on product market imperfections, entry deterrence, and strategic interaction. The strategic conflict approach uses the tools of game theory and thus implicitly views competitive outcomes as a function of the effectiveness with which firms keep their rivals off balance through strategic investments, pricing strategies, signaling, and the control of information. Both the competitive forces and the strategic conflict approaches appear to share the view that rents flow from privileged product market positions.

Another distinct class of approaches emphasizes building competitive advantage through capturing entrepreneurial rents stemming from fundamental firm-level efficiency advantages. These approaches have their roots in a much older discussion of corporate strengths and weaknesses; they have taken on new

---

[1] For a review of the fundamental questions in the field of strategy, see Rumelt, Schendel, and Teece (1994).

life as evidence suggests that firms build enduring advantages only through efficiency and effectiveness, and as developments in organizational economics and the study of technological and organizational change become applied to strategy questions. One strand of this literature, often referred to as the 'resource-based perspective,' emphasizes firm-specific capabilities and assets and the existence of isolating mechanisms as the fundamental determinants of firm performance (Penrose, 1959; Rumelt, 1984; Teece, 1984; Wemerfelt, 1984).[2] This perspective recognizes but does not attempt to explain the nature of the isolating mechanisms that enable entrepreneurial rents and competitive advantage to be sustained.

Another component of the efficiency-based approach is developed in this paper. Rudimentary efforts are made to identify the dimensions of firm-specific capabilities that can be sources of advantage, and to explain how combinations of competences and resources can be developed, deployed, and protected. We refer to this as the 'dynamic capabilities' approach in order to stress exploiting existing internal and external firm specific competences to address changing environments. Elements of the approach can be found in Schumpeter (1942), Penrose (1959), Nelson and Winter (1982), Prahalad and Hamel (1990), Teece (1976, 1986a, 1986b, 1988) and in Hayes, Wheelwright, and Clark (1988): Because this approach emphasizes the development of management capabilities, and difficult-to-imitate combinations of organizational, functional and technological skills, it integrates and draws upon research in such areas as the management of R&D, product and process development, technology transfer, intellectual property, manufacturing, human resources, and organizational learning. Because these fields are often viewed as outside the traditional boundaries of strategy, much of this research has not been incorporated into existing economic approaches to strategy issues. As a result, dynamic capabilities can be seen as an emerging and potentially integrative approach to understanding the newer sources of competitive advantage.

We suggest that the dynamic capabilities approach is promising both in terms of future research potential and as an aid to management endeavoring to gain competitive advantage in increasingly demanding environments. To illustrate the essential elements of the dynamic capabilities approach, the sections that follow compare and contrast this approach to other models of strategy. Each section highlights the strategic insights provided by each approach as well as the

---

[2] Of these authors, Rumelt may have been the first to self-consciously apply a resource to the field of strategy. Rumelt (1984:561) notes that the strategic firm 'is characterized by a bundle of linked and idiosyncratic resources and resource conversion activities.' Similarly, Teece (1984:95) notes: 'Successful firms possess one or more forms of intangible assets, such as technological or managerial knowhow. Over time, these assets may expand beyond the point of profitable reinvestment in a firm's traditional market. Accordingly, the firm may consider deploying its intangible assets in different product or geographical markets, where the expected returns are higher, if efficient transfer modes exist.' Wernerfelt, (1984) was early to recognize that this approach was at odds with product market approaches and might constitute a distinct paradigm of strategy.

different competitive circumstances in which it might be most appropriate. Needless to say, these approaches are in many ways complementary and a full understanding of firm-level, competitive advantage requires an appreciation of all four approaches and more.

MODELS OF STRATEGY EMPHASIZING THE EXPLOITATION OF MARKET POWER

Competitive Forces

The dominant paradigm in strategy at least during the 1980s was the competitive forces approach. Pioneered by Porter (1980), the competitive forces approach views the essence of competitive strategy formulation as 'relating a company to its environment . . . [T]he key aspect of the firm's environment is the industry or industries in which it competes.' Industry structure strongly influences the competitive rules of the game as well as the strategies potentially available to firms.

In the competitive forces model, five industry level forces—entry barriers, threat of substitution, bargaining power of buyers, bargaining power of suppliers, and rivalry among industry incumbents-determine the inherent profit potential of an industry or subsegment of an industry. The approach can be used to help the firm find a position in an industry from which it can best defend itself against competitive forces or influence them in its favor (Porter, 1980: 4).

This 'five-forces' framework provides a systematic way of thinking about how competitive forces work at the industry level and how these forces determine the profitability of different industries and industry segments. The competitive forces framework also contains a number of underlying assumptions about the sources of competition and the nature of the strategy process. To facilitate comparisons with other approaches, we highlight several distinctive characteristics of the framework.

Economic rents in the competitive forces framework are monopoly rents (Teece, 1984). Firms in an industry earn rents when they are somehow able to impede the competitive forces (in either factor markets or product markets) which tend to drive economic returns to zero. Available strategies are described in Porter (1980). Competitive strategies are often aimed at altering the firm's position in the industry *vis-a-vis* competitors and suppliers. Industry structure plays a central role in determining and limiting strategic action.

Some industries or subsectors of industries become more 'attractive' because they have structural impediments to competitive forces (e.g., entry barriers) that allow firms better opportunities for creating sustainable competitive advantages. Rents are created largely at the industry or subsector level rather than at the firm level. While there is some recognition given to firm specific assets, differences among firms relate primarily to scale. This approach to strategy reflects its incubation inside the field of industrial organization and in par-ticular the industrial structure school of Mason and Bain [3] (Teece, 1984).

Strategic Conflict

The publication of Carl Shapiro's 1989 article, confidently titled 'The Theory of Business Strategy,' announced the emergence of a new approach to business strategy, if not strategic management. This approach utilizes the tools of game theory to analyze the nature of competitive interaction between rival firms. The main thrust of work in this tradition is to reveal how a firm can influence the behavior and actions of rival firms and thus the market environment.[4] Examples of such moves are investment in capacity (Dixit, 1980), R&D (Gilbert and Newberry, 1982), and advertising (Schmatensee, 1983). To be effective, these strategic moves require irreversible commitments.[5] The moves in question will have no effect if they can be costlessly undone. A key idea is that by manip-ulating the market environment, a firm may be able to increase its profits.

This literature, together with the contestability literature (Baumol, Panzar, and Willig, 1982), has led to a greater appreciation of the role of sunk costs, as opposed to fixed costs, in determining competitive outcomes. Strategic moves can also be designed to influence rivals' behavior through signaling. Strategic sig-naling has been examined in a number of contexts, including predatory pricing (Kreps and Wilson, 1982a, 1982b) and limit pricing (Milgrom and Roberts, 1982a, 1982b). More recent treatments have emphasized the role of commit-ment and reputation (e.g., Ghemawat, 1991) and the benefits of firms simulta-neously pursuing competition and cooperation[6] (Brandenburger and Nalebuff, 1995, 1996).

In many instances, game theory formalizes long-standing intuitive argu-ments about various types of business behavior (e.g., predatory pricing, patent races), though in some instances it has induced a substantial change in the con-ventional wisdom. But by rationalizing observed behavior by reference to suit-ably designed games, in explaining everything these models also explain nothing, as they do not generate testable predictions (Sutton, 1992). Many specific game-

---

[3] In competitive environments characterized by sustainable and stable mobility and struc-tural barriers, these forces may become the determinants of industry-level profitability. However, competitive advantage is more complex to ascertain in environments of rapid technological change where specific assets owned by heterogeneous firms can be expected to play a larger role in explaining rents.

[4] The market environment is all factors that influence market outcomes (prices, quanti-ties, profits) including the beliefs of customers and of rivals, the number of potential tech-nologies employed, and the costs or speed with which a rival can enter the industry.

[5] For an excellent discussion of committed competition in multiple contexts, see Ghemawat (1991).

[6] Competition and cooperation have also been analyzed outside of this tradition. See, for example, Teece (1992) and Link, Teece and Finan (1996).

theoretic models admit multiple equilibrium, and a wide range of choice exists as to the design of the appropriate game form to be used. Unfortunately, the results often depend on the precise specification chosen. The equilibrium in models of strategic behavior crucially depends on what one rival believes another rival will do in a particular situation. Thus the qualitative features of the results may depend on the way price competition is modeled (e.g., Bertrand or Coumot) or on the presence or absence of strategic asymmetries such as first-mover advantages. The analysis of strategic moves using game theory can be thought of as 'dynamic' in the sense that multiperiod analyses can be pursued both intuitively and formally. However, we use the term 'dynamic' in this paper in a different sense, referring to situations where there is rapid change in technology and market forces, and 'feedback' effects on firms.[7]

We have a particular view of the contexts in which the strategic conflict literature is relative to strategic management. Firms that have tremendous cost or other competitive advantage *vis-a-vis* their rivals ought not be transfixed by the moves and countermoves of their rivals. Their competitive fortunes will swing more on total demand conditions, not on how competitors, deploy and redeploy their competitive assets. Put differently, when there are gross asymmetries in competitive advantage between firms, the result of game-theoretic analysis are likely to be obvious and uninteresting. The stronger competitor will generally advance, even if disadvantaged by certain information asymmetries. To be sure, incumbent firms can be undone by new entrants with a dramatic cost advantage, but no 'gaming' will overturn that outcome. On the other hand, if firms' competitive positions are more delicately balanced, as with Coke and Pepsi, and United Airlines and American Airlines, then strategic conflict is of interest to competitive outcome. Needless to say, there are many such circumstances, but they are rare in industries where there is rapid technological change and fast-shifting market circumstances.

In short, where competitors do not have deep-seated competitive advantages, the moves and countermoves of competitors can often be usefully formulated in game-theoretic terms. However, we doubt that game theory can comprehensively illuminate how Chrysler should compete against Toyota and Honda, or how United Airlines can best respond to Southwest Airlines since Southwest's advantage is built on organization attributes which United cannot readily replicate.[8] Indeed, the entrepreneurial side of strategy—how significant new rent streams are created and protected—is largely ignored by the game-theoretic approach.[9] Accordingly, we find that the approach, while

---

[7] Accordingly, both approaches are dynamic, but in very different senses.

[8] Thus even in the air transport industry game-theoretic formulations by no means capture all the relevant dimensions of competitive rivalry. United Airlines' and United Express's difficulties in competing with Southwest Airlines because of United's inability to fully replicate Southwest's operation capabilities is documented in Gittel (1995).

[9] Important exceptions can be found in Brandenburger and Nalebuff (1996) such as their emphasis on the role of complements. However, these insights do not flow uniquely from game theory and can be found in the organizational economics literature (e.g., Teece, 1986a, 1986b; de Figueiredo and Teece. 1996).

important, is most relevant when competitors are closely matched[10] and the population of relevant competitors and the identity of their strategic alternatives can be readily ascertained. Nevertheless, coupled with other approaches it can sometimes yield powerful insights.

However, this research has an orientation that we are concerned about in terms of the implicit framing of strategic issues. Rents, from a game theoretic perspective, are ultimately a result of managers' intellectual ability to 'play the game.' The adage of the strategist steeped in this approach is 'do unto others before they do unto you.' We worry that fascination with strategic moves and Machiavellian tricks will distract managers from seeking to build more enduring sources of competitive advantage. The approach unfortunately ignores competition as a process involving the development, accumulation, combination, and protection of unique skills and capabilities. Since strategic interactions are what receive focal attention, the impression one might receive from this literature is that success in the marketplace is the result of sophisticated plays and counterplays, when this is generally not the case at all.[11]

In what follows, we suggest that building a dynamic view of the business enterprise- something missing from the two approaches we have so far identified—enhances the probability of establishing an acceptable descriptive theory of strategy that can assist practitioners in the building of long-run advantage and competitive flexibility. Below, we discuss first the resource-based perspective and then an extension we call the dynamic capabilities approach.

MODELS OF STRATEGY EMPHASIZING EFFICIENCY

Resource-Based Perspective

The resource-based approach sees firms with superior systems and structures being profitable, not because they engage in strategic investments that may deter entry and raise prices above long-run costs, but because they have markedly lower costs, or offer markedly higher quality or product performance. This approach focuses on the rents accruing to the owners of scarce firm-specific resources rather than the economic profits from product market positioning.[12] Competitive advantage lies 'upstream' of product markets and rests on the firm's idiosyncratic and difficult-to-imitate resources.[13]

---

[10] When closely matched in an aggregate sense, they may nevertheless display asymmetries which game theorists can analyze.

[11] The strategic conflict literature also tends to focus practitioners on product market positioning rather than on developing the unique assets which make possible superior product market positions (Dierickx and Cool, 1989).

[12] In the language of economics, rents flow from unique firm specific assets that cannot readily be replicated, rather than from tactics which deter entry and keep competitors off balance. In short, rents are Ricardian.

[13] Teece (1982: 46) saw the firm as having 'a variety of end products which it can produce with its organizational technology.'

One can find the resources approach suggested by the earlier preanalytic strategy literature. A leading text of the 1960s (Learned *et al.*, 1969) noted that 'the capability of an organization is its demonstrated and potential ability to accomplish against the opposition of circumstance or competition, whatever it sets out to do. Every organization has actual and potential strengths and weaknesses; it is important to try to determine what they are and to distinguish one from the other.' Thus what a firm can do is not just a function of the opportunities it confronts; it also depends on what resources the organization can muster.

Learned *et al.* proposed that the real key to a company's success or even to its future development lies in its ability to find or create 'a competence that is truly distinctive.'[14] This literature also recognized the constraints on firm behavior and, in particular, noted that one should not assume that management 'can rise to any occasion.' These insights do appear to keenly anticipate the resource-based approach that has since emerged, but they did not provide a theory or systematic framework for analyzing business strategies. Indeed, Andrews (1987: 46) noted that 'much of what is intuitive in this process is yet to be identified.' Unfortunately, the academic literature on capabilities stalled for a couple of decades.

New impetus has been given to the resource based approach by recent theoretical developments in organizational economics and in the theory of strategy, as well as by a growing body of anecdotal and empirical literature [15] that highlights the importance of firm-specific factors in explaining firm performance. Cool and Schendel (1988) have shown that there are systematic and significant performance differences among firms which belong to the same strategic group within the U.S. pharmaceutical industry. Rumelt (1991) has shown that intra-industry differences in profits are greater than inter-industry differences in profits, strongly suggesting the importance of firm-specific factors and the relative unimportance of industry effects.[16] Jacobsen (1988) and Hansen and Wemerfelt (1989) made similar findings.

A comparison of the resource-based approach and the competitive forces approach (discussed earlier in the paper) in terms of their implications for the strategy process is revealing. From the first perspective, an entry decision looks roughly as follows: (1) pick an industry (based on its 'structural attractiveness'); (2) choose an entry strategy based on conjectures about competitors' rational

---

[14] Elsewhere Andrews (1987: 47) defined a distinctive competence as what an organization can do particularly well.

[15] Studies of the automobile and other industries displayed differences in organization which often underlay differences amongst firms. See, for example, Womack, Jones, and Roos, 1991; Hayes and Clark, 1985; Barney, Spender and Reve, 1994; Clark and Fujimoto, 1991; Henderson and Cockburn, 1994; Nelson, 1991; Levinthal and Myatt, 1994.

[16] Using FFC line of business data, Rumelt showed that stable industry effects account for only 8 percent of the variance in business unit returns. Furthermore, only about 40 percent of the dispersion in industry returns is due to stable industry effects.

strategies; (3) if not already possessed, acquire or otherwise obtain the requisite assets to compete in the market. From this perspective, the process of identifying and developing the requisite assets is not particularly problematic. The process involves nothing more than choosing rationally among a well-defined set of investment alternatives. If assets are not already owned, they can be bought. The resource-based perspective is strongly at odds with this conceptualization.

From the resource-based perspective, firms are heterogeneous with respect to their resources/capabilities/endowments. Further, resource endowments are 'sticky:' at least in the short run, firms are to some degree stuck with what they have and may have to live with what they lack.[17] This stickiness arises for three reasons. First, business development is viewed as an extremely complex process.[18] Quite simply, firms lack the organizational capacity to develop new competences quickly (Dierickx and Cool, 1989). Secondly, some assets are simply not readily tradeable, for example, tacit know-how (Teece, 1976, 1980) and reputation (Dierickx and Cool, 1989). Thus, resource endowments cannot equilibrate through factor input markets. Finally, even when an asset can be purchased, firms may stand to gain little by doing so. As Barney (1986) points out, unless a firm is lucky, possesses superior information, or both, the price it pays in a competitive factor market will fully capitalize the rents from the asset.

Given that in the resources perspective firms possess heterogeneous and sticky resource bundles, the entry decision process suggested by this approach is as follows: (1) identify your firm's unique resources; (2) decide in which markets those resources can earn the highest rents; and (3) decide whether the rents from those assets are most effectively utilized by (a) integrating into related market(s), (b) selling the relevant intermediate output to related firms, or (c) selling the assets themselves to a firm in related businesses (Teece, 1980, 1982).

The resource-based perspective puts both vertical integration and diversification into a new strategic light. Both can be viewed as ways of capturing rents on scarce, firm-specific assets whose services are difficult to sell in intermediate markets (Penrose, 1959; Williamson, 1975; Teece, 1980, 1982, 1986a, 1986b; Wernerfelt, 1984). Empirical work on the relationship between performance and diversification by Wernerfelt and Montgomery (1988) provides evidence for this proposition. It is evident that the resource-based perspective focuses on strategies for exploiting existing firm-specific assets.

However, the resource-based perspective also invites consideration of managerial strategies for developing new capabilities (Wernerfelt, 1984). Indeed, if control over scarce resources is the source of economic profits, then it follows that such issues as skill acquisition, the management of knowledge and know-how (Shuen, 1994), and learning become fundamental strategic issues. It is in this second dimension, encompassing skill acquisition, learning, and accumulation of

---

[17] In this regard, this approach has much in common with recent work on organizational ecology (e.g., Freeman and Boeker, 1984) and also on commitment (Ghemawat, 1991: 17–25).

[18] Capability development, however, is not really analyzed.

organizational and intangible or 'invisible' assets (Itami and Roehl, 1987), that we believe lies the greatest potential for contributions to strategy.

The Dynamic Capabilities Approach: Overview

The global competitive battles in high-technology industries such as semi-conductors, information services, and software have demonstrated the need for an expanded paradigm to understand how competitive advantage is achieved. Well-known companies like IBM, Texas Instruments, Philips, and others appear to have followed a 'resource based strategy' of accumulating valuable technology assets, often guarded by an aggressive intellectual property stance. However, this strategy is often not enough to support a significant competitive advantage. Winners in the global marketplace have been firms that can demonstrate timely responsiveness and rapid and flexible product innovation, coupled with the management capability to effectively coordinate and redeploy internal and external competences. Not surprisingly, industry observers have remarked that companies can accumulate a large stock of valuable technology assets and still not have many useful capabilities.

We refer to this ability to achieve new forms of competitive advantage as 'dynamic capabilities' to emphasize two key aspects that were not the main focus of attention in previous strategy perspectives. The term 'dynamic' refers to the capacity to renew competences so as to achieve congruence with the changing business environment; certain innovative responses are required when time-to-market and timing are critical, the rate of technological change is rapid, and the nature of future competition and markets difficult to determine. The term 'capabilities' emphasizes the key role of strategic management in appropriately adapting, integrating, and reconfiguring internal and external organizational skills, resources, and functional competences to match the requirements of a changing environment.

One aspect of the strategic problem facing an innovating firm in a world of Schumpeterian competition is to identify difficult-to-imitate internal and external competences most likely to support valuable products and services. Thus, as argued by Dierickx and Cool (1989), choices about how much to spend (invest) on different possible areas are central to the firm's strategy. However, choices about domains of competence are influenced by past choices. At any given point in time, firms must follow a certain trajectory or path of competence development. This path not only defines what choices are open to the firm today, but it also puts bounds around what its internal repertoire is likely to be in the future. Thus, firms, at various points in time, make long term, quasi-irreversible commitments to certain domains of competence.[19]

---

[19] Deciding, under significant uncertainty about future states of the world, which long-term paths to commit to and when to change paths is the central strategic problem confronting the firm. In this regard, the work of Ghemawat (1991) is highly germane to the dynamic capabilities approach to strategy.

The notion that competitive advantage requires both the exploitation of existing internal and external firm-specific capabilities, and developing new ones is partially developed in Penrose (1959), Teece (1982), and Wernerfelt (1984). However, only recently have researchers begun to focus on the specifics of how some organizations first develop firm-specific capabilities and how they renew competences to respond to shifts in the business environments.[20] These issues are intimately tied to the firm's business processes, market positions, and expansion paths. Several writers have recently offered insights and evidence on how firms can develop their capability to adapt and even capitalize on rapidly changing environments.[21] The dynamic capabilities approach seeks to provide a coherent framework which can both integrate existing conceptual and empirical knowledge, and facilitate prescription. In doing so, it builds upon the theoretical foundations provided by Schumpeter (1934), Penrose (1959), Williamson (1975, 1985), Barney (1986), Nelson and Winter (1982), Teece (1988), and *Teece et al.* (1994).

TOWARD A DYNAMIC CAPABILITIES FRAMEWORK

Terminology

In order to facilitate theory development and intellectual dialogue, some acceptable definitions are desirable. We propose the following.

Factors of Production

These are 'undifferentiated' inputs available in disaggregate form in factor markets. By undifferentiated we mean that they lack a firm-specific component. Land, unskilled labor, and capital are typical examples. Some factors may be available for the taking, such as public knowledge. In the language of Arrow, such resources must be 'nonfugitive.'[22] Property rights are usually well-defined for factors of production.

Resources[23]

Resources are firm-specific assets that are difficult if not impossible to imitate. Trade secrets and certain specialized production facilities and engineering

---

[20] See, for example, Iansiti and Clark (1994) and Henderson (1994).
[21] See Hayes *et al.* (1988), Prahalad and Hamel (1990), Dierickx and Cool (1989), Chandler (1990), and Teece (1993).
[22] Arrow (1996) defines fugitive resources as ones that can move cheaply amongst individuals and firms.
[23] We do not like the term 'resource' and believe it is misleading. We prefer to use the term firm-specific asset. We use it here to try and maintain links to the literature on the resource-based approach which we believe is important.

experience are examples. Such assets are difficult to transfer among firms because of transactions costs and transfer costs, and because the assets may contain tacit knowledge.

Organizational Routines/Competences

When firm-specific assets are assembled in integrated clusters spanning individuals and groups so that they enable distinctive activities to be performed, these activities constitute organizational routines and processes. Examples include quality, miniaturization, and systems integration. Such competences are typically viable across multiple product lines, and may extend outside the firm to embrace alliance partners.

Core Competences

We define those competences that define a firm's fundamental business as core. Core competences must accordingly be derived by looking across the range of a firm's (and its competitors) products and services.[24] The value of core competences can be enhanced by combination with the appropriate complementary assets. The degree to which a core competence is distinctive depends on how well endowed the firm is relative to its competitors, and on how difficult it is for competitors to replicate its competences.

Dynamic Capabilities

We define dynamic capabilities as the firm's ability to integrate, build, and reconfigure internal and external competences to address rapidly changing environments. Dynamic capabilities thus reflect an organization's ability to achieve new and innovative forms of competitive advantage given path dependencies and market positions (Leonard-Barton, 1992).

Products

End products are the final goods and services produced by the firm based on utilizing the competences that it possesses. The performance (price, quality, etc.) of a firm's products relative to its competitors at any point in time will depend upon its competences (which over time depend on its capabilities).

Markets and Strategic Capabilities

Different approaches to strategy view sources of wealth creation and the essence of the strategic problem faced by firms differently. The competitive forces framework sees the strategic problem in terms of industry structure, entry deter-

---

[24] Thus Eastman Kodak's core competence might be considered imaging, IBM's might be considered integrated data processing and service, and Motorola's untethered communications.

rence, and positioning; game-theoretic models view the strategic problem as one of interaction between rivals with certain expectations about how each other will behave;[25] resource-based perspectives have focused on the exploitation of firm-specific assets. Each approach asks different, often complementary questions. A key step in building a conceptual framework related to dynamic capabilities is to identify the foundations upon which distinctive and difficult-to-replicate advantages can be built, maintained, and enhanced.

A useful way to vector in on the strategic elements of the business enterprise is first to identify what is not strategic. To be strategic, a capability must be honed to a user need[26] (so there is a source of revenues), unique (so that the products/services produced can be priced without too much regard to competition) and difficult to replicate (so profits will not be competed away). Accordingly, any assets or entity which are homogeneous and can be bought and sold at an established price cannot be all that strategic (Barney, 1986). What is it, then, about firms which undergirds competitive advantage?

To answer this, one must first make some fundamental distinctions between markets and internal organization (firms). The essence of the firm, as Coase (1937) pointed out, is that it displaces market organization. It does so in the main because inside the firms one can organize certain types of economic activity in ways one cannot using markets. This is not only because of transaction costs, as Williamson (1975, 1985) emphasized, but also because there are many types of arrangements where injecting high-powered (market like) incentives might well be quite destructive of cooperative activity and learning.[27] Inside an organization, exchange cannot take place in the same manner that it can outside an organization, not just because it might be destructive to provide high-powered individual incentives, but because it is difficult if not impossible to tightly calibrate individual contribution to a joint effort. Hence, contrary to Arrow's (1969) view of firms as quasi markets, and the task of management to inject markets into firms, we recognize the inherent limits and possible counterproductive results of attempting to fashion firms into simply clusters of internal markets. In particular, learning and internal technology transfer may well be jeopardized.

Indeed, what is distinctive about firms is that they are domains for organizing activity in a nonmarket-like fashion. Accordingly, as we discuss what is distinctive about firms, we stress competences/capabilities which are ways of organizing and getting things done which cannot be accomplished merely by

---

[25] In sequential move games, each player looks ahead and anticipates his rival's future responses in order to reason back and decide action, i.e., look forward, reason backward.
[26] Needless to say, users need not be the current customers of the enterprise. Thus a capability can be the basis for diversification into new product markets.
[27] Indeed, the essence of internal organization is that it is a domain of unleveraged or low-powered incentives. By unleveraged we mean that rewards are determined at the group or organization level, not primarily at the individual level, in an effort to encourage team behavior, not individual behavior.

using the price system to coordinate activity.[28] The very essence of most capabilities/competences is that they cannot be readily assembled through markets (Teece, 1982, 1986a; Zander and Kogut, 1995). If the ability to assemble competences using markets is what is meant by the firm as a nexus of contracts (Fama, 1980), then we unequivocally state that the firm about which we theorize cannot be usefully modeled as a nexus of contracts. By 'contract' we are referring to a transaction undergirded by a legal agreement, or some other arrangement which clearly spells out rights, rewards, and responsibilities. Moreover, the firm as a nexus of contracts suggests a series of bilateral contracts orchestrated by a coordinator. Our view of the firm is that the organization takes place in a more multilateral fashion, with patterns of behavior and learning being orchestrated in a much more decentralized fashion, but with a viable headquarters operation.

The key point, however, is that the properties of internal organization cannot be replicated by a portfolio of business units amalgamated just through formal contracts as many distinctive elements of internal organization simply cannot be replicated in the market.[29] That is, entrepreneurial activity cannot lead to the immediate replication of unique organizational skills through simply entering a market and piecing the parts together overnight. Replication takes time, and the replication of best practice may be illusive. Indeed, firm capabilities need to be understood not in terms of balance sheet items, but mainly in terms of the organizational structures and managerial processes which support productive activity. By construction, the firm's balance sheet contains items that can be valued, at least at original market prices (cost). It is necessarily the case, therefore, that the balance sheet is a poor shadow of a firm's distinctive competences.[30] That which is distinctive cannot be bought and sold short of buying the firm itself, or one or more of its subunits.

There are many dimensions of the business firm that must be understood if one is to grasp firm-level distinctive competences/capabilities. In this paper we merely identify several classes of factors that will help determine a firm's distinctive competence and dynamic capabilities. We organize these in three categories: processes, positions, and paths. The essence of competences and capabilities is embedded in organizational processes of one kind or another. But the content of these processes and the opportunities they afford for developing competitive advantage at any point in time are shaped significantly by

---

[28] We see the problem of market contracting as a matter of coordination as much as we see it a problem of opportunism in the fact of contractual hazards. In this sense, we are consonant with both Richardson (1960) and Williamson (1975, 1985).

[29] As we note in Teece *et al.* (1994), the conglomerate offers few if any efficiencies because there is little provided by the conglomerate form that shareholders cannot obtain for themselves simply by holding a diversified portfolio of stocks.

[30] Owners' equity may reflect, in part, certain historic capabilities. Recently, some scholars have begun to attempt to measure organizational capability using financial statement data. See Baldwin and Clark (1991) and Lev and Sougiannis (1992).

the assets the firm possesses (internal and market) and by the evolutionary path it has adopted/inherited. Hence organizational processes, shaped by the firm's asset positions and molded by its evolutionary and co-evolutionary paths, explain the essence of the firm's dynamic capabilities and its competitive advantage.

Processes, Positions, and Paths

We thus advance the argument that the competitive advantage of firms lies with its managerial and organizational processes, shaped by its (specific) asset position, and the paths available to it.[31] By managerial and organizational processes, we refer to the way things are done in the firm, or what might be referred to as its routines, or patterns of current practice and learning. By position we refer to its current specific endowments of technology, intellectual property, complementary assets, customer base, and its external relations with suppliers and complementors. By paths we refer to the strategic alternatives available to the firm, and the presence or absence of increasing returns and attendant path dependencies.

Our focus throughout is on asset structures for which no ready market exists, as these are the only assets of strategic interest. A final section focuses on replication and imitation, as it is these phenomena which determine how readily a competence or capability can be cloned by competitors, and therefore distinctiveness of its competences and the durability of its advantage. The firm's processes and positions collectively encompass its competences and capabilities. A hierarchy of competences/capabilities ought to be recognized, as some competences may be on the factory floor, some in the R&D labs, some in the executive suites, and some in the way everything is integrated. A difficult-to-replicate or difficult-to-imitate competence was defined earlier as a distinctive competence. As indicated, the key feature of distinctive competence is that there is not a market for it, except possibly through the market for business units. Hence competences and capabilities are intriguing assets as they typically must be built because they cannot be bought.

Organizational and Managerial Processes

Organizational processes have three roles: coordination/integration (a static concept); learning (a dynamic concept); and reconfiguration (a transformational concept). We discuss each in turn.

---

[31] We are implicitly saying that fixed assets, like plant and equipment which can be purchased off-the-shelf by all industry participants, cannot be the source of a firm's competitive advantage. Inasmuch as financial balance sheets typically reflect such assets, we point out that the assets that matter for competitive advantage are rarely reflected in the balance sheet, while those that do not are.

Coordination/Integration   While the price system supposedly coordinates the economy,[32] managers coordinate or integrate activity inside the firm. How efficiently and effectively internal coordination or integration is achieved is very important (Aoki, 1990).[33] Likewise for external coordination.[34] Increasingly, strategic advantage requires the integration of external activities and technologies. The growing literature on strategic alliances, the virtual corporation, and buyer supplier relations and technology collaboration evidences the importance of external integration and sourcing.

There is some field-based empirical research that provides support for the notion that the way production is organized by management inside the firm is the source of differences in firms' competence in various domains. For example, Garvin's (1988) study of 18 room air-conditioning plants reveals that quality performance was not related to either capital investment or the degree of automation of the facilities. Instead, quality performance was driven by special organizational routines. These included routines for gathering and processing information, for linking customer experiences with engineering design choices, and for coordinating factories and component suppliers.[35] The work of Clark and Fujimoto (1991) on project development in the automobile industry also illustrates the role played by coordinative routines. Their study reveals a significant degree of variation in how different firms coordinate the various activities required to bring a new model from concept to market. These differences in coordinative routines and capabilities seem to have a significant impact on such performance variables as development cost, development lead times, and quality. Furthermore, Clark and Fujimoto tended to find significant firm-level differences in coordination routines and these differences seemed to have persisted for a long time. This suggests that routines related to coordination are firm-specific in nature.

Also, the notion that competence/capability is embedded in distinct ways of coordinating and combining helps to explain how and why seemingly minor technological changes can have devastating impacts on incumbent firms' abilities to compete in a market. Henderson and Clark (1990), for example, have shown that incumbents in the photolithographic equipment industry were sequentially

---

[32] The coordinate properties of markets depend on prices being "sufficient" upon which to base resource allocation decisions.

[33] Indeed, Ronald Coase, author of the pathbreaking 1937 article 'The nature of the firm,' which focused on the costs of organizational coordination inside the firm as compared to across the market, half a century later has identified as critical the understanding of 'why the costs of organizing particular activities differs among firms' (Coase, 1988: 47). We argue that a firm's distinctive ability needs to be understood as a reflection of distinctive organizational or coordinative capabilities. This form of integration (i.e., inside business units) is different from the integration between business units; they could be viable on a stand-alone basis (external integration). For a useful taxonomy, see Iansiti and Clark (1994).

[34] Shuen (1994) examines the gains and hazards of the technology make-vs.-buy decision and supplier codevelopment.

[35] Garvin (1994) provides a typology of organizational processes.

devastated by seemingly minor innovations that, nevertheless, had major impacts on how systems had to be configured. They attribute these difficulties to the fact that systems-level or 'architectural' innovations often require new routines to integrate and coordinate engineering tasks. These findings and others suggest that productive systems display high interdependency, and that it may not be possible to change one level without changing others. This appears to be true with respect to the 'lean production' model (Womack *et al,* 1991) which has now transformed the Taylor or Ford model of manufacturing organization in the automobile industry.[36] Lean production requires distinctive shop floor practices and processes as well as distinctive higher-order managerial processes. Put differently, organizational processes often display high levels of coherence, and when they do, replication may be difficult because it requires systemic changes throughout the organization and also among interorganizational linkages, which might be very hard to effectuate. Put differently, partial imitation or replication of a successful model may yield zero benefits.[37]

The notion that there is a certain rationality or coherence to processes and systems is not quite the same concept as corporate culture, as we understand the

[36] Fujimoto (1994: 18-20) describes key elements as they existed in the Japanese auto industry as follows: 'The typical volume production system of effective Japanese makers of the 1980s (e.g., Toyota) consists of various intertwined elements that might lead to competitive advantages. Just-in-Time (JIT), Jidoka (automatic defect detection and machine stop), Total Quality Control (TQC), and continuous improvement (Kaizen) are often pointed out as its core subsystems. The elements of such a system include inventory reduction mechanisms by Kanban system; levelization of production volume and product mix (heijunka); reduction of 'muda' (non-value adding activities), 'mura' (uneven pace of production) and muri (excessive workload); production plans based on dealers' order volume (genyo scisan); reduction of die set-up time and lot size in stamping operation; mixed model assembly; piece-by-piece transfer of parts between machines (ikko-nagashi); flexible task assignment for volume changes and productivity improvement (shojinka); multi-task job assignment along the process flow (takotei-mochi); U-shape machine layout that facilitates flexible and multiple task assignment, on-the-spot inspection by direct workers (tsukurikomi); fool-proof prevention of defects (poka-yoke); real-time feedback of production troubles (andon); assembly line stop cord; emphasis on cleanliness, order and discipline on the shop floor (5-S); frequent revision of standard operating procedures by supervisors; quality control circles standardized tools for quality improvement (e.g., 7 tools for QC, QC story); worker involvement in preventive maintenance; (Total Productive Maintenance); low cost automation or semi-automation with just-enough functions; reduction of process steps for saving of tools and dies, and so on. The human-resource management factors that back up the above elements include stable employment of core workers (with temporary workers in the periphery); long-term training of multi-skilled (multitask) workers; wage system based in part on skill accumulation; internal promotion to shop floor supervisors; cooperative relationships with labor unions; inclusion of production supervisors in union members; generally egalitarian policies for corporate welfare, communication and worker motivation. Parts procurement policies are also pointed out often as a source of the competitive advantage.

[37] For a theoretical argument along these lines, see Milgrom and Roberts (1990).

latter. Corporate culture refers to the values and beliefs that employees hold; culture can be a *de facto* governance system as it mediates the behavior of individuals and economizes on more formal administrative methods. Rationality or coherence notions are more akin to the Nelson and Winter (1982) notion of organizational routines. However, the routines concept is a little too amorphous to properly capture the congruence amongst processes and between processes and incentives that we have in mind. Consider a professional service organization like an accounting firm. If it is to have relatively high-powered incentives that reward individual performance, then it must build organizational processes that channel individual behavior; if it has weak or low-powered incentives, it must find symbolic ways to recognize the high performers, and it must use alternative methods to build effort and enthusiasm. What one may think of as styles of organization in fact contain necessary, not discretionary, elements to achieve performance.

Recognizing the congruencies and complementarities among processes, and between processes and incentives, is critical to the understanding of organizational capabilities. In particular, they can help us explain why architectural and radical innovations are so often introduced into an industry by new entrants. The incumbents develop distinctive organizational processes that cannot support the new technology, despite certain overt similarities between the old and the new. The frequent failure of incumbents to introduce new technologies can thus be seen as a consequence of the mismatch that so often exists between the set of organizational processes needed to support the conventional product/service and the requirements of the new. Radical organizational reengineering will usually be required to support the new product, which may well do better embedded in a separate subsidiary where a new set of coherent organizational processes can be fashioned.[38]

Learning Perhaps even more important than integration is learning. Learning is a process by which repetition and experimentation enable tasks to be performed better and quicker. It also enables new production opportunities to be identified.[39] In the context of the firm, if not more generally, teaming has several key characteristics. First, learning involves organizational as well as individual skills.[40] While individual skills are of relevance, their value depends upon their employment, in particular organizational settings. Learning processes are intrinsically social and collective and occur not only through the imitation and emulation of individuals, as with teacher-student or master-apprentice, but also because of joint contributions to the understanding of complex problems.[41] Learning requires common codes of communication and coordinated search pro-

---

[38] See Abernathy and Clark (1985).

[39] For a useful review and contribution, see Levitt and March (1988).

[40] Levinthal and March, 1993. Mahoney (1992) and Mahoney and Pandian (1995) suggest that both resources and mental models are intertwined in firm-level learning.

[41] There is a large literature on learning, although only a small fraction of it deals with organizational learning. Relevant contributors include Levitt and March (1988), Arayris and Schon (1978), Levinthal and March (1981), Nelson and Winter (1982), and Leonard-Barton (1995).

cedures. Second, the organizational knowledge generated by such activity resides in new patterns of activity, in 'routines,' or a new logic of organization. As indicated earlier, routines are patterns of interactions that represent successful solutions to particular problems. These patterns of interaction are resident in group behavior, though certain subroutines may be resident in individual behavior. The concept of dynamic capabilities as a coordinative management process opens the door to the potential for interorganizational learning. Researchers (Doz and Shuen, 1990; Mody, 1993) have pointed out that collaborations and partnerships can be a vehicle for new organizational learning, helping firms to recognize dysfunctional routines, and preventing strategic blindspots.

Reconfiguration and Transformation   In rapidly changing environments, there is obviously value in the ability to sense the need to reconfigure the firm's asset structure, and to accomplish the necessary internal and external transformation (Amit and Schoemaker, 1993; Langlois, 1994). This requires constant surveillance of markets and technologies and the willingness to adopt best practice. In this regard, benchmarking is of considerable value as an organized process for accomplishing such ends (Camp, 1989). In dynamic environments, narcissistic organizations are likely to be impaired. The capacity to reconfigure and transform is itself a learned organizational skill. The more frequently practiced, the easier accomplished.

Change is costly and so firms must develop processes to minimize low payoff change. The ability to calibrate the requirements for change and to effectuate the necessary adjustments would appear to depend on the ability to scan the environment, to evaluate markets and competitors, and to quickly accomplish reconfiguration and transformation ahead of competition. Decentralization and local autonomy assist these processes. Firms that have honed these capabilities are sometimes referred to as 'high-flex'.

Positions   The strategic posture of a firm is determined not only by its learning processes and by the coherence of its internal and external processes and incentives, but also by its specific assets. By specific assets we mean for example its specialized plant and equipment. These include its difficult-to-trade knowledge assets and assets complementary to them, as well as its reputational and relational assets. Such assets determine its competitive advantage at any point in time. We identify several illustrative classes.

Technological Assets   While there is an emerging market for know-how (Teece, 1981), much technology does not enter it. This is either because the firm is unwilling to sell it[42] or because of difficulties in transacting in the market for know-how (Teece, 1980). A firm's technological assets may or may not be protected by the standard instruments of intellectual property law. Either way, the

---

[42] Managers often evoke the 'crown jewels' metaphor. That if the technology is released, the kingdom will be lost.

ownership protection and utilization of technological assets are clearly key differentiators among firms. Likewise for complementary assets.

Complementary Assets   Technological innovations require the use of certain related assets to produce and deliver new products and services. Prior commercialization activities require and enable firms to build such complementarities (Teece, 1986b). Such capabilities and assets, while necessary for the firm's established activities, may have other uses as well. These assets typically lie downstream. New products and processes either can enhance or destroy the value of such assets (Tushman, Newman, and Romanelli, 1986). Thus the development of computers enhanced the value of IBM's direct sales force in office products, while disk brakes rendered useless much of the auto industry's investment in drum brakes.

Financial Assets   In the short run, a firm's cash position and degree of leverage may have strategic implications. While there is nothing more fungible than cash, it cannot always be raised from external markets without the dissemination of considerable information to potential investors. Accordingly, what a firm can do in short order is often a function of its balance sheet. In the longer run, that ought not be so, as cash flow ought be more determinative.

Reputational Assets   Firms, like individuals, have reputations. Reputations often summarize a good deal of information about firms and shape the responses of customers, suppliers, and competitors. It is sometimes difficult to disentangle reputation from the firm's current asset and market position. However, in our view, reputational assets are best viewed as an intangible asset that enables firms to achieve various goals in the market. Its main value is external, since what is critical about reputation is that it is a kind of summary statistic about the firm's current assets and position, and its likely future behavior. Because there is generally a strong asymmetry between what is known inside the firm and what is known externally, reputations may sometimes be more salient than the true state of affairs, in the sense that external actors must respond to what they know rather than what is knowable.

Structural Assets   The formal and informal structure of organizations and their external linkages have an important bearing on the rate and direction of innovation, and how competences and capabilities co-evolve (Argyres, 1995; Teece, 1996). The degree of hierarchy and the level of vertical and lateral integration are elements of firm-specific structure. Distinctive governance modes can be recognized (e.g., multiproduct, integrated firms; high 'flex' firms; virtual corporations; conglomerates), and these modes support different types of innovation to a greater or lesser degree. For instance, virtual structures work well when innovation is autonomous; integrated structures work better for systemic innovations.

Institutional Assets   Environments cannot be defined in terms of markets alone. While public policies are usually recognized as important in constraining what firms can do, there is a tendency, particularly by economists, to see these as acting through markets or through incentives. However, institutions themselves are a critical element of the business environment. Regulatory systems, as well as intellectual property regimes, tort laws, and antitrust laws, are also part of the environment. So is the system of higher education and national culture. There are significant national differences here, which is just one of the reasons geographic location matters (Nelson, 1994). Such assets may not be entirely firm specific; firms of different national and regional origin may have quite different institutional assets to call upon because their institutional/policy settings are so different.

Market (Structure) Assets   Product market position matters, but it is often not at all determinative of the fundamental position of the enterprise in its external environment. Part of the problem lies in defining the market in which a firm competes in a way that gives economic meaning. More importantly, market position in regimes of rapid technological change is often extremely fragile. This is in part because time moves on a different clock in such environments.[43] Moreover, the link between market share and innovation has long been broken, if it ever existed (Teece, 1996). All of this is to suggest that product market position, while important, is too often overplayed. Strategy should be formulated with regard to the more fundamental aspects of firm performance, which we believe are rooted in competences and capabilities and shaped by positions and paths.

Organizational Boundaries   An important dimension of 'position' is the location of a firm's boundaries. Put differently, the degree of integration (vertical, lateral, and horizontal) is of quite some significance. Boundaries are not only significant with respect to the technological and complementary assets contained within, but also with respect to the nature of the coordination that can be achieved internally as compared to through markets. When specific assets or poorly protected intellectual capital are at issue, pure market arrangements expose the parties to recontracting hazards or appropriability hazards. In such circumstances, hierarchical control structures may work better than pure arms-length contracts.[44]

---

[43] For instance, an Internet year might well be thought of as equivalent to 10 years on many industry clocks, because as much change occurs in the Internet business in a year that occurs in say the auto industry in a decade.

[44] Williamson (1996: 102–103) has observed, failures of coordination may arise because 'parties that bear a long term bilateral dependency relationship to one another must recognize that incomplete contracts require gap filling and sometimes get out of alignment. Although it is always in the collective interest of autonomous parties to fill gaps, correct errors, and affect efficient realignments, it is also the case that the distribution of the resulting gains is indeterminate. Self-interested bargaining predictably obtains. Such bargaining is itself costly. The main costs, however, are that transactions are maladapted to the environment during the bargaining interval. Also, the prospect of ex post bargaining invites ex ante prepositioning of an inefficient kind.'

Paths

Path Dependencies   Where a firm can go is a function of its current position and the paths ahead. Its current position is often shaped by the path it has traveled. In standard economics textbooks, firms have an infinite range of technologies from which they can choose and markets they can occupy. Changes in product or factor prices will be responded to instantaneously, with technologies moving in and out according to value maximization criteria. Only in the short run are irreversibilities recognized. Fixed costs—such as equipment and overheads—cause firms to price below fully amortized costs but never constrain future investment choices. 'Bygones are bygones.' Path dependencies are simply not recognized. This is a major limitation of macroeconomic theory.

The notion of path dependencies recognizes that 'history matters.' Bygones are rarely bygones, despite the predictions of rational actor theory. Thus a firm's previous investments and its repertoire of routines (its 'history') constrain its future behavior.[45] This follows because learning tends to be local. That is, opportunities for learning will be 'close in' to previous activities and thus will be transaction and production specific (Teece, 1988). This is because learning is often a process of trial, feedback, and evaluation. If too many parameters are changed simultaneously, the ability of firms to conduct meaningful natural quasi experiments is attenuated. If many aspects of a firm's learning environment change simultaneously, the ability to ascertain cause-effect relationships is confounded because cognitive structures will not be formed and rates of learning diminish as a result. One implication is that many investments are much longer term than is commonly thought.

The importance of path dependencies is amplified where conditions of increasing returns to adoption exist. This is a demand-side phenomenon, and it tends to make technologies and products embodying those technologies more attractive the more they are adopted. Attractiveness flows from the greater adoption of the product amongst users, which in turn enables them to become more developed and hence more useful. Increasing returns to adoption has many sources including network externalities (Katz and Shapiro, 1985), the presence of complementary assets (Teece, 1986b) and supporting infrastructure (Nelson, 1996), learning by using (Rosenberg, 1982), and scale economies in production and distribution. Competition between and amongst technologies is shaped by increasing returns. Early leads won by good luck or special circumstances (Arthur, 1983) can become amplified by increasing returns. This is not to suggest that first movers necessarily win. Because increasing returns have multiple sources, the prior positioning of firms can affect their capacity to exploit increasing returns. Thus, in Mitchell's (1989) study of medical diagnostic imaging, firms already controlling the relevant complementary assets could in theory start last and finish first.

---

[45] For further development, see Bercovitz, de Figueiredo, and Teece, 1996.

In the presence of increasing returns, firms can compete passively, or they may compete strategically through technology-sponsoring activities.[46] The first type of competition is not unlike biological competition amongst species, although it can be sharpened by managerial activities that enhance the performance of products and processes. The reality is that companies with the best products will not always win, as chance events may cause 'lock-in' on inferior technologies (Arthur, 1983) and may even in special cases generate switching costs for consumers. However, while switching costs may favor the incumbent, in regimes of rapid technological change switching costs can become quickly swamped by switching benefits. Put differently, new products employing different standards often appear with alacrity in market environments experiencing rapid technological change, and incumbents can be readily challenged by superior products and services that yield switching benefits. Thus the degree to which switching costs cause 'lock-in' is a function of factors such as user learning, rapidity of technological change, and the amount of ferment in the competitive environment.

Technological Opportunities   The concept of path dependencies is given forward meaning through the consideration of an industry's technological opportunities. It is well recognized that how far and how fast a particular area of industrial activity can proceed is in part due to the technological opportunities that lie before it. Such opportunities are usually a lagged function of foment and diversity in basic science, and the rapidity with which new scientific breakthroughs are being made.

However, technological opportunities may not be completely exogenous to industry, not only because some firms have the capacity to engage in or at least support basic research, but also because technological opportunities are often fed by innovative activity itself. Moreover, the recognition of such opportunities is affected by the organizational structures that link the institutions engaging in basic research (primarily the university) to the business enterprise. Hence, the existence of technological opportunities can be quite firm specific.

Important for our purposes is the rate and direction in which relevant scientific frontiers are being rolled back. Firms engaging in R&D may find the path dead ahead closed off, though breakthroughs in related areas may be sufficiently close to be attractive. Likewise, if the path dead ahead is extremely attractive, there may be no incentive for firms to shift the allocation of resources away from traditional pursuits. The depth and width of technological opportunities in the

---

[46] Because of huge uncertainties, it may be extremely difficult to determine viable strategies early on. Since the rules of the game and the identity of the players will be revealed only after the market has begun to evolve, the pay-off is likely to lie with building and maintaining organizational capabilities that support flexibility. For example, Microsoft's recent about-face and vigorous pursuit of Internet business once the Netscape phenomenon became apparent is impressive, not so much because it perceived the need to change strategy, but because of its organizational capacity to effectuate a strategic shift.

neighborhood of a firm's prior research activities thus are likely to impact a firm's options with respect to both the amount and level of R&D activity that it can justify. In addition, a firm's past experience conditions the alternatives management is able to perceive. Thus, not only do firms in the same industry face 'menus' with different costs associated with particular technological choices, they also are looking at menus containing different choices.[47]

Assessment

The essence of a firm's competence and dynamic capabilities is presented here as being resident in the firm's organizational processes, that are in turn shaped by the firm's assets (positions) and its evolutionary path. Its evolutionary path, despite managerial hubris that might suggest otherwise, is often rather narrow.[48] What the firm can do and where it can go are thus rather constrained by its positions and paths. Its competitors are likewise constrained. Rents (profits) thus tend to flow not just from the asset structure of the firm and, as we shall see, the degree of its imitability, but also by the firm's ability to reconfigure and transform.

The parameters we have identified for determining performance are quite different from those in the standard textbook theory of the firm, and in the competitive forces and strategic conflict approaches to the firm and to strategy.[49] Moreover, the agency theoretic view of the firm as a nexus of contracts would put no weight on processes, positions, and paths. While agency approaches to the firm may recognize that opportunism and shirking may limit what a firm can do, they do not recognize the opportunities and constraints imposed by processes, positions, and paths.

Moreover, the firm in our conceptualization is much more than the sum of its parts—or a team tied together by contracts.[50] Indeed, to some extent individuals can be moved in and out of organizations and, so long as the internal processes and structures remain in place, performance will not necessarily be impaired. A shift in the environment is a far more serious threat to the firm than is the loss of key individuals, as individuals can be replaced more readily than organizations can be transformed. Furthermore, the dynamic capabilities view of the firm would suggest that the behavior and performance of particular firms may be quite hard to replicate, even if its coherence and rationality are observable. This matter and related issues involving replication and imitation are taken up in the section that follows.

---

[47] This is a critical element in Nelson and Winter's (1982) view of firms and technical change.

[48] We also recognize that the processes, positions, and paths of customers also matter. See our discussion above on increasing returns, including customer learning and network externalities.

[49] In both the firm is still largely a black box. Certainly, little or no attention is given to processes, positions, and paths.

[50] See Alchian and Demsetz (1972).

Replicability and Imitability of Organizational Processes and Positions

Thus far, we have argued that the competences and capabilities (and hence competitive advantage) of a firm rest fundamentally on processes, shaped by positions and paths. However, competences can provide competitive advantage and generate rents only if they are based on a collection of routines, skills, and complementary assets that are difficult to imitate.[51] A particular set of routines can lose their value if they support a competence which no longer matters in the marketplace, or if they can be readily replicated or emulated by competitors. Imitation occurs when firms discover and simply copy a firm's organizational routines and procedures. Emulation occurs when firms discover alternative ways of achieving the same functionality.[52]

Replication

To understand imitation, one must first understand replication. Replication involves transferring or redeploying competences from one concrete economic setting to another. Since productive knowledge is embodied, this cannot be accomplished by simply transmitting information. Only in those instances where all relevant knowledge is fully codified and understood can replication be collapsed into a simple problem of information transfer. Too often, the contextual dependence of original performance is poorly appreciated, so unless firms have replicated their systems of productive knowledge on many prior occasions, the act of replication is likely to be difficult (Teece, 1976). Indeed, replication and transfer are often impossible absent the transfer of people, though this can be minimized if investments are made to convert tacit knowledge to codified knowledge. Often, however, this is simply not possible.

In short, competences and capabilities, and the routines upon which they rest, are normally rather difficult to replicate.[53] Even understanding what all the relevant routines are that support a particular competence may not be transparent. Indeed, Lippman and Rumelt (1992) have argued that some sources of competitive advantage are so complex that the firm itself, let alone its competitors, does not understand them.[54] As Nelson and Winter (1982) and Teece (1982)

---

[51] We call such competences distinctive. See also Dierickx and Cool (1989) for a discussion of the characteristics of assets which make them a source of rents.

[52] There is ample evidence that a given type of competence (e.g., quality) can be supported by different routines and combinations of skills. For example, the Garvin (1988) and Clark and Fujimoto (1991) studies both indicate that there was no one 'formula' for achieving either high quality or high product development performance.

[53] See Szulanski's (1995) discussion of the intrafirm transfer of best practice. He quotes a senior vice president of Xerox as saying 'you can see a high performance factory or office, but it just doesn't spread. I don't know why.' Szulanski also discusses the role of benchmarking in facilitating the transfer of best practice.

[54] If so, it is our belief that the firm's advantage is likely to fade, as luck does run out.

have explained, many organizational routines are quite tacit in nature. Imitation can also be hindered by the fact few routines are 'stand-alone;' coherence may require that a change in one set of routines in one part of the firm (e.g., production) requires changes in some other part (e.g., R&D).

Some routines and competences seem to be attributable to local or regional forces that shape firms' capabilities at early stages in their lives. Porter (1990), for example, shows that differences in local product markets, local factor markets, and institutions play an important role in shaping competitive capabilities. Differences also exist within populations of firms from the same country. Various studies of the automobile industry, for example, show that not all Japanese automobile companies are top performers in terms of quality, productivity, or product development (see, for example, Clark and Fujimoto, 1991). The role of firm-specific history has been highlighted as a critical factor explaining such firm level (as opposed to regional or national-level) differences (Nelson and Winter, 1982). Replication in a different context may thus be rather difficult.

At least two types of strategic value flow from replication. One is the ability to support geographic and product line expansion. To the extent that the capabilities in question are relevant to customer needs elsewhere, replication can confer value.[55] Another is that the ability to replicate also indicates that the firm has the foundations in place for learning and improvement. Considerable empirical evidence supports the notion that the understanding of processes, both in production and in management, is the key to process improvement. In short, an organization cannot improve that which it does not understand. Deep process understanding is often required to accomplish codification. Indeed, if knowledge is highly tacit, it indicates that underlying structures are not well understood, which limits learning because scientific and engineering principles cannot be as systematically applied.[56] Instead, learning is confined to proceeding through trial and error, and the leverage that might otherwise come from the application of scientific theory is denied.

Imitation

Imitation is simply replication performed by a competitor. If self-replication is difficult, imitation is likely to be harder. In competitive markets, it is the ease of imitation that determines the sustainability of competitive advantage. Easy imitation implies the rapid dissipation of rents.

---

[55] Needless to say, there are many examples of firms replicating their capabilities inappropriately by applying extant routines to circumstances where they may not be applicable, e.g., Nestle's transfer of developed-country marketing methods for infant formula to the third World (Hartley, 1989). A key strategic need is for firms to screen capabilities for their applicability to new environments.

[56] Different approaches to learning are required depending on the depth of knowledge. Where knowledge is less articulated and structured, trial and error and learning-by-doing are necessary, whereas in mature environments where the underlying engineering science is better understood, organizations can undertake more deductive approaches or what Pisano (1994) refers to as 'learning-before-doing.'

Factors that make replication difficult also make imitation difficult. Thus, the more tacit the firm's productive knowledge, the harder it is to replicate by the firm itself or its competitors. When the tacit component is high, imitation may well be impossible, absent the hiring away of key individuals and the transfers of key organization processes.

However, another set of barriers impedes imitation of certain capabilities in advanced industrial countries. This is the system of intellectual property rights, such as patents, trade secrets, and trademarks, and even trade dress.[57] Intellectual property protection is of increasing importance in the United States, as since 1982 the legal system has adopted a more pro-patent posture. Similar trends are evident outside the United States. Besides the patent system, several other factors cause there to be a difference between replication costs and imitation costs. The observability of the technology or the organization is one such important factor. Whereas vistas into product technology can be obtained through strategies such as reverse engineering, this is not the case for process technology, as a firm need not expose its process technology to the outside in order to benefit from it.[58] Firms with product technology, on the other hand, confront the unfortunate circumstances that they must expose what they have got in order to profit from the technology. Secrets are thus more protectable if there is no need to expose them in contexts where competitors can learn about them.

One should not, however, overestimate the overall importance of intellectual property protection; yet it presents a formidable imitation barrier in certain particular contexts. Intellectual property protection is not uniform across products, processes, and technologies, and is best thought of as islands in a sea of open competition. If one is not able to place the fruits of one's investment, ingenuity, or creativity on one or more of the islands, then one indeed is at sea.

We use the term appropriability regimes to describe the ease of imitation. Appropriability is a function both of the ease of replication and the efficacy of intellectual property rights as a barrier to imitation. Appropriability is strong when a technology is both inherently difficult to replicate and the intellectual property system provides legal barriers to imitation. When it is inherently easy to replicate and intellectual property protection is either unavailable or ineffectual, then appropriability is weak. Intermediate conditions also exist.

---

[57] Trade dress refers to the 'look and feel' of a retail establishment, e.g., the distinctive marketing and presentation style of The Nature Company.

[58] An interesting but important exception to this can be found in second sourcing. In the microprocessor business, until the introduction of the 386 chip, Intel and most other merchant semi producers were encouraged by large customers like IBM to provide second sources, i.e., to license and share their proprietary process technology with competitors like AMD and NEC. 'The microprocessor developers did so to assure customers that they had sufficient manufacturing capability to meet demand at all times.

CONCLUSION

The four paradigms discussed above are quite different, though the first two have much in common with each other (strategizing) as do the last two (economizing). But are these paradigms complementary or competitive? According to some authors, 'the resource perspective complements the industry analysis framework' (Amit and Schoemaker, 1993: 35). While this is undoubtedly true, we think that in several important respects the perspectives are also competitive. While this should be recognized, it is not to suggest that there is only one framework that has value. Indeed, complex problems are likely to benefit from insights obtained from all of the paradigms we have identified plus more. The trick is to work out which frameworks are appropriate for the problem at hand. Slavish adherence to one class to the neglect of all others is likely to generate strategic blindspots. The tools themselves then generate strategic vulnerability. We now explore these issues further. Table 6.1 summarizes some similarities and differences.

Efficiency Versus Market Power

The competitive forces and strategic conflict approaches generally see profits as stemming from strategizing—that is, from limitations on competition which firms achieve through raising rivals' costs and exclusionary behavior (Teece, 1984). The competitive forces approach in particular leads one to see concentrated industries as being attractive—market positions can be shielded behind entry barriers, and rivals costs can be raised. It also suggests that the sources of competitive advantage lie at the level of the industry, or possibly groups within an industry. In text book presentations, there is almost no attention at all devoted to discovering, creating, and commercializing new sources of value.

The dynamic capabilities and resources approaches clearly have a different orientation. They see competitive advantage stemming from high-performance routines operating 'inside the firm,' shaped by processes and positions. Path dependencies (including increasing returns) and technological opportunities mark the road ahead. Because of imperfect factor markets, or more precisely the nontradability of 'soft' assets like values, culture, and organizational experience, distinctive competences and capabilities generally cannot be acquired; they must be built. This sometimes takes years—possibly decades. In some cases, as when the competence is protected by patents, replication by a competitor is ineffectual as a means to access the technology. The capabilities approach accordingly sees definite limits on strategic options, at least in the short run. Competitive success occurs in part because of policies pursued and experience and efficiency obtained in earlier periods.

Competitive success can undoubtedly flow from both strategizing and economizing,[59] but along with Williamson (1991) we believe that, economizing

---

[59] Phillips (1971) and Demsetz (1974) also made the case that market concentration resulted from the competitive success of more efficient firms, and not from entry barriers and restrictive practices.

TABLE 6.1 Paradigm of strategy: Salient characteristics

Paradigm	Intellectual roots	Representative authors addressing strategic management questions	Nature of rents	Rationality assumptions of managers	Fundamental units of analysis	Short-run capacity for strategic reorientation	Role of industrial structure	Focal concern
(1) Attenuating competitive forces	Mason, Bain	Porter (1980)	Chamberlinean	Rational	Industries, firms, products	High	Exogenous	Structural conditions and competitor positioning
(2) Strategic conflict	Machiavelli, Schelling, Cournot, Nash, Harsanyi, Shapiro	Ghemawat (1986) Shapiro (1989) Brandenburger and Nalebuff (1995)	Chamberlinean	Hyper-rational	Firms, products	Often infinite	Endogenous	Strategic interactions
(3) Resource-based perspectives	Penrose, Selznick, Christensen, Andrews	Rumelt (1984) Chandler (1966) Wernerfelt (1984) Teece (1980, 1982)	Ricardian	Rational	Resources	Low	Endogenous	Asset fungibility
(4) Dynamic capabilities perspective	Schumpeter, Nelson, Winter, Teece	Dosi, Teece, and Winter (1989) Prahalad and Hamel (1990) Hayes and Wheelwright (1984) Dierickx and Cool (1989) Porter (1990)	Schumpeterian	Rational	Processes, positions, paths	Low	Endogenous	Asset accumulation, replicability and inimitability

is more fundamental than strategizing . . . or put differently, that economy is the best strategy.[60] Indeed, we suggest that, except in special circumstances, too much 'strategizing' can lead firms to underinvest in core competences and neglect dynamic capabilities, and thus harm long-term competitiveness.

Normative Implications

The field of strategic management is avowedly normative. It seeks to guide those aspects of general management that have material effects on the survival and success of the business enterprise. Unless these various approaches differ in terms of the framework and heuristics they offer management, then the discourse we have gone through is of limited immediate value. In this paper, we have already alluded to the fact that the capabilities approach tends to steer managers toward creating distinctive and difficult-to-imitate advantages and avoiding games with customers and competitors. We now survey possible differences, recognizing that the paradigms are still in their infancy and cannot confidently support strong normative conclusions.

Unit of Analysis and Analytic Focus

Because in the capabilities and the resources framework business opportunities flow from a firm's unique processes, strategy analysis must be situational.[61] This is also true with the strategic conflict approach. There is no algorithm for creating wealth for the entire industry. Prescriptions they apply to industries or groups of firms at best suggest overall direction, and may indicate errors to be avoided. In contrast, the competitive forces approach is not particularly firm specific; it is industry and group specific.

Strategic Change

The competitive forces and the strategic conflict approach, since they pay little attention to skills, know-how, and path dependency, tend to see strategic choice occurring with relative facility. The capabilities approach sees value augmenting strategic change as being difficult and costly. Moreover, it can generally only occur incrementally. Capabilities cannot easily be bought; they must be

---

[60] We concur with Williamson that economizing and strategizing are not mutually exclusive. Strategic ploys can be used to disguise inefficiencies and to promote economizing outcomes, as with pricing with reference to learning curve costs. Our view of economizing is perhaps more expansive than Williamson's as it embraces more than efficient contract design and the minimization of transactions costs. We also address production and organizational economies, and the distinctive ways that things are accomplished inside the business enterprise.

[61] On this point, the strategic conflict and the resources and capabilities are congruent. However, the aspects of 'situation' that matter are dramatically different, as described earlier in this paper.

built. From the capabilities perspective, strategy involves choosing among and committing to long-term paths or trajectories of competence development.

In this regard, we speculate that the dominance of competitive forces and the strategic conflict approaches in the United States may have something to do with observed differences in strategic approaches adopted by some U.S. and some foreign firms. Hayes (1985) has noted that American companies tend to favor 'strategic leaps' while, in contrast, Japanese and German companies tend to favor incremental, but rapid, improvements.

Entry Strategies

Here the resources and the capabilities approaches suggest that entry decisions must be made with reference to the competences and capabilities which new entrants have, relative to the competition. Whereas the other approaches tell you little about where to look to find likely entrants, the capabilities approach identifies likely entrants. Relatedly, whereas the entry deterrence approach suggests an unconstrained search for new business opportunities, the capabilities approach suggests that such opportunities lie close in to one's existing business. As Richard Rumelt has explained it in conversation, 'the capabilities approach suggests that if a firm looks inside itself, and at its market environment, sooner or later it will find a business opportunity.'

Entry Timing

Whereas the strategic conflict approach tells little about where to look to find likely entrants, the resources and the capabilities approach identifies likely entrants and their timing of entry. Brittain and Freeman (1980) using population ecology methodologies argued that an organization is quick to expand when there is a significant overlap between its core capabilities and those needed to survive in a new market. Recent research (Mitchell, 1989) showed that the more industry specialized assets or capabilities a firm possesses, the more likely it is to enter an emerging technical subfield in its industry, following a technological discontinuity. Additionally, the interaction between specialized assets such as firm-specific capabilities and rivalry had the greatest influence on entry timing.

Diversification

Related diversification—that is, diversification that builds upon or extends existing capabilities—is about the only form of diversification that a resources/capabilities framework is likely to view as meritorious (Rumelt, 1974; Teece, 1980, 1982; Teece *et al.*, 1994). Such diversification will be justifiable when the firms' traditional markets decline.[62] The strategic conflict approach is

---

[62] Cantwell shows that the technological competence of firms persists over time, gradually evolving through firm-specific learning. He shows that technological diversification has been greater for chemicals and pharmaceuticals than for electrical and electronic-related fields., and he offers as an explanation the greater straight-ahead opportunities in electrical and electronic fields than in chemicals and pharmaceuticals. See Cantwell (1993).

likely to be a little more permissive; acquisitions that raise rivals' costs or enable firms to effectuate exclusive arrangements are likely to be seen as efficacious in certain circumstances.

Focus and Specialization

Focus needs to be defined in terms of distinctive competences or capability, not products. Products are the manifestation of competences, as competences can be molded into a variety of products. Product market specialization and decentralization configured around product markets may cause firms to neglect the development of core competences and dynamic capabilities, to the extent to which competences require accessing assets across divisions.

The capabilities approach places emphasis on the internal processes that a firm utilizes, as well as how they are deployed and how they will evolve. The approach has the benefit of indicating that competitive advantage is not just a function of how one plays the game; it is also a function of the 'assets' one has to play with, and how these assets can be deployed and redeployed in a changing market.

Future Directions

We have merely sketched an outline for a dynamic capabilities approach. Further theoretical work is needed to tighten the framework, and empirical research is critical to helping us understand how firms get to be good, how they sometimes stay that way, why and how they improve, and why they sometimes decline.[63] Researchers in the field of strategy need to join forces with researchers in the fields of innovation, manufacturing, and organizational behavior and business history if they are to unlock the riddles that lie behind corporate as well as national competitive advantage. There could hardly be a more ambitious research agenda in the social sciences today.

ACKNOWLEDGMENTS

Research for this paper was aided by support from the Alfred P. Sloan Foundation through the Consortium on Competitiveness and Cooperation at the University of California, Berkeley. The authors are grateful for helpful comments from two anonymous referees, as well as from Raffi Amit, Jay Barney, Joseph Bower, Henry Chesbrough, Giovanni Dosi, Sumantra Goshal, Pankaj Ghemawat, Connie Helfat, Rebecca Henderson, Dan Levinthal, Richard Nelson,

---

[63] For a gallant start, see Miyazaki (1995) and McGrath *et al* (1996). Chandler's (1990) work on scale and scope, summarized in Teece (1993), provides some historical support for the capabilities approach. Other relevant studies can be found in a special issue of *Industrial and Corporate Change* 3(3), 1994, that was devoted to dynamic capabilities.

Margie Peteraf, Richard Rosenbloom, Richard Rumelt, Carl Shapiro, Oliver Williamson, and Sidney Winter. Useful feedback was obtained from workshops at the Haas School of Business, the Wharton School, the Kellogg School (Northwestern), the Harvard Business School, and the International Institute of Applied Systems Analysis (IIASA) in Vienna, the London School of Economics, and the London Business School.

REFERENCES

Abernathy, W. J. and K. Clark (1985). 'Innovation: Mapping the winds of creative destruction', *Research Policy,* 14, pp. 3–22.

Alchian, A. A. and H. Demsetz (1972). 'Production, information costs, and economic organization', *American Economic Review,* 62, pp. 777–795.

Amit, R. and P. Schoemaker (1993). 'Strategic assets and organizational rent', *Strategic Management Journal,* 14(1), pp. 33–46.

Andrews, K. (1987). *The Concept of Corporate Strategy* (3rd ed.). Dow Jones–Irwin, Homewood, IL.

Aoki, M. (1990). 'The participatory generation of information rents and the theory of the firm'. In M. Aoki, B. Gustafsson and O. E. Williamson (eds.), *The Firm as a Nexus of Treaties.* Sage, London, pp. 26–52.

Argyres, N. (1995). 'Technology strategy, governance structure and interdivisional coordination', *Journal of Economic Behavior and Organization,* 28, pp. 337–358.

Argyris, C. and D. Schon (1978). *Organizational Learning.* Addison-Wesley, Reading, MA.

Arrow, K. (1969). 'The organization of economic activity: Issues pertinent to the choice of market vs. nonmarket allocation'. In *The Analysis and Evaluation of Public Expenditures: The PPB System,* 1. U.S. Joint Economic Committee, 91st Session. U.S. Government Printing Office, Washington, DC, pp. 59–73.

Arrow, K. (1996) 'Technical information and industrial structure', *Industrial and Corporate Change,* 5(2), pp. 645–652.

Arthur, W. B. (1983). 'Competing technologies and lock-in by historical events: The dynamics of allocation under increasing returns', working paper WP-83–90, International Institute for Applied Systems Analysis, Laxenburg, Austria.

Bain, J. S. (1959). *Industrial Organization.* Wiley, New York.

Baldwin, C. and K. Clark (1991). 'Capabilities and capital investment: New perspectives on capital budgeting', Harvard Business School working paper #92–004.

Barney, J. B. (1986). 'Strategic factor markets: Expectations, luck, and business strategy', *Management Science,* 32(10), pp. 1231–1241.

Barney, J. B., J.-C. Spender and T. Reve (1994). *Crafoord Lectures,* Vol. 6. Chartwell-Bratt, Bromley, U.K. and Lund University Press, Lund, Sweden.

Baumol, W., J. Panzar and R. Willig (1982). *Contestable Markets and the Theory of Industry Structure.* Harcourt Brace Jovanovich, New York.

Bercovitz, J. E. L., J. M. de Figueiredo and D. J. Teece (1996). 'Firm capabilities and managerial decision-making: A theory of innovation biases'. In R. Garud, P. Nayyar and

Z. Shapira (eds), *Innovation: Oversights and Foresights*. Cambridge University Press, Cambridge, U.K., pp. 233–259.

Brandenburger, A. M. and B. J. Nalebuff (1996). *Competition*. Doubleday, New York.

Brandenburger, A. M. and B. J. Nalebuff (1995). 'The right game: Use game theory to shape strategy', *Harvard Business Review*, 73(4), pp. 57–71.

Brittain, J. and J. Freeman (1980). 'Organizational proliferation and density-dependent selection'. In J. R. Kimberly and R. Miles (eds.), *The Organizational Life Cycle*. Jossey-Bass, San Francisco, CA, pp. 291–338.

Camp, R. (1989). *Benchmarking: The Search for Industry Best Practices that Lead to Superior Performance*. Quality Press, Milwaukee, WI.

Cantwell, J. (1993). 'Corporate technological specialization in international industries'. In M. Casson and J. Creedy (eds.), *Industrial Concentration and Economic Inequality*. Edward Elgar, Aldershot, pp. 216–232.

Chandler, A. D., Jr. (1966). *Strategy and Structure*. Doubleday, Anchor Books Edition, New York.

Chandler, A. D., Jr. (1990). *Scale and Scope: The Dynamics of Industrial Competition*. Harvard University Press, Cambridge, MA.

Clark, K. and T. Fujimoto (1991). *Product Development Performance: Strategy, Organization and Management in the World Auto Industries*. Harvard Business School Press, Cambridge, MA.

Coase, R. (1937). 'The nature of the firm', *Economica*, 4, pp. 386–405.

Coase, R. (1988). 'Lecture on the Nature of the Firm, III', *Journal of Law, Economics and Organization*, 4, pp. 33–47.

Cool, K. and D. Schendel (1988). 'Performance differences among strategic group members', *Strategic Management Journal*, 9(3), pp. 207–223.

de Figueiredo, J. M. and D. J. Teece (1996). 'Mitigating procurement hazards in the context of innovation', *Industrial and Corporate Change*, 5(2), pp. 537–559.

Demsetz, H. (1974). 'Two systems of belief about monopoly'. In H. Goldschmid, M. Mann and J. F. Weston (eds.), *Industrial Concentration: The New Learning*. Little, Brown, Boston, MA, pp. 161–184.

Dierickx, I. and K. Cool (1989). 'Asset stock accumulation and sustainability of competitive advantage', *Management Science*, 35(12), pp. 1504–1511.

Dixit, A. (1980). 'The role of investment in entry deterrence', *Economic Journal*, 90, pp. 95–106.

Dosi, G., D. J. Teece and S. Winter (1989). 'Toward a theory of corporate coherence: Preliminary remarks', unpublished paper, Center for Research in Management, University of California at Berkeley.

Doz, Y. and A. Shuen (1990). 'From intent to outcome: A process framework for partnerships', INSEAD working paper.

Fama, E. F. (1980). 'Agency problems and the theory of the firm', *Journal of Political Economy*, 88, pp. 288–307.

Freeman, J. and W. Boeker (1984). 'The ecological analysis of business strategy'. In G. Carroll and D. Vogel (eds.), *Strategy and Organization*, Pitman, Boston, MA, pp. 64–77.

Fujimoto, T. (1994). 'Reinterpreting the resource-capability view of the firm: A case of the development production systems of the Japanese automakers', draft working paper, Faculty of Economics, University of Tokyo.

Garvin, D. (1988). *Managing Quality.* Free Press, New York.

Garvin, D. (1994). 'The processes of organization and management', Harvard Business School working paper #94–084.

Ghemawat, P. (1986). 'Sustainable advantage', *Harvard Business Review,* **64**(5), pp. 53–58.

Ghemawat, P. (1991). *Commitment: The Dynamics of Strategy.* Free Press, New York.

Gilbert, R. J. and D. M. G. Newberry (1982). 'Preemptive patenting and the persistence of monopoly', *American Economic Review,* **72**, pp. 514–526.

Gittell, J. H. (1995). 'Cross functional coordination, control and human resource systems: Evidence from the airline industry', unpublished Ph.D. thesis, Massachusetts Institute of Technology.

Hansen, G. S. and B. Wernerfelt (1989). 'Determinants of firm performance: The relative importance of economic and organizational factors', *Strategic Management Journal,* **10**(5), pp. 399–411.

Hartley, R. F. (1989). *Marketing Mistakes.* Wiley, New York.

Hayes, R. (1985). 'Strategic planning: Forward in reverse', *Harvard Business Review,* **63**(6), pp. 111–119.

Hayes, R. and K. Clark (1985). 'Exploring the sources of productivity differences at the factory level'. In K. Clark, R. H. Hayes and C. Lorenz (eds.), *The Uneasy Alliance: Managing the Productivity-Technology Dilemma.* Harvard Business School Press, Boston, MA, pp. 151–188.

Hayes, R. and S. Wheelwright (1984). *Restoring Our Competitive Edge: Competing Through Manufacturing.* Wiley, New York.

Hayes, R., S. Wheelwright and K. Clark (1988). *Dynamic Manufacturing: Creating the Learning Organization.* Free Press, New York.

Henderson, R. M. (1994). 'The evolution of integrative capability: Innovation in cardio-vascular drug discovery', *Industrial and Corporate Change,* **3**(3), pp. 607–630.

Henderson, R. M. and K. B. Clark (1990). 'Architectural innovation: The reconfiguration of existing product technologies and the failure of established firms', *Administrative Science Quarterly,* **35**, pp. 9–30.

Henderson, R. M. and I. Cockburn (1994). 'Measuring competence? Exploring firm effects in pharmaceutical research', *Strategic Management Journal,* Summer Special Issue, **15**, pp. 63–84.

Iansiti, M. and K. B. Clark (1994). 'Integration and dynamic capability: Evidence from product development in automobiles and mainframe computers', *Industrial and Corporate Change,* **3**(3), pp. 557–605.

Itami, H. and T. W. Roehl (1987). *Mobilizing Invisible Assets.* Harvard University Press, Cambridge, MA.

Jacobsen, R. (1988). 'The persistence of abnormal returns', *Strategic Management Journal,* **9**(5), pp. 415–430.

Katz, M. and C. Shapiro (1985). 'Network externalities, competition and compatibility', *American Economic Review,* **75**, pp. 424–440.

Kreps, D. M. and R. Wilson (1982a). 'Sequential equilibria', *Econometrica,* **50**, pp. 863–894.

Kreps, D. M. and R. Wilson (1982b). 'Reputation and imperfect information', *Journal of Economic Theory,* **27**, pp. 253–279.

Langlois, R. (1994). 'Cognition and capabilities: Opportunities seized and missed in the history of the computer industry', working paper, University of Connecticut. Presented at the conference on Technological Oversights and Foresights, Stern School of Business, New York University, 11–12 March 1994.

Learned, E., C. Christensen, K. Andrews and W. Guth (1969). *Business Policy: Text and Cases*. Irwin, Homewood, IL.

Leonard-Barton, D. (1992). 'Core capabilities and core rigidities: A paradox in managing new product development', *Strategic Management Journal*, Summer Special Issue, **13**, pp. 111–125.

Leonard-Barton, D. (1995). *Wellsprings of Knowledge*. Harvard Business School Press, Boston, MA.

Lev, B. and T. Sougiannis (1992). 'The capitalization, amortization and value-relevance of R&D', unpublished manuscript, University of California, Berkeley, and University of Illinois, Urbana-Champaign.

Levinthal, D. and J. March (1981). 'A model of adaptive organizational search', *Journal of Economic Behavior and Organization*, **2**, pp. 307–333.

Levinthal, D. A. and J. G. March (1993). 'The myopia of learning', *Strategic Management Journal*, Winter Special Issue, **14**, pp. 95–112.

Levinthal, D. and J. Myatt (1994). 'Co-evolution of capabilities and industry: The evolution of mutual fund processing', *Strategic Management Journal*, Winter Special Issue, **15**, pp. 45–62.

Levitt, B. and J. March (1988). 'Organizational learning', *Annual Review of Sociology*, **14**, pp. 319–340.

Link, A. N., D. J. Teece and W. F. Finan (October 1996). 'Estimating the benefits from collaboration: The Case of SEMATECH', *Review of Industrial Organization*, **11**, pp. 737–751.

Lippman, S. A. and R. P. Rumelt (1992) 'Demand uncertainty and investment in industry-specific capital', *Industrial and Corporate Change*, **1**(1), pp. 235–262.

Mahoney, J. (1995). 'The management of resources and the resources of management', *Journal of Business Research*, **33**(2), pp. 91–101.

Mahoney, J. T. and J. R. Pandian (1992). 'The resource based view within the conversation of strategic management', *Strategic Management Journal*, **13**(5), pp. 363–380.

Mason, E. (1949). 'The current state of the monopoly problem in the U.S.', *Harvard Law Review*, **62**, pp. 1265–1285.

McGrath, R. G., M-H. Tsai, S. Venkataraman and L. C. MacMillan (1996). 'Innovation, competitive advantage and rent: A model and test', *Management Science*, **42**(3), pp. 389–403.

Milgrom, P. and J. Roberts (1982a). 'Limit pricing and entry under incomplete information: An equilibrium analysis', *Econometrica*, **50**, pp. 443–459.

Milgrom, P. and J. Roberts (1982b). 'Predation, reputation and entry deterrence', *Journal of Economic Theory*, **27**, pp. 280–312.

Milgrom, P. and J. Roberts (1990). 'The economics of modern manufacturing: Technology, strategy, and organization', *American Economic Review*, **80**(3), pp. 511–528.

Mitchell, W. (1989). 'Whether and when? Probability and timing of incumbents' entry into emerging industrial subfields', *Administrative Science Quarterly*, **34**, pp. 208–230.

Miyazaki, K. (1995). *Building Competences in the Firm: Lessons from Japanese and European Optoelectronics.* St. Martins Press, New York.

Mody, A. (1993). 'Learning through alliances', *Journal of Economic Behavior and Organization,* 20(2), pp. 151–170.

Nelson, R. R. (1991). 'Why do firms differ, and how does it matter?' *Strategic Management Journal,* Winter Special Issue, 12, pp. 61–74.

Nelson, R. R. (1994). 'The co-evolution of technology, industrial structure, and supporting institutions', *Industrial and Corporate Change,* 3(1), pp. 47–63.

Nelson, R. (1996). 'The evolution of competitive or comparative advantage: A preliminary report on a study', WP–96–21, International Institute for Applied Systems Analysis, Laxemberg, Austria.

Nelson, R. and S. Winter (1982). *An Evolutionary Theory of Economic Change.* Harvard University Press, Cambridge, MA.

Penrose, E. (1959). *The Theory of the Growth of the Firm.* Basil Blackwell, London.

Phillips, A. C. (1971). *Technology and Market Structure.* Lexington Books, Toronto.

Pisano, G. (1994). 'Knowledge integration and the locus of learning: An empirical analysis of process development', *Strategic Management Journal,* Winter Special Issue, 15, pp. 85–100.

Porter, M. E. (1980). *Competitive Strategy.* Free Press, New York.

Porter, M. E. (1990). *The Competitive Advantage of Nations.* Free Press, New York.

Prahalad, C. K. and G. Hamel (1990). 'The core competence of the corporation', *Harvard Business Review,* 68(3), pp. 79–91.

Richardson, G. B. H. (1960, 1990). *Information and Investment.* Oxford University Press, New York.

Rosenberg, N. (1982). *Inside the Black Box: Technology and Economics.* Cambridge University Press, Cambridge, MA

Rumelt, R. P. (1974). *Strategy, Structure, and Economic Performance.* Harvard University Press, Cambridge. MA.

Rumelt, R. P. (1984). 'Towards a strategic theory of the firm'. In R. B. Lamb (ed.), *Competitive Strategic Management.* Prentice-Hall, Englewood Cliffs, NJ, pp. 556–570.

Rumelt, R. P. (1991). 'How much does industry matter?', *Strategic Management Journal,* 12(3), pp. 167–185.

Rumelt, R. P., D. Schendel and D. Teece (1994). *Fundamental Issues in Strategy.* Harvard Business School Press, Cambridge, MA.

Schmalensee, R. (1983). 'Advertising and entry deterrence: An exploratory model', *Journal of Political Economy,* 91(4), pp. 636–653.

Schumpeter, J. A. (1934). *Theory of Economic Development.* Harvard University Press, Cambridge, MA.

Schumpeter, J. A. (1942). *Capitalism, Socialism and Democracy.* Harper, New York.

Shapiro, C. (1989). 'The theory of business strategy', *RAND Journal of Economics,* 20(l), pp. 125–137.

Shuen, A. (1994). 'Technology sourcing and learning strategies in the semiconductor industry', unpublished Ph.D. dissertation, University of California, Berkeley.

Sutton, J. (1992). 'Implementing game theoretical models in industrial economies'. In A. Del Monte (ed.), *Recent Developments in the Theory of Industrial Organization.* University of Michigan Press, Ann Arbor, MI, pp. 19–33.

Szulanski, G. (1995). 'Unpacking stickiness: An empirical investigation of the barriers to transfer best practice inside the firm', *Academy of Management Journal,* Best Papers Proceedings, pp. 437–441.

Teece, D. J. (1976). *The Multinational Corporation and the Resource Cost of International Technology Transfer.* Ballinger, Cambridge, MA.

Teece, D. J. (1980). 'Economics of scope and the scope of the enterprise', *Journal of Economic Behavior and Organization,* 1, pp. 223–247.

Teece, D. J. (1981). 'The market for know-how and the efficient international transfer of technology', *Annals of the Academy of Political and Social Science,* 458, pp. 81–96.

Teece, D. J. (1982). 'Towards an economic theory of the multiproduct firm', *Journal of Economic Behavior and Organization,* 3, pp. 39–63.

Teece, D. J. (1984). 'Economic analysis and strategic management', *California Management Review,* 26(3), pp. 87–110.

Teece, D. J. (1986a). 'Transactions cost economics and the multinational enterprise', *Journal of Economic Behavior and Organization,* 7, pp. 21–45.

Teece, D. J. (1986b). 'Profiting from technological innovation', *Research Policy,* 15(6), pp. 285–305.

Teece, D. J. (1988). 'Technological change and the nature of the firm'. In G. Dosi, C. Freeman, R. Nelson, G. Silverbero, and L. Soete (eds.), *Technical Change and Economic Theory.* Pinter Publishers, New York, pp. 256–281.

Teece, D. J. (1992). 'Competition, cooperation, and innovation: Organizational arrangements for regimes of rapid technological progress', *Journal of Economic Behavior and Organization,* 18(1), pp. 1–25.

Teece, D. J. (1993). 'The dynamics of industrial capitalism: Perspectives on Alfred Chandler's *Scale and Scope (1990)*', *Journal of Economic Literature,* 31(1), pp. 199–225.

Teece, D. J. (1996). 'Firm organization, industrial structure, and technological innovation', *Journal of Economic Behavior and Organization,* 31, pp. 193–224.

Teece, D. J. and G. Pisano (1994). 'The dynamic capabilities of firms: An introduction', *Industrial and Corporate Change,* 3(3), pp. 537–556.

Teece, D. J., R. Rumelt, G. Dosi and S. Winter (1994). 'Understanding corporate coherence: Theory and evidence', *Journal of Economic Behavior and Organization,* 23, pp. 1–30.

Tushman, M. L., W. H. Newman and E. Romanelli (1986). 'Convergence and upheaval: Managing the unsteady pace of organizational evolution', *California Management Review,* 29(1), pp. 29–44.

Wernerfelt, B. (1984). 'A resource-based view of the firm', *Strategic Management Journal,* 5(2), pp. 171–180.

Wernerfelt, B. and C. Montgomery (1988). 'Tobin's Q and the importance of focus in firm performance', *American Economic Review,* 78(1), pp. 246–250.

Williamson, O. E. (1975). *Markets and Hierarchies.* Free Press, New York.

Williamson, O. E. (1985). *The Economic Institutions of Capitalism.* Free Press, New York.

Williamson, O. E. (1991). 'Strategizing, economizing, and economic organization', *Strategic Management Journal,* Winter Special Issue, 12, pp. 75–94.

Williamson, O. E. (1996) *The Mechanisms of Governance*. Oxford University Press, New York.

Womack, J., D. Jones and D. Roos (1991). *The Machine that Changed the World*. Harper-Perennial, New York.

Zander, U. and B. Kogut (1995). 'Knowledge and the speed of the transfer and imitation of organizational capabilities: An empirical test', *Organization Science*, **6(1)**, pp. 76–92.

7

Organizational Knowledge, Collective Practice and Penrose Rents

J.-C. Spender

Abstract—Recent developments in the resource-based theory of the firm have suggested that organizational knowledge is the key to competitive advantage. We argue for several different types of knowledge, developing a two-by-two matrix using the explicit-implicit and individual-social distinctions. Resource-based theory characteristically overlooks the collective knowledge and skills required to coordinate the resources into a viable bundle. It overlooks, therefore, the synergistic aspects of the organization as a system of practice. We argue that these are emergent, a result of fundamental collective learning and remembering capabilities, and the key to the firm's sustainable competitive advantage. We conclude by raising the paradox embedded in Penrose's theory of the growth of the firm, that if the collective resources built up by learning by doing give rise to Penrose rents, they are also appropriable.

THE KNOWLEDGE-BASED THEORY OF THE FIRM

Following the institutional economic groundwork established by Commons (1924) and Williamson (1975), much current discussion about the firm treats it as a 'bundle' of heterogeneous resources. At the same time, strategy is the search for such differentiation as can be turned to competitive advantage. It follows that resource differences may well provide a useful theory of business strategy. Recent work on the resource-based theory of the firm (Wernerfelt, 1984; Barney, 1986; Teece, 1987; Prahalad and Hamel, 1990; Peteraf, 1993) has led us to distinguish the firm's important or 'core' resources, such as technological

From International Business Review, Vol. 3, No. 4, 1994, pp. 353–367. Reprinted by permission of Elsevier Science Ltd., Oxford, England.

117

capability, advantageous location, high market share, product design and customer loyalty, which underpin the firm's super-normal profit or rent stream and
strategic advantage, from those resources which are peripheral, such as its communication, computer and production facilities, which merely support or complement the core.

It is immediately obvious that this kind of theory of the firm must also
explain how the firm acquires its core resources since, in efficient markets, any
firm attempting to buy them meets sellers aware of their value. The seller will
then capitalize the rent stream attached to the resource and raise the price so as
to prevent the transfer of the rent potential to the firm (Rumelt, 1987, p. 142).
Following Barney (1986) we label this the 'strategic factor market' argument.
The implication is that the firm's rent-yielding resources must be acquired in
some other way, such as through luck, initial disposition or economic irrational-
ity, or across imperfect or less than efficient markets.

Given that firms typically possess many types of resource, with different
locations, designs, methods, and customers, this kind of resource based discussion shifts our attention from the specifics of the core resources onto the manner
and circumstances of their acquisition and the methods of protecting them from
being appropriated by competitors or eroded by misuse. Analysts tend to focus
on the specifics of the acquisition and protection mechanisms, such as patents
and contracts, and treat the resources themselves in ways that make it difficult
to know how they could be measured or even recognized. Barney (1991, p. 105)
has argued that core resources must be valuable, rare, inimitable and non-
substitutable. Likewise Peteraf (1993, p. 186) has proposed that the 'cornerstones of competitive advantage', in addition to resource heterogeneity, are
mobility barriers and *ex ante* and *en post* limits to competition.

The resource-based shift may be an error. Focusing only on the acquisition
and protection of core resources, we overlook how the resources are applied, i.e.
how a potential resource-based competitive advantage is transformed into revenue. The processes of resource acquisition and protection merely create and sustain the rent-potential, not the revenue. Thus rent-based theory contains
assumptions similar to the distinction between formulation and implementation
in strategy theory. There it is assumed that all important aspects of the implementation activity can be thought through beforehand, that the implementer will
later build an explicit model of the implementation's practical details. Hence the
details can be ignored in the strategic analysis, they are of no strategic account.
Yet we know how the kingdom was lost for the want of a nail and that the devil
is in the details. In the same way the theory of resource application and protection cavalierly overlooks the process of transforming resources into revenue.
When we overlook the resource application processes we miss what it means to
bundle the resources together so that they become a firm. We overlook the core
of our theory of the firm, the process of coordinating the organization's activities.

Resource-based theory has paid little attention to the construction and
management of the bundle. At first sight it seems intuitively obvious that the
firm's bundle should consist of more than one resource and that at least one
resource must be 'core' in that it has rent potential. We might think about land,

labor and capital as three distinctive and different types of resource combined in a classical enterprise. Rents might be earned if any of these three were in short supply. Resources which are not core are either complementary, by which we mean that they were acquired at prices that stripped them of any rent-potential they might have had for their previous owners. Or they might be slack, by which we mean they have been acquired but have yet to be applied and brought into the organizational process. It follows that it is the manner of application that determines whether a particular resource is core, complementary or slack.

But it could also be that none of the resources have rent-potential when they separated from the other resources in the bundle. The firm's only advantage may lie in the superior coordination of its resource set. Penrose (1959, p. 25), exploring this line of thought, interposed coordination between the firm and its inputs remarking that "it is never the resources themselves that are the inputs to the production process, only the services that the resources can render." Clearly the manner of coordination and application determines the service. Hence the difficulty presented by the strategic factor market argument, of developing a satisfactory theory based only on the acquisition and protection of rent-yielding resources, drives us toward a Penrosian approach in which coordinating capability, i.e. management is the principal source of competitive advantage. This places the managerial function in a rather different light, especially in an age so taken up with technology as the source of competitive advantage. But the difference would be of no account if the necessary coordinating capability had to be acquired in an efficient market like any other resource. Strategy would then be about the acquisition of this crucial resource and about how to prevent its owner, such as an incoming CEO, from appropriating all of the resultant rent-stream.

This paper argues that while senior management's abilities may sometimes be the principal scarce resource, and the widespread evidence of excessive executive income suggests that it is often so perceived, we argue that it is not generally the case. It may also happen that a particular rent-yielding resource, such as mining rights or a patent, may be the clue to a particular firm's advantage. Again, this is not the most general case since others might equally well have pursued the exploration or research that produced this advantage. A theory of effective exploration or research does not constitute a satisfactory basis for a general theory of the firm either. It merely leads to an infinite regress as we attempt to find the reason why one prospector or research scientist succeeded where others failed. This regress only stops when we introduce luck or initial endowment.

In this paper we follow Penrose (1959) and Barnard (1938) and focus on the firm as the intended outcome of coordinating a set of resource-based activities. In particular we argue that the core of the rent-producing firm is its ability to learn by doing, so that the core coordinating capabilities emerge during the process of coordination rather than before. The impulse to carry these emergent capabilities forward to new coordination tasks is the dynamic behind Penrose's theory of the growth of the firm. Penrose's theory contrasts with Chandler's (1962). In the latter it is the accumulated profits that drive the growth of the firm. Thus we shift the search for competitive advantage from the resources and capabilities which are logically prior to the firm's activities towards those which are the product of its unique set of activities. In particular we begin to focus on the firm as a dynamic body of knowledge in action.

ORGANIZATIONAL KNOWLEDGE

Many authors have shared Penrose's (1959, p. 53) and Arrow's (1962, 1974) interest in learning-by-doing (e.g. March and Simon, 1958; Cyert and March, 1963; Argyris and Schon, 1978; Nelson and Winter, 1982; Winter, 1987). It seems obvious that firms and their employees do learn. Not only do they learn how to design products and make particular processes work, they also learn about coordination, both between the firm's constituent activities and with its external environment. The learning organization, which must have some mechanism for increasing its stock of knowledge can be illuminated by contrast with a bureaucracy which requires all the knowledge articulated in its structure and rules to be present prior to its establishment. Weber (in Pugh, 1984, p. 26) argued that bureaucracy is control on the basis of knowledge. A pure bureaucracy's only learning is *ex post* about the gap between its achieved performance and its *ex ante* goals. Its fundamental knowledge, such as its goals and *modus operandi*, is logically prior and is generated exogenously, leading Weber to remark that the question is always who controls the bureaucratic mechanism (in Pugh, 1984, p. 25), i.e. who creates or otherwise owns its fundamental knowledge.

This kind of argument draws attention to the locus of organizational knowledge and, as with the rent-based approach: to the processes by which knowledge is transferred from its origin to the firm. Given the unproblematic bridge suggested by bureaucratic theory, that individuals supply the firm with all the knowledge required, it is not necessary to deal seriously with the idea of learning at the collective level. The firm is simply the consequence of learning at the individual level. All the subsequent learning is at the individual level too (Cohen and Sproull, 1991). Many writers interested in organizational learning seem satisfied with this view, assuming that organizational change follows individual learning about, for instance, why the goals are not being met. Simon (1991, p. 125) has endorsed this convention and argued that all learning is individual. Similarly Huber (1991, p. 89) implied that organizational learning is simply a terminological convention for that learning at the individual level which is transferred unproblematically to the organization. These authors presumed that the individual acted in his/her organizational role, learning on behalf of the organization. The relationship between the individual and the firm is simple.

Of course, this discussion involves more than learning. It involves notions of organizational mind, knowledge and memory. Many authors, such as Walsh and Ungson (1991, p. 59) have noted that organizational analysts are unclear about whether there can be any kind of knowledge at the organizational level. Allport (1924, p. 4) and Argyris and Schön (1978, p. 11) argued against. Sandelands and Stablein (1987, p. 136) were less sure.

The technical problem is to deal with reification, especially its anthropomorphic aspects. There is little reason to think that organizations have human-like capabilities of consciousness, wit, feeling, and so forth. Walsh and Ungson (1991 , p. 60) struggled with the problem of reification and argued that the purely organizational properties, as opposed to those of its members, are inter-subjectively shared and sustained through the use of common language. The implication is that organizational knowledge can be observed at the level of the individual member. It follows that organizational knowledge is of the same type as that of the individuals. The bridge between the individual and the organiza-tion is simple. No transformation takes place as the learning individual's knowl-edge becomes organizational. It is merely selected and aggregated. This is broadly the position adopted by March and the many researchers that he has influenced. Specifically March (1991, p. 74) argued that organizational learning is about aligning its knowledge with external reality. The organization remem-bers through its routines and standard procedures, and learns by institutionaliz-ing individuals' beliefs when they correspond better with reality than the organization's prior beliefs. Individuals learn both from the organization, into which they become socialized, and from their own experience. Here March adopted a rational positivist approach that, like many systems theorists, treats organizations as basically similar to individuals, albeit at a different level of analysis.

COLLECTIVE KNOWLEDGE

Contrasting with March's and Simon's individualistic position, Sandelands and Stablein (1987) adopted a subtler approach derived from Durkheim's (1964, 1970) notion of the *conscience collective*. Durkheim argued that every society is constituted by collective ways of acting and thinking that appear as concrete social facts to those that are socialized into that society. The conscious aspects of individual activity are shaped by the taken-for-granted structure of social life. This structure is not at the individual level of analysis. The individual and the society are not of the same genus. Indeed the individual is typically only dimly conscious of the nature of his or her society. It remains to the sociologist to sur-face its hidden or latent structures. Following Durkheim, Halbwachs (1992) and Connerton (1989) explored the degree to which the individual's memory is col-lective, though held individually, it is shaped and sustained by social practices. Absent these practices, memory distorts and fades.

The twin features of Durkheim's model, activity and unconsciousness, take us beyond the individual's conscious reasoning and provide the clues for a sub-tler theory of organizational knowledge. First, we know that a model and the thing modeled are not the same. In the same way a decision differs from the activity which it precipitates. The creation of activity demands a practical grasp of particulars, while decisions are framed in terms of abstractions and symbols. This is one dimension of the gap between decision and activity.

But Durkheim also suggested that we are unconscious of much of the knowledge that we bring to activities undertaken in a social context. Thus the knowledge necessary to create an intentional and coordinated pattern of activity differs from that which individuals are able to bring to their decision making. We must conclude that competent intentional activity is a form of practical knowledge in its own right and that it often differs from the kind of abstract and symbolic knowledge applied in decision analysis. The temptation to reify the organization as a cognizing and decision-making entity is the result of seeing decision-making as the organization's only significant activity. The detail of its practical activities, and the rest of the knowledge and skills necessary to its effective performance, is overlooked. Since, in the terms introduced by Toennies (1971), organizations are both *gesellschaftlich* the result of human intention, and *gemeinschaftlich*, systems of social activity, real organizations must comprise several different types of knowledge. Much will be explicit and individual, as bureaucratic theory suggests. But much will be social in the sense of being at the level of the collective, in this case the organization, and embedded in its practices. Only part of this latent social knowledge will have been made explicit and thus captured in symbols and language.

Sandelands and Stablein (1987, p. 136) arrived at their definition of the organization as the set of intentional interrelations between the activities of the individual by adopting Asch's (1952) earlier definition. They argued that this treated organizations as sets of behaviors rather than sets of individuals, focusing particularly on the relationships between these behaviors. In fact bureaucratic theory also treats organizations as behaviors. The difference is that in the latter case the behaviors are explicitly rational, directed by rules or at least intendedly so. Rational theories of organization have no need to go beyond this definition of behavior. Sandelands and Stablein's purpose, in contrast, was to go beyond these bounds and define additional categories of behavior which are the result of interactions with others' behaviors. These interactions are not bound by the rules given by the organization's designers. The additional behaviors are emergent, unintended and social. They are institutional in the sense of Selznick's (1957) use of the term. Here we move towards a notion of culture as a system of collective practice, one that contrasts vividly with the Schein (1983) based notion of culture as a system of shared cognitions (Allaire and Firsirotu, 1984).

Weick and Roberts (1993), in their analysis of the flight deck activities aboard an aircraft carrier, focused on the 'mindfulness' of the system of collective practice. They offered three key analytic notions: contributing, representing, and subordinating. Collective mind, as they termed the system of practice, emerged as the individuals forming the group constructed their activity (contributing) by envisaging the activity system (representing), and focussing on the system's interactions and interdependencies rather than their own interests and objectives (subordinating). Weick and Roberts (1993, p. 374) distinguished the development of collective mind from the classical concepts of group development. The latter defines group in terms of a movement from individual isolation through mere inclusion, via group control to affection. Affect is distinguished from cognition. They argued that there can be well-developed groups without collective mind, such as messianic cults and those showing groupthink (Janis, 1983). Collective mind without group formation might also occur, such as in firm production teams, airline cockpit crews and the *ad hoc* teams that respond to crises (Rochlin, 1989). Weick and Roberts argued that emergent collective systems of mindful practice make up for the failure of bureaucratic design principles under conditions of tight coupling and high interactive complexity which Perrow (1984) identified as the sources of systemic failure. They contrasted 'high reliability organizations', with Perrow's notion of 'normal accidents' (Bierly and Spender, 1994). Weick and Roberts (1993, p. 377) suggested provocatively that the underlying difference between organizational forms is the degree to which they facilitate or inhibit the development of collective mind.

Though grounded in the tradition of Durkheim and Halbwachs, the Weick and Roberts approach focused on the 'mindful' at the risk of overlooking the 'mindless', or rather the intuitive and unconscious aspects of collective systems of practice. They distinguished mindful from habitual practice on the ground that the latter merely reproduces itself while the former is dynamic, changing as the individual actors learn. As the group matures it institutionalizes and, they argued its inter-relating becomes routine and habitual. They dismissed by assumption any less than conscious type of collective learning, such as that which precedes the emergence of new social institutions. They seemed to deny the emergent characteristics of social groups, whether those emergent characteristics might be either cognitive or behavioral. Ironically Sandelands and Stablein (1987, p. 152), quoted Weick's earlier work to illustrate how the collective mind might know more than the sum of the individuals and thereby go beyond the mindful. The story is that native caribou hunters decide where to hunt by 'reading' the burnt bones of previously caught caribou. Being effectively random and meaningless, this process is an institutionalized form of hunting control which helps preserve the hunters' delicate ecosystem. Merton (1957) illustrated the latent functions of native rain-dances in a similar way. What the collective knows is simply not explicitly known to any of the members, even the witch doctors and tribal leaders who are expressly concerned with the collective benefits of the knowledge. Nelson and Winter (1982, p. 134), who explored the significance of practice as an aspect of organizational knowledge, argued that much of the organization's knowledge is embedded in its practices in the form of routines and operating procedures, allowed for the possibility that the collective has knowledge which is unknown to any of the members.

We can summarize this section by saying that collective knowledge is probably unlike that of individuals. It is not merely shared individual knowledge. It is likely to be embedded in the organization's institutionalized collective practices and thus deals with the interaction between the individuals' practice rather than with what they can report explicitly. It is likely to be emergent and arise after the individuals begin to engage in collective practice. It is likely to be implicit and become evident through practice rather than through explicit analysis. We can summarize the different types of organizational knowledge in the following matrix (Figure 7.1).

Conscious knowledge is that which can be reported explicitly by the individual members. Automatic knowledge is that which they bring to the creation

	Individual	*Social*
Explicit	Conscious	Objectified
Implict	Automatic	Collective

FIGURE 7.1 The Different Types of Knowledge in Organizational Analysis (Spender, 1993) p. 39

of practice but are unable to report. Thus, to quote Polanyi (1967), individuals know more than they can say and manifest that knowledge through their actions. Objectified knowledge is that which is wholly explicit and diffused through the organization. Its archetype is scientific knowledge, but it might also be more localized in, for instance, the company's rules and operating guidelines. Our focus in this section has been on the collective category. The argument is that organizations are systems of intentional practice, but not all of that practice is the result of conscious analysis. Much, possibly most, of this body of collective practices is emergent, path-dependent, compelling evidence of the history and evolution of the organization. It forms the taken-for-granted context of organizational activity. It is indicated by the term organizational culture, but it gives this term a meaning different from the more general use which reflects Schein's concept of shared cognition. It remains for us to consider the relationship between collective practice, Penrose rents and competitive advantage.

THE ECONOMIC CONSEQUENCES OF COLLECTIVE KNOWLEDGE

In the first section, we considered the difficulty of explaining the firm's competitive advantage in terms of its individual resources. The quality of coordination between resources may be crucial. This emerges as the firm's managers grapple with the challenges of implementing decisions which draw heterogeneous resources and skills into a system of directed practice. The result is a resource of a quite different type, one that inheres in the activity itself, is a property of the firm rather than of any of its individual members, is firm- and context-specific, and is intimately connected to, though not determined by, the existing pattern of skills and resources. Clearly Penrose regarded this as the most important type of knowledge and made it the basis of her theory of the growth of the firm.

Alchian and Demsetz (1972) called this kind of collective practice 'team production'. They argued that team production is the result of several features common to firms: (a) several different types of resource are used; (b) the product is not a simple sum of the separable outputs of each cooperating resource; (c) not all the resources belong to one person. They pointed out that these characteristics gave rise to metering problems, of knowing how to reward the individual resource owners or their contribution and to control shirking among those whose rewards might exceed their contributions. Thus team production would only be used where the additional governance costs would be exceeded by the benefits of team production. The fact that teams are so popular suggests that their benefits are considerable. Alchian and Demsetz also argued, of course, that the firm provided a governance structure within which the bilateral contracts between input resource owners would minimize the costs of monitoring total production and so maximize its benefits.

The notion of the whole being more than the parts, and that there are emergent properties in social systems and in organizations, is well known. To many analysts it recalls the term 'synergy' and the work of Ansoff (1965). In a well known sentence Ansoff (1965, p. 75) noted that synergy is often defined in the business literature as the $2 + 2 = 5$ effect. This was unfortunate, since it suggested that synergy is a misunderstanding of the formality of mathematics. At best it suggests that synergy is associated with some kind of mathematical space-warp. What Ansoff missed completely was what Ward, the originator of the modern meaning of the term, actually wanted to capture.

Ward was an influential nineteenth century US botanist and polymath who was also one of the founders of modern sociology. He noted that natural systems display a sense of order, integrity and wholeness which overcomes the obvious heterogeneity of their parts. He also noted that this would only occur in the presence of energy, a literal interpretation of the Second Law of Thermodynamics and the notion of entropy. Casting about for an appropriate term to describe the bindings or order-energy of natural systems Ward (1903) wrote:

> there is a universal principle, operating in every department of nature and at every stage of evolution, which is conservative, creative and constructive. . . . I have at last fixed upon the word synergy, as the term best adapted to express its twofold character of 'energy' and 'mutuality' or the systematic and organic 'working together' of the antithetical forces of nature (p. 170).

In short, synergy is the consequence of the energy expended in creating order. It is locked up in the viable system created, be it an organism or a social system. It is at the level of the system. It is not discernible at the level of the system. It is not discernible at the level of the system's components. Whenever the system is dismembered to examine its components, this binding energy dissipates. An ordered library offers systemic possibilities, such as rapid search, selection, and aggregation, that cannot be explained by looking at the books themselves. These possibilities only exist because of the investment made in defining and creating interrelations between the books, their physical arrangement and the catalogues.

We argue, of course, for a likeness between synergy and Penrose rents, between organizations and natural systems. Penrose (1971, p. 3) was extremely critical of the use of biological analogies in economics. Her principal concern was that these analogies, such as the life cycle theory, were often used to deny the significance of managerial choice (Penrose, 1971, p. 12). This environmental determinism, which many attribute to Marshall, was carried to its logical extremes in the work of the population ecologists (e.g. Hannan and Freeman, 1989). But Penrose's theory of the growth of the firm was also grounded in biological analogy. Penrose (1971) argued for a theory:

> which, in common with the biological variant, insists that a predisposition to grow is inherent in the very nature of firms, but which, in contrast [to many biological models] makes growth depend on human motivation—in the usual case on the businessman's search for profits. (p. 30)

While the intention to grow is a necessary aspect of her theory, it is far from sufficient. She went on to argue that growth was limited by the firm's ability to build up the effective management team that would enable the firm to expand as a coordinated unit (Penrose, 1971, p. 62). Just as Chandler (1977) argued for the significance of investment in administration, so Penrose saw the fundamental importance of extending energy and resources in developing effective coordination. The results were that the firm would then do more with less, provide more services with the same or fewer resources. Organizational learning, in particular the development of collective knowledge, is crucial.

Given that there are several types of organizational knowledge, it is clear that there are several types of learning. Each can lead to more effective coordination. The Scientific Management agenda (Taylor, 1911) was to generate explicit models of all the firm's processes and then optimize its operations through the application of sound analytic techniques. This strategy, which is alive and well today, belongs in the upper part of the matrix shown in Fig. 7.1. The success of scientific management, and its modern variants such as operational research and quality control, has shown us that the process of objectification can be very powerful.

But Penrose (1959, p. 53) was equally interested in the emergent practice based developments that are suggested by the term *learning-by-doing*. This knowledge emerged subsequent to activity and both added to previous knowledge and changed the firm's ability to use its knowledge. The term learning-by-doing came into general use among economic theorists after Arrow's (1962) article. His purpose was to emphasize the improved service aspect. Drawing on Wright's work on learning curves in aircraft construction, Arrow pointed to what he called the Horndahl effect, a reference to a steel plant in Sweden which showed a steady 2% per annum increase in productivity over a 15 year period without any capital investment whatsoever. Clearly learning-by-doing involves improving practice and collective knowledge in the face of uncertainty. The practice precedes the knowing and the learning strategy lies in the lower half of the matrix in Fig. 7.1. It is also important to distinguish learning-by-doing, as defined here, from trial and error which is the lay term or systematic discovery.

The scientific method is to form hypotheses which are then subject to empirical test. The trials are not random, they are determined and evaluated through explicit theorizing. This kind of learning lies in the upper part of the matrix and we might call it the Popperian learning strategy (Popper, 1968) in contrast to the collective Penrosian strategy or to individual *bricolage* (Levi-Strauss, 1969; Harper, 1987).

In this section we argued that collective knowledge, implicit and embedded in organizational practice, is a powerful source of economic advantage. It is context specific, shaped by the particular uncertainties and possibilities of the situation which management faced. It is firm-specific since it is an internally generated solution to a particular set of conditions. It is unlikely to have value or relevance to other organizations or to other times. Thus it is probably highly perishable. While Penrose argued that its being carried forward is the dynamic behind the growth of the firm, it also calls for sustained investment and maintenance in the way that Chandler suggested.

THE TRANSFER OF ORGANIZATIONAL KNOWLEDGE

If there is no surplus collective knowledge, there would be no collective resource to drive the growth of the firm. However if there is a surplus, then it must be transferred from one context to another for it to matter. If organizations comprise different types of knowledge, then, as we have argued above and elsewhere, there will be different kinds of learning (Spender, 1994). Learning is the core of the process of knowledge transfer. Imitation especially is a form of learning guided by others. Thus, recalling the first section of the paper, we approach a paradox. On the one hand, following Penrose's line of argument, we see that organizations are driven by the kinds of knowledge which can be transferred into different contexts. On the other hand, such knowledge presents appropriation risks, lest competitors acquire it, or the executives that possess it leave and set up imitative firms.

The explicit knowledge in the upper half of the matrix is potentially appropriable by definition. Thus organizations develop mobility barriers to prevent its transfer. But, at the same time, firms want to transfer this knowledge to particular others in ways that they can control and so secure the associated rents. Thus these mobility barriers must not simply inhibit transfer, they must do so selectively under the firm's control. The mobility barrier must divide the favored from the feared. Typically there must be internal transfer from the location in which the knowledge is developed to that in which it must be applied. Here we define the firm as comprising at least two dialectically intertwined sets of practices, knowledge generation and knowledge application (Spender, 1999). The methods chosen to protect the knowledge generated must not inhibit internal transfer (Leonard-Barton 1990). Yet they must inhibit transfer to outsiders, except under contract.

Sometimes the firm's knowledge strategy is in the lower half of the matrix, embedded in practice. Under these circumstances it is probably inappropriate to speak of the knowledge or technology being transferred. Rather the objective is to generate successful practice in some other context (Spender, 1993b). Organizational practice is normally partially explicit, so that part of the knowledge can be abstracted and moved. But part of the knowledge will be implicit (Nelson and Winter, 1982, p. 134), learned and remembered by doing. Where it consists of an individual's skills and automatic capabilities, the principal method by which it can be applied to a new context is by moving the individual concerned. This is a common nostrum among knowledge-transfer specialists. But, as we have seen, that individual's memory is sustained through collective practices and a move may lead to the erosion or transformation of his or her automatic knowledge. More likely, the change will force the individual into developing a new set of relationships and into the development of a new system of practice. Inevitably this leads to a transformation of the original skill-set.

If the practices are collective and truly implicit, they become nontransferable. Even moving the whole group fails because of the change in the context and infrastructure which sustains the previous practices. This is obvious when large groups of people such as villages, tribes or factories are removed to different locations. A basic learning capacity is needed to generate a new set of collective practices in a new situation. Cohen and Levinthal's (1990) notion of absorptive capacity pointed out part of what this implies. Resources must be allocated and the short-term pressures of knowledge application must not be allowed to drive out the longer-term processes of knowledge generation. But Cohen and Levinthal are not sensitive to the significance of practice. They presume all organizational knowledge can be made explicit. They deal with the less important types of knowledge.

The nub of learning-by-doing under new circumstances is to apply the most fundamental human capability, that of being able to act purposively under conditions of uncertainty. Weick illustrated this with his story of the map, the wrong map, which nevertheless precipitated the lost soldiers into the activity which eventually saved them. Here we see activity preceding any level of explicit understanding. The key, as some authors have indicated, lies in the higher level capability of learning to learn, an intuition about what kinds of action to initiate (Bereiter and Scardamalia, 1993). Here, when uncertainties are at their most extreme, collective knowledge and its ability to shape practice counts for a great deal (Spender, 1989). The practices developed will be shaped to the new situation so they are unlikely to bear a close resemblance to previous practices. Thus transfer inevitably means novelty. While transferability can be inhibited to some extents, those with this fundamental capacity to learn will generally be able to find a way to imitate, co-invent, re-engineer and otherwise leverage from whatever knowledge is available.

Sometimes the transfer of collective knowledge can be achieved by careful management of the boundaries around the system of practice. Instead of simply transferring people and expecting them to generate novel practices in the new context, the boundaries around the initial system of practice can be enlarged so as to embrace others who then, with a sort of mitosis divide off to become a separate organism. The fundamental example is that of the master with an apprentice. The apprentice is first drawn into the master's system of practice and then, alter the achievement of a masterpiece, achieves an independent identity. Firms are increasingly using such joint ventures and strategic appliances as a method of effecting the movement of collective practice though, as the many failures indicate, this requires considerable coordinating capability (Hull and Slowinski, 1990; Spender et al., forthcoming).

CONCLUSION

One modern view of the firm sees it as a bundle of resources. It follows that the firm's competitive capability is related to the components of this bundle. In this paper we argue that collective knowledge rather than the acquired resources that lies at the heart of the firm's competitive advantage. Different types of knowledge give rise to different types of economic rent. While the individual participant's knowledge and skills can be treated like any other resource and so become the basis of Pareto rents, the difficulty is to explain how the firm ever acquires and protects such resources. We argue that this kind of resource-based theory overlooks the application of the resources, in particular the process of coordination that converts the resources into services and gives the bundle its integrity. We turn to Penrose's theory of the firm and her argument that this coordinating capacity is the essence of the firm and both the impetus and the constraint to its growth. Once developed through learning by doing, it gives rise to Penrose rents. The Penrose model allows us to approach the paradox that for these rents to be generated, the coordinating capabilities need to be transferable to new contexts. But when such capabilities are transferable, they become appropriable.

REFERENCES

Alchian, A. A. and Demsetz, H. (1972) Production, Information Costs, and Economic Organization. *American Economic Review,* Vol. 62, pp. 777–795.

Adlaire, Y. and Firsirotu, M. E. (1984) Theories of Organization Culture. *Organization Studies.* Vol. 5, pp. 193– 226.

Allport, F. H. (1924) *Social Psychology.* Houghton Mifflin, Boston, Massachusetts.

Ansoff, H. I. (1965) *Corporate Strategy.* McGraw-Hill, New York.

Argyris, C. and Schön, D. A. (1978) *Organizational Learning. A Theory of Action Perspective.* Addison-Wesley, Reading, Massachusetts.

Arrow, K. (1962) The Economic Implications of Learning by Doing. *Review of Economic Studies, Vol.* 29, pp. 155–173.

Arrow, K. J. (1974) *The Limits of Organization.* W. W. Norton, New York.

Asch, S. E. (1952) *Social Psychology.* Prentice-Hall, Englewood Cliffs, New Jersey.

Barnard, C. I. (1938) *The Functions of the Executive.* Harvard University Press, Cambridge, Massachusetts.

Barney, J. B. (1986) Strategic Factor Markets: Expectations, Luck, and Business Strategy. *Management Science*, Vol. 32, pp. 1231–1241.

Barney, J. B. (1991) Firm Resources and Sustained Competitive Advantage. *Journal of Management*, Vol. 17, No. 1, pp. 99–120.

Bereiter, C. and Scardamalia, M. (1993) *Surpassing ourselves: An Inquiry into the Nature and Implications of Expertise.* Open Court, Chicago, Illinois.

Bierly, P. E. and Spender, J.-C. (1984) The Culture of High Reliability Organizations: The Case of the Nuclear Submarine. *Journal of Management,* forthcoming.

Chandler, A. D. (1962) *Strategy and Structure: Chapters in the History to the American Industrial Enterprise.* MIT Press, Cambridge, Massachusetts.

Chandler, A. D. (1977) *The Visible Hand: The Managerial Revolution in American Business.* Belknap Press, Cambridge, Massachusetts.

Cohen, W. M. and Levinthal, D. A. (1990) Absorptive Capacity: A New Perspective on Learning and Innovation. *Administrative Science Quarterly,* Vol. 35, pp. 128–152.

Cohen, M. D. and Sproull, L. S. (1991) Editors' Introduction to the Special Issue on Organizational Learning. *Organization Science,* Vol. 2, No. 1.

Commons, J. R. (1924) *The Legal Foundations of Capitalism.* Macmillan, New York.

Connerton, P. (1989) *How Societies Remember.* Cambridge University Press, Cambridge.

Cyert, R. M. and March, J. G. (1963) *A Behavioral Theory of the Firm.* Prentice-Hall, Englewood Cliffs, New Jersey.

Durkheim, E. (1964) *The Rules of Sociological Method.* Free press, New York.

Durkheim, E. (1970) *Suicide—A Study in Sociology.* Routledge & Kegan Paul, London.

Halbwachs, M. (1992) *On Collective Memory.* University of Chicago Press, Chicago, Illinois.

Hannan, M. T. and Freeman, J. (1989) *Organizational Ecology.* Harvard University Press, Cambridge, Massachusetts.

Harper, D. A. (1987) *Working Knowledge: Skill and Community in a Small Shop.* University of Chicago Press, Chicago, Illinois.

Huber, G. (1991) Organizational Learning: The Contributing Process and the Literature. *Organization Science.* Vol. 2, No. 1, pp. 88–115.

Hull, F. and Slowinski, G. (1990) Partnering with Technology Entrepreneurs. *Research and Technology Management,* Nov.–Dec., pp. 16–20.

Janis, I. L. (1983) *Groupthink: Psychological Studies of Policy Decisions and Fiascoes,* 2nd Ed. Houghton Mifflin Co., Boston, Massachusetts.

Leonard-Barton, D. (1990) The Intraorganizational Environment: Point-to-point versus Diffusion, in Williams, F. and Givson, D. V. (Eds.), *Technology Transfer: A Communications Perspective,* pp. 43–62. Sage Publications, Newbury Park, California.

Levi-Strauss, C. (1962) *The Savage Mind.* University of Chicago Press, Chicago, Illinois.

March, J. G. (1991) Exploration and Exploitation in Organizational Learning. *Organization Science,* Vol. 2, pp. 71–87.

March J. G. and Simon, H. A. (1958) *Organizations.* Wiley, New York.

Merton, R. K. (1957) *Social theory and Social Structure.* Free Press, New York.

Nelson, R. R. and Winter, S. G. (1982) *An Evolutionary Theory of Economic Chance.* Belknap Press, Cambridge, Massachusetts.

Penrose, E. T. (1959) *The Theory of the Growth of the Firm.* Wiley, New York.

Penrose, E. T. (1971) *The Growth of Firms, Middle East Oil and Other Essays.* Frank Cass, London.

Perrow, C. (1984) *Normal Accidents: Living with High-risk Technologies.* Basic Books, New York.

Peteraf, M. A. (1993) The Cornerstones of Competitive Advantage: A Resource-base View. *Strategic Management Journal,* Vol. 14, pp. 179–191.

Polanyi, M. (1967) *The Tacit Dimension.* Anchor Books, Garden City, New York.

Popper, K. (1968) *The Logic of Scientific Discovery.* Hutchinson, London.

Prahalad, C. K. and Hamel G. (1990) The Core Competence of the Corporation. *Harvard Business Review,* Vol. 68 No. 3, pp. 79–91.

Pugh, D. S. (Ed.) (1984) *Organization Theory: Selected Readings.* Penguin Books, Harmondsworth, UK.

Rochlin, G. I. (1989) Informal Organizational Networking as a Crisis-avoidance Strategy: US Naval Flight Operations as a Case Study. *Industrial Crisis Quarterly,* Vol. 3, pp. 159–176.

Rumelt, R. P. (1987) Theory, Strategy, and Entrepreneurship, in Teece, D. J. (Ed.), *The Competitive Challenge,* pp. 137–158. Ballinger, Cambridge, Massachusetts.

Sandelands, L. E. and Stablein, R. E. (1987) The Concept of Organization Mind, in Bacharach, S. and DiTomaso, N. (Eds.), *Research in the Sociology of Organizations,* Vol. 5, pp. 135–161. JAI Press, Greenwich, Connecticut.

Schein, E. H. (1983) Organizational Culture. *Organizational Dynamics,* Vol. 12, pp. 13–28.

Selznick, P. (1957) *Leadership in Administration: A Sociological Interpretation.* Harper & Row, New York.

Simon, H. A. (1991) Bounded Rationality and Organizational Learning. *Organization Science,* Vol. 2, pp. 125–134.

Spender, J.-C. (1989) *Industry Recipes: The Nature and Sources of Managerial Judgement.* Basil Blackwell, Oxford.

Spender, J.-C. (1992) Limits to Learning from the West: How Western Management Advice May Prove Limited in Eastern Europe. *The International Executive,* Vol. 34, pp. 389–410.

Spender, J.-C. (1993a) Competitive Advantage from Tacit Knowledge? Unpacking the Concept and Its Strategic Implications. *Academy of Management Best Paper Proceedings,* pp. 37–41.

Spender, J.-C. (1993b) Using a 5-step Knowledge Based Approach to Manage Technology Transfer. *T'Squared, Newsletter of the Technology Transfer Society,* Vol. 18, No. 9, pp. 1–5.

Spender, J.-C. (1994) Knowing, Managing and Learning: A Dynamic Managerial Epistemology. *Management Learning,* Vol. 25, No. 3, pp. 387–412.

Spender, J.-C., Slowinski, G., Farris, G. and Hull, F. (forthcoming) Handling the Uncertainty in R&D Alliances, in Balkin, D. (Ed.), *Advances in High-technology Management.* JAI Press, Greenwich, Connecticut.

Taylor, F. W. (1911) *The Principles of Scientific Management.* Harper & Brothers, New York.

Teece, D. J. (1987) Profiting from Technological Innovation: Implications for Integration, Collaboration, Licensing, and Public Policy, Teece, D.J. (Ed.). *The Competitive Challange,* pp. 185–210. Ballinger, Cambridge, Massachusetts.

Toennies, F. (1971) *On Sociology: Pure, Applied and Empirical.* University of Chicago Press, Chicago, Illinois.

Walsh, J. P. and Ungson, G. R. (1991) Organizational Memory. *Academy of Management Review,* Vol. 16, pp. 57–91.

Ward, L. F. (1903) *Pure Sociology.* Macmillan, New York.

Weick, K. E. and Roberts, K. H. (1993) Collective Mind in Organizations: Heedful Interrelating on Flight Decks. *Administrative Science Quarterly,* Vol. 38, pp. 357–381.

Wernerfelt, B. (1984) A Resource-based View of the Firm. *Strategic Management Journal,* Vol. 5, pp. 171–180.

Williamson, O. E. (1975) *Markets and Hierarchies: Analysis and Antitrust Implications.* Free Press, New York.

Winter, S. G. (1987) Knowledge and Competence as Strategic Assets, in Teece, D. J. (Ed.), *The Competitive Challenge,* pp. 159–184. Ballinger, Cambridge, Massachusetts.

8

Prospering in Dynamically-Competitive Environments: Organizational Capability as Knowledge Integration

Robert M. Grant

Abstract—Unstable market conditions caused by innovation and increasing intensity and diversity of competition have resulted in organizational capabilities rather than served markets becoming the primary basis upon which firms establish their long-term strategies. If the strategically most important resource of the firm is knowledge, and if knowledge resides in specialized form among individual organizational members, then the essence of organizational capability is the integration of individuals' specialized knowledge.

This paper develops a knowledge-based theory of organizational capability, and draws upon research into competitive dynamics, the resource-based view of the firm, organizational capabilities, and organizational learning. Central to the theory is analysis of the mechanisms through which knowledge is integrated within firms in order to create capability. The theory is used to explore firms' potential for establishing competitive advantage in dynamic market settings, including the role of firm networks under conditions of unstable linkages between knowledge inputs and product outputs. The analysis points to the difficulties in creating the "dynamic" and "flexible-response capabilities" which have been deemed critical to success in hyper competitive markets.

From *Organization Science*, Vol. 7, No. 4, 1996, pp. 375–387. Reprinted by permission of The Institute of Management Sciences (INFORMS), 2 Charles St., Suite 300, Providence, RI 02904 USA.

INTRODUCTION

The growing intensity and dynamism of competition across product markets has had profound implications for the evolution of strategic management thought during the 1980s and 1990s. Increasing turbulence of the external business environment has focused attention upon *resources* and *organizational capabilities* as the principal source of sustainable competitive advantage and the foundation for strategy formulation. As the markets for resources have become subject to the same dynamically-competitive conditions that have afflicted product markets, so *knowledge* has emerged as the most strategically-significant resource of the firm. This paper seeks to extend our understanding of the determinants of competitive advantage in dynamically competitive market environments by analyzing the role of knowledge in organizational capability. Building upon four major theoretical streams: competition as a dynamic process, the resource-based view of the firm, organizational capabilities and competences and organizational knowledge and learning, this paper establishes the rudiments of a knowledge-based theory of the firm. At the heart of this theory is the idea that the primary role of the firm, and the essence of organizational capability, is the *integration of knowledge*. The paper explores how knowledge is integrated to form organizational capability, and goes on to identify characteristics of capabilities which are associated with creating and sustaining competitive advantage in dynamically-competitive markets, including the achievement of *flexible integration* across multiple knowledge bases. Finally, I consider the relative merits of internal versus external knowledge integration and the benefits of firm networks in coping with hypercompetitive market conditions.

BACKGROUND

The displacement of static theories of competition associated with neoclassical microeconomics and the "structure-conduct-performance" school of industrial economics by the more dynamic approaches associated with the Austrian school of economics, especially with Schumpeter's concept of competition as a process of "creative destruction" (Schumpeter 1934), has had profound implications for strategic management thought (Jacobsen 1992). During the early part of the 1980s, strategy analysis was focused upon the quest for monopoly rent through industry and segment selection and the manipulation of market structure to create market power (Porter 1980). However, if market structure is in a state of flux, and if monopoly rents quickly succumb to new sources of competition, approaches to strategy based upon choices of product markets and positioning within them are unlikely to yield profit advantages that are more than temporary. The impact of the resource-based view of the firm on strategic management thinking can be attributed to two factors. First, given the lack of evidence that monopoly power is an important source of profit (Rumelt 1991), Ricardian rents (returns to resources over and above their opportunity costs) appear to be the primary source of interfirm profitability differences. Second, if external markets are in a state of flux, then the internal resources and capabilities of a firm would appear to be a more stable basis for strategy formulation than the external customer focus that has traditionally associated with the marketing-orientation to strategy (Levitt 1960).

This emphasis on the "supply-side" rather than the "demand side" of strategy has been closely associated with recent work on organizational capabilities. Prahalad and Hamel (1990) argue that sustainable competitive advantage is dependent upon building and exploiting "core competences"—those capabilities which are fundamental to a firm's competitive advantage and which can be deployed across multiple product markets. Porter's recent work emphasizes the need for firms and countries to broaden and upgrade their internal advantages in order to sustain and extend competitive advantages (Porter 1991, 1992).

While extreme forms of dynamic competition (termed "hypercompetition" by D'Aveni 1994) are characteristic of product markets, dynamically competitive conditions also are present in the markets for resources. Indeed, competitive conditions in product markets are driven, in part, by the conditions of competition in the markets for resources (Barney 1986). Thus, the speed with which positions of competitive advantage in product markets are undermined depends upon the ability of challengers to acquire the resources needed to initiate a competitive offensive. Sustainability of competitive advantage therefore requires resources which are *idiosyncratic* (and therefore scarce), and not easily *transferable* or *replicable* (Grant 1991). These criteria point to knowledge (tacit knowledge in particular) as the most strategically-important resource which firms possess (Quinn 1992). Thus, this paper's focus upon knowledge and its integration is justified by two assumptions about the success in dynamically-competitive market environments:

> First, under dynamic competition, superior profitability is likely to be associated with resource and capability-based advantages than with positioning advantages resulting from market and segment selection and competitive positions based upon some form of "generic strategy";

> Second, such resource and capability-based advantages are likely to derive from superior access to and integration of specialized knowledge.

The literature on organizational knowledge and learning has explored the role of organizations in the acquisition, processing, storage, and application of knowledge (Argyris and Schon 1978, Levitt and March 1988, Organization Science 1991, Starbuck 1992). The primary emphasis of this literature is on the acquisition of information by organizations. Nonaka (1994) proposes a theory of knowledge creation built around dynamic interaction between two dimensions of knowledge transfer: transformations from tacit to explicit knowledge and vice-versa; and transfers between individual, group, organizational, and interorganizational levels. However, as Spender (1992) recognizes, firms are engaged not only in knowledge creation but also in knowledge application. The distinction between these two processes is crystallized in Demsetz's (1991) observation that efficiency in the acquisition of knowledge requires that individuals specialize in specific areas of knowledge, while the application of knowledge to produce goods and services requires the bringing together of many areas of specialized knowledge.

Much of the research into the management issues concerning the integration of different types of specialized knowledge has been within the context of new product development (Nonaka 1990, Clark and Fujimoto 1991, Wheelwright and Clark 1992). While some innovations are the result of the application of new knowledge, others result from reconfiguring existing knowledge to create "architectural innovations" (Henderson and Clark 1990, Henderson and Cockburn 1995). This ability of the firm to "generate new combinations of existing knowledge" and "to exploit its knowledge of the unexplored potential of the technology" is what Kogut and Zander (1992, p. 391) describe as "combinative capabilities."

The theory of organizational capability which follows represents an extension and synthesis of these contributions, based upon the idea that the essence of organizational capability is the integration of individuals' specialized knowledge.

THE MODEL: ORGANIZATIONAL CAPABILITY AS KNOWLEDGE INTEGRATION

My model of organizational capability rests upon basic assumptions regarding the characteristics of knowledge and its deployment. From these assumptions I develop propositions concerning the nature of organizational capability, the linkage of capability to organizational structure, and the determinants of competitive advantage.

ASSUMPTIONS

The focus of this paper is upon a single resource: knowledge. This emphasis is justified by the assumptions that, first, knowledge accounts for the greater part of value added,[1] second, barriers to the transfer and replication of knowledge endow it with strategic importance. I define knowledge broadly to include both "explicit" knowledge which can be written down, and "tacit" knowledge

[1] The part of national income attributable to knowledge may be calculated as wages and salaries over and above that which would be earned by unskilled manual labor, plus royalties and license fees. To this a major part of profit can be added, since profit is a return to the resources owned by the firm, a major part of which comprise or embody the knowledge of people. International differences in living standards and productivity are mainly due to differences in human capital. Denison's research into international differences in growth rates found that, in the case of Britain, advances in knowledge accounted for 46 percent increases in real national income per person employed between 1950 and 1960 (Denison 1968).

which cannot. The emphasis is on tacit knowledge since, in the form of "know-how", skills, and "practical knowledge" of organizational members, tacit knowledge is closely associated with production tasks, and raises the more interesting and complex issues regarding its transfer both within and between organizations.

The key managerial issues arising from the characteristics of knowledge stem from the observation that tacit knowledge is acquired by and stored within individuals. Due to the cognitive limits of the human brain, knowledge is acquired in a highly specialized form: an increase in depth of knowledge implies reduction in breadth. Advances in knowledge tend to be associated with increased specialization. However, production—the creation of value through transforming input into output—requires a wide array of knowledge, usually through combining the specialized knowledge of a number of individuals.

INTEGRATING KNOWLEDGE TO FORM ORGANIZATIONAL CAPABILITY

These assumptions provide the basis for a knowledge based view of the firm. If knowledge is a critical input into all production processes, if efficiency requires that it is created and stored by individuals in specialized form, and if production requires the application of many types of specialized knowledge, then the primary role of the firm is the integration of knowledge. But why are institutions called "firms" needed for the integration of knowledge? It is because the alternatives are too inefficient. An individual's ability to integrate knowledge is constrained by cognitive limits: it is not feasible for each individual to try to learn the knowledge possessed by other specialists. Integration across markets is difficult: in the case of explicit knowledge it is difficult to appropriate the value of the knowledge through market contracts; in the case of tacit knowledge, transfer is both difficult and necessitates transaction-specific investment. This view of the firm as an institution for knowledge integration establishes a view of the firm based upon close integration between organizational members implying stability, propinquity and social relationships, but it does not readily yield precision definition of the firm and its boundaries. For this reason, Demsetz (1991) refers to "firm-like organizations."

Integration of specialist knowledge to perform a discrete productive task is the essence of organizational capability, defined as a firm's ability to perform repeatedly a productive task which relates either directly or indirectly to a firm's capacity for creating value through effecting the transformation of inputs into outputs. Most organizational capabilities require integrating the specialist knowledge bases of a number of individuals. A hospital's capability in cardiovascular surgery is dependent upon integrating the specialist knowledge of surgeons, anaesthetist, radiologist, operating-room nurses, and several types of technicians. L.L. Bean's order processing capability, Rubbermaid's new product development capability and McDonald's Restaurants' capability in preparing and serving hamburgers are all examples of organizational capabilities requiring the integration of specialized knowledge across quite large numbers of employees.

THE ARCHITECTURE OF CAPABILITIES

The integration of knowledge into organizational capabilities may be viewed as a hierarchy. This hierarchy is not one of authority and control, as in the traditional concept of an administrative hierarchy, but is a hierarchy of integration. At the base of the hierarchy is the specialized knowledge held by individual organizational members. At the first level of integration are capabilities which deal with specialized tasks. Moving up the hierarchy of capabilities, the span of specialized knowledge being integrated broadens: task-specific capabilities are integrated into broader functional capabilities—marketing, manufacturing, R & D, and financial. At higher levels of integration are capabilities which require wide-ranging cross-functional integration—new product development involves especially wide ranging integration (Clark and Fujimoto 1991). Figure 8.1 illustrates this concept of hierarchy of capabilities by providing a vertical segment of the hierarchically arranged organizational capabilities of a manufacturer of private-branch telephone exchanges (PBXs).

The wider the span of knowledge being integrated, the more complex are the problems of creating and managing organizational capability. The "quick response capability" which Richardson (1996) identifies among apparel suppliers Benetton, The Gap, and Giordano is an important competitive advantage primarily because it is difficult to achieve-it involves integrating across multiple vertical stages. The difficulties experienced by the Bell operating companies in transferring the new capabilities developed in their overseas businesses back to their domestic operations can be attributed to the fact that many of these new capabilities (e.g. wireless communication, fiber-optics, marketing within competitive markets, and managing joint ventures) require integration across broad-spans of knowledge and expertise (Smith 1996).

Although higher-level capabilities involve the integration of lower-level capabilities, such integration can only be achieved through integrating individual knowledge. This is precisely why higher level capabilities are so difficult to perform. New product development requires the integration of an extremely broad basis of knowledge, but communication constraints imply that the number of individuals who can be directly involved in the process is small.[2] Cross-functional product development teams are not so difficult to set up, the challenge (as confirmed by Imai et al. 1985 and Clark and Fujimoto 1991) is for the team to

[2] A key distinction between an administrative hierarchy and the hierarchy of capabilities is that, in the administrative hierarchy, the span of control can remain constant throughout the hierarchy. In the hierarchy of capabilities, the fact that each layer of capabilities cannot directly integrate the preceding layer of capabilities and must return to the base in terms of integrating individual's knowledge, means that the span of integration increases as one ascends the hierarchy.

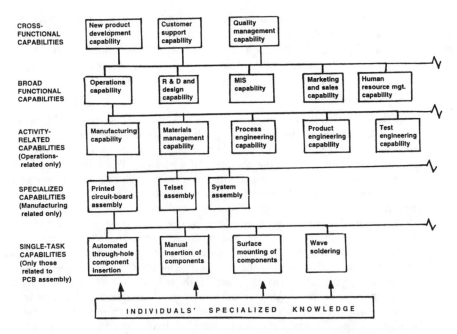

FIGURE 8.1 Organizational Capabilities of a PBX Producer: A Partial Vertical Segment

access the breadth and depth of functional knowledge pertinent to the product, and integrate that knowledge.

In most companies, hierarchies of capabilities do not correspond closely with their authority-based hierarchies as depicted by organization charts. In particular, some top management capabilities such as capital budgeting, strategic planning, and government lobbying may involve a limited scope of knowledge integration, and hence are closer to the base than to the apex of the capability structure. At the same time, if knowledge is to be integrated effectively by the firm, the architecture of capabilities must have some correspondence with the firm's structure of authority, communication, and decision making, whether formal or informal. For example, Clark and Fujimoto find that, within automobiles, superior capabilities in new product development require product managers with substantial influence and decision making authority—what they term "heavyweight product managers." The need for organizational capabilities to be supported by firm structure poses difficulties for the creation of new capabilities. In the case of the Bell telephone companies, new capabilities were created outside the formal structure through "garbage can" processes (Smith 1996).

MECHANISMS FOR INTEGRATING KNOWLEDGE

How is knowledge integrated by firms to create organizational capability? Explicit knowledge involves few problems of integration because of its inherent communicability. Advances in information technology have greatly facilitated the integration of explicit knowledge through increasing the ease with which explicit knowledge can be codified, communicated, assimilated, stored, and retrieved (Rockart and Short 1989). However, the most interesting and complex issues concern the integration of tacit knowledge. The literature points to two primary integration mechanisms:

(i) Direction. Demsetz (1991, p. 172) identifies direction as the principal means by which knowledge can be communicated at low cost between "specialists and the large number of other persons who either are nonspecialists or who are specialists in other fields." To optimize the operation of a McDonald's restaurant, it is more efficient for McDonald's to create an operating manual which covers almost every aspect of the restaurant's management than to educate every McDonald's manager in cooking, nutrition, hygiene, engineering, marketing, production management, human resource management, psychology, accounting and finance, and the other specialist areas of knowledge embodied in standard operating rules.

The more complex an activity, the greater the number of locations in which that activity must be replicated, and the more stringent the performance specifications for the outcome of that activity, the greater is the reliance on knowledge integration through direction. British Airways operates aircraft maintenance facilities in 67 locations distributed across the globe. Service and repair at these facilities is guided by a host of highly formalized procedures and directives based upon the standards established by the major regulatory authorities (the Federal Aviation Authority, the British Civil Aeronautics Board, and others), guidance and technical information provided by aircraft manufacturers, and the company's own policies and procedures. These directives, policies, and procedures embody the technical knowledge of a large number of specialists.

(ii) Organizational Routines. Direction involves codifying tacit knowledge into explicit rules and instructions. But since a characteristic of tacit knowledge is that "we can know more than we can tell" (Polanyi 1966), converting tacit knowledge into explicit knowledge in the form of rules, directives, formulae, expert systems, and the like inevitably involves substantial knowledge loss.

An organizational routine provides a mechanism for coordination which is not dependent upon the need for communication of knowledge in explicit form. March and Simon (1958, p. 142) "regard a set of activities as routinized to the extent that choice has been simplified by the development of a fixed response to a defined stimuli." Such patterns of stimulus and response may lead to highly complex and variable patterns of seemingly-automatic behavior. Within our knowledge-based view, the essence of an organizational routine is that individuals develop sequential patterns of interaction which permit the integration of their specialized knowledge without the need for communicating that knowledge.

Observation of any work team, whether it is a surgical team in a hospital operating room or a team of mechanics at a grand prix motor race, reveals closely coordinated working arrangements where each team member applies his or her specialist knowledge, but where the patterns of interaction appear automatic. This coordination relies heavily upon informal procedures in the form of commonly-understood roles and interactions established through training and constant repetition, supported by a series of explicit and implicit signals (see Pentland and Rueter 1994, for a careful analysis). The advantage of routine over direction is in economizing on communication and a greater capacity to vary responses to a broad range of circumstances.

COMPETITIVE ADVANTAGE IN DYNAMiCALLY-COMPETITIVE ENVIRONMENTS

Creating and Sustaining Advantage

Under conditions of dynamic competition, the potential of organizational capabilities to earn rents for the firm through establishing sustainable competitive advantage depends upon their capacity for both creating and sustaining advantage. Competitive advantage is determined by a combination of supply-side and demand-side factors. On the demand side, a firm's productive activities must correspond to a market need. On the supply side, the firm must have the capabilities not only to serve that market need, but to serve it more effectively or efficiently than other firms. For simplicity's sake, let us abstract from demand-side considerations and focus exclusively upon the supply side: the ability to create unique advantages and to protect these advantages against imitation.

The first observation is that the critical source of competitive advantage is knowledge integration rather than knowledge itself. Specialized knowledge cannot, on its own, provide a basis for sustainable advantage, first, because specialized knowledge resides in individuals, and individuals are transferable between firms; second, because the rents generated by specialized knowledge are more likely to be appropriated by individuals than by the firm. Of course, some knowledge (patents, copyrights, trade secrets) is proprietary to the firm, and is appropriable. However, empirical evidence suggests that the value of proprietary knowledge depreciates quickly through obsolescence and imitation (Levin et al. 1987). Hence, even in technology-intensive industries, the key to sustainable advantage is not proprietary knowledge itself, but the technological capabilities which permit the generation of new knowledge.

If knowledge integration is the basis for competitive advantage under dynamic market conditions, what are the characteristics of knowledge integration associated with the creation and sustenance of such an advantage? I identify three characteristics of knowledge integration pertinent to the competitive advantage and the rents associated with such advantage:

(i) The *efficiency of integration*—the extent to which the capability accesses and utilizes the specialist knowledge held by individual organizational members;

(ii) by the *scope of integration*—the breadth of specialized knowledge the organizational capability draws upon;

(iii) the *flexibility of integration*—the extent to which a capability can access additional knowledge and reconfigure existing knowledge.

My goal is to explore the performance requirements of systems of knowledge integration conducive to attaining competitive advantage. Given the uniqueness of each firm's stock of specialized knowledge and the idiosyncrasy of each firm's institutional heritage, it is impossible to specify the organizational arrangements conducive to the formation of organizational capability through knowledge integration. Critical to the analysis of this paper is an equifinality view (Van de Ven and Drazin 1985) that, recognizing uniqueness of knowledge bases and institutional conditions, firms can achieve equally effective, yet highly differentiated approaches to knowledge integration. The key contribution of our analysis is in recognizing the common requirements of these different approaches.

The Efficiency of Integration

Competitive advantage depends upon how productive firms are in utilizing the knowledge stored within individual organizational members, which is dependent upon the ability of the firm to access and harness the specialized knowledge of its members. Three factors are important in determining the efficiency with which a firm integrates the specialized knowledge available within it:

(a) The Level of Common Knowledge

Both direction and routine require communication between individuals. Demsetz (1991) identifies the prerequisite for communication between different specialists as the presence of common knowledge between them. If specialized knowledge must be reduced to common knowledge in order to communicate it, there is inevitably substantial information loss. The size of this loss depends upon the level and sophistication of common knowledge. A basic prerequisite is a common language. Direction is almost entirely ability upon detailed articulation of instructions. Routines typically rely upon a much more limited set of cues and responses which serve not so much as to communicate knowledge, but to permit a sequencing of individual's application of knowledge inputs. For both integration mechanisms, efficiency of communication depends upon commonality of vocabulary, conceptual knowledge, and experience between individual specialists. Shared behavioral norms form a central part of the common knowledge which facilitates communication and understanding (Garfinkel 1967, Zucker 1987). Generally speaking, the wider the scope of knowledge being integrated (and, hence, the greater the diversity of the individuals involved), the lower is the level of common knowledge, and the more inefficient the communication and integration of knowledge. Thus, the effectiveness of social networks among biotechnologists as mechanisms for communicating and integrating knowledge reflected their high level of common knowledge arising from their comparatively narrow spread of knowledge and commonality of behavioral norms (Liebeskind et al. 1996). Organizational culture may be regarded as a form of common knowledge, one of the functions of which is to facilitate knowledge integration within the company.

(b) Frequency and Variability of Task Performance

The efficiency with which organizational integrate the specialized knowledge of team members depends upon the sophistication of the system of signaling and responsiveness which develops between team members as a result of repetition and improvement. The efficiency of an organizational routine derives from the fact that:

> While each organization member must know his job, there is no need for anyone to know anyone else's job. Neither is there a need for anyone to be able to articulate or conceptualize the procedures employed by the organization as a whole (Nelson and Winter 1982, p. 105).

The critical requirement is the "ability to receive and interpret a stream of incoming messages from other members and from the environment" (Ibid, p. 100). Integrative efficiency depends upon the effectiveness of this communication in eliciting appropriate responses from each organization member. This is a function of the frequency with which the particular pattern of coordinated activity is performed. The greater the variation in the routine which is required in response to variation in environmental circumstances, the lower is integrating efficiency likely to be. The ineffectiveness of the response by the National Guard to the Los Angeles riots of 1992 and the Russian Army to the Chechnya rebellion of 1994/95 reflects, in part, the infrequence with which these organizations were required to suppress insurrection.

(c) Structure

Efficiency of knowledge integration requires economizing upon the amount of communication needed to effect integration. Organization structures need to be designed with a view to organizing activities such as to reduce the extent and intensity of communication needed to achieve knowledge integration. Bureaucracy is a structure which (under certain circumstances) maximizes the efficiency of knowledge integration in an organization where direction is the predominant integrating mechanism. A key feature of organizational innovations such as Henry Ford's moving assembly line, the kanban system for just-in-time scheduling, multidivisional structure (or "M-form") is their promotion of efficiency through achieving higher levels of coordination with lower levels of communication.

The principle of modularity is fundamental to the structuring of organizations to achieve communication efficiencies. Simon's observation that:

> . . . division of labor means factoring the total system of decisions that need to be made into relatively independent subsystems, each one of which can be designed with only minimal concern for its interactions with the others (Simon 1973, p. 270),

and Williamson's "principle of hierarchical decomposition" (Williamson 1981, p. 1550), may be viewed as organizational conditions for optimizing the efficiency of knowledge integration.

Modularity is especially important in organizing highly complex capabilities which involve broad-scope knowledge integration. Clark and Fujimoto (1991) show how the hugely complex task of developing a new model of automobile is facilitated by means of organizing the task:

- into sequential phases (concept development, vehicle design and layout, component design, prototype building, process engineering);

- by function (marketing, product engineering, test engineering, process engineering);
- by product segment (body, chassis, engine, transmission, electrics and electronics).

The problem of many conventional approaches to modularity is that they rest heavily upon time-sequencing. Under conditions of hypercompetition such as sequencing is simply too time consuming. The organizational challenge is creating modularity which permits either overlapping phases or full simultaneity.

The Scope of Integration

Increases in the span of knowledge which are integrated within an organizational capability increases the potential for both establishing and sustaining competitive advantages through two sources:

(i) Different types of specialized knowledge are *complements* rather than *substitutes* in production. Up to the point of diminishing relevance, the marginal revenue product of a unit of specialist knowledge increases with the addition of different types of knowledge.

(ii) The greater the scope of knowledge being integrated within a capability, the greater the difficulty faced by competitors in replicating that capability due to increases in "*causal ambiguity*" (Lippman and Rumelt 1982) and time-based diseconomies of replication (Dierickx and Cool 1989). The complexities associated with broad-scope integration are further increased when different types of knowledge require different patterns of integration. Toyota's lean production system combines cost efficiency, quality, flexibility, and innovation. These different performance dimensions involve different types of integration. While cost efficiency may be best served through organization around "sequential interdependence," flexibility is likely to require more complex patterns of "reciprocal interdependence" (Thompson 1967, p. 40). Similar complexities of integration are likely among suppliers of fashion apparel which combine low costs with fashion-based differentiation and quick response capability (Richardson 1996).

The Flexibility of Integration

While integration across a wide scope of specialist knowledge is important in sustaining competitive advantage, hypercompetitive conditions ultimately result in all positions of competitive advantage being eroded by imitative or innovative competition. Hence, maintaining superior performance ultimately requires the continual renewal of competitive advantages through innovation and the development of new capabilities. Within the context of our model, there are two dimensions to such renewal: extending existing capabilities to encompass additional types of knowledge, and reconfiguring existing knowledge into new types of capability.

The ease with which existing capabilities can be extended to encompass new knowledge depends heavily upon the characteristics of knowledge with regard to communicability. If new knowledge is explicit, or if tacit knowledge can be articulated in explicit form, then integrating new knowledge does not pose major difficulties. In designing its 777 passenger plane, Boeing was able to greatly extend its knowledge of electronics and new materials through an advanced CAD system which provided a common language for specialists across widely different knowledge areas and different companies to communicate and integrate. By contrast, General Motors' upgrading of its manufacturing capability to encompass the knowledge embodied in Toyota's system of lean production was a slow and painful process because much of that knowledge was tacit and the routines for its integration were deeply embedded with Toyota's history and culture.

The reconfiguration of existing knowledge through new patterns of integration is more complex, but may be even more important in creating competitive advantage. Such knowledge reconfiguration is central to Abernathy and Clark's (1985) concept of *"architectural innovation."* Subsequent research by Henderson and Clark (1990) and Henderson and Cockburn (1995) identifies the critical role of *"architectural knowledge"*—the "integration of knowledge across disciplinary and organizational boundaries within the firm" (Henderson 1995, p. 3)—in driving such innovation. Her studies of pharmaceuticals and the semiconductor photolithographic alignment equipment industry provide strong support for the role of broad-scope knowledge integration in supporting superior performance.

Such architectural innovations are concerned not only with product and process innovations, but also with *strategic innovations* which reconfigure knowledge into new approaches to competing. Such "new-game strategies" (Baron 1981) are not specific to technology-based industries. Baden-Fuller and Stopford (1994, Chapter 3) show that strategic innovation is fundamental to creating competitive advantage in mature business environments. In fashion clothing for example, Benetton and The Limited have created "quick response capability" through innovative approaches to value-chain reconfiguration (Richardson 1996).

Most examples of firms' reconfiguring knowledge into architectural innovations (EMI's CT scanner, the Polaroid instant camera, the Apple Macintosh, Pilkington's float glass process, Lanier's "virtual reality") and strategic innovations (Nucor in steel, Benetton in apparel, Starbuck's in coffee houses) point to these innovations as isolated successes rather than evidence of flexible capabilities which have the capacity to continuously and repeatedly reconfigure knowledge in new patterns of interaction. Given the difficulties inherent in integrating tacit knowledge and dependence of such integration upon routines and communication patterns developed over time, establishing organizational arrangements needed to achieve the "flexible integration" proposed by Henderson (1995) and "meta-flexibility" proposed by Volberda (1996) represents a formidable challenge to management. Continuous innovation in dynamically-competitive environments (e.g., Rubbermaid in plastic housewares, 3M in adhesive and thin-film products, Sony in consumer electronics, Motorola in communication products) tends to be the result of the deployment and extension of a continuing core of capabilities rather than the constant creation of new capabilities. Achieving flexible integration, either through continually integrating new tacit knowledge or through constantly reconfiguring existing knowledge, is likely to impose substantial costs in terms of reducing the efficiency of knowledge integration. The implication is that radical, discontinuous change in industry environments (such as the micro revolution in computing and the possible displacement of internal combustion engines by electric motors in autos) is likely to be accompanied by the decline of established market leaders. The noteworthy feature of IBM's performance during the 1980s and 1990s is not so much its decline during the 1990s, but its remarkable success in microcomputers during the 1980s.

INTERNAL VERSUS EXTERNAL INTEGRATION: THE CASE FOR NETWORKS

The need for flexibility in organizational capabilities poses complex issues with regard to firm boundaries and choices between internal and external knowledge integration. In common with other types of transactions, there are three basic alternatives for knowledge transfer and integration: internalization within the firm, market contracts, and relational contacts (which in multiple form create firm networks). Given uncertainties over appropriability and valuation, market contracts are typically inefficient means for transferring knowledge. In Demsetz's (1991) analysis, market transactions are only efficient in transferring knowledge when that knowledge is embodied within a product. Such transfer of product-embodied knowledge across markets is efficient when the effective utilization of the product by buyers is not dependent upon the buyers needing access to the knowledge embodied within the product. Thus, within the context of fashion apparel (Richardson 1996), Benetton does not need to integrate knowledge of the application of computer science to computer-aided design into its design capability, if it can purchase CAD software adequate to its needs. On the other hand, expertise in fashion design is tacit, and it cannot be embodied into expert-system software. Thus, Benetton cannot purchase fashion design knowledge packaged into software, neither can Benetton rely upon purchasing individual fashion designs from independent designers because of the need for garment design to integrate multiple knowledge bases: fashion design flair, Benetton's own market knowledge, and manufacturing expertise. The implication is that Benetton is likely to require internalization of at least some of fashion design capability. Similarly, in the case of the regional Bell companies' expansion into wireless communication. If knowledge concerning wireless switching and siting of cellular bases is not capable of embodiment within marketable products and services, then these companies will, ultimately, be required to extend their capabilities to embody such knowledge (Smith 1996).

Relational contracts, either in individual strategic alliances or broader interfirm networks, are an intermediate solution justified by a number of intermediate situations. For example, explicit knowledge which is not embodied in specific products cannot be efficiently transferred through market contracts, but diffusion of its sources or uncertainty over its applicability to the firm's products may not justify the internalization of its producers within the firm. Networks, either of firms or of individuals, may be well-suited to the transfer and integration of such knowledge. Thus, in biotechnology, social networks of scientists provide a powerful vehicle for the transfer of scientific knowledge since such networks provide the reputational assets and the repeated-game characteristics necessary to avoid the inefficiencies associated with market exchanges (Liebeskind et al. 1996).

Interfirm collaboration through relational contracts is also likely to provide efficient mechanisms for knowledge integration where there is a lack of perfect correspondence between the knowledge base of the firm and its set of products. The scope of a firm may be defined in terms of its range of knowledge or its range of products. Where the boundaries of both knowledge and products correspond perfectly, not only are firm boundaries unambiguous, but knowledge resources are fully utilized. Where a perfect correspondence does not exist, or where uncertainty exists over the linkages between knowledge and products, then two consequences follow:

(a) ambiguity is created over the optimal boundaries of the firm;
(b) internal provision of the full range of specialized knowledge needed for a particular set of products must result in the inefficient exploitation of at least some of that specialist knowledge.

In such circumstances, interfirm collaboration can increase the efficiency with which specialized knowledge is utilized. A consequence of hypercompetition is uncertainty over links between knowledge inputs and product outputs. In biotechnology, new knowledge may have applications in "human health, crop production and protection, chemical feedstock production and processing, food processing, and waste management" (Liebeskind et al. 1996). As a result, "these sources of technological and competitive uncertainty make it extremely difficult to determine which scientific knowledge is potentially valuable and which is not" (Ibid). While my analysis points to the superiority of intrafirm relationships in integrating knowledge, the importance of networks in sourcing biotechnological knowledge suggests that the inefficiencies of interorganizational relationships are outweighed by the flexibility advantages associated with a wider set of knowledge-product linkages.

A final consideration concerns the speed with which new capabilities can be built and extended. Even if relational contracts are imperfect vehicles for integrating knowledge, a critical concern is that they can permit knowledge to be transferred and integrated with a comparatively short time. If competitive advantage in dynamic market settings is critical dependent upon establishing first-mover advantage then the critical merit of firm networks is in providing speed of access to new knowledge. Such considerations proved to be critically important both in biotechnology (Liebeskind et al. 1996) and in telecommunications (Smith 1996). In fashion apparel where the need to access new knowledge was less apparent, firm networks did not provide any clear advantage over vertical integration (Richardson 1996).

Similar considerations explain the establishment of the Nordvest Forum regional learning network (Hanssen-Bauer and Snow 1996). Although such interorganizational contacts have limited potential for integrating knowledge across companies, such a network permits fuller utilization of knowledge by permitting firms to share knowledge that has application outside of each firm's product set. Second, it encourages investments in knowledge acquisition in the face of uncertainty over knowledge-product linkages.

SUMMARY AND CONCLUSION

I have established that knowledge is the preeminent resource of the firm, and that organizational capability involves the integration of multiple knowledge bases. The resulting theory of organizational capability provides a more cogent description of firm competence and analyzes more precisely than hitherto the relationship of organizational capability to competitive advantage in markets where market leadership and power is continually undermined by competition and external change. I show that the processes through which firms integrate specialized knowledge are fundamental to their ability to create and sustain competing advantage. The "Summary: Knowledge-based Theory of Organizational Capability" boxed feature summarizes this theory of organizational capability and its implications for competitive advantage in hypercompetitive environments.

While making some progress in integrating prior research on organizational learning and organizational resources and capabilities, much remains to be done at both the empirical and the theoretical level, especially in relation to understanding the organizational processes through which knowledge is integrated. For example, while organizational routines are generally recognized as important mechanisms for coordination within firms, with a few notable exceptions (e.g. Pentland 1992, Pentland and Rueter 1994), detailed study of the operation of organizational routines is limited. Further progress is critically dependent upon closer observation of the processes through which tacit knowledge is transferred and integrated.

Despite its limited achievements so far, this analysis offers considerable potential—especially in building bridges between strategic management and organization theory and design. Conventional notions of organizational structure rest heavily upon concepts such as division of labor, unity of command, and grouping of similar tasks. The view of the firm as an integrator of knowledge provides a rather different perspective on the functions of organization structure. The analysis can also offer insight into many current developments in management practice. Cross-functional product development teams, TQM, and organizational change programs such as GE's "workout" can be viewed as attempts to change organizational structure and processes to achieve better integration across broad spectra of specialized knowledge. The trend towards "empowerment" takes account of the

BOX 8.1 Summary: The Knowledge-based Theory of Organizational Capability

ASSUMPTIONS

* Knowledge is the principal productive resource of the firm.
* Of the two main types of knowledge, explicit and tacit, the latter is especially important due to its limited transferability.
* Tacit knowledge is acquired by and stored within individuals in highly specialized form.
* Production requires a wide array of knowledge.

PROPOSITIONS

1. *The nature of the firm.* The fundamental role of the firm is the integration of individuals' specialist knowledge. Organizational capabilities are the manifestation of this knowledge integration.

2. *Capability and structure.* The capabilities of the firm are hierarchically structured according to the scope of knowledge which they integrate. Effectiveness in creating and managing broad-scope capabilities requires correspondence between the scope of knowledge and the structures needed for managing such integration.

3. *Integration mechanisms.* Two primary mechanisms exist to integrate knowledge: direction and routine. Reliance upon direction increases with complexity of the activity, the number of locations in which the activity is performed, and the stringency of performance specifications. The advantage of routine in integrating tacit knowledge is in economizing upon communication and permitting flexible responses to changing circumstances.

4. *Capability and competitive advantage.*

(A) The competitive advantage conferred by an organizational capability depends, in part, upon the efficiency of knowledge integration which is a function of: (a) the level of common knowledge among organizational members; (b) frequency and variability of the activity; (c) a structure which economizes on communication (e.g., through some form of modularity).

(B) An organizational capability's potential for establishing and sustaining competitive advantage increases with the span of knowledge integrated.

(C) Sustaining competitive advantage under conditions of dynamic competition requires continuous innovation which requires flexible integration through either (a) extending existing capabilities to encompass new knowledge, or (b) reconfiguring existing knowledge within new patterns of integration. Since efficient integration of tacit knowledge requires experience through repetition, achieving flexible integration represents a formidable management challenge.

IMPLICATION: FIRM NETWORKS UNDER HYPERCOMPETITION

Firm networks based upon relational contracts are an efficient and effective basis for accessing knowledge:

– where knowledge can be expressed in explicit form;
– where there is a lack of perfect correspondence between the knowledge domain and product domain of individual firms, or uncertainty over the product-knowledge linkages;
– where speed in extending the knowledge base of the firm is critical in creating competitive advantage.

nature of knowledge acquisition and storage in firms: if each employee possesses unique specialized knowledge and if each employee has access to only part of every other employee's knowledge base, then top-down decision making must be a highly inefficient means of knowledge integration. The task is to devise decision processes that permit integration of the specialized knowledge held throughout the organization—not just in the boardroom, but on the shop floor as well.

The paper offers little solace to managers grappling with the uncertainties and demands of hypercompetitive environments. While establishing that, under conditions of intense and dynamic competition, internal capabilities provide a more stable basis for strategy than market positioning, my analysis points to the difficulties inherent in achieving the dynamic capabilities which for many are the "solution" to the problem of sustaining competitive advantage under conditions of hypercompetition. Volberda (1996) identifies these dynamic capabilities with "the repertoire of flexibility increasing capabilities that management possesses." But, if such capabilities depend upon integration across a broad span of largely-tacit knowledge, then a firm's strategic flexibility is limited by two factors: first, its repertoire of capabilities is unlikely to extend far beyond those currently deployed within existing business activities; second, the time horizon and uncertainty associated with creating new capabilities. The "flexible integration" and network relationships I propose as responses to this problem identify what is required, but offer little guidance as to the management actions needed to achieve flexibility in knowledge integration.

Acknowledgments

I am grateful to Jon Hanssen-Bauer, Duane Helleloid, Arie Lewin, Julia Liebeskind, Steve Postrel, James Richardson, Ann Smith, and Henk Volberda for helpful comments and suggestions.

REFERENCES

Abernathy, W. J. and K. B. Clark (1985), "Innovation: Mapping the Winds of Creative Destruction," *Research Policies,* 14, 3–22.

Argyris, C. and D. A. Schon (1978), *Organizational Learning,* Reading, MA: Addison-Wesley.

Baden-Fuller, C. and J. M. Stopford (1994), *Rejuvenating the Mature Enterprise,* Boston, MA: Harvard Business School Press.

Barney, J. (1986), "Strategic Factor Markets: Expectations, Luck and Business Strategy," *Management Science,* 32, 1231–1241.

Buaron, R. (1981), "New-game Strategies," *McKinsey Quarterly,* Fall, 24–40.

Clark, K. B. and T. Fujimoto (1991), *Product Development Performance,* Boston, MA: Harvard Business School Press.

Demsetz, H. (1991). "The Theory of the Firm Revisited," in O. E. Williamson and S. Winter (Eds.), *The Nature of the Firm,* New York: Oxford University Press, 159–178.

Denison, E. F. (1968), "Economic Growth," in R. E. Caves (Ed.), *Britain's Economic Prospects,* Washington: Brookings Institution.

Dierickx, I. and K. Cool (1989), "Asset Stock Accumulation and Sustainability of Competitive Advantage," *Management Science,* 35,1504–1513.

Garfinkel, H. (1967), *Studies in Ethnomethodology,* Englewood Cliffs, NJ: Prentice-Hall.

Grant, R. M. (1991), "The Resource-based Theory of Competitive Advantage: Implications for Strategy Formulation", *California Management Review,* 33, 3, 114–135.

Hanssen-Bauer, J. and C. C. Snow (1996), "Responding to Hypercompetition: The Structure and Processes of a Regional Learning Network Organization," *Organization Science,* 7, 4, 413–427.

Henderson, R. and K. Clark (1990), "Architectural Innovation: The Reconfiguration of Existing Product Technologies and the Failure of Established Firms," *Administrative Science Quarterly,* 35, 9–31.

Henderson, R. and I. Cockburn (1995), "Measuring Competence? Exploring Firm Effects in Pharmaceutical Research," *Strategic Management Journal,* 15, Winter, 63–84.

Imai, K., I. Nonaka, and H. Takeuchi (1985), "Managing the New Product Development Process: How Japanese Companies Learn and Unlearn," in K. Clark, R. Hayes, and C. Lorenz (Eds.), *The Uneasy Alliance,* Boston, MA: Harvard Business School Press.

Jacobsen, R. (1992), "The 'Austrian' School of Strategy," *Academy of Management Review,* 17, 782–805.

Kogut, B. and U. Zander (1992), "Knowledge of the Firm, Combinative Capabilities, and the Replication of Technology," *Organization Studies,* 3, 383–397.

Levin, R. C., A. K. Klevorick, R. R. Nelson, and S. G. Winter (1987), "Appropriating the Returns from Industrial Research and Development," *Brookings Papers on Economic Activity,* 3, 783–820.

Levitt, B. and J. G. March (1988), "Organizational Learning," *Annual Review of Sociology,* 14, 319–340.

Levitt, T. (1960), "Marketing Myopia," *Harvard Business Review,* July—August. 24–47,

Liebeskind, J. P., A. Oliver, L. Zucker, and M. Brewer (1996), "Social Networks, Learning, and Flexibility: Sourcing Scientific Knowledge in New Biotechnology Firms," *Organization Science,* 7, 4, 428–443.

Lippman, S. and R. Rumelt (1982), "Uncertain Imitability- An Analysis of Interfirm Differences in Efficiency Under Uncertainty," *Bell Journal of Economics,* 13, 418–438.

March, J. and H. Simon (1958), *Organizations,* New York: Wiley.

Nelson, R. and S. Winter (1982), *An Evolutionary Theory of Economic Change.* Cambridge: Belknap.

Nonaka, I. (1990), "Redundant, Overlapping Organization: A Japanese Approach to Managing the Innovation Process." *California Management Review,* 32, Spring, 27–38.

———. (1994), "A Dynamic Theory of Organizational Knowledge Creation," *Organization Science,* 5, 1, 14–37.

Organization Science (1991), Special Issue, "Organizational Learning: Papers in Honor of (and by) James G. March," 2, 1, 1–163.

Pentland, B. T. (1992), "Organizing Moves in Software Support," *Administrative Science Quarterly,* 37, 527–548.

———. and H. H. Rueter (1994), "Organizational Routines as Grammars of Action," *Administrative Science Quarterly,* 39, 484–510.

Polanyi, M. (1966), *The Tacit Dimension,* New York: Anchor Day.

Porter, M. E. (1991), *The Competitive Advantage of Nations.* New York: Free Press.

———. (1992), "Towards a Dynamic Theory of Strategy," *Strategic Management Journal,* 12, Winter Special Issue, 95–118.

Prahalad, C. K. and G. Hamel (1990), "The Core Competences of the Corporation," *Harvard Business Review,* May–June, 79–91.

Quinn, J. B. (1992), *Intelligent Enterprise,* New York: Free Press.

Richardson, J. (1996), "Vertical Integration and Rapid Response in Fashion Apparel," *Organization Science,* 7, 4, 400–412.

Rockart, J. F. and J. E. Short (1989), "IT in the 1990s: Managing Organizational Interdependence," *Sloan Management Review,* 30, 2, 17–33.

Rumelt, R. P. (1991), "How Much Does Industry Matter?", *Strategic Management Journal,* 12, 167–185.

Schumpeter, J. A. (1934), *The Theory of Economic Development,* Cambridge, MA: Harvard University Press.

Simon, H. A. (1973), "Applying Information Technology to Organization Design," *Public Administration Review,* 106, 467–482.

———. (1991), "Bounded Rationality and Organizational Learning," *Organization Science,* 2, 125–134.

Smith, A. and C. Zeithaml (1996), "Baby Bells, Garbage Cans, and Hypercompetition," *Organization Science* 7, 4, 388–399.

Spender, J-C. (1992), "Limits to Learning from the West: How Western Management Advice May Prove Limited in Eastern Europe," *International Executive,* 34, 5, September/ October, 389–410.

Starbuck, W. H. (1992), "Learning by Knowledge-intensive Firms," *Journal of Management Studies,* 29, 713–739.

Thompson, J. D. (1967), *Organizations in Action,* New York: McGraw-Hill.

Van de Ven, A. H. and R. Drazin (1985), "The Concept of Fit in Contingency Theory," in L. L. Cummins and B. Staw (Eds.), Research in *Organizational Behavior,* 7, Greenwich, CT: JAI Press, 333–365.

Volberda, H. W. (1996), "Towards the Flexible Form: How to Remain Vital in Hyper competitive Environments," *Organization Science,* 7, 4, 359–374.

Wheelwright, S. C. and K. B. Clark (1992), *Revolutionizing Product Development,* New York: Free Press.

Williamson, O. E. (1975), *Markets and Hierarchies,* Englewood Cliffs, NJ: Prentice-Hall.

———. (1981), "The Modern Corporation: Origins, Evolution, Attributes," *Journal of Economic Literature,* 19, 1537–1568.

Winter, S. G. (1987), "Knowledge and Competence as Strategic Assets," in D. Tecce (Ed.), *The Competitive Challenge*, Cambridge, MA: Ballinger.

Zucker, L. (1987), "Institutional Theories of Organizations," *Annual Review of Sociology*, 13, 443–464.

Part Three

Characteristics of
Knowledge as a
Strategic Asset

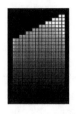

9

Knowledge and Competence as Strategic Assets

Sidney G. Winter

An asset, my dictionary says, may be defined as "a useful thing or quality." Among commentators on corporate strategy, it is widely accepted that knowledge and competence are useful things for a company to have. At times, particular approaches to the acquisition and profitable exploitation of productive knowledge—such as the experience curve—have been the central focus of strategic discussion. At other times, explicit attention to the place of knowledge considerations in the strategic picture has waned, perhaps to the point where such issues have "dropped through the cracks" of strategic analysis (see Peters 1984: 115). But they certainly cannot drop very far below the analytical surface because any discussion of innovation and indeed the activity of strategic analysis itself implicitly concedes their importance.

The dictionary offers an alternative definition of an asset as "a single item of property." In some cases, this second meaning may be applicable, along with the first, to knowledge held by a business firm. A basic patent, for example, may certainly be a useful thing for a company to have, and at the same time it may represent a discrete bundle of legally defined and enforceable property rights; such an item of property can be conveyed from one owner to another just as a stock certificate or a deed can. In general, however, it is decidedly problematic whether the realities denoted by such terms as *knowledge, competence, skills, know-how,* or *capability* are the sorts of things that can be adequately discussed as items of property. The word item is suggestive of a discreteness, of a potential for severance from the prevailing context, that is frequently not characteristic of the skills of individuals and organizations. The term intellectual property is established in legal parlance, but there are never-

From "Knowledge and Competence as Strategic Assets," Chapter 8 in David J. Teece (ed.), *The Competitive Challenge: Strategies for Industrial Innovation and Renewal,* Ballinger Publishing Company, Cambridge, MA, 1987, pp. 159–184.

theless often profound ambiguities in both principle and practice regarding the scope and locus of the rights associated with the possession of knowledge.

Thus, of the two definitions of assets, one is plainly applicable to the knowledge and competence of a business firm, while the other is of uncertain applicability. This situation does not pose a problem for lexicographers, but it does pose a problem for analysts of strategy. The reason is that the disciplines of economics, accounting, and finance have developed and defined the asset concept in ways that are largely specializations of the second dictionary definition (which, of course, is itself a specialization of the first definition). Where the second definition does not apply, the tool kits of those important disciplines contain little that affords a useful analytical grip on strategic issues. Systematic analysis is crippled, and many important issues are addressed only with the general purpose tools of aphorism and anecdote.

This chapter attempts to bridge the gap between the two meanings of asset as they relate to the knowledge and competence of a business firm. The first section introduces a state description approach to strategy that borrows elements from optimal control theory and from evolutionary economics. The next two sections develop this approach, with particular emphasis on its relationship to the valuation of the firm's productive system, link the state description approach to the diverse set of organizational phenomena denoted by knowledge, competence, and kindred terms, and explore some distinctions among these phenomena that are of major importance for strategy. The next section draws on the Yale survey of corporate R&D managers to suggest the extent to which the key mechanisms affecting the creation and diffusion of productive knowledge differ from one branch of manufacturing industry to another. The final section briefly reviews the major themes of the chapter.

STRATEGIC STATE DESCRIPTION

An organizational strategy, I propose, is a summary account of the principal characteristics and relationships of the organization and its environment—an account developed for the purpose of informing decisions affecting the organization's success and survival. This formulation emphasizes the normative intent of strategic analysis and rejects the notion that there are strategies that have "evolved implicitly" (Porter 1980: xiii) or that strategy is a "nonrational concept" (Greiner 1983: 13). There may of course be strategies that are clearly formulated but then rejected or ignored, that are not written down but are nevertheless successfully pursued, or that lead to abject failure rather than to success. These realistic possibilities are consistent with a view of strategic analysis as a form of "intendedly rational" (Simon 1957: xxiv) behavior directed toward pragmatically useful understanding of the situation of the organization as a whole. By contrast, mere habits of thought or action, managerial or otherwise, are not strategies. Such habits may as easily be parts of an (unintended) problem as parts of an (intended) solution.

The propensity to perceive habits as strategies may well derive from the valid observation that much of the behavior of an organization is quasiautomatic and neither requires the attention of top management on a day-to-day basis nor, when it receives such attention, responds to it in a straightforward and constructive way. This phenomenon is most frequently noted in connection with organizational resistance to change—that is, as a problem facing change agents. But it is also cited as a factor on the bright side, contributing to excellence in organizational performance or as indicative of the positive results achievable when lower levels of the organization are successfully imbued with appropriate operational versions of organizational goals. Thus, as Peters (1984: 111) says:

> Distinctive organizational performance, for good or ill, is almost entirely a function of deeply engrained repertoires. The organization, within its marketplace, is the way it acts from moment to moment—not the way it thinks it might act or ought to act.

Peters's statement is quite consistent with the viewpoint on organizations that is basic to the evolutionary economic theory developed by Richard Nelson and myself (Nelson and Winter 1982: 134–36). The same view is a fundamental constituent of the approach to strategy set forth in this chapter. Nevertheless, it should be clear that this view is potentially quite subversive of the whole undertaking of normative strategic analysis. The more deeply ingrained the organizational repertoires, the less clear it is what important decisions remain for an analyst to advise on or an executive to execute. When apparent choice situations of apparent strategic significance confront the organization, perhaps outcomes are fully determined by some combination of habit and impulse.[1]

This is exactly the way the organizational world is envisaged, for purposes of descriptive theorizing, in evolutionary economics. In that theoretical world, strategic analysis in the sense defined here has no place, although of course there is abundant scope for *ex post facto* discussion of which habits and impulses proved successful. As a response to a need for guidance in the real world, this fatalistic perspective has obvious and severe limitations.

A key step in strategic thinking is the identification of the attributes of the organization that are considered subject to directed change and the implicit or explicit acknowledgment that some attributes do not fall in that category. As the Alcoholics Anonymous serenity prayer puts it, "God grant me the serenity to accept the things I cannot change, courage to change the things I can, and

---

[1] The habits may well be sophisticated skills and the impulses leaps of passionate faith. Peters, in the paper cited, puts forward normative conclusions that emphasize the role of corporate leaders in the related tasks of (1) selecting, in an uncertain world, directions of skill development that will lead to longterm profitability and (2) guiding the development of these skills through the enunciation and legitimation of appropriate subgoals. He seems to be skeptical of the usefulness of any (intendedly) rational analytic framework in connection with step 1.

wisdom to know the difference." Substitute for courage the words managerial attention and related resources supporting strategic decision making and you have here the beginnings of a paradigm for strategic analysis, its role being to help with the wisdom part. Of course, the sort of wisdom contributed by an economist will include the observations that change per se is presumably not the goal, that change will often be a matter of degree, and that the trick is to allocate the available change capacity in the right way.

STATE DESCRIPTION AS A GENERALIZED ASSET PORTFOLIO

The concept of the state of a dynamic system has a long history in control theory and related subjects (Bellman 1957; Pontryagin et al. 1962; and a vast literature of applications). The distinction between the state variables of a system and the control variables is roughly the distinction between aspects of the system that are not subject to choice over a short time span and aspects that are. The values chosen for control variables, however, do affect the evolution of the state variables over larger time spans. As far as the internal logic of a control theory model is concerned, the list of state variables constitutes a way of describing the system that is sufficiently precise and comprehensive so that the motion of the system through time is determined, given the settings of the control variables and the state of the external environment at each point of time.

In general, a variety of alternative state descriptions provide formally equivalent approaches to a given problem. Also, the conceptual distinctions among state variables, control variables, and the environment can become blurred in the sense that particular considerations may be treated under different headings in formulations of two very closely related problems. There is, for example, little substantial difference between a given feature of the environment and a system state variable that is alterable only over a very narrow range.

In evolutionary economics, the notion of state description is extended to cover behavioral patterns that most economists or management scientists would instinctively place in the control variable category. Behavior is conceived as governed by *routines* (or alternatively, by "deeply ingrained repertoires") rather than deliberate choice. The object of a theoretical exercise is not to discover what is optimal for a firm, but to understand the major forces that shape the evolution of an industry (Nelson and Winter 1982: 18–19):

> The core concern of evolutionary theory is with the dynamic process by which behavior patterns and market outcomes are jointly determined over time. The typical logic of these evolutionary processes is as follows: At each point of time, the current operating characteristics of firms, and the magnitudes of their capital stocks and other state variables, determine input and output levels. Together with market supply and demand conditions that are exogenous to the firms in question, these firm decisions determine market prices of inputs and outputs. The profitability of each individual firm is thus determined. Profitability operates, through firm investment rules, as one

major determinant of rates of expansion and contraction of individual firms. With firm sizes thus altered, the same operating characteristics would yield different input and output levels, hence different prices and profitability signals, and so on. By this selection process, clearly, aggregate input and output and price levels for the industry would undergo dynamic change even if individual firm operating characteristics were constant. But operating characteristics, too, are subject to change, through the workings of the search rules of firms. Search and selection are simultaneous, interacting aspects of the evolutionary process: the same prices that provide selection feedback also influence the directions of search. Through the joint action of search and selection, the firms evolve over time, with the condition of the industry in each period bearing the seeds of its condition in the following period.

It is clear that *among* the things that are candidate variables inclusion for a state description of a business firm are the amounts of the firm's tangible and financial assets, the sorts of things that are reflected on the asset side of a balance sheet. It is equally clear that the conception of a firm state description in evolutionary theory goes well beyond the list of things conventionally recognized as assets. Theoretical studies employing control theory techniques, by economists and management scientists, have established characteristics of optimal behavior in problems in which state variables correspond closely to things recognizable as assets—for example, inventory or capacity levels—but also things that are not so recognized, at least in financial accounting—for example, stocks of customers, employees, and advertising or R&D capital. There is, therefore, a relationship but also a conceptual gap between the concepts of a *state description* and a collection (or *portfolio*) of assets. There is likewise a relationship but also a gap between evolutionary theory's notion of a state description for a *business firm*, a description that is comprehensive in principle, however limited or stylized it may be in a particular analytical application, and the descriptions that derive from the conventions of asset accounting or from the focused objectives that necessarily govern the construction of a control theory model, whether for theoretical or practical use. In particular, the state description concept in evolutionary theory, and the concept of a routine more specifically, direct attention to the problem of reflecting the knowledge and competence of a firm in a state description—but offer only minimal guidance as to how this might be done.

ORGANIZATIONAL GOALS

The bridges that are to be constructed across the gaps just referred to must be anchored, at least for the time being, in a strong commitment regarding the goals of the organizations whose strategic problems are to be analyzed. The discussion will relate only to organizations for which present value maximization, or expected present value maximization, adequately characterizes the organizational goat as perceived by the actor or actors for whose guidance the analysis is conducted. It is to be hoped that some of the illumination will extend well beyond the range of the assumptions adopted here, but how far that may be the case is an issue that must be left open.[2]

The assumption of a present-value goal for the organization places this analysis in a simple and orthodox tradition in economic theorizing. This tradition of viewing the firm as a unitary actor with well defined preferences has long been challenged by organization theorists and social scientists outside of economics, and by a few economists of heretical bent (such as Cyert and March 1963). Increasingly, this tradition has been abandoned by numerous theoretical economists of diverse points of view, and the assumption made here might well be regarded as a throwback.[3]

There are indeed some key issues in the strategic management of knowledge assets that relate to whether the firm can hold together in the face of conflict among the diverse interests of the participants. Although these issues are touched on below, for the most part they remain on the agenda for future work. The assumption that the present value of the concern is maximized is maintained for the time being in the spirit of dividing the difficulties.

The major restrictions on the scope of this discussion having been duly noted, it is now time to emphasize its generality. The concept of a system state is highly flexible, yet within the confines established by a present value criterion it can easily be linked to the conventional (second definition) concept of an asset. A complete and accurate state description for a business firm is plainly an unattainable goal outside the confines of a theoretical model. Yet the idea of seeking a normatively useful state description is realistic and familiar. When the normative purpose in view involves the direction of the entire organization, an attempt at strategic state description may be helpful.

Theories of strategy, accounting principles, and many other aspects of business practice can be understood as providing conceptual structures for state descriptions that are practical and often quantitative but clearly partial. The value of these schemes, at least regarding the strategic guidance they provide, is often limited by the weakness of their connections to economically relevant conceptions of assets and returns on assets. Relatedly, and perhaps more significantly, they are but weakly connected to the most basic of all paradigms for

[2] There is a well known device for extending the range of goals represented in an optimization problem beyond that reflected by the formal criterion of the problem: Introduce constraints requiring that acceptable levels of other goal variables be achieved (see Simon 1964). This device is one available method for extending the propositions developed here. For example, "Maximize present value subject to acting in compliance with the law" is formally a close cousin of "Maximize present value," although it may be a very different thing substantively.

[3] In one way or another, most contemporary theorists actively concerned with the theory of the firm and its internal organization seem to have adopted the nexus-of-contracts view. For a concise statement of this view, see the opening paragraph of Fama and Jensen (1985).

making money—"buy low, sell high."[4] The strategic state description paradigm developed here does not suffer from these limitations, but, as emphasized below, it cannot escape the fact that any implementable state description scheme is necessarily partial.

STATE DESCRIPTION AND VALUATION

Full Imputation

The mathematics of optimal control theory reflects a long-familiar heuristic principle in economic thinking, the principle of full imputation. This principle states that a proper economic valuation of a collection of resources is one that precisely accounts for the returns the resources make possible.[5] For present purposes, the simplest relevant application of this principle is "an asset (def. 2) should be valued at time at T at the present value of the net returns it will yield from T onward." A more exact formulation, appropriate for present purposes, is that the owner(s) of an asset should value it at the present value of the net future returns it generates under present ownership, where the interest rate(s) employed in the discounting reflect the lending opportunities open to the owners. This is an owners' reservation price valuation; if more than this is offered for the asset, the owners should take it. In the optimal control theory context with a present value criterion, a more complex version of this same proposition attributes the maximized present value attainable from the system to its initial state together with features of the environment and the laws of change. Of course, the policy choices made affect the present value achieved—but since optimal control theory points the way to optimal choices of these policy variables, once these choices are made the policy followed is not explicitly a determinant of value.

The adoption of this valuation principle carries the direct implication that the notion that an excess return or (economic) profit can be earned by holding an asset is illusory. Properly valued assets yield only normal returns, where properly valued refers to the owner's reservation price defined above. If there is a gain

---

[4] As a classroom example of this problem, I like to cite the following passage from a BCG publication, regarding the appropriate treatment of "dogs": "They can never be satisfactorily profitable and should be liquidated in as clever and graceful a manner as possible. Outright sale to a buyer with different perceptions can sometimes be accomplished" (Conley 1970: 13, emphasis supplied). This is sound advice—but, of course, equally sound for stars, cash cows, and question marks as for dogs, if the buyer's perceptions differ sufficiently in the right direction. On the other hand, if no such buyer can be found for a dog, it is not at all clear that selling it makes sense.

[5] In economic theory, the issue and principle of full imputation may be traced back at least to Wicksteed's concern with the exhaustion-of-the-product problem in production theory (Wicksteed 1894). For a sophisticated discussion of profitability and imputation, see Triffin (1949: ch. 5).

or loss, the full imputation principle declares it to be a capital gain or loss associated with having acquired the asset at a price below or above its true value—
that is, it is in the nature of a success or failure in speculation.

What sort of speculation is involved, and what are the sources of success
in this activity? One clear possibility is blind luck in the making of decisions to
buy or sell. Perhaps success also can be explained by superior knowledge, competence, insight, skill, or information.[6] But the guidance provided by the full
imputation principle suggests that the words *can be explained by* might reasonably be replaced by *should be imputed to*—a conceptual maneuver that makes
the full imputation fuller than it was before, restores blind chance as the sole
source of net returns, and leaves us with a conception of the assets involved in
the situation that is broader and more remote from financial accounting conventions than it was before. The subtleties of this imputation dialectic—full
imputation for one process discloses unaccounted returns in a casualty
antecedent process, which then calls for a fuller imputation—must be confronted
if strategic analysis is to have solid foundations in economic reasoning.

Whether confronted or not, they are key issues when the strategic options
include acceptance or rejection of a bid to purchase the company, and in the
wider range of cases involving transactions in functioning business units, large or
small. Rational action in such situations demands attention to the question of
what future earning power actually "comes with" the entity whose ownership is
transferred. That question cannot be answered without inquiring deeply into the
sources of earning power—that is, without confronting the imputation problem.

The subtleties are particularly fundamental to understanding the strategic
role of knowledge and competence. For, as is discussed further in the next section, policies affecting the growth or decline of knowledge and competence assets
can have major effects on earning power over time but may do so without pos-
ing the question "What is this worth?" with the clarity with which it is posed in
a major transaction.

State Descriptions, Optimization, and Heuristic Frames

Strategic analysis would present no challenge if only two conditions were
satisfied; (1) if it were easy to identify the real problem faced by the organization
(that is, to correctly identify and assess the state variables, control variables, constraints, and laws of change affecting the organizational system) and (2) if the
problem thus identified were easily solved. Once these easy steps were taken, any
apparent superiority or inferiority in actual organizational performance over time
would reflect the play of pure chance. In fact, because of the bounded rationality
of individuals and organizations, neither of these conditions is remotely satisfied
in the real world. It is therefore inevitable that real strategic analysis involve
highly simplified and perhaps fragmented conceptualization of what the strategic

[6] Failure can be explained by deficiencies in these various respects—although luck seems
to be more widely acknowledged as an explanation for failure than for success.

problem is and that the solution to the identified problem involve a continuing process of situational analysis, decision making, action taking, and evaluation of the results. Difficulties in implementation appear, which is to say that some of the things conceived as control variables do not have the anticipated effects on things conceived as state variables or that presumed control variables themselves turn out to be not so controllable after all. Surprises occur as environmental situations arise that were not conceived as possible or were regarded as of negligibly low probability. Failures to comprehend fully the internal logic of the strategic problem may become manifest in coordination failures and intraorganizational conflict.

Since strategic analysis is necessarily imperfect in the real world, there is always room for improvement. In general, there is room for improvement both at the stage of problem definition (since the real problem, nicely formulated, is not handed to the analyst on a platter) and at the stage of problem solution (since it is not necessarily a trivial matter to derive the policy implications of a statement of the strategic problem, however clearly formulated). Because bounded rationality limits achievement at both stages, the relations between the two are more subtle than the simple define problem/solve problem scheme might suggest. Stage one must be conducted with a view both to capturing the key features of the strategic situation and with a view to the available capabilities for deriving specific conclusions in stage two. As a result, there is a tension or tradeoff between flexibility and scope on the one hand versus problem-solving power on the other.

I will use the term *heuristic frame* to refer to a collection of possible approaches to a particular strategic problem whose members are related by the fact that they all rely on the same conception of the state variables and controls that are considered central to the problem. A heuristic frame corresponds to a degree of problem definition that occupies an intermediate position on the continuum between a long and indiscriminate list of things that might matter at one end and a fully formulated control, theoretic model of the problem at the other. Within a heuristic frame, there is room for a wide range of more specific formulations of the problem—but there is also enough structure provided by the frame itself to guide and focus discussion. On the other hand, a rich variety of different heuristic frames may represent plausible approaches to a given problem. Commitment to a particular frame is thus a highly consequential step in strategic analysis and one that deserves careful consideration.

Most of the approaches to strategic problems that are to be found in the literature do not involve explicit reference to state descriptions and heuristic frames or emphasize the possibility of translating the analysis into the language, if not the formalism, of control theory. (Therein lies, of course, the claim to novelty of the strategic state description approach presented here.) Many strategic perspectives can, however, be recast in this form without too much sacrifice of content and often with the benefit of revealing gaps, limitations, or vagueness in the particular perspective. The danger of neglecting alternative heuristic frames may also be highlighted.

Consider, for example, the classic BCG doctrine based on the experience curve. At the level of the individual line of business, this doctrine identifies unit cost and cumulative output to date as the key state variables and current output as the control. The connection from output to unit cost is mediated by cumulative output and the experience curve; an obvious identity relates current output and cumulative output to the new value of cumulative output. Market share can seemingly play alternative roles in the scheme, being sometimes a surrogate for output as the control variable (especially in situations in which multiple outputs are involved), sometimes a surrogate for cumulative output as a determinant of cost (where shares have been constant over an extended period), sometimes a control variable causally antecedent to current output (where the step between producing more output and getting it sold is itself strategically problematic), and sometimes a state variable subsequent to unit cost (low cost makes high share attainable, and high share makes high profits attainable). At the corporate level, the state description is the list of lines of business, with each line characterized by a market growth rate and a market share. Allocations of investment funds to the various lines of business are among the control variables. An allocation to a line of business relieves the cash constraint on the control variable for that line, making possible an increase of market through a capacity increase, advertising campaign, price cut, or whatever. Acquisitions and divestitures are also corporate level controls, making possible direct changes in the corporate-level state variables.

The general character of the normative guidance that is loosely derived from this scheme presumably needs no review. One notable feature of most accounts of the BCG approach in the literature is the absence of discussion of the costs at which changes in state variables are affected, at either the line of business or corporate level; needless to say, there is also no discussion of balancing costs and benefits at the margin. A second feature is the sparsity of the description of the environment, which treats market share as the only significant characteristic of rivals and also does not address features of the market itself that, along with growth, might affect profitability—such as the price elasticity of demand. Spelling out the heuristic frame of the BCG analysis, and noting the character of the questions that would need to be answered to complete a control-theoretic formulation thus leads rather quickly to the identification of what seem to be important gaps; it is proposed that the same critical approach might be helpful more generally.

Applying the full imputation principle within the BCG heuristic frame tells us what the value of a company depends on. It depends on the unit cost and cumulative output levels in all the individual lines of business, considered in conjunction with the environmental facts of market sizes, market growth rates, and sizes of leading rivals—plus, of course, the net financial assets of the company. If the heuristic frame were fully and correctly expanded into an optimal control problem, and that problem were in turn correctly solved, then (for the purposes of strategic analysis) these considerations and net financial assets would be the only determinants of the company's value; nothing would be left of the strategic problem but to carry out the optimal policy. Actually, since problem formulations and solutions are the imperfect products of bounded rationality, there will almost certainly be room for influencing the value of the company through a different implementation of the strategic approach defined by a particular heuristic frame.

More central to the purposes of the present paper is the observation that a quite different heuristic frame might be adopted. An alternative frame provides a different list of things that influence profitability in the long run and of how these relate to things that are controllable in the short run. A different approach to valuation, and perhaps a very different result, is implied. Whether the new strategic valuation is lower or higher is not indicative of the merit of the change of frame; what matters is whether the guidance obtained from the new frame serves the company better or worse in obtaining actual returns than the guidance obtained from the old. In particular, a change of heuristic frame may be a response to recognition that the old frame embodies an overoptimistic view of the strategic situation and the present value it implies is unrealizable.

DESCRIBING KNOWLEDGE STATES

Simple descriptors of knowledge states, often involving a single variable, have played an important role both in the theory of economic growth and in empirical research on R&D, the determinants of profitability, and related topics.[7] Although considerable insight has been derived from these studies, both the theory and the evidence are generally at too aggregative a level to be more than the suggestive for the purposes of strategic analysis. The domain of strategic choice certainly includes, for example, the choice of a level of R&D expenditure, but such a choice ordinarily interacts with the details of project selection.

It is therefore necessary to confront the difficulties that arise from the complexity and diversity of the phenomena denoted by such terms as knowledge, competence, skill, and so forth. When we use such terms, we hardly ever know precisely what we are talking about (except when we are expert in the area under discussion), and there is sometimes a nagging concern that we are too far from the complex details to be making sense at all. The purpose of this discussion is to alleviate this situation in some degree—to introduce some distinctions that clarify the conceptual issues surrounding knowledge and competence as strategic assets.

---

[7] A noteworthy example of the latter genre is Salinger (1984), which gives impressive evidence that an R&D stock (accumulated expenditure) variable is an important determinant of profitability when the latter is measured by Tobin's q. This approach to assessing profitability is in much better conformity with the valuation discussion in this chapter than approaches based exclusively on accounting measures.

TAXONOMIC DIMENSIONS

Suppose that we have under discussion something that we tentatively think of as a knowledge or competence asset. Figure 9.1 below lays out some dimensions along which we could try to place this asset and thus come to a clearer understanding of what the thing is and what its strategic significance might be. In general, a position near the left end of any of the continua identified in the figure is an indicator that the knowledge may be difficult to transfer (thus calling into question its status as an asset in the second sense), whereas a position near the right end is indicative of ease of transfer. This interpretation is elaborated below.

The first of the continua listed in Figure 9.1 ranges from highly tacit to fully articulable knowledge. Individual skills are often highly tacit in the sense that "the aim of a skillful performance is achieved by the observance of a set of rules which are not known as such to the person following them" (Polanyi 1962: 49, emphasis in original). "Not known as such" here means that the person could not provide a useful explanation of the rules. Fully articulable knowledge, on the other hand, can be communicated from its possessor to another person in symbolic form, and the recipient of the communication becomes as much "in the know" as the originator.

The reality of the phenomenon of tacit knowing at the level of individual skills is obvious from introspective evidence; its sources and significance were explored in depth in Nelson and Winter (1982). An article in the New York Times (Blakeslee 1985) cited recent scientific evidence that different brain structures are involved in memory for the "procedural" knowledge underlying skills as opposed to memory for the "declarative knowledge" of facts, and provided a striking example of the distinction. A brain-damaged man retained his ability to play a good game of golf (something that he obviously could not transfer to

Tacit	———	Articulable
not teachable	——— teachable	
	not articulated ———	articulated
Not observable in use	———	Observable in use
Complex	———	Simple
An element of a system	———	Independent

FIGURE 9.1 Taxonomic Dimensions of Knowledge Assets

another person by mere communication), but could not recall where the ball had just landed or keep track of his score (fully articulable knowledge that his damaged memory could not retain).

Knowledge possessed by an organization may be tacit knowledge in the sense, first, that the possession arises from the association with the organization of an individual for whom the knowledge in question is tacit. Related articulable knowledge may be possessed by other members of the organization, to the effect that "We have someone who knows about (or can do) that." Second, the fact that the myriads of relationships that enable the organization to function in a coordinated way are reasonably understood by (at most) the participants in the relationship and a few others means that the organization is certainly accomplishing its aims by following rules that are not known as such to most participants in the organization. Third, in a metaphorical sense an organization's knowledge is tacit to the extent that its top decisionmakers are uninformed regarding the details of what happens when their decisions are implemented. The decisionmakers are the symbol-processing brains of the organization, the symbols they deal in may suggest very little of what the nerves, bones, and muscles actually do—even though, in the reality to which the metaphor relates, the nerves, bones, and muscles may be quite capable of describing it to each other.

Tacit skills may be teachable even though not articulable. Successful teaching presupposes the willingness of the pupil to engage in a series of trial performances of the skill and to attend to the teacher's critique of the errors made in these trials. Teachers may also provide model performances of the skill, which provide the pupil with an opportunity for imitative learning. Instruction of this sort may accomplish a radical reduction in the time and effort required for skill acquisition, relative to what would be required by the pupil proceeding on trial and error alone but the situation nevertheless is vastly different from one in which knowledge is fully conveyed by communication alone.

A second subdimension identified in Figure 9.1 is the distinction between articulable knowledge that is articulated and articulable knowledge that is not. The latter situation may be illustrated by the case of a complex computer program that has gone through a number of major revisions since its documentation was last brought up to date. Simple answers to questions about the program's functioning could be articulated in principle but may not be articulable in fact if the information is no longer in someone's memory. Similar situations seem to arise frequently in manufacturing, where the actual process or product design being followed deviates systematically from the symbolically recorded design or plan. Personnel turnover or simple lapse of time may erase the organization's memory of the actual process or design if the production routine is not regularly exercised and thus remembered by doing. A related phenomenon is that a deviation from the nominal standard may remain unarticulated because it includes features that are to the advantage of an individual organization member but perhaps not to the organization as a whole.

In Figure 9.1, the fact that the not articulated position is placed to the left of the teachable position is intended to suggest the point that the failure to articulate what is articulable may be a more severe handicap for the transfer of knowledge than tacitness itself.

Observability in use, the second of the major continua in Figure 9.1, involves the extent of disclosure of underlying knowledge that is necessitated by use of the knowledge. The design of a product is a secret that is hard to keep if the product is made available for purchase (and inspection) by all comers in an open market. In general, the question at issue involves the opportunities that use makes available to someone who wishes to discover the underlying knowledge. The resources that such an individual has to apply to the task, relative to the costs of observation, should be taken into account in operationalizing this conceptual dimension. Also, the question of whether the observation is taking place with or without the cooperation of the organization or individual observed is a key contextual feature of the discovery task.

The complexity/simplicity dimension has to do with the amount of information required to characterize the item or knowledge in question. Here, as elsewhere in information theory, the notion of an amount of information must be interpreted in terms of the alternative possibilities from which a particular case must be distinguished. For example, the item in question might superficially have to do with the design of an automobile. But perhaps everything about the design is familiar throughout the relevant context except the ceramic material used in the spark plugs, which itself is distinguished from possible alternatives by its name. In that context, the apparently complex is actually simple.

Similar issues arise in connection with the final dimension. A single module in a microcomputer qualifies intuitively as an element of a system. A pocket calculator is at the opposite end of the spectrum; it is useful standing alone. In a context where all other elements of the microcomputer system are readily available, however, the individual module might be said to be useful by itself.

STRATEGIC SIGNIFICANCE

As suggested above, the left-hand ends of the continua in Figure 9.1 are unfavorable to knowledge transfer: Transfer of tacit knowledge, if possible at all, requires teaching; an element of a system may not be helpful if transferred without the rest of the system, and so forth. Ease of transfer is itself a decidedly ambiguous variable. From the strategic point of view, it is crucial here to distinguish voluntary from involuntary transfers of knowledge. Among the most important peculiarities of knowledge and competence as assets is that secure control of such assets is often very difficult to maintain. No one can walk out the gate of a steel plant or a refinery taking the economic value of the physical installation with him in his pocket, leaving a hollow shell behind. The same is not true of an R&D lab, since the pocket may contain an articulated statement of a simple item of knowledge whose value is substantially independent of the value of other knowledge that remains behind in the lab. And even though what is in the pocket may be only a copy of something that remains in the lab, it may suffice to make the original a hollow shell without economic value.

A recent Fortune article (Flax 1984) provides a handy list of twenty-one ways that companies snoop on their rivals, ranging from such familiar methods as hiring away rivals' employees and reverse engineering their products to more esoteric or exotic techniques such as getting customers to put out phony bid requests and buying competitors' garbage for analysis. Because it focuses on "snooping" activity, the list omits one major route by which knowledge may escape from control, the "fissioning" of the company as new, entrepreneurial enterprises are founded by its former employees.[8] For the same reason, it also omits the important category of voluntary disclosure through patent applications, advertising, and contract bidding.

The key strategic questions are (1) What sorts of knowledge and competence asset, are worth developing and (2) how is value to be derived from those assets? As will be emphasized below, intrinsic differences among knowledge bases and other circumstances of different areas of technology and organization are important determinants of where newly developed assets tend to fall along the taxonomic dimensions identified above. To the extent this is true, the implications for strategic choice relate to which areas to be in. These implications in turn must be assessed in light of the previous section's emphasis on the initial state of the system as a fundamental determinant of value: If the company in question is in the toy business, it is not helpful to observe that the prospects for protecting knowledge assets are better in the chemical business. Less dramatic transformations of a company's knowledge and competence, however, may usefully be guided by asking where the new areas under consideration tend to fall along the taxonomic dimensions of Figure 9.1.

There do exist important opportunities for affecting the positions that particular knowledge developments take on these dimensions. The degree of articulation of anything that is articulable is partially controllable. The possibilities for controlling observability and resisting reverse engineering are illustrated by the practice of "potting" integrated circuit devices—encasing them in a resin that cannot be removed without destroying the device (Shapley 1978). In the case of process knowledge, hazards associated with observability in use may be reduced not only by restricting observation opportunities to employees but also by compartmentalizing knowledge within the company and restricting the opportunity for a full overview to a select few. The emphasis that Teece (1986) places on control of co-specialized assets in the protection of gains from innovation is interpretable in the present framework as involving recognition that virtually any innovation is at least potentially an element of a system in one or more ways. Acquiring control of the complementary elements of the system is a way to move away from independence and its attendant hazards of involuntary transfer.

---

[8] The term fissioning is used by Charles A. Ziegler (1985: 104), who provides an interesting account of the process, concluding that "it can be unwise for corporate leaders to overestimate the efficacy of legal precautions and countermeasures and to underestimate the debilitating effect on the parent firm that successful fissioning can produce."

Features that restrain involuntary transfer tend to inhibit voluntary transfer; likewise, actions undertaken to facilitate voluntary transfer may well facilitate involuntary transfer also. It is here that the question of how value is to be derived becomes crucial. On the assumption that value is maximized by exploiting the knowledge within the firm (and at approximately the current scale), the general rule is to keep to the left in Figure 9.1, to the extent possible. If, on the other hand, the appropriate course is to rapidly expand the use of the same knowledge within the company or to enter licensing agreements or partnerships concerning the technological or organizational competencies involved, then it is at least necessary to restrain the tendency to keep to the left and perhaps better to keep to the right. These observations do not suggest the full complexity of the problem because actually the value-maximizing choice of mode of exploitation of the knowledge is interdependent with the cost and effectiveness of directing its development to the left or to the right. If, for example, it appears unlikely that a process secret can be kept for long, regardless of the effort put into the attempt, then either rapid growth to exploit leadtime or licensing arrangements, may be a superior exploitation mode. Such a choice may imply a drastic change in how the development is handled because many arrangements that would support the secrecy approach become counterproductive. Finally, the answer to the antecedent question of whether an entire area of activity is worth entering in the first place depends on the value achievable from an appropriate simultaneous choice of position on the taxonomic dimensions and mode of exploitation of the knowledge.

HEURISTIC FRAMES

The foregoing discussion is far from exhaustive either with respect to the dimensions on which knowledge states might be described or with respect to the control variables that can be employed to alter them. Under the former heading, for example, there is obviously a need for an approach to describing the amount of knowledge or competence held in a particular area; under the latter, there is the whole domain of the legal system and its various mechanisms that support or hamper efforts to protect knowledge assets. The discussion is at least suggestive of a general approach to the development of heuristic frames appropriate to the development and protection of knowledge and competence assets in a particular line of business. Consider once again the example of BCG experience curve doctrine. Mechanisms that have been suggested to account for the experience curve effect include skill development by individual workers and design improvements in both products and processes. Each of these three is no doubt real, but they represent very different sorts of knowledge assets in the taxonomic scheme of Figure 9.1 and are accordingly developed and tended by quite different means (control variables).

THE DIVERSITY OF INDUSTRIAL CONTEXTS

This section sets forth evidence that U.S. manufacturing industries present a diverse array of environments in terms of the characteristics of the productive knowledge on which they depend and the means that are effective in protecting knowledge assets. One obvious strategic implication of this diversity is that lessons derived from experience in one industry may be very misleading guides to knowledgerelated strategic choices in another. Also, while the across-industry variation is demonstrably lame, this does not imply that the within-industry variation is small. (Indeed, as just pointed out, the slope of a single experience curve may reflect a variety of mechanisms.) Consideration of the across-industry variation suggests that there may be a payoff to a more discriminating approach to the problems of a single business unit—a willingness to recognize, for example, that a particular situation arising in some branch of chemical manufacturing may be "like semiconductors" even though most of the situations encountered there are, naturally, "like chemicals."[9]

The evidence presented here derives from the Yale survey of R&D executives. This survey project, headed by Richard Levin in collaboration with Alvin Klevorick, Richard Nelson, and myself, obtained answers from R&D executives to a wide range of questions regarding the appropriability of gains from innovation and the sources of technological opportunity in the industries with which they are familiar. To circumvent problems of confidentiality regarding the practices of individual companies, the survey addressed respondents in their capacity as experts on innovation in particular lines of business, rather than as authorities on the practices of their own companies. We obtained 650 responses from executives involved in R&D management in 130 lines of business. There are eighteen lines of business, noncoincidentally including most of the major R&D performing industries, for which we received ten or more responses.[10]

The first questions of the survey asked respondents to record, on a seven-point Likert scale, their view of the effectiveness of various means of protecting

[9] There are analogous implications for public policy. For example, in the light of the evidence presented below, it is clear that patent policy is a tool of dramatically different significance in different industries. It is, accordingly, an inappropriate focus for policy attention arising from general (as opposed to industry-specific) concerns about the innovativeness of U.S. industry (see Levin 1985).

[10] The lines of business were those defined by the Federal Trade Commission, which correspond primarily to four-digit SIC manufacturing industries, occasionally to groups of four-digit industries or to three-digit industries. Lines of business that report zero R&D expenditures were excluded from the sample, as were highly heterogeneous ones. The starting point for our list of R&D performing firms was the *Business Week* annual R&D survey list, which includes all publicly traded firms that report R&D expenses in excess of 1 percent of sales or $35 million. This gives the survey excellent coverage as measured by R&D expenditure but largely omits the perspective of small, entrepreneurial firms. For further details on the design of the survey and an overview of its results, see Levin, et al. (1984).

the returns from innovation in their various lines of business. Table 9.1 records the exact phrasing of the question, along with mean effectiveness scores for patents to prevent duplication obtained from the eighteen industries for which we had ten or more responses.

The first notable feature of these results is that, with the single exception of petroleum refining, patents are consistently rated as more effective in protecting product innovations than process innovations. To interpret this pattern requires consideration of how the observability-in-use dimension of a knowledge asset interacts with the patent law. In general (and practices like "potting" notwithstanding), the design information embodied in a product is discoverable through reverse engineering by any purchaser who wants to apply the necessary resources. Contractual arrangements to forestall reverse engineering are effective in only a few cases involving narrow markets where all buyers are identified to the seller. Also, design information is articulable. By contrast, physical access to a production process can be restricted, and much process knowledge is tacit or unarticulated. Although there are cases in which knowledge of the process can be inferred from reverse engineering of the product, the central situation is that process knowledge need not be observable in use unless the producer permits it. Finally, there are many cases in which complex processes yield simple products.

TABLE 9.1 Effectiveness Ratings of Patents of Patents to Prevent Duplication

Question: In this line of business, how effective is each of the following means of capturing and protecting the competitive advantages of new or improved processes/products? (1) Patents to prevent competitors from duplicating the product, (2) Patents to secure royalty income, (3) Secrecy, (4) Lead time (being first with a new process/product), (5) Moving quickly down the learning curve, (6) Superior sales or service efforts. Scale: 1 = "not at all effective," 4 = "moderately effective," 7 = "very effective." (Mean scores are given for eighteen industries with ten or more respondents.)

Line of Business[a]	New Processes	New Products
Pulp, paper, and paperboard	2.58	3.33
Inorganic chemicals	4.59	5.24
Organic chemicals	4.05	6.05
Drugs	4.88	6.53
Cosmetics	2.94	4.06
Plastic materials	4.58	5.42
Plastic products	3.24	4.93
Petroleum refining	4.90	4.33
Steel mill products	3.50	5.10
Pumps and pumping equipment	3.18	4.36
Motors, generators, and controls	2.70	3.55
Computers	3.33	3.43
Communications equipment	3.13	3.65
Semiconductors	3.20	4.50
Motor vehicle parts	3.65	4.50
Aircraft and parts	3.14	3.79
Measuring devices	3.60	3.89
Medical instruments	3.20	4.73

a. See Table 9–2 for SIC codes

On all these grounds, knowledge embodied in products is inherently more subject to involuntary transfer than process knowledge—the patent system aside.

As is apparent from Table 9.1, patenting is not always an effective response to this inherent vulnerability of product information. In relation to process knowledge, however, the patent system has specific and severe disabilities. Processes that involve an inarticulable "mental step" are not patentable. Insights into process arrangements that are of such broad scope as to amount to "ideas" or "scientific principles" are not patentable. Most important, a patent on a process that is not observable in use (without consent) is difficult to enforce because infringement is not directly observable and can at best be inferred, in the first instance, from circumstantial evidence. Finally, the patent application itself discloses information that might otherwise be protected by secrecy. In sum, patent protection is ineffective for processes relative to products because tacitness and nonobservability are more characteristic of process than of product innovations. In addition, secrecy is a strong alternative to patenting for processes but a weak alternative for products.

A second significant observation derivable from Table 9.1 is that highly effective patent protection is by no means a necessary condition for technological progressiveness. At least, this is the conclusion that follows if we assume that common perception is correct in assessing such industries as computers, semiconductors, communications equipment, and aircraft as being highly innovative. Of the eight mean scores characterizing patent effectiveness for processes and products in these four industries, only one (semiconductor products) is above the humdrum midlevel—"moderately effective." A thorough analysis of this phenomenon is beyond the scope of the present discussion, but it is worth noting the obvious inference that if these industries manage to be innovative in spite of the lack of effective patent protection, other mechanisms presumably protect the gains from innovation. Some reflection on the nature of these industries and another glance at Figure 9.1 produce the suggestion that the prevalence of "complexity" and the status "part of a system" may play a key role in protecting innovative gains in these areas.

A third prominent feature of Table 9.1 is the high scores for patent effectiveness shown for a group of industries that are within the SIC chemicals group (SIC 28). Although the importance of patents in this area comes as no surprise—especially in the case of drugs—the survey results are nevertheless striking for the closeness of the association between patent effectiveness and the chemical industry. In Table 9.1, SIC 28 accounts for all four out of the top four mean scores in the product column, and four out of the top five in the process column—and the intruder (with the top score) is a close relative of the chemi-

---

[11] The anomalies relative to this relationship are cosmetics (actually "perfumes, cosmetics and toilet preparations") (an industry which does not seem to share the characteristics of the chemicals club in spite of being SIC 2844) and steel mill products (SIC 331), which score high on patent effectiveness for new products in spite of being remote from the chemicals club.

cal business, petroleum refining.[11] Out of the full sample of 130 lines of business, there are only four for which patents are rated more effective than any of the non-patent means of protecting gains from product innovation. Two of those are drugs and pesticides, one is represented by a single respondent, the other is meat products (three respondents).

At least a part of this pattern is easily accounted for by reference to the taxonomic dimensions of Figure 9.1. Chemical products are plainly far to the right on the dimensions of articulability, observability in use, and independence (meaning in this case that there are markets for individual products as defined by the molecular structure). Indeed, with modem analytical techniques, chemical products (whether simple or complex) are essentially an open book to the qualified and well equipped observer. In the absence of patents, this sort of knowledge would be highly subject to involuntary transfer. On the other hand, essentially the same characteristics make the property right conferred by a chemical product patent peculiarly sharply defined, distinctively invulnerable to "inventing around." (As is documented elsewhere in the survey results, "inventing around" is the leading reason given for ineffectiveness of patent protection.)

The rationale for the distinctive position of chemicals industries with respect to patent protection of new processes seems much less clear. Relatively tight process-product links may well be involved; for example, it may be unusually easy to infer process patent infringement from examination of the product.

A different perspective on the diversity of industrial contexts is provided by Table 9.2. This shows, for the same industries as Table 9.1, the method of protecting gains from process and product innovation that ranked highest in mean score. Note that one of the possible responses, patents to secure royalty income, never shows up in first place.[12] Patents to prevent duplication rank first only in drugs and in organic chemical products.

Surprisingly, only in organic chemicals does secrecy hold first place as a means of protecting process innovation. Everywhere else, it is lead time or learning curve effects in the process column and lead time or sales and service efforts in the product column.

Finally, it should be noted explicitly that the industries in which we obtained ten or more responses from R&D executives are industries that are doing a substantial amount of R&D—and some mechanism must be protecting the results of that effort or it would not be going on. There is another industrial environment, not represented in Tables 9.1 and 9.2, where appropriability is low and not much R&D is done. This does not mean that knowledge and competence are strategically insignificant. It means that emphasis shifts from the production of innovation to the adoption of innovations produced elsewhere and to the competent use of competitive weapons other than innovation.

---

[12] By contrast, the analysis of situations in which patents are used to secure royalty income does occupy a very prominent place in the theoretical economics of innovation.

TABLE 9.2 Highest-Rated Methods of Protecting Gains from Innovation

Key: PD = patents to prevent competitors from duplicating the product, S = secrecy, LT = lead time, LC = moving quickly down the learning curve, SS = superior sales or service efforts. Numbers in parentheses are SIC codes for the line of business. (Industries and question are the same as in Table 9.1 .)

Line of Business	Processes	Products
Pulp, paper, and paperboard (261, 262, 263)	LC	SS
Inorganic chemicals (2812, 2819)	LT	LT
Organic chemicals (286)	S	PD
Drugs (283)	PD	PD
Cosmetics (2844)	LT	LT
Plastic materials (2821)	LT	SS
Plastic products (307)	LC	SS
Petroleum refining (291)	LC	SS
Steel mill products (331)	LC	SS
Pumps and pumping equipment (3561)	LT	LT
Motors, generators, and controls (3621, 3622)	LT	SS
Computers (3573)	LT	LT
Communications equipment (3661, 3662)	LT	SS
Semiconductors (3674)	LC	LT
Motor vehicle parts (3714)	LC	LT
Aircraft and parts (3721, 3728)	LT	LT
Measuring devices (382)	LT-LC	SS
Medical instruments (3841, 3842)	LT	SS

SUMMARY

Considering the acknowledged importance of knowledge and competence in business strategy and indeed in the entire system of contemporary human society, it is striking that there seems to be a paucity of language useful for discussing the subject. Within each microcosm of expertise or skill, there is of course a specialized language in which that subject—or at least the articulable parts of it—can be discussed. At the opposite extreme, there is terminology of very broad scope. There are words like *information, innovation, skill, technology transfer, diffusion, learning,* and (of course) *knowledge* and *competence.* These name parts of the realm of discourse but do not do much to point the way toward advancing the discourse. The problems of managing technological and organizational change surely lie between these two extremes of low and high generality, and in that range there seems to be a serious dearth of appropriate terminology and conceptual schemes. Such, at least, has been the promise of this paper.

Like evolutionary theory, from which it partly derives, the approach to strategy sketched in earlier sections has a healthy appetite for facts. The first implementation challenge it poses is that of strategic state description—the development of a strategically useful characterization of those features of the organization that are not subject to choice in the short run but are influencable in the long run and are considered key to its development and success. From evolutionary theory comes the idea that a state description may include organizational behavioral patterns or routines that are not amenable to rapid change, as well as a more conventionally defined assets. It is by this route that a variety of considerations that fall under the rubrics *knowledge* and *competence* may enter the strategic state description. From the optimal control theory side comes, first, the insistence that a scheme intended to provide policy guidance must have some choices to relate to; there must be some control variables that affect the development of the state variables. Second, granting the adoption of present value or expected present value as a criterion, control theory provides an approach to the valuation of strategic assets, conventional, and unconventional. In particular, it offers the full imputation challenge of seeking out the present acorns from which the future golden oaks are expected to grow—information likely to be useful in the proper tending of the acorns.

Both control theory and evolutionary theory invoke the notion of state description in the context of formal modeling, and both pursue conclusions logically within the context of the model once it is set down. Without denying the possible usefulness of a formal modeling approach to particular strategic problems, I have proposed the informal, looser and more flexible concept of a heuristic frame—essentially, the control theory approach stripped down to a list of state descriptors and controls. The word heuristic serves as a reminder that a control theory model or any other elaboration of a heuristic frame is an elaboration of an educated guess about what matters and what can be controlled. The making of that guess may be the key step. A change of heuristic frame may make all the difference in terms of identifying those acorns from which future value will grow and in so doing dramatically affect the value actually realized. It is in the choice of heuristic frame, above all, that creative insight into strategic problems plays its role.

Another challenging problem is the subtask of the strategic state description task that involves the characterization of knowledge and competence assets. Such assets are extraordinarily diverse, not only (obviously) in their specific details but also in a number of identifiable dimensions of strategic significance. Some assets are subject to major hazards of involuntary transfer; others may prove highly resistant to affirmative efforts to transfer them pursuant to a sale or exchange. Among the control variables involved in the management of these assets are some that affect the hazards of involuntary transfer or the feasibility of voluntary transfer. It was suggested that the opposition between these two control goals is fundamental.

Finally, the diversity of knowledge contexts found in U.S. manufacturing industry (documented with evidence from the Yale survey of R&D executives) can be analyzed using the chapter's taxonomic scheme. It underscores the point that different approaches to the management of knowledge and competence assets, for understandable reasons, predominate in different industries.

The themes introduced in this chapter are not fully developed. There is much more to be done and said. If the gaps and loose ends are obvious, that at least suggests that a heuristic frame for the analysis of knowledge and competence assets has been put in place.

REFERENCES

Bellman, R. 1957. *Dynamic Programming*. Princeton, N.J.: Princeton University Press.

Blakeslee, S. 1985. "Clues Hint at Brain's Two Memory Maps. "*New York Times* (February 19): C1.

Conley, P. 1970. *Experience Curves as a Planning Tool*. Boston: Boston Consulting Group.

Cyert, R.M., and J.G. March. 1963. *A Behavioral Theory of the Firm*. Englewood Cliffs, N.J.: PrenticeHall.

Dorfman, R., P.A. Samuelson, and R.M. Solow. 1958. *Linear Programming and Economic Analysis*. New York: McGraw-Hill.

Fama, E.F., and M.C. Jensen. 1985. "Organizational Form and Investment Decisions." *Journal of Financial Economics* 14: 101–19.

Flax, S. 1984. "How to Snoop on Your Competitors." *Fortune* (May 14): 29–33.

Greiner, L. E. 1983. "Senior Executives as Strategic Actors." *New Management* 1: 11–15.

Levin, R. 1985. "Patents in Perspective." *Antitrust Law Journal* 53: 519–22.

Levin, R., A.K. Klevorick, R.R. Nelson, and S.G. Winter. 1984. "Survey Research on R&D Appropriability and Technological Opportunity." Working paper, Yale University.

Nelson, R.R., and S.G. Winter. 1982. *An Evolutionary Theory of Economic Change*. Cambridge, Mass.: Belknap Press of the Harvard University Press.

Peters, T.J. 1984. "Strategy Follows Structure: Developing Distinctive Skills." In *Strategy and Organization: A West Coast Perspective*, edited by G. Carroll and D. Vogel. Mansfield, Mass.: Pitman.

Polanyi, M. 1962. *Personal Knowledge: Toward a PostCritical Philosophy*. New York: Harper Torchbooks.

Pontryagin, L.S., V.G. Boltyanskii, R.V. Gamkrelidze, and E.F. Mischenko. 1962. *The Mathematical Theory of Optimal Processes*. New York: Interscience.

Porter, M.E. 1980. *Competitive Strategy: Techniques for Analyzing Industries and Competitors*. New York: Free Press.

Salinger, M.A. 1984. "Tobin's *q* Unionization, and the Concentration-Profits Relationship." *The Rand Journal of Economics* 15: 159–70.

Shapley, D. 1978. "Electronics Industry Takes to 'Potting' Its Products for Market." *Science* 202, 848–49.

Simon, H.A. 1957. *Administrative Behavior*, 2d ed. New York: Free Press.

―――. 1964. "On the Concept of Organizational Goal." *Administrative Science Quarterly* 9: 1–22.

Teece, D.J. 1986. "Capturing Value from Technological Innovation: Integration's Strategic Partnering and Licensing Decisions." Working paper, University of California, Berkeley.

Triffin, R. 1949. *Monopolistic Competition and General Equilibrium Theory*. Cambridge, Mass.: Harvard University Press.

Wicksteed, P. 1894. *An Essay on the Coordination of the Laws of Distribution.* London: Macmillan.

Ziegler, C. A. 1985. "Innovation and the Imitative Entrepreneur." *Journal of Economic Behavior and Organization* 6: 103–21.

10
The Strategic Analysis of Intangible Resources

Richard Hall

Sustainable competitive advantage results from the possession of relevant capability differentials. The feedstock of these capability differentials is intangible resources which range from patents and licenses, to reputation and know-how. A framework of intangible resources has been produced which formed the basis for a national survey of chief executives in the U.K. Some of the more significant findings of the survey were that: employee know-how and reputation are perceived as the resources which make the most important contribution to business success; and that for most companies operations is the most important area of employee know-how. This article argues, by means of both theoretical reasoning and empirical evidence, that the analysis of intangible resources should play a major role in the strategic management process.

INTRODUCTION

Intangible resources range from the intellectual property rights of patents, trademarks, copyright and registered design; through contracts; trade secrets; public knowledge such as scientific works; to the people dependent, or subjective resources of know-how; networks; organizational culture, and the reputation of product and company.

The difficulty encountered by the accountancy profession when it attempts to value 'homegrown' brand-names which have not been the subject of an exchange (Barwise, *et al*, 1989) raises the more fundamental question regarding the significance of any quantification of shareholders' funds which does not recognize the value of intangible assets. For example the valuation of the shareholders' funds of a private, as opposed to a state owned, university is only trivially related to the value of the land and buildings which it owns; the resources which are of strategic

From *Strategic Management Journal*, Vol. 13, 1992, pp. 135–144. Reproduced by permission of John Wiley & Sons Limited.

significance are reputation, research momentum, etc., as it is these factors which govern the future earning potential. An indication of the significance of intangibles can be obtained from a comparison of the balance sheet valuation of a publicly quoted company and its stock market valuation.

Handy (1990) suggests that businesses will need to become more like universities with respect to the emphasis which is placed on being information /knowledge positive as well as being cash positive. Itami and Roehl (1987) have argued that a characteristic of all successful organizations is the recognition that there is a learning process which runs in parallel to all operations, and that all activities present the potential to both enhance, or degrade, the know-how and reputation elements of the intangible resources. They also argue that at a strategic level this view leads to the selection of strategies which will enrich the 'know-how stock' of the core competencies of the business.

Companies have sustainable competitive advantage when they consistently produce product/delivery systems with attributes which correspond to the key buying criteria for the majority of the customers in their targeted market. These attributes, which will include price, quality, aesthetics, functionality, availability image, etc., will be offered in a package which optimizes, for this majority, the ratio of 'perceived value: delivered cost' (Gilbert and Strebel, 1989).

Coyne (1986) identifies the sources of sustainable competitive advantage as being four types of capability differential, viz.: 'functional differential', 'positional differential', 'cultural differential' and 'regulatory differential'. (Coyne's article uses the terminology 'business system gap', 'position gap', 'organization quality gap' and 'regulatory/legal gap'.) This article develops Coyne's model of capability differentials by extending it to identify, and categorize, the intangible resources which act as the feedstock to the capability differentials.

Capability Differentials Based on Competencies

Functional differential results from the knowledge, skill and experience of employees, and others in the value chain such as suppliers, distributors, stockbrokers, lawyers, advertising agents etc. When know-how can be utilized to produce products which will maintain, and preferably win, market share, then it can be said to be creating a relevant functional differential.

Cultural differential applies to the organization as a whole. It incorporates the habits, attitudes, beliefs and values, which permeate the individuals and groups which comprise the organization. When the organization's culture results in, for example: a perception of high quality standards, an ability to react to challenge, an ability to change, an ability to put the customer first etc.; then that culture is a contributor to competitive advantage.

Capability Differentials Based on Assets

Positional differential is a consequence of past actions which, for example, have produced a certain reputation with customers, a certain advantageous location of facilities, etc. These states contribute not only to competitive advantage, but also to defendable position, because of the long time it would usually take a competitor, starting from scratch, to match them.

Regulatory differential results from the possession of legal entities such as: intellectual property rights, contracts, trade secrets, etc. These resources also make a major contribution to defendable position because of the ability afforded to the owners to defend them in law.

In summary therefore functional and cultural differentials are based on competencies, or skills, such as advertising, or zero defect production; whilst positional and regulatory differentials are related to assets which the business owns, such as brand names, or physical locations. The first two differentials are therefore concerned with 'doing', whilst the second two are concerned with 'having'. The resources which produce the four differentials are described in this article as 'intangible resources', and the nature and characteristics of these intangible resources are examined in the following section.

THE NATURE AND CHARACTERISTICS OF INTANGIBLE RESOURCES

Intangible resources may be classified as 'assets' or 'skills'. Assets, which are obviously things which one owns, include the intellectual property rights of: patents, trademarks, copyright and registered designs; as well as contracts, trade secrets and data bases. The intangible resource of reputation may also be classified as an asset due to its characteristic of 'belongingness', and whilst it may be defendable to attack with respect to defamation and libel, it cannot be said to have the property rights of, say a trademark, which can be bought and sold. Skills, or competencies, include the know-how of employees (as well as suppliers and advisers), and the collective aptitudes which add up to organizational culture. When a company is taken over the acquirer can be confident that he has acquired the acquiree's intangible resources such as patents, but he cannot be certain that he will retain the intangible resources of know-how, culture, or networks which can ultimately 'walk away'.

Intangible Resources Which Are Assets

Intangible resources which are assets, and which enjoy legal protection, are: intellectual property rights; contracts; and trade secrets which are subject to the laws of confidentiality and contract. These categories are considered in the following sections.

Trade Marks

Of the four main categories of intellectual property, the trade mark is the oldest. The earliest evidence of a maker's mark is on pottery made 7,000 years ago. Property rights for trade marks were incorporated in Roman law, where the emphasis was on protecting the customers from being cheated with fraudulent goods, rather than protecting the reputation of the manufacturer, as is the case today. Trade and service marks afford protection in the use of devices, names, signatures etc. used to describe a product or service. In an age when the brand name can represent the essence of the ideas and feelings associated with a product, the protection afforded by the trade mark can be crucial to the well being of a company so that it may avoid unfair competition and the 'borrowing' of its reputation by rivals, To have a mark registered in the U.K. the requirements are that it has to be: distinctive, not descriptive of the product, and different from other marks. Generally speaking a trade mark cannot be a surname or a geographical name. Unlike patents and copyright which have a finite duration, trade marks can be renewed indefinitely.

Patents

The formal recognition of an inventor's right of ownership to his invention, was first conceived in Venice in 1421 when the state granted a monopoly to Phillipo Brunillesci in respect of his invention of a floating architectural crane. This was followed in England in 1449 when Henry VI granted a monopoly to one John of Utyman who was installing the stained glass windows in Eton College chapel.

When a patent is granted a 'deal' is struck between the state and the inventor whereby the inventor is granted a monopoly in the exploitation of his invention for a limited period of time in the state's territory, in return for the inventor disclosing his invention and it being made available to the world at large. The very word 'patent' derives from the Latin 'literae patentes' meaning open letter. It can be seen therefore that the basis of patent protection is the concept of the ownership of a new idea (the invention); and consequent upon the demonstration of that ownership, the establishment of a 'contract' between the state and the inventor. The information contained in patents is clearly intended for the benefit of the public, and in fact patent data bases constitute one of the richest, albeit esoteric, information crops which it is possible to harvest.

Copyright

The need for copyright did not arise until the invention of the printing press in the 16th century, when the copying of documents became easy. In England a monopoly was granted to the Stationers' Company. Members of this company were the only people who could print documents, and in exchange for this monopoly they undertook to censor, on political and religious grounds, everything which was printed. This is another example of a 'deal' being struck between the state and the owner of the intellectual property. Nowadays no such 'contract' applies, as in the U.K. copyright is usually automatic, so long as date and exclusivity of authorship can be demonstrated.

Whereas patents are meant to protect an inventive idea, copyright is meant to protect an embodiment of that idea. For example the plots of 'The Taming of the Shrew' and 'Romeo and Juliet' are Shakespeare's original ideas, and 'Kiss Me Kate' and 'West Side Story' are embodiments, fashioned by others, of those ideas. These separate embodiments have their own protection in copyright. Copyright protects literary, dramatic, musical and artistic works, sound recordings, films and broadcasts by giving legal rights to the originators so that they may control the copying, adaptation, publishing, performing and broadcasting of the material (Hodkinson, 1987). Additionally in the U.K. it is sometimes possible to protect the design of an industrial product by means of the copyright which resides in the original drawings on which the product is based. Copyright is a collection of separate legal rights each of which is specific to the type of material in question.

Registered Designs

A registered design enables the 'eye appeal' of a commercial article to be protected. Design registration is concerned only with appearance, and designs may be two dimensional, e.g. a fabric print; or three dimensional, e.g. a soft drink bottle. Designs which are purely functional, and which lack 'eye appeal', will not be registrable; however it may be possible to obtain copyright protection for some functional designs, as mentioned above. For a design to be registrable it must not have been published or offered for sale.

Contracts

Contracts, in the form of agency agreements, license agreements, property leases, etc. can constitute one of the most important resource categories of some businesses, e.g. Pan American's landing rights at Heathrow. A contract is an agreement between two or more persons (or other legal entities) intended to create a legal obligation between them and to be legally enforceable. The law of contract exists to regulate all kinds of business and economic relationships, sale, hiring, employment, construction, etc. (Walker, 1980). Contracts are therefore the embodiment of an agreement, which define the terms of that agreement so that each party understands, and can protect and enforce, his rights.

Trade Secrets

Trade secrets cover a wide range of confidential information from technical secrets such as formulae, know-how, and processes, to information about a firm's customers, employees, sales strategies, etc.

> The law on trade secrets in the U.K. is almost entirely judge-made, no statute governs it... 'The basic requirement for information to qualify for protection is that it must be information which is not publicly or generally known in the industry or business concerned and which is communicated to the recipient for only a limited purpose, or received by the recipient in circumstances which objectively he should know impose a restriction on the uses to which that information may be put. It is not possible to protect trade secrets from independent discovery by a third party, as is the case with patents, but the unauthorized use or disclosure of the information, if directly or indirectly obtained from the owner or licensee, can often be restrained. (Hodkinson, 1987:14).

Trade secrets therefore depend on the imposition, sometimes unilaterally, of personal obligations on others, either by means of the law of confidentiality, or the law of contract. The nature of this contract, which may be implicit or explicit, can give one party (say the employer) rights, whilst the other party (say the employee) may experience restrictions.

Reputation

Unlike the intangible resources treated above, reputation has little significance in a legal context other than the redress obtainable with respect to libel and defamation. It is clearly not possible to buy or to sell reputation except insofar as it may be construed to reside in a registered brand name. Reputation, which represents the knowledge and emotions held by individuals about, say, a product range, can be a major factor in achieving competitive advantage through differentiation; it also contributes to a defendable position because of the time which can be involved in matching a reputation which is strong in both fame and esteem; fame can be bought with advertising spending in the short term, but esteem has to be earned, usually over a long period of time.

Networks

Networks are those personal relationships which transcend the requirements of organizational structure, commercial relationships, etc.; they are to do with sharing information and purpose to mutual advantage (Hastings, Mindel and Young, 1989). The networks which employees institute may be internal, or external, to the organization. Internal networking is essential in large organizations if synergy is to be achieved. External networks with customers, suppliers, government agencies, research institutes, and even competitors are essential if the changing environment is to be effectively monitored.

The Balance Sheet Valuation of Brand Names

When the reputation of a company, or product, is encapsulated in a brand name, or mark, then it should be protected by registration as a trademark; such registration, unlike that of patents, can be everlasting if renewed as required by the British Patent Office. Insofar as registered trademarks enjoy property rights, i.e. ownership can be established, and the asset is separable from the business, then it is feasible to assign a valuation to such an asset in the balance sheet. This has been done in the U.K. in recent years by such companies as Guinness, and Ranks Hovis McDougal. In the former case the accountancy profession had little difficulty with the move as the valuation could be related to the goodwill element of the consideration involved in the Guinness takeover of Distillers, (the accountancy discipline prefers all asset valuations be traceable to an exchange). The profession therefore had more difficulty with the Ranks Hovis McDougal valuation of their homegrown brand-names which were valued by consultants at a figure which virtually trebled shareholders' funds without the test of an exchange. In spite of contrary guidance from the Accounting Standards Committee the practice of valuing brand names without the test of an exchange continues in some companies and the controversy is unresolved. Whatever the eventual outcome in terms of accounting practice it is now well recognized that intangible assets can represent the bulk of the worth of many companies.

Intangible Resources Which Are Skills

Intangible resources which are skills include: the know-how of employees, suppliers, distributors; and the culture of the organization which enables it to cope with change, put the customer first, etc.

Know-how

The know-how of employees, (and suppliers, distributors, etc.), is the intangible resource which results in distinctive competencies. Distinctive competencies are those capabilities which the organization possesses which set it apart from its competitors. For example it can be argued that the competitive advantage which Jaguar Cars enjoys is the differentiation achieved by the reputation of the 'Jaguar' name; the distinctive competence which the company enjoys, however, is the ability to build a special type of quality car. This ability is founded on the skill and experience, or know-how of the employees.

Culture

Culture constitutes the beliefs, knowledge, attitudes of mind and customs to which individuals are exposed in an organization, as a result of which they acquire a language, values, habits of behavior and thought. The culture of an organization both sets it apart from others, and also binds its members together; it may work to the organization's advantage or to its disadvantage. To a degree culture is a function of the type of activity which the organization is engaged upon, to a degree it is a function of the lifecycle stage which the organization has reached; but increasingly it is being recognized that an organization's culture is the product, consciously or unconsciously produced, of the senior management's beliefs. Indeed some would argue that the main task of senior management in the future will be the promotion of organizational cultures which thrive on change (Kanter, 1983).

A Framework of Intangible Resources

In addition to being categorized as assets or skills, intangible resources may be categorized as being people dependent and people independent. These two perspectives can be presented in the context of capability differentials as shown in Figure 10.1.

CAPABILITY DIFFERENTIALS				
FUNCTIONAL	CULTURAL	POSITIONAL	REGULATORY	
Know-How of: Employees, Suppliers, & Distributors.	Perception of Quality, Ability to Learn, et..			S K I L L S
		Reputation, Networks.		
		Databases.		A S S E T S
			Contracts, Licences, Trade Secrets, Intellectual Property Rights.	

On the left margin (top block, vertical text): DEPENDENT PEOPLE INDEPENDENT
On the left margin (bottom block, vertical text): INDEPENDENT PEOPLE DEPENDENT

FIGURE 10.1 A Framework of Intangible Resources & Capability Differentials

CHIEF EXECUTIVES' PERCEPTIONS OF THE ROLE OF INTANGIBLE RESOURCES

In order to determine the relative contribution which each intangible resource makes to the success of business a national survey of chief executives in the U.K. was carried out.

The only executive who can be responsible for the totality of intangible resources, from patents to company reputation, is the Chief Executive Officer (CEO). The survey was therefore addressed to CEOs in the U.K. and it set out to determine: the chief executives' perceptions of the relative importance of the contributions which each intangible resource makes to the success of the business, the replacement periods associated with these resources, and the most important areas of employee know-how.

The survey was addressed to 847 chief executives throughout the U.K., representing the following sectors: manufacturing consumer products, manufacturing industrial products, retailing, transport, distribution and services. The addressees were supplied by Dun and Bradstreet Limited who made random selections from specified Standard Industrial Classification numbers, with the sole condition that the organizations should employ more than 100 people. The composition of the 95 respondents was as follows: manufacturing 31; trading 14; transport 16; services 21; diversified 13. This represented an 11 percent response rate, which was the rate anticipated from this type of population.

The questionnaire possessed a longitudinal dimension insofar as some data was elicited both for 1987, and for 1990, (this data related to: sales, employees, and the importance of the contribution which each resource made to the success of the business). The existence of this data meant that three performance groups (measured in terms of the 'increase in sales/employee 1987-90') could be identified. These were classified as: 'Low' < 14 percent (N = 30); 'Medium' 15-29 percent (N = 26); 'High' > 30 percent (N = 26).

It is interesting to note in passing that many more service companies reported a high increase in total sales revenue (1987-90) than did the other sectors. 65 percent of service companies reported sales revenue increases greater than 60 percent; whereas only 30 percent of the companies in the other sectors reported an increase greater than 60 percent. However, the productivity performance of the service sector (as measured by the increase in sales/employee in the same period) did not differ significantly from the other sectors; *in fact in terms of the increase in sales/employee 1987-90 all commercial and industrial sectors were equally represented in the three performance groups.*

Contribution to the Success of the Business

The question 'What contribution did (in 1987), and does (in 1990), the reputation of your company make to the overall success of the business?' was also asked with respect to the following 12 resources: reputation of products; know-how of employees; know-how of suppliers; know-how of distributors; networks; data bases; public knowledge; trade secrets; contracts; intellectual property; specialist physical resources; and organizational culture. (Respondents were asked to rate the contribution from: insignificant 1 to crucial 10).

The importance of the contribution which each intangible resource is reported as making to the overall success of the business is shown in Table 10.1.

This analysis of the total sample shows company reputation, product reputation and employee know-how as the most important contributors to company success; these, together with culture and networks were ranked above specialist physical resources. When the absolute weighting scores, and the rankings derived therefrom, were analyzed for 1990 there was a surprising unanimity over the subgroups analyzed, e.g. manufacturers, traders, service companies; independents, subsidiaries; and over the 'Low', 'Medium' and 'High' performance groups. This suggests that the ranking of the contributions of the different intangible resources identified by this research is predictable for the majority of companies, irrespective of sector, status, or performance characteristics.

It is interesting to note that 'Data bases' moved from 10th position in the ranking in 1987 to 7th position in the ranking in 1990, reflecting the growing importance of information technology to business success.

Replacement Periods

The question 'Given a reasonably high priority how many years would it take to recreate the current reputation of your company if you had to start from scratch?' was also asked with respect to: The reputation of product range; The

TABLE 10.1 Relative Importance of the Contribution Made by Each Intangible Resource to the Overall Success of the Business in 1987 and 1990; Total Sample (N=95)

	Ranking	
	1 Most Important	13 Least Important
Intangible resource	1990	1987
Company reputation	1	1
Product reputation	2	2
Employee know-how	3	3
Culture	4	5
Networks	5	4
Specialist physical resources	6	6
Data bases	7	10
Supplier know-how	8	7
Distributor know-how	9	8
Public knowledge	10	9
Contracts	11	11
Intellectual property rights	12	13
Trade secrets	13	12

know-how of employees; the know-how of suppliers; the know-how of distributors; and networks.

The average replacement period estimated for each intangible resource is shown in Table 10.2.

The significance of this question is in the fact that the possession of resources, such as reputation, with a long replacement period can contribute significantly to the defendability of one's position.

The three intangible resources which were rated as most important (Question 1) viz. 'company reputation', 'product reputation', and 'employee know-how', were also perceived as having the longest replacement periods, with reputation significantly longer than the rest; however, the CEOs of the 'High' performance group took a more sanguine view of the time it would take to replace company reputation than did the CEOs of the other two groups, although they all took the same view with respect to the replacement time associated with product reputation.

The Most Important Function

CEOs were asked 'Which is the single most important area of employee know-how?' The results are shown in Table 10.3.

TABLE 10.2 Replacement Periods

| | Replacement Period (years) | | | |
| | | Performance Groups | | |
Intangible resource	Total sample	Low	Medium	High
Company reputation	10.8	13.0	14.0	8.1
Product reputation	6.0	6.8	6.4	6.3
Employee know-how	4.6	4.4	4.6	4.7
Networks	3.4	3.0	3.9	3.3
Supplier know-how	3.1	2.4	4.4	3.0
Data bases	2.1	2.0	2.8	1.6
Distributor know-how	1.6	1.2	1.9	1.8

Operations was perceived as the most important area of employee know-how by the CEOs of all sectors with the exception of retailing and manufacturing consumer products, where in both cases sales and marketing was viewed as the most important area of employee know-how. This finding suggests that the research and teaching of operations should be upgraded in importance in many business schools.

In view of these responses it is sensible to ask the question 'Should the analysis of intangible resources be formalized in terms of research, teaching and strategic management practice?' This issue is explored in the next section.

THE ANALYSIS OF INTANGIBLE RESOURCES

Aaker (1989) identifies the route to sustainable competitive advantage as being a process of managing assets (intangible and tangible), and skills, which involves the following three stages: firstly the identification of the relevant assets and skills by observing successes and failures; secondly the selection of those assets and skills which will be relevant to the future needs of the market; and thirdly the implementation of programs which will develop, enhance and/or protect these assets and skills. Itami and Roehl (1987) suggest that a key element of strategy is the management of invisible assets (know-how, reputation etc.), and he suggests that every turn of the business cycle should add value to the know-how base of the organization in the areas of core competencies; this leads to the view that an organization needs to make strategic decisions regarding which know-how areas it wishes to enhance, in the same way as it decides which tangible asset areas it wishes to enhance. If the organization is going to learn by doing then there are clear indications with respect to make/buy decisions, for example, because any

TABLE 10.3 Percentage of CEOs Quoting the Function as the Most Important Area of Employee Know-How

	Total sample %	Performance groups			Manfg. cons. prods %	Retailing
		Low %	Medium %	High %		
Operations	43	47	44	45	27	8
Sales & marketing	29	28	23	33	46	46
Technology	17	19	27	11	18	31
Finance	6	3	3	4	0	15
Other	5	3	3	7	9	0
Total	100	100	100	100	100	100

policy of subcontracting work which incorporates core competence may deny the organization the ongoing opportunity to learn by doing.

Prahalad and Hamel (1990) question the basis for the formation of strategic business units (SBUS) which are predicated on market considerations, and suggest that the key consideration in any business is the identification, development and leverage of the core competence(s) of the business. If the core competence of toilet preparations to a detergents corporation is surface chemistry, this core competence may be underutilized, or at worst dissipated, if it is spread across the detergent, toilet preparations, drugs etc. divisions which have been set up as autonomous product/market orientated businesses. Indeed Prahalad and Hamel (1990) suggest that the market share with which a business should be concerned is not that achieved by its finished products, but that which reflects the exploitation of its core competence; and they argue that in the case of Black and Decker this is its share of the world market in small electric motors. Prahalad and Hamel (1990) list three tests which should be applied to identify a core competence: firstly it should provide potential access to a wide variety of markets, i.e. it possesses leverage potential, secondly it should be relevant to the customers' key buying criteria, and thirdly it should be difficult for competitors to imitate. They suggest that few companies will lead in more than six core competencies.

We have seen that Coyne (1986) identified the sources of sustainable competitive advantage as being four types of capability differential: 'regulatory differential', 'positional differential', 'functional differential' and 'cultural differential'. It is possible to extend Coynes' model of capability differentials by identifying the intangible resources which act as the 'feedstock' to each differential. This extension is shown in Figure 10.2.

The main thrust of the theoretical argument in this article is that intangible resources are the 'feedstock' of the four capability differentials, and that an understanding of the role of the intangible resources in a business may be achieved by analyzing the competitive advantage observed in the market place, the capability differentials which produce this advantage, and the intangible

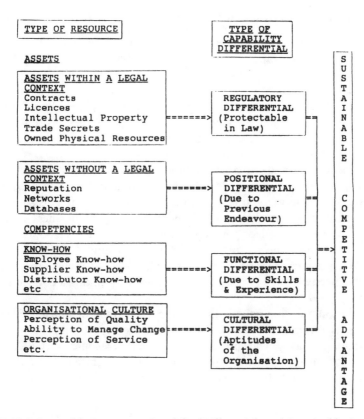

FIGURE 10.2 Intangible Resources, Capability Differentials and Sustainable Competitive Advantage

resources which act as the wellsprings. The model presented in Figure 10.2 has proved effective in teaching and research situations in achieving these objectives because it quickly imparts an understanding of the subject matter, provides a framework for analysis, and acts as a checklist. When the essence of the business has been identified in this fashion then the key management responsibilities are concerned with exploitation, development and protection of the essential intangible resources.

Where the organization is a collection of SBUs the model may be particularly useful in determining for each SBU which are its key intangible resources. Thereafter the analysis can be used to identify the degree to which the current organization and management practices are productive or counterproductive with respect to the exploitation, development and safeguarding of the key resources.

CONCLUSIONS

The following conclusions may be drawn from the foregoing:

The Perceptions of Chief Executives

All CEOs rated company reputation, product reputation, and employee know-how as the most important contributors to overall success, and there is no significant difference in the rankings awarded by the different sectors, or performance groups.

Company reputation, product reputation and employee know-how were also identified as the resources which would take the longest to replace if they had to be replaced from scratch; suggesting that they have considerable significance with respect to the sustainability of advantage.

The most important area of employee know-how was viewed as being Operations, except by CEOs in retailing and manufacturing consumer products who viewed sales and marketing as the most important area. This suggests that operations should be afforded greater importance in many business schools.

The emphasis placed on employee know-how by the respondents to the survey is in tune with the writing of Prahalad and Hamel (1990) on core competencies. They suggest that strategic thinking has been over concerned with taking a market perspective, and too little concerned with taking a core competence perspective.

Reputation, which is usually the product of years of demonstrated superior competence, is a fragile resource; it takes time to create, it cannot be bought, and it can be damaged easily. The emphasis placed on this resource by CEOs suggests that a key task of management is to make sure that every employee is disposed to be both a promoter and a custodian of the reputation of the organization which employs him.

The Management of Intangible Resources

It is too soon to say whether the views expressed in this paper, and by other authors, will result in changes in management practice, for example in terms of organizational responsibility for intangibles. There are grounds for believing that the analysis technique, represented by the model presented in Figure 10.2, which traces the linkage between competitive advantage, capability differentials and intangible resources is an effective means of achieving a deeper understanding of the key intangible resources of a business, and in consequence what needs to be done with respect to their exploitation, protection and development.

REFERENCES

Aaker, D. A. 'Managing assets and skills: The key to a sustainable competitive advantage', *California Management Review*, Winter 1989, pp. 91–106.

Barwise, P., C. Higson, A. Likierman and P. Marsh. 'Accounting for brands', The London Business School and The Institute of Chartered Accountants of England and Wales, 1989.

Coyne, K. P. 'Sustainable competitive advantage What it is and what it isn't', *Business Horizons,* Jan./Feb. 1986, pp. 54–61.

Gilbert, X. and Paul Strebel. 'Taking advantage of industry shifts', *European Management Journal,* 7(4), 1989, pp. 398–402.

Handy, C. *The Age of Unreason,* Arrow Books Ltd., Random Century Group, London, 1989.

Hastings, R., R. Mindel and C. Young. 'The Know-how Organization of the 1990's' Paper presented at E.F.M.D. Conference in Barcelona: Knowledge as a Corporate Asset, 1989.

Hodkinson, K. *Protecting and Exploiting New Technology and Designs,* E. & F.N. Spon, London, 1987.

Itami, H. and T. W. Roehl, *Mobilizing Invisible Assets.* Harvard University Press, Cambridge, MA, 1987.

Kanter, R. M. *The Change Masters,* Unwin/Counterpoint, 1989.

Prahalad, C. K. and G. Hamel. 'The Core Competence of the Corporation', *Harvard Business Review,* May-June 1990, pp. 79–91.

Walker, D. M. *The Oxford Companion to Law,* Clarendon Press, Oxford, 1980.

11

Knowledge, Strategy, and the Theory of the Firm

Julia Porter Liebeskind

This paper argues that firms have particular institutional capabilities that allow them to protect knowledge from expropriation and imitation more effectively than market contracting. I argue that it is these generalized institutional capabilities that allow firms to generate and protect the unique resources and capabilities that are central to the strategic theory of the firm.

Possession is nine-tenths of the law.

—(Anonymous)

INTRODUCTION

For many strategy scholars, organizational economics in general, and transaction-costs economics in particular, remains a dissatisfying theoretical framework for theorizing about the relationship between organization and competitive advantage. Perhaps the most important source of this dissatisfaction is the apparent failure of transaction-costs theory to accommodate the central notion that strategy scholars hold about firms—that firms' principal purpose is to generate rents through creating and sustaining sources of competitive advantage (Bowman, 1974; Rumelt, 1984, 1987; Barney, 1986). One weakness of transaction-costs economics in this regard is its emphasis on static comparative analysis and on identifying generalized boundary conditions that exist between firms and markets. These emphases bypass the usual concerns of strategy research, which are focused on dynamic rent-seeking behavior, and the ownership and exploitation of unique assets and capabilities. In addition, transaction-costs theory is

From *Strategic Management Journal*, Vol. 17, Winter Special Issue, 1996, pp. 93–107. Reproduced by permission from John Wiley & Sons Limited.

concerned primarily with transactions that involved fixed, tangible assets.[1] Strategy researchers, instead, understand rents as deriving in large part from intangible assets such as organizational learning, brand equity, and reputation (Penrose, 1959; Rumelt, 1984, 1987; Barney, 1986; Spender, 1994; Grant, 1996). In particular, transaction-costs theory has paid scant attention to the question of knowledge. Yet knowledge is arguably the most important asset that firms possess—a key source of both Ricardian and monopoly rents (Penrose, 1959; Winter, 1988). Without taking knowledge into account, then, transaction-costs economics stands in danger of becoming a theory that provides only marginally useful connections between organization on the one hand and competitive advantage on the other.

In this paper, I argue that transaction-costs theory can be extended to accommodate the notion of knowledge in a way that is useful for strategy research. I argue that firms, *as institutions,* play a critical role in creating and sustaining competitive advantage: that of protecting valuable knowledge. Specifically, because property rights in knowledge are weak, and are costly to write and enforce, firms are able to use an array of organizational arrangements that are not available in markets to protect the value of knowledge. Thus firms can (a) differentially prevent expropriation of knowledge and (b) differentially reduce the observability of knowledge and its products, thereby protecting against imitation. In this way, firms are able to create 'possession rights' to knowledge that are just as valuable, if not more valuable, than the limited property rights to knowledge accorded under the law.

This argument has some important implications for strategy research. First, it suggests that the condition of 'uniqueness' that is so central to strategy theory depends critically upon the deployment of protective organizational arrangements by firms. Thus, the organization of a firm can serve as an important—if not critical—'isolating mechanism' (Rumelt, 1984). Consequently, the fact that resources and capabilities are distributed asymmetrically across firms may be attributed not only to luck, success in search, history or inherent causal ambiguity (Lippman and Rumelt, 1982; Nelson and Winter, 1982; Rumelt, 1984; Barney, 1986), but also to the fact that some firms are able to protect their knowledge from expropriation or imitation more effectively than other firms.

Second, considering firms as institutions that are able to protect the value of knowledge provides a direct connection between the organizational characteristics of firms on the one hand, and their dynamic strategic behavior on the other. By protecting knowledge, firms may serve to induce investment in strategic innovation, because incentives to innovate depend on the degree to which the innovator can appropriate future rent streams. In addition, if some firms are able to protect the value of their knowledge more effectively than other firms, these firms will have more high-powered incentives to innovate. Thus, we should

---

[1] Thus, transaction-costs theories of the firm in general appear to be far more appropriate to explaining the scope of manufacturing firms, than service firms or 'knowledge work' firms such as consulting practices and research firms. One exception is Teece (1980, 1986), who argues that knowledge is an important determinant of the scope of the firm.

expect to observe a long-run correlation between a firm's rate of innovation and its success at protecting the knowledge that it generates.

Third, by identifying some of the mechanisms firms can use to protect knowledge, the argument in this paper provides some concreteness to theories of the scope of the firm that are based on knowledge-protection arguments (Teece, 1980, 1986). This potentially allows for a more detailed development of predictions about the circumstances under which internalization of knowledge transactions will, or should, take place.

KNOWLEDGE AND RENTS

Knowledge

In this paper, I define knowledge as *information whose validity has been established through tests of proof.* Knowledge can therefore be distinguished from opinion, speculation, beliefs, or other types of unproven information.[2] This definition of knowledge is intentionally very broad: it can include such codified knowledge products as written documents and blueprints, as well as tacit knowledge such as uncodified routines.

Knowledge and Rents

New knowledge is produced by investment in innovation and tests of proof. Because innovation and tests of proof are costly, and because new knowledge production is inherently an uncertain process (i.e., innovation and tests of proof cannot be relied upon to produce valuable new knowledge), valuable knowledge is unlikely to be distributed evenly across innovators, so that its ownership can potentially earn both Ricardian and monopoly rents (Winter, 1988).

Ricardian rents are earned by firms when one firm possesses factors of production that are more productive than those of other firms carrying out the same activity. When Ricardo wrote his original treatise on rents (Ricardo, 1926 [1821]), he used the example of 'good land' as a rent-bearing resource. Good land produces more output per acre than poor land, so unit costs of agricultural production are lower. In the modern world, however, most factors of production are not naturally occurring factors such as land, but are deliberately created factors such as machines, trained workers, and systems of work organization. Thus, superior knowledge allows a firm to build a better piece of machinery, train its workers more effectively, or devise a more productive system of work organization (Penrose, 1959; Spender, 1994). Ricardian rents in modern industrial com-

---

[2] This is the Socratic/Platonic definition of knowledge *eidos*—which can be contrasted with opinions or beliefs—*doxa*. This distinction is important because knowledge establishes reliable relationships between inputs or circumstances on the one hand and outcomes on the other: what we 'know' we can use repeatedly without further experimentation or proof.

petition, then, are commonly generated from the knowledge of the firm. Similarly, a firm with superior product design knowledge can produce a unique product and earn monopoly rents.

Of course, there are other sources of Ricardian and monopoly rents such as luck, chance, and history (Lippman and Rumelt, 1982; Rumelt, 1984; Barney, 1986). However, luck, chance, and history cannot be managed. Therefore, it is difficult to conceive of a circumstance in which a firm can be said to earn a rent from its deliberate actions—i.e., its managerial strategy—without attributing that rent at least in part to the knowledge which allowed the relevant process or product to be created.

However, the argument that rents derive first and foremost from the knowledge of a firm depends critically on the assumption that a firm can protect its knowledge from appropriation or imitation by its competitors; that is, a firm can exclude others from using its knowledge.[3] By definition, an asset cannot be expropriated—stolen—unless a thief has access to it either directly, or through third parties acting on her behalf. Similarly, for an asset to be imitated, it must at least be observed by the imitator or by a third party. In many instances, imitation will only be possible if the asset itself can be used or experienced. For example, it may be relatively easy to imitate clock production because the machinery can be disassembled, and its working can be easily observed.[4] On the other hand, it may be far more difficult to imitate the production of a Wolfgang Puck pizza, because the quality of the pizza is determined not only by the recipe (which may be imitated through experimentation or expropriated by theft), but also by the process by which the pizza and its ingredients are made, which can only be observed directly. Thus, to the degree that observability of products or processes can be reduced, causal ambiguity is increased, and the costs of imitation are increased accordingly.

The Problem of Knowledge Protection

For many types of asset, exclusion is a relatively simple matter. First of all, many assets can be *defined according to property laws,* so that ownership can be asserted unambiguously. In particular, tangible assets such as land, buildings,

---

[3] Rents will only accrue to an asset if it can be used exclusively by a single individual or entity; if a number of different individuals can use the asset, its rent will be dissipated (Demsetz, 1967; Barzel, 1991). For instance, in the case of Ricardo's 'good land', a rent can be earned only when the land is owned individually and when others are excluded from its use. If the good land were held in common, as under the feudal system, no rent would be earned (Demsetz, 1967; Barzel, 1991). Even if the good land were held individually, the value of that ownership would be dissipated if it were very costly to exclude others from its use (Field, 1989). In this case, other parties—such as deer or thieves—could consume the crops, eroding the productivity differential between good land and poor. Exclusion, then, is critical to the capability of any asset to earn a rent for its owner.

[4] Indeed, the first example of Japanese imitation of a 'Western' technology took place in the eighteenth century, when Japanese craftsmen imported and imitated clockmaking technology (Boorstin, 1983).

and equipment are all considered property under the law. These assets can then be protected by social institutions that enforce property ownership (e.g., the courts). Tangible property can also be given additional, private protection at relatively low cost. For example, land can be fenced, and machinery and equipment can be locked inside a building, or fitted with starter keys.

A second feature that renders most tangible assets protectable is that they are *clearly observable, and have finite productive capacity,* so that expropriation can be easily detected. For example, an owner can observe whether or not an outsider is using her machinery, or has stolen it altogether. Thus, it is relatively simple to monitor property rights in tangible assets.

However, protecting knowledge is more problematic. First of all, *property rights in knowledge—patents, copyrights, and trade secrets—are very narrowly defined under the law, and are costly to write and enforce.*[5] For example, patents have a limited life, and apply only to products that are entirely original and have proven efficacy. Also, patents are published, and so reveal the knowledge of a firm to its rivals.[6]

Patents are only issued after a costly proving process,[7] and can be challenged by other parties, and even overturned.[8] Copyrights create ownership rights only for certain encoded products such as written documents, music, artwork, films, photographs, software, and technical drawings. Copyrights also have a limited life, and are costly to enforce, because the plaintiff must prove novelty of their copyrighted product for any suit for infringement to be successful. Finally, trade secrets laws apply only to knowledge that is codified and is in continuous use; 'noncontinuous' knowledge such as contract bids, plans or prototypes, and tacit knowledge, are not protected.[9] In addition, unlike patents or

[5] Due to restrictions on the length of this article, I provide only a very cursory discussion of the limits to intellectual property and trade secrets law here. For a detailed discussion of this topic, please see (for example) Seidel and Panich (1973); Cheung (1982); Barrett (1991); Besen and Raskind (1991); and Friedman, Landes, and Posner (1991). My comments here refer to U.S. laws on intellectual property and trade secrecy. However, intellectual property laws are similar in many other developed countries.

[6] Publishing is a problem because it allows competitor firms to 'invent around' an issued patent. Empirical research shows that patents provide effective protection against imitation only in the pharmaceutical and chemical industries (Mansfield, 1985; Levin *et al.,* 1987).

[7] The inventors of any given patent are determined in the U.S.A. by the federal Patent and Trademark Office (PTO). If an inventor cannot be clearly identified, the PTO will not issue a patent. For instance, the PTO took over 4 years to issue the Cohen-Boyer gene-splicing patent (1978-82) due to concerns over discovery credit, as well as other matters.

[8] For example, Texas Instruments (TI) opposed a broad software patent issued by the Patent Office in 1994. As a result of TI's efforts, this patent was overturned 2 years later.

[9] According to the first Restatement of Torts, section 757 comment b, a 'trade secret' is 'any formula, pattern, device or compilation of information which is used in one's business, and which gives him an opportunity to obtain an advantage over competitors who do not know or use it'. Trade secrets laws do not create property fights in knowledge *per se,* but are similar to laws of theft in that they create sanctions for illegal possession of codified materials. See Seidel and Panich (1973), Cheung (1982), Barrett (1991), Besen and Raskind (1991), and Friedman, Landes, and Posner (1991) for further details.

copyrights, trade secrets laws do not protect against a rival using 'fair' methods to replicate the knowledge concerned, and use it, nor are they binding on third parties. The problem of protecting knowledge through property rights or trade secrets protections is summarized in Table 11.1. The table shows that these protections are extremely limited or nonexistent for knowledge that is only partially original, or is tacit, or is long lived. Thus, there is a large body of knowledge that may be valuable to a given owner, but that cannot be protected from expropriation and/or imitation under the law.

Knowledge is also difficult to protect because *it is difficult to detect its expropriation, or illegal imitation.* For one, unlike most tangible assets, knowledge is inherently mobile, because it resides in the heads of individuals (Grant, 1996). Therefore, knowledge can only be rendered immobile by deliberate actions. For instance, a blueprint can be easily transferred from one person to another by hand, by mail, or by computer; the blueprint is rendered immobile only if steps are taken such as locking it up in a safe; storing it in a computer file where access is strictly limited; or writing it in indecipherable code. Similarly, knowledge about a manufacturing technology or a new product in development is accessible to the workers and managers involved, while final products can be observed by any buyer. In addition, knowledge is a public good (Arrow, 1962); one item of knowledge can be used by many individuals or organizations at the

TABLE 11.1 Limits to Legal Protections for Knowledge

	Patents	*Copyrights*	*Trade Secrets*
A. *Limits to scope*			
Codified knowledge only qualifies; tacit or inchoate knowledge is excluded	X	X	X
Applies only to products: processes excluded		X	
Applies only to entirely original products or processes	X	X	
Protection has limited lifetime	X	X	
No protection against *de novo* imitation by third parties			X
No protection against observation/publicity	X		
B. *Costs of definition, registration, and enforcement*			
Costly to define and/or register	X		
Costly to enforce	X	X	X
Requires supplementary protections to be enforceable			X

same time, without diminishing its productivity for any one user. Thus, illegal use of knowledge can be very difficult and costly to detect.

The fact that knowledge is more easily expropriated or imitated than other types of asset is not a problem when it can be generated and commercialized by a single person. For example, a chef who produces unique and magnificent cakes can protect his knowledge by locking up his recipe and keeping other people out of his kitchen. However, in many instances, producing valuable knowledge will require the input of proprietary, personal knowledge from a number of different individuals, each of whom must exchange some of her knowledge with other team members.[10] In this case, if one member of a knowledge production team can obtain and absorb the knowledge of other team members, she has an incentive to expropriate that knowledge for her own use or to 'leak' it to competitors, eliminating the monopoly on that knowledge that the team might otherwise possess. In other instances, knowledge will require 'complementary' assets to be commercialized, such as manufacturing equipment or marketing expertise (Teece, 1986). Here, the owner of the proprietary knowledge must typically exchange it with the owner of the complementary assets for commercialization to proceed. For example, a scientist must reveal some of his research findings to a venture capitalist to obtain funding for development research. Again, there is an opportunity for the owner of the complementary asset to expropriate the knowledge for her own use and benefit.

Given the considerable limitations to intellectual property and trade secrets protections, and their costs, it may be more effective and more efficient to conduct knowledge transactions within firms than across markets, where legal protections are the only protections that are broadly available and enforceable.[11]

FIRMS AND KNOWLEDGE PROTECTION

Transaction-costs economics suggests that a firm may have three types of advantage relative to markets for managing, or 'governing,' knowledge transactions. First, by unifying ownership of knowledge and other assets within a firm, the incentives of the contracting parties can be better aligned, attenuating incentives for opportunistic behavior. Second, a firm can substitute an employment contract for a market contract for human capital services, increasing the scope of control over knowledge workers' actions and/or reducing the costs of such control by replacing legal contracting with managerial fiat. Third, a firm can

---

[10] Examples of team production of knowledge are scientific discovery teams, product design teams; strategic planning teams; and consulting teams.

[11] It is possible that 'social networks' may provide some protection against expropriation or imitation in knowledge transactions in some specialized circumstances, such as exchange of valuable knowledge within certain professional networks. For an example, see Liebeskind *et al.* (1996).

alter the futurity of rewards relative to market contracts, thereby reducing employee mobility.

Incentive Alignment and Knowledge Protection

In general, market contracts that govern exchanges of goods and services are costly to write and enforce (Coase, 1937; Klein, 1980). Consequently, such contracts are typically 'incomplete': some terms and conditions of the anticipated exchange are left uncontracted, subject to later negotiation between the parties (Williamson, 1979). These uncontracted dimensions of the exchange, which are in essence property rights, are called 'residual rights of control' (Grossman and Hart, 1986; Hart and Moore, 1990). When residual rights of control accrue to separate parties, these parties may have incentives to use them in their own favor, motivating self-interested and even opportunistic behavior. When the ownership of the assets involved in a transaction is unified within a single firm, instead, the firm becomes the sole owner of the residual rights, allowing these rights to be administered by a single managerial hierarchy.

In the traditional 'incomplete contracting' situation, residual rights of control can earn 'quasi-rents' when an exchange is characterized by specific asset investments (Klein, Crawford, and Alchian 1978; Grossman and Hart, 1986). In the case of knowledge transactions, however, the nature of the contracting problem is different: it resides in the fact that many types of valuable knowledge cannot be defined as property under the law. This *lack of contractability* then creates incentives for parties to knowledge exchanges to expropriate uncontractable but valuable knowledge from one another. Consider, for example, the case of two scientists who are involved in a joint research project aimed at discovering a new patentable substance.[12] In the course of this research, the two must exchange their research findings with one another for the project to progress. However, prior to the issue of a patent, neither scientist can legally protect their knowledge against expropriation by the other. Meanwhile, each scientist has a strong financial incentive to expropriate the other's knowledge and gain sole patent rights. Knowing this, the two scientists will rationally restrict the amount of knowledge they share with each other, and the success of the research project will be jeopardized. However, if the two scientists form a jointly owned firm together with a third party to conduct the project, and agree in advance to invest all intellectual property stemming from the collaboration in the firm, their incentives to expropriate unprotected knowledge from one another are attenuated.[13] In essence, the firm converts uncontractable property interests into contractable corporate ownership interests that can be monitored and enforced through the

---

[12] This example is drawn from a real-life situation.

[13] Note that in this case the third party is acting to retain residual rights of control for the benefit of the firm (vs. other parties), rather than allocating them as in the usual arguments (e.g., Grossman and Hart, 1986).

courts by the interested third party owner, as well as the two scientists themselves. Similar considerations apply to knowledge transactions with owners of complementary assets; in this case, the firm can also constitute a credible gain-sharing contract between the parties.[14] Thus, internalization of knowledge transactions within a firm can extend protection of knowledge where legal protections are absent or are costly to write and enforce because incentives to expropriate are reduced.[15] Essentially, firms create quasi-property rights in knowledge. I call these quasi-rights 'possession rights.'

Employment and Knowledge Protection

A second institutional capability that allows firms to protect knowledge is their ability to write employment contracts—be they formal, written contracts or unwritten contracts. When an individual becomes an 'employee,' she is agreeing, contractually, to obey the orders of her employer. Thus, a primary feature of an employment contract is rules—rules that pertain to the duties to be performed, the reporting hierarchy, and a myriad other items. Through such rules, a firm can restrict the actions of an employee in ways that would not be permitted in a market contract for human capital services (Masten, 1988). Thus, employment supports the enforcement of possession rights to knowledge. Two types of rules are particularly important in relation to knowledge protection: employee conduct rules, and job designs.

Employee Conduct Rules

A number of commonly found employee conduct rules serve to reduce the mobility of employees, and thereby reduce the mobility of the knowledge they possess. First, most employment contracts stipulate that a full-time employee must work exclusively for the employer in question for the duration of her employment. This restriction would be considered anti-competitive in a market contract, as it would prevent a worker from practicing her trade freely and may result in market foreclosure. Second, employment contracts frequently contain confidentiality or nondisclosure clauses, whereby the employee agrees in writing not to discuss the business of a firm with outsiders, and even with

---

[14] Incentives to expropriate in this case may be attenuated by competition for inventions (Anton and Yao, 1994).

[15] One interesting question I do not have space to explore here is: when will knowledge workers from firms themselves (as in the case of the two scientists), and by implication, hire capital and management as they need, and when will the owners of capital hire knowledge workers? This is a bilateral bargaining game. Thus, theory suggests that owners of highly valuable knowledge will be able to hire capital and will collect the rents to their own knowledge, whereas workers who use the knowledge of a firm will be hired by management and capital, who will garner the rents. For a discussion of this issue in relation to corporate ownership, see Blair (1995).

other employees. In market exchanges, such broad confidentiality agreements may also be considered anti-competitive, and are likely to be considered as infringing rights to privacy and to free speech (Alderman and Kennedy, 1995). Third, a firm can demand that an employee conduct her work in a particular place within its premises (and not enter other areas of its premises), and that the employee communicate with, and report to, particular other employees (and not communicate with other specific employees). Finally, a firm may write an employment contract that contains a 'non-compete' clause that forbids an employee from working for a competitor for a given period of time after leaving the firm.

Firms may also have lower costs of monitoring and enforcing such conduct rules. In market transactions, one party to a contract has only limited rights to monitor the activities of another. Within firms, rights to monitor are far more extensive: a firm can legally monitor its employees' telephone conversations, e-mail communications, and mail; use visual monitoring systems; and monitor and search individuals who enter and exit its premises.[16] In addition, requiring that work be conducted in a particular place and with particular others reduces the costs of monitoring employee actions: it is far more difficult and costly to monitor employees when they work alone, or in unsupervised premises.

With regard to enforcement, legal protections for knowledge can only be prosecuted once incontrovertible proof of expropriation is available. Within firms, instead, employees may be sanctioned for actions that merely appear to increase the chance that expropriation may take place. For instance, an employee can be dismissed for visiting another firm's premises without permission, without any evidence indicating that she imparted valuable information during the visit. In addition, violations of intellectual property rights and trade secrets laws must be prosecuted through the courts—an expensive, lengthy, and public process. Instead, firms can resolve disputes that pertain to internal transactions of knowledge at low cost, rapidly, and in privacy. While dismissal is a less severe sanction than being convicted of a crime, dismissal nonetheless can have severe economic consequences, and therefore may serve as a sufficient deterrent to expropriation in many circumstances. Indeed, the reduced costs of monitoring and enforcing restrictions within a firm may alone justify internalizing knowledge transactions.

One example of a firm that makes extensive use of employee conduct rules to protect its knowledge from competitors is Proctor & Gamble (P&G): the firm's management forbids its employees to discuss business in public places where they may be overheard; forbids its plant managers from belonging to industry associations; and even forbids employees from tagging their luggage to indicate that they work for the company, for fear that this will attract unwelcome attention (Swayse, 1994). However, less draconian restrictions are a common feature of firms' employee conduct rules. For instance, most firms restrict their employees from discussing important company business with outsiders.

[16] These statements are generalized. In some jurisdictions, firms have more extensive rights to monitor employees than in others.

Job Design

Many security systems follow a design in which access to valuable knowledge can only be obtained when a number of subsystems have been put in place. Consider the simplest of all security systems, a safe. Here, a person who wants to open the safe must (a) know where the safe is located; (b) know what it contains; (c) have access to the place where the safe is located; and (d) possess a key to the safe, or have other means of opening it. By compartmentalizing this information in some way, theft can be more effectively prevented. For instance, a person may illegally obtain the key to the safe, but have no idea where it is located. Almost all types of security architecture are characterized by such 'disaggregation.'[17]

Within a firm, disaggregation can be achieved by adjusting job designs. Consider, for example, the team production of a highly valuable software program. If knowledge protection were not an issue, this program might best be produced by four programmers working in close collaboration. However, this job design would allow all four workers access to the final product. The firm can reduce this number to one by mandating that the four programmers work separately on different subcomponents of the system, and by having their work supervised and integrated by a single manager. The key advantage of the firm here is that it can mandate job specialization and enforce it through the employment contract. Parties to market contracts cannot credibly commit to such specialization, because they have incentives to acquire and expropriate the knowledge of others.

Disaggregation of tasks in this way is a common feature of many firms (and other organizations) that possess highly valuable knowledge. For instance, in defense contracting, the production of defense systems (such as aircraft, rockets, missiles, or satellites) is frequently disaggregated. Thus, employees of a division providing some part of an intelligence-gathering satellite system will receive incomplete blueprints and will not be a party to meetings that discuss the satellite's overall design.[18] Similarly, laboratory technicians in a pharmaceutical firm will be given a substance to test without being given information about its therapeutic properties.[19] Note that this disaggregation of tasks will require the concomitant disaggregation of the firm's production technology. For example, an assembly operation may be divided into separate stages to limit observation of the complete process. Task disaggregation efforts can also be reinforced by spatial isolation: valuable knowledge-production or knowledge-use processes can be located far away from the other activities of a firm, or from outsiders. Thus a well-known software firm has located its new product development department in a remote area of Oregon, while the premises of Lockheed's famous 'Skunk

---

[17] Disaggregation has developed to its highest level within the government security establishment; organizations such as the Central Intelligence Agency and the Executive Offices of the U.S. Government have very sophisticated systems of disaggregation established for the purpose of protecting sensitive knowledge. See, for example, Andrew (1995).

[18] Information provided to the author in interviews.

[19] Information provided to the author in interviews.

Works' are closed to all but Skunk Works employees (Rich and Janos, 1994); other Lockheed workers are excluded.[20]

A firm's hierarchy also serves to disaggregate knowledge. For instance, information on takeovers, mergers, and other sensitive business negotiations is typically restricted to managers who work in the corporate office. To the degree that upper echelon managers have worked for a firm for a long time, so that their personal characteristics are known, this hierarchical knowledge structure can be designed to conform with the established trustworthiness of the managers involved (Luhman, 1988; McCleod and Malcolmsen, 1988).

Reordering Rewards and Knowledge Protection

A third institutional capability that may allow a firm an advantage in protecting knowledge relates to their ability to reorder rewards over time. In markets, the owner of a property can sell that property freely at any time she wishes, provided the property is unencumbered by other claims. In particular, an individual is free to sell her human capital services to any buyer that she wishes at any point in time. This right to sell is particularly problematical in relation to knowledge protection. Because knowledge—and most particularly, legally unprotected knowledge—resides in the heads of individuals, an individual who possesses valuable knowledge always has an incentive to sell her knowledge to the highest bidder, most especially by leaving a firm and going to work for a rival.

An employment contract can place only limited restrictions on an employee's freedom to leave the firm. However, because a firm is a long-lived institutional form, a firm may be able to increase an employee's costs of leaving by deferring the timing at which an individual receives payments for her knowledge—so-called 'golden handcuffs' (Milgrom and Roberts, 1992). These deferred rewards include deferred stock options; pension plans with delayed vesting; and promotions over time. All these arrangements impose exit costs on employees (Milgrom and Roberts, 1992).[21]

---

[20] Before the advent of the corporate form, craft guilds operated as 'quasi-firms' in protecting the production of silk and other fine crafted goods in Italy and elsewhere. Exclusion from observation played a key role in protecting these crafts. For example, in the early seventeenth century, the London Pewterer's Company sanctioned 'divers of the company who worketh openly in shoppes'. (Welch, 1902: 34). The company forced one of its members to erect a partition in his shop to conceal the practice of his craft from passersby. Only apprentices, the equivalent of employees of the guild, were allowed to discover the 'secrets' of the guild's manufacturing processes (Greif, Milgrom, and Weingast, 1994).

[21] The question arises why scientists should accept such contracts. The answer is, because they know that these contracts protect the knowledge of the firm, and so increase their own wealth in the long-run. These contracts are therefore incentive compatible. For a discussion of the role of firms in resolving individual preference inconsistencies over time, see Postrel and Rumelt (1994).

It is important to note that deferred rewards will reduce employee mobility only to the degree that the firm can commit to paying them in future periods. For instance, a deferred stock option will only serve as an inducement to stay with a firm if the stock value of the firm is expected to appreciate more over time than that of its rivals. Similarly, expectations of promotion within a given firm must be more attractive than those of rival firms. Thus, deferred reward schemes will be more credible when the firm offering them is financially stable; when the firm is committed to not laying off its employees; when the firm hires only from within (thereby protecting promotion prospects); and when the firm is protected from takeover.[22]

By providing credible long-term incentives, a firm also increases the incentive for an employee to invest in forming personal relationships with other employees, thereby increasing the likelihood that an employee will become emotionally attached to other employees or to the organization as a whole. These attachments will also increase the employee's costs of exit (Bowlby, 1969; Abt, 1988). Although these mechanisms of attachment are second-order effects that depend on expectations of long-lived employment, they may nonetheless play a critical role in inhibiting employee mobility. Long-term employment also allows management to observe the behavior of an employee over a long period of time, and better determine their trustworthiness (Luhman, 1988; McCleod and Malcolmsen, 1988).

Finally, long-term employment increases an employee's exposure to a firm's acculturation mechanisms. Firms can influence employees' attitudes in numerous different ways, such as advocating certain personal values or attitudes (e.g., loyalty to the firm), and providing social rewards to individuals who demonstrate certain desirable behaviors (e.g., maintaining confidentiality). Attempts to influence attitudes are more effective, the longer an individual is exposed to them, and the less that individual is exposed to countervailing influences (Cialdini, 1984; Simpson, 1994). Long-term employment serves both these ends.

The Costs of Knowledge Protection

While firms may be able to protect knowledge from expropriation and imitation more effectively than markets, all of the protective capabilities discussed in this section have their costs. The most important of these are increases in sunk costs, increases in administration costs, and the costs of loss of communication.

Any investment in a firm-specific asset is a sunk cost. Thus, if these investments cannot be amortized over the expected useful life of the asset in question, they will increase a firm's costs of doing business. Investments in knowledge protection infrastructure are particularly susceptible to obsolescence, because out-

---

[22] One effective protection from takeover is having a large proportion of shares owned by employees (Blair, 1995). Thus, there is a close relationship between ownership structure and credible, high-powered, deferred rewards.

siders have incentives to circumvent the protections they offer. For instance, a computer protection system may be rapidly compromised by advances in code-breaking technology. Similarly, an investment in a secret research facility in a remote location will become worthless when a competitor firm moves into the same area. However, arguably the most important source of sunk costs in terms of knowledge protection is employment: commitments to employ knowledge workers for long periods of time have high direct costs, relative to short-term contracting. These commitments also have high indirect costs in the form of reduced flexibility. Because commitments to existing employees must be upheld to maintain credibility in the future, a firm cannot simply lay off some workers and hire others should its employment needs change. As a result, when the knowledge required to conduct a business successfully changes rapidly from period to period, the costs of internalizing knowledge workers may become prohibitive (Teece, 1986, 1992).

Internalization of knowledge transactions will also necessarily incur costs of organization, both direct and indirect. For instance, monitoring employee conduct rules may not only require a firm to install costly monitoring technologies of various kinds; it may also de-motivate employees, and lead to difficulties in hiring and retention (Strickland, 1958; Deci and Ryan, 1985; Liebeskind, 1995).

Finally, many of the mechanisms that serve to protect knowledge transactions within a firm do so by impeding communication (Liebeskind, 1995). Such a loss of communication can, however, be very costly. First of all, communication enhances coordination: recent evidence from such organizational innovations as concurrent engineering and product design teams show that teamwork significantly increases innovation, productivity and speed-to-market. (See, for example, Allen, Lee, and Tushman, 1980; Hayes and Clark, 1988; Eisenhardt, 1989; Jelinek and Schoonhoven, 1990; Henderson and Cockburn, 1994; Adler, 1995.). Therefore, if communication is impeded by protection considerations, productivity and speed-to-market can be expected to fall. Indeed, communication of knowledge is considered so important to the achievement of these strategic goals that much of the existing literature on knowledge management within firms (e.g., Nonaka, 1994; Spender, 1994) and within strategic alliances (e.g., Grant, 1995, 1996) places primary emphasis on improving communication of knowledge.

Second, communication may increase a firm's access to new knowledge. In many industries, new knowledge arises from a variety of different sources, such as university research laboratories; small research or design firms; or individual experts outside the firm. Firms in these industries may need to be able to access these external sources of knowledge in order to stay abreast of the competition (Von Hippel, 1988; Foray, 1991; Teece, 1992; Saxenian, 1994; Liebeskind et al., 1996). However, accessing external sources of knowledge may require the firm to reveal some of its own valuable knowledge (e.g., Schrader, 1991). For instance, a pharmaceutical firm that sponsors a university professor to conduct research on its behalf may need to provide that professor with some proprietary information or research materials for the research to progress. Similarly, if the firm wants the professor to provide advice on one of its internal research programs, that advice will be more valuable if the professor is given more detailed information.

Finally, the value of a firm's knowledge itself may depend on the degree to which that knowledge is communicated to outsiders. In particular, publication of new, private knowledge exposes it to the rigors of 'social proof,' providing a comprehensive and unbiased test of its validity (Kuran, 1993; David, 1992). Impeding publication, then, can be costly. For instance, a product design firm may be able to significantly reduce its costs of development by showing early-stage designs to potential customers. Similarly, a manufacturing firm may save many millions of dollars by sharing its process innovation ideas with competitors who may already have tried and failed to implement similar technologies.

DISCUSSION

Synthesis

In this paper, I have argued that firms have generalized institutional capabilities that may allow them to protect knowledge from expropriation and imitation more effectively than the limited and costly legal protections than are available in markets. These capabilities and their consequences for knowledge protection are summarized in Table 11.2. However, I have also argued that it is costly for a firm to protect its knowledge. Thus, the costs and benefits of protection must be weighed very carefully.

TABLE 11.2 The Institutional Capabilities of Firms and Their Implications for Knowledge Protection

Institutional capability	Knowledge protection benefits relative to market contracting
1. *Incentive alignment*	Extends the scope of control over knowledge, transactions to include residual rights and their associated rewards Reduces the cost of negotiating and enforcing rights
2. *Employment* (a) Employee conduct rules	Extend the scope of control over individuals' actions Reduce employee mobility, reducing the mobility of knowledge and increasing the effectiveness of employee monitoring
(b) Job designs	Allow for protection of knowledge through disaggregation and the coordination of disaggregated production
3. *Re-ordering*	Increasing futurity of incentives reduces employee mobility

First of all, firms must resolve the question of *what knowledge should be protected and what should not*. Because knowledge protection is costly, over-protection will incur excess costs. Thus, to economize, firms should only protect their unique, valuable knowledge which can repay the costs of protection; other knowledge should not be protected. However, exactly what knowledge of a firm is valuable to that firm may be difficult to discern, especially in the early stages of knowledge creation. Once knowledge has been commercialized processes or products, its value may be more easily ascertained.

The second critical question for a firm is *what mechanism or combination of mechanisms should be used to protect its valuable knowledge*. Using too many protective measures at the same time will incur excess costs; insufficient protec-tion, on the other hand, may result in significant losses of value. Moreover, some mechanisms will be more effective than others, depending on the particular cir-cumstances of the firm. Because protection may inhibit the very knowledge flows that are essential for innovation to take place, firms also may need to make dif-ficult trade-off decisions between protection on the one hand, and innovation on the other. This 'innovation—protection trade-off,' however, may be more or less stark, depending on the protective mechanisms used.

Consider, for example, a new biotechnology firm (NBF). This firm is con-ducting business in a rapidly, evolving technological environment biotechnol-ogy—where the sources of innovation are diffuse, research costs are high, investment funds are limited, and there are many competitors (Liebeskind *et al.*, 1996). For these new firms, sourcing a large part of their knowledge from uni-versity scientists can economize on R&D costs and may increase their chances of making a new discovery by allowing them access to star scientists (Zucker, Darby, and Brewer, 1994; Liebeskind *et al.*, 1996). In conducting these external exchanges of knowledge, however, an NBF increases the likelihood that its own knowledge will be expropriated or exposed to observation, more particularly so because university scientists are acculturated and motivated to publicize their research findings. For instance, Werth (1995) describes how scientists at one NBF, Vertex, struggled over the issue of collaborating with an external scientist, Stuart Schreiber of Harvard University:

> The combination of Schreiber's personality and ambition posed [an] immedi-ate threat. . . . Schreiber loved to talk about himself and what he was think-ing, and how he had the world's ear. 'I am not concerned that Stuart will find a compound that will compete with ours' Boger [Vertex's CEO] said. 'I am concerned he may tell everyone in the world what we're doing.'. . . Boger feared that Schreiber was persistently naive about the need for secrecy. (Werth, 1995: 71)

Thus, NBFs must manage external access to their valuable knowledge very carefully. First of all, these firms have rules regarding presentations at profes-sional meetings and journal publications that are aimed at restricting dissemi-nation of their most valuable research findings (Hicks, 1995; Rabinow, 1996). NBFs also restrict outsiders' use of their research materials (Eisenberg, 1987; Werth, 1995; Rabinow, 1996). However, an NBF must exchange some information and research materials in order to advance its own scientific research and to fulfill norms of reciprocity within the scientific community (Eisenberg, 1987; Schrader, 1991). Thus, NBFs also typically offer very high-powered deferred incentives to their employee scientists, which motivate them to act in the long-term interests of the firm when conducting research collaborations with outsiders.

Where the costs of communication loss with outsiders are lower, a firm may depend more on employee conduct rules and adjustments to use rights to protect its valuable knowledge. Consider, for example, the investment firm, D. E. Shaw & Co. (Welsh, 1996):

> Shaw's penchant for secrecy is legendary. . . . To make sure that nothing gets out that isn't supposed to get out, Shaw has all his employees sign nondisclosure agreements, and these gag orders do their job well. . . .
>
> The secrecy is understandable when it comes to the firm's proprietary technology—what Shaw calls 'our life's blood.' Shaw's market-beating [security-trading] algorithms are so secret, even limited partners [in the firm] such as Morgan Miller . . . aren't entirely sure what's going on behind the curtain. (Welsh, 1996: 1 10)

While the basic argument of this paper has been that firms are able to protect knowledge more effectively, or protect knowledge at lower costs, than legal protections, there may be situations where legal protections are more effective or less costly than internalization. For instance, if a process is patentable, patenting may prove less costly than using a firm's institutional capabilities, so long as patent rights are sufficiently broad that the entire process is protected, and so long as a firm expects to develop a new process before patent rights expire. Patent rights will play a particularly important role in protecting knowledge that is embedded in a firm's products, because this knowledge must perforce be publicized, if the products are to be sold to a broad market.[23] In other cases, combining firm protections with legal protections may outperform the use of one or the other. For instance, a firm may deliberately file for a patent on part of a valuable process technology, and use various organizational arrangements to conceal the other parts of the technology from its competitors.

Finally, while the discussion here has focused on identifying some general institutional capabilities of firms, it is important to note that these capabilities are highly dependent on the legal regulatory context in which a firm operates. For instance, in some jurisdictions, a firm may be able to control the actions of its employees more extensively than in other jurisdictions. Similarly, noncompete and confidentiality clauses may be more binding in some jurisdictions than in others. In some jurisdictions, protections may be weak; in others, enforcing legal protections may be prohibitively costly, or there may be a lack of effective enforcement institutions. We should expect to observe that the scope of firm will

---

[23] There are instances where a firm will restrict sales of its products to reduce the chance of expropriation or imitation. Such restriction is most feasible when products are customized.

vary according to such differences. Specifically, in a legal-regulatory context where legal protections are narrow, enforcement costs are high, or enforcement mechanisms are weak, we should expect to observe more knowledge transactions carried out within firms concomitantly, where legal protections are more broad reaching, enforcement costs are relatively low, and enforcement mechanisms are strong, we should expect to observe more knowledge transactions carried out through contracting between firms or individuals.

Implications

The argument that firms can protect knowledge from expropriation or imitation more effectively than market contracting has a number of important implications for strategy theory and research. First of all, it has implications for the strategic theory of the firm. According to Bowman (1974) and Rumelt (1984, 1987), firms' primary purpose is to create, exploit and defend sources of economic rents. The managerial strategies of firms, then, can be understood as representing rent-seeking behavior, directed both at innovation—the discovery or creation of new processes and products—and at the discovery or creation of 'isolating mechanisms' that serve to protect a firm's innovations from expropriation or imitation by rivals (Rumelt, 1984). The argument in this paper suggests that a firm's own organization is a critically important isolating mechanism. I have argued that firms can both extend the scope of knowledge protection, and/or reduce the costs of such protection, relative to legal protections. Thus, firms are able to replace the limited and costly property rights in knowledge with far more extensive possession rights.

Although this argument is generated by appealing to the generalized institutional capabilities of firms, it is important to note that *it is only because firms have these generalized protective capabilities that we observe so many different types of unique assets.* If all knowledge were rapidly and costlessly imitable, no firm would possess unique assets outside those whose protection were provided by laws of property definition and protection, or which were inherently very difficult to imitate. However, by deploying their generalized institutional capabilities, firms can ensure that knowledge that arises within their organizational boundaries—be it arrived at through luck, history, or deliberate investment remains their own, unique asset for extended periods of time. In this way, my argument provides a clear link between the generalized institutional capabilities of firms on the one hand, and the unique capabilities and resources of any given firm on the other.

Of course, not all firms may be equally competent at deploying their institutional capabilities to protect their knowledge. Just as some firms may be more efficient at coordinating knowledge flows, some firms may also be more efficient than others at impeding knowledge flows to rival firms. Thus, one reason we would expect to observe differences in profits among firms is that firms have differences in their protective capabilities.

The argument presented here also has implications for dynamic strategic behavior by firms. Incentives to invest in innovation—be it process innovation aimed at earning Ricardian rents or product innovation aimed at earning monopoly rents—depend on the degree to which a firm can appropriate the expected rent streams. Thus, because firms can protect their knowledge from expropriation and imitation, it can be understood that *it is the generalized institutional capabilities of firms that engender and promote strategic innovation.*

We should also expect to observe higher rates of innovation in those firms that have superior organizational capabilities in terms of knowledge protection. However, innovation and protection will only be correlated to the degree that a firm can devise organizational arrangements that resolve the innovation–protection trade-off. To the degree that these organizational arrangements are difficult and costly to identify, and to the degree that they can themselves be protected from expropriation or innovation, firms with these arrangements in place will also earn Ricardian rents. Thus, over time, we should expect to observe firms investing in generating organizational arrangements that promote innovation on the one hand, while protecting innovative outputs on the other.

Finally, by describing the mechanisms that firms can use to protect knowledge, this paper provides some concreteness to Teece's (1986) argument that, if knowledge can only be commercialized when it is combined with complementary assets, it will be more valuable when it is commercialized within a firm. Argyres (1996) provides evidence that appropiability considerations influence internalization. More generally, we observe relatively little industrial R&D being conducted in R&D-specialized firms; most industrial R&D is conducted within the boundaries of vertically integrated firms.[24] The argument here also suggests that *managing* knowledge within strategic alliances may be particularly problematical, unless the alliance can be structured in a way that obviates the parties' incentives to expropriate knowledge from one another.

CONCLUDING REMARKS

While this paper has focused on the relationships between knowledge, strategy, and the theory of the firm, issues of knowledge protection have broad implications for strategy theory and research, as I have attempted to illustrate in this final section. Moreover, knowledge protection is likely to become an increasingly important issue to our field. There is a widespread consensus that we are moving towards an economy where competitive advantage will be determined by knowledge rather than by access to raw materials and cheap labor. In this econ-

---

[24] One possible exception is NBFs. However, many NBFs are becoming vertically integrated over time, either through the acquisition of complementary assets themselves (e.g., Amgen), or through partial or complete mergers with large pharmaceutical firms that possess such assets (e.g., Genentech's acquisition by Hoffman LaRoche).

omy, knowledge protection will play a critical role, just as much as innovation. In addition, global expansion has increased many firms' exposure to expropriation and imitation efforts. Within the U.S.A. and other countries, overseas firms (and governments) are becoming increasingly involved in industrial espionage activities. Meanwhile, U.S. and European firms undergoing global expansion are finding that, in many countries, legal protections against expropriation and imitation are extremely weak. Thus, protective organizational arrangements can be vitally important to sustaining competitive advantage in the global competitive context. This paper has taken a first step towards developing some arguments about the protective institutional capabilities of firms. Hopefully, it will serve to stimulate more work on this interesting and economically important topic.

Acknowledgments

Thanks to Nick Argyres, Vai-Lam Mui, Gabriel Szulanski, Todd Zenger, and the Editors of this Special Issue for providing detailed comments on various drafts of this and related papers. Thanks also to Jennifer Bethel, Rajesh Chandy, Timur Kuran, Josh Lemer, Sharon Traweek, and seminar participants at the University of Southern California, the University of California, Irvine, and the University of California, Riverside for useful comments and suggestions. Any errors are mine alone.

REFERENCES

Abt, T. (1988). *Progress Without Loss of Soul*. Chiron Press, Wilmette, IL.

Adler, P. (1995). 'Interdepartmental interdependence and coordination: The case of the design/ manufacturing interface', *Organization Science*, 6, pp. 147–167.

Alderman, E. and C. Kennedy (1995). *The Right to Privacy*. Alfred A. Knopf, New York.

Allen, T., D. M. Lee and M. L. Tushman (1980). 'R& D performance as a function of internal communication, project management, and the nature of work', *IEEE Transactions on Engineering Management*, EM–27(1), pp. 2–12.

Andrew, C. (1995). *For the President's Eyes Only*. Harper Collins, New York.

Anton, J.J. and D.A. Yao (1994). 'Expropriations and inventions: Appropriate rents in the absence of property fights', *American Economic* Review, 84, pp.190–209.

Argyres, N. (1996). 'Some evidence of firm capabilities in vertical integration decisions', *Strategic Management Journal*, 17(5), pp. 395–410.

Arrow, K. (1962). 'Economic welfare and the allocation of resources for invention'. In *The Rate and Direction of Inventive Activity*. National Bureau of Economic Research, Princeton, NJ, pp. 609–625.

Barney, J. (1986). 'Strategic factor markets: Expectations, luck, and business strategy', *Management Science*, 32, pp. 1231–1241.

Barrett, M. (1991). *Intellectual Property*. Smith's Review, Larchmont, NY.

Barzel, Y. (1991). *Economic Analysis of Property Rights*. Cambridge University Press, Cambridge, U.K.

Besen, S. M. and L. J. Raskind (1991). 'An introduction to the law and economics of intellectual property', *Journal of Economic Perspectives,* 5, pp. 327.

Blair, M. (1995). *Ownership and Control: Re-thinking Corporate Governance for the 21st Century.* Brookings Institution, Washington, DC.

Boorstin, D. (1983). *The Discoverers.* Random House, New York.

Bowlby, J. (1969). *Attachment and Loss.* (2 Volumes). Basic Books, New York.

Bowman, E. H. (1974). 'Epistemology, corporate strategy, and academe', *Sloan Management Review,* 15, pp. 35–50.

Cheung, S. (1982). 'Property fights in trade secrets', *Economic Inquiry,* 20, pp. 40–53.

Cialdini, R. (1984). *Influence: The Psychology of Persuasion.* William Morrow, New York.

Coase, R. (1937). 'The nature of the firm', *Economia,* 4, pp. 386–405.

David, P. A. (1992). 'Reputation and agency in the historical emergence of the institutions Of "Open Science"', unpublished manuscript, Stanford University.

Deci, E. and R. M. Ryan (1985). *Intrinsic Motivation and Self-determination in Human Behavior.* Plenum Press, New York.

Demsetz, H. (1967). 'Towards a theory of property rights', *American Economic Review,* 57, pp. 347–359.

Eisenberg, R. (1987). 'Proprietary rights and the norms of science in biotechnology research', *Yale Law Journal,* 97, pp. 177–231.

Eisenhardt, K. (1989). 'Making fast decisions in high velocity environments', *Academy of Management Journal,* 32, pp. 543–576.

Field, B. (1989). 'The evolution of property fights', *Kyklos,* 42, pp. 319–345.

Foray. D. (1991). 'The secrets of industry are in the air: Industrial cooperation and the organizational dynamics of the innovative firm', *Research Policy,* 20, pp. 393–406.

Friedman, D.D., W.M. Landes and R.A. Posner (1991). 'Some economics of Trade Secret Law', *Journal of Economic Perspectives,* 5, pp. 61–72.

Grant, M. (1995). 'A knowledge-based theory of interfirm collaboration', *Best Papers Proceedings.* 55th Annual Meeting of the Academy of Management, Vancouver, Canada, pp. 17–21.

Grant, R. (1996). 'Prospering in dynamically-competitive environments: Organizational capability as knowledge integration', *Organization Science,* 7, pp. 375–387.

Grief, A., P. Milgrom and B. R. Weingast (1994). 'Coordination, commitment and enforcement: The case of the Merchant Guild', *Journal of Political Economy,* 102, pp. 745–777.

Grossman, S. and O. Hart (1986). 'The costs and benefits of ownership: A theory of vertical and lateral integration', *Journal of Political Economy,* 94, pp. 691–719.

Hart, O. and J. Moore (1990). 'Property rights and the nature of the firm', *Journal of Political Economy,* 98, pp. 1119–1158.

Hayes, R. and K. Clark (1988). *Dynamic Manufacturing.* Free Press, New York.

Henderson, R. and I. Cockburn (1994). 'Measuring core competence? Evidence from the pharmaceutical industry', *Strategic Management Journal,* Winter Special Issue, 15, pp. 63–84.

Hicks, D. (1995). 'Published papers, tacit competencies and corporate management of the public/private character of knowledge', *Journal of Industrial and Corporate Change,* 4, pp. 401–424.

Jelinek, M. and C. B. Schoonhoven (1990). *The Innovation Marathon*. Basil Blackwell, Oxford, U.K.

Klein, B. (1980). 'Transaction cost determinants of "unfair" contractual relationships', *American Economic Review*, 70, pp. 356–362.

Klein, B., R. G. Crawford and A. A. Alchian (1978). 'Vertical integration, appropriable rents, and the competitive contracting process', *Journal of Law and Economics*, 21, pp. 271–296.

Kuran, T. (1993). 'The unthinkable and the unthought', *Rationality and Society*, 5, pp. 473–505.

Levin, R., K. Klevofick, R. Nelson and S. Winter (1987). 'Appropriating the returns from individual research and development', *Brookings Papers on Economic Activity*, 3, pp. 783–820.

Liebeskind, J. (1995). 'Keeping organizational secrets: Institutional protective mechanisms and their costs', University of Southern California working paper.

Liebeskind, J. P., A. L. Oliver, L. Zucker and M. Brewer (1996). 'Social networks, learning and flexibility: Sourcing scientific knowledge in new biotechnology firms', *Organization Science*, 7 (forthcoming).

Lippman, S. and R. P. Rumelt (1982). 'Uncertain imitability: An analysis of interfirm differences in profitability under competition', *Bell Journal of Economics*, 13, pp. 418–438.

Luhman, N. (1988). 'Familiarity, confidence, and trust'. In D. Gambetta (ed.), *Trust: Making and Breaking Cooperative Relations*. Basil Blackwell, Oxford, U.K., pp. 94–108.

Mansfield, E. (1985). 'How rapidly does new technology leak out?', *Journal of Industrial Economics*, 34, pp. 217–224.

Masten, S. (1988). 'A legal basis for the firm', *Journal of Law, Economics and Organization*, 4, pp. 3–47.

McCleod, W. B. and J. Malcolmsen (1988). 'Reputation and hierarchy in dynamic models of employment', *Journal of Political Economy*, 96, pp. 832–854.

Milgrom, P. and J. Roberts (1992). *Economics, Organization and Management*. Prentice-Hall, Englewood Cliffs, NJ.

Nelson, R. and S. Winter (1982). *An Evolutionary Theory of Economic Change*. Harvard University Press, Cambridge, MA.

Nonaka, I. (1994). 'A dynamic theory of organizational knowledge creation', *Organization Science*, 5, pp. 14–37.

Penrose, E. (1959). *The Theory of the Growth of the Firm*. Wiley, New York.

Postrel, S. and R. P. Rumelt (1994). 'Incentive, routines, and self-command', *Industrial and Organizational Change*, 3, pp. 397–425.

Rabinow, P. (1996). *Making PCR*. University of Chicago Press, Chicago, IL.

Ricardo, D. (1926 [1821]). *Principles of Political Economy and Taxation*. Everyman, London.

Rich, B. and L. Janos (1994). *Skunk Works: A Personal Memoir of my Years at Lockheed*. Little, Brown, Boston, MA.

Rumelt, R. P. (1984). 'Towards a strategic theory of the firm'. In R. B. Lamb (ed.), *Competitive Strategic Management*. Prentice-Hall, Englewood Cliffs, N.J.

Rumelt, R. P. (1987). 'Theory, strategy, and entrepreneurship'. In D. Teece (ed.), *The Competitive Challenge*. Ballinger, Cambridge, MA, pp. 556–570.

Saxenian, A. (1994). *Regional Advantage*. Harvard University Press, Cambridge, MA.

Schrader, S. (1991). 'Informal technology transfer between firms: Cooperation through information trading', *Research Policy*, **20**, pp. 153–170.

Seidel, A. and R. Panich (1973). *What the Practitioner Should Know about Trade Secrets and Employment Agreements*. American Law Institute, Philadelphia, PA.

Simpson, C. *(1994)*. *Science of Coercion: Communication Research and Psychological Warfare 1945–1960*. Oxford University Press, Oxford, U.K.

Spender, J.-C. (1994). 'Organizational knowledge, collective practice and Penrosian rents,' *International Business Review*, **3**, pp. 353–367.

Spender, J.-C. (1996). 'Organizational knowledge, learning and memory: Three concepts in search of a theory', *Journal of Organizational Change Management*, **9**, pp. 67–79.

Strickland, L. H. (1958). 'Surveillance and trust', *Journal of Personality*, **26**, pp. 200–215.

Swayse, A. (1994). *Soap Opera: The Inside Story of Proctor & Gamble*. Simon & Schuster, New York.

Teece, D. (1980). 'Economies of scope and the scope of the enterprise', *Journal of Economic Behavior and Organization*, **1**, pp. 223–247.

Teece, D. (1986). 'Profiting from technological innovation', *Research Policy*, **15**, pp. 286–305.

Teece, D. (1992). 'Competition, cooperation and innovation: Organizational arrangements for regimes of rapid technological progress', *Journal of Economic Behavior and Organization*, **18**, pp. 1–25.

Von Hippel, E. (1988). *The Sources of Innovation*. Oxford University Press, New York.

Welch, C. (1902). A *History of the Worshipful Company of Pewterers of the City of London*. Blades, East & Blades, London.

Welsh, T. (5 February 1996). 'Extreme investing', *Fortune*, pp. 108–112.

Werth, B. (1995). *The Billion Dollar Molecule*. Simon & Schuster/Touchstone, New York.

Williamson, O. E. (1979). 'Transaction cost economics: The governance of contractual relations', *Journal of Law and Economics*, **22**, pp. 3–61.

Winter, S. (1988). 'Knowledge and competence as strategic assets'. In D. Teece (ed.), *The Competitive Challenge: Strategies for Industrial Innovation and Renewal*. Ballinger, Cambridge, MA.

Zucker, L., M. Darby and M. Brewer (1994). 'Intellectual capital and the birth of U.S. biotechnology enterprises', NBER working paper no. 4653. NBER. Cambridge, MA.

Part Four
Knowledge and Strategy

12

Tacit Knowledge: The Key to the Strategic Alignment of Intellectual Capital

Hubert Saint-Onge

In an environment of shortened business cycles and rapid technological change, the intellectual capital framework represents the primary value-creation dynamics of the firm. It is this focus on the intellectual that has dubbed our times "the knowledge era." At the Canadian Imperial Bank of Commerce (CIBC), we have been working for a number of years to understand the concept of intellectual capital. Our work has led us to a definition of intellectual capital, the exploration of the roles of both explicit and tacit knowledge in the three constituent elements of intellectual capital, and, finally, to the development of ways of encouraging value creation in these elements in support of our business strategies.

INTELLECTUAL CAPITAL DEFINED

A firm's intellectual capital includes three elements:

- Human capital—the capabilities of the individuals required to provide solutions to customers.
- Customer capital—the depth (penetration), width (coverage), attachment (loyalty), and profitability of customers.
- Structural capital—the capabilities of the organization to meet market needs.

From *Strategy and Leadership*, March/April 1996, pp. 10–14. Reprinted by permission.

Hubert Saint-Onge is vice president, Learning Organization and Leadership Development, for the Ontario-based Canadian Imperial Bank of Commerce (CIBC). Mr. Saint Onge's role is to enhance the organization's capability to achieve its business strategies through the development of the CIBC Leadership Centre.

There are two levels of knowledge held within these areas: explicit and tacit knowledge. Explicit knowledge is articulated knowledge—the words we speak, the books we read, the reports we write, the data we compile.

The greater level of knowledge in an organization, however, is tacit—unarticulated. Tacit knowledge includes the intuition, perspectives, beliefs, and values that people form as a result of their experiences. Out of the beliefs and assumptions in our individual mindsets, we make decisions and develop patterns of behavior for everything we do. Our mindsets feed on themselves both positively and negatively—we believe what we see, and we see what we believe.

At the individual level, tacit knowledge forms a mental grid—a unique set of beliefs and assumptions through which we filter and interpret what we see and do. The grid guides our "auto-pilot" and our behavior. It acts like a lens that filters our interpretation and understanding of our personal experiences and communication and places boundaries around our behavior. In this way it delimits our performance and, thus, our results.

In an organization, tacit knowledge is made up of the collective mindsets of everyone in the organization. Out of its experience, the organization assumes a unique set of beliefs and assumptions through which it *collectively* filters and interprets how it sees the world and reacts to it. Based on these beliefs and assumptions, the organization adopts values, principles, and "ways of doing things." Although the collective mindsets of an organization remain largely implicit, or unspoken and taken for granted, they still have a great impact on the collective perceptions and behaviors of the members.

Tacit knowledge shapes the way the leaders of the organization perceive their industry and their firm's place within it; tacit knowledge determines how the organization makes decisions and shapes the collective behaviors of the members.

Tacit knowledge can be both good and bad for an individual or an organization. Holding commonly understood values and assumptions allows us to function quickly and reliably without debating each issue or forming a new process for each action. But when the environment changes or the process becomes inefficient, neither individuals nor organizational leaders may be able to recognize the need for change.

FROM DATA TO WISDOM

The speed of change in this knowledge era requires that we place greater importance on the systemic renewal of the tacit knowledge for the sustainability of the firm. Renewing tacit knowledge means finding ways of making meaning from knowledge. In order to create value in intellectual capital, we must understand how knowledge is formed and how people and organizations learn to use knowledge wisely. Figure 12.1 displays graphically the process of how data are converted to wisdom.

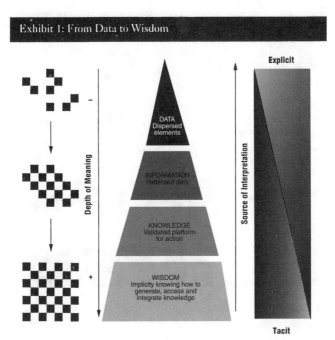

FIGURE 12.1 From Data to Wisdom

Data arrive in our lives and on our desks as dispersed elements. It is only when we compile this data into a meaningful pattern that we have information. As information is converted into a valid basis for action, it becomes knowledge. Upon achieving wisdom, we implicitly know how to generate, access, and integrate knowledge as a guide for action. As individuals and organizations move through the constructs from data to wisdom, their depth of meaning increases and their interpretation shifts from being highly explicit at the data stage to entirely tacit at the point of wisdom.

A firm's tacit knowledge, as embedded in its culture, provides the nodes or entry points through which information is transmitted and processed into knowledge. The collective mindsets making up the organizational culture furnish the filters through which that knowledge is accessed for future application. If we are to have effective communication and the exchange of explicit knowledge within an organizational culture, then we must begin by having at least a minimal level of congruence in tacit knowledge. (See Figure 12.2.) A diversity of individual mindsets is valuable in providing varying perspectives on the business. However, to facilitate knowledge exchange and the most effective strategy development and implementation we must have a level of congruence that allows these individual perspectives to understand one another and to work together toward common goals.

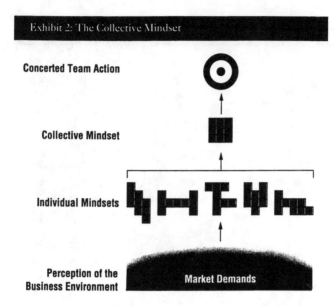

FIGURE 12.2 The Collective Mindset

Tacit knowledge takes a different form in each segment of a firm's intellectual capital:

- In human capital, it is the mindsets of individuals—their assumptions, biases, values, and beliefs.
- In customer capital, it is the individual and collective mindsets of customers that shape their perceptions of value provided by any given products or services.
- In structural capital, it is the collective mindsets of the organization's members that shape the culture of that organization, including its norms and values.

It is extremely important that the tacit knowledge of the three groups be congruent in all aspects that affect the firm's activities. Communication between any of the parties—individual members of the organization, customers, and the organization as a whole—will be disrupted if discontinuities in tacit knowledge exist. As a result, words and concepts in the communication could take on different meanings and lead to counter-productive actions. Aligning some part of the tacit knowledge of these three groups provides pathways along which meaning can be exchanged effectively, and communication will lead to responses that enhance mutual understanding and create an effective platform for partnership.

THE STRATEGY/CULTURE LINK

As shown in Figure 12.3, the structural capital of a firm consists of four elements:

- Systems—the way in which an organization's processes (information, communication, decision-making) and outputs (products/services and capital) proceed.
- Structure—the arrangement of responsibilities and accountabilities that defines the position of and relationship between members of an organization.
- Strategy—the goals of the organization and the ways it seeks to achieve them.
- Culture—the sum of individual opinions, shared mindsets, values, and norms within the organization.

Tacit knowledge has an impact on all four of these elements, but it springs from the organization's culture. Thus, what we are or wish to be as an organization, what we know and understand, and what we must and may do, all combine to create our organizational behavior. (Organizational culture is often insufficiently defined solely by its artifacts, e.g., position titles, office size and location, forms of address, and the presence or absence of specific perquisites. These artifacts—or behaviors—are, in reality, simply a manifestation of the collective values and beliefs held by members of the organization.)

There is a stronger linkage between strategy and culture than is generally assumed. In the beginning, an organization's culture acts as a powerful filter on its perceptions of the business environment and, thus, contributes to the shape of the business strategies that are adopted. Later, when specific strategies are in place, they cannot be successfully implemented if the culture does not shape the organization's behavior in ways that are congruent with these strategies.

The largest barrier to success in implementing change is the lack of fit between strategies and the organization's structures and culture. Organizations often respond to their business environment by adopting new strategies and developing the structures and processes to make them work. Because the

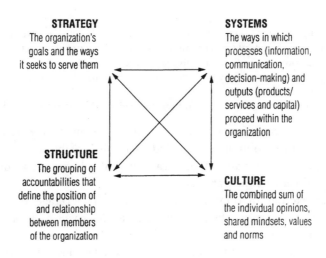

STRATEGY
The organization's goals and the ways it seeks to serve them

SYSTEMS
The ways in which processes (information, communication, decision-making) and outputs (products/services and capital) proceed within the organization

STRUCTURE
The grouping of accountabilities that define the position of and relationship between members of the organization

CULTURE
The combined sum of the individual opinions, shared mindsets, values and norms

FIGURE 12.3 Elements of Structural Capital

"culture" element tends to be more implicit, however, it is usually ignored. Management has relatively little understanding of how to intervene in order to make the necessary culture changes. Ultimately, the competitive advantages meant to be derived from new strategies and the accompanying organizational changes will not be realized if they are not supported by an organizational culture that is appropriately aligned.

The creative tension between the strategic requirements presented by the external environment and the internal capabilities of the organization are the prime engine that drives organizational learning. In order to keep pace with a fast changing business environment, organizations have to continuously regenerate their core strategies. If their strategies are out of phase with the business environment, the enhancement of internal effectiveness will not significantly improve performance, while on the other hand, the adoption of strategies must take into account the capabilities of the organization to implement them.

MANAGING TACIT KNOWLEDGE AT CIBC

The role of the CIBC Leadership Centre is to provide the organization with systematic practices for the generation and renewal of intellectual capital. Our mission is to enhance the capability of the organization to realize its business strategies by enabling managers and teams to fulfill their leadership role in congruence with corporate values in order to better serve our customers.

The renewal of tacit knowledge implies learning. It implies changing mental images in relating to customers, in relating to employees, and in assessing the external environment. Realigning mindsets is an active management process that includes:

- Focusing the organization on the essence of its competitive advantage.
- Motivating the people by communicating the value of the target.
- Leaving room for individual and team contributions.
- Sustaining enthusiasm by providing new operational definitions as circumstances change.
- Consistently using the target and the strategies to guide resource allocation.

The Centre's strategic goals are to build commitment to shared vision and purpose, to enhance communication and ownership of business strategies, to entrench corporate values and shape organizational culture, and to develop core managerial and leadership strategies.

We have found that business teams have the leverage to turn limited resources into great results when management is congruent with defined values, driven by ambitious targets, rooted in reality, and focused on results. Within the organization, it is possible to reshape tacit knowledge through participation in group sessions that systematically surface individually or collectively held assumptions about how to deal with the business, customers, or employees; make explicit the beliefs that underlie these assumptions; and then determine how these beliefs and values may need to change in order to accomplish objectives in the new business environment.

GETTING THERE FROM HERE

In its essence, we believe that in order to manage knowledge—or intellectual capital—we must become better collaborators. The work we have done in trying to understand the deep-seated values of individuals in our organizations tells us that many managers are currently incapable of collaborating because of their mental orientation and their lack of interpersonal skills. They have never been exposed to environments with a level of interdependence that would encourage them to develop the interpersonal skills that collaboration requires.

Collaboration and a skillful exchange of knowledge—an exchange that brings about learning—cannot occur if participants cannot hear and listen actively. They must be able to detect the assumptions of others in a conversation, and they must be able to recognize their own assumptions and understand how these assumptions guide their reactions.

At CIBC, we have put 3,200 managers through a program that is based on changing their mindsets from "If I give them (my employees) half a chance, they'll do something wrong" to "If I give them half a chance, they'll do something right." This program is a building block for cultural change. It is impossible to have effective knowledge exchange in a command and control structure. We all know and understand that fact intellectually, but to go from the cliche to the actual application requires hard work. We strive to find ways of closing the chasm between what people say and what they do.

Our philosophy about making some of these difficult changes is "middle-up-down." We begin with a team of predisposed middle-level managers in a part of the business that is considered strategic to the enterprise. Often, it will not be in a mainstream business because of the greater risk in considering something new. It may be even better to take on a business unit that is experiencing significant problems. We then work with unit management to formulate a plan to systematically transform the business.

This business unit becomes our middle-up-down beachhead and demonstrates how huge strides can be made in bottom-line results when the assumptions that shape the business are aligned with the new realities of the business environment.

So, start in the middle—choose a beachhead. Work with the group on tacit knowledge renewal, explicit knowledge exchange, organizational structure, teamwork, and levels of collaboration. Eventually, senior management will notice and start to ask questions. We create the tension at the middle level, present it to the senior level, and then, with senior management's blessing, we generalize the changes down into the rest of the organization.

At CIBC, we were able to go from a traditional banking culture to what we call the inverted pyramid in 3½ years. Now the business environment has changed and we believe we must move from the inverted pyramid to a partnership culture. We are in the process of generalizing elements of the new culture to align it more closely with the requirements of our evolving business strategies.

Our vision is to create a dynamic forum where everyone is a leader. We will achieve this vision through learning: individual learning at all levels of the organization, team learning that focuses on aligning mindsets and transferring knowledge and skills, organization learning that seeks alignment and facilitates the evolution of our corporate culture toward the full realization of a performance-oriented environment, and customer learning that offers customers an avenue for input on changing needs and an opportunity to become an integral part of our total learning process.

We believe that by understanding tacit knowledge we have found ways to build a dynamic internal cohesiveness that will enhance future performance. In addition, as the organization periodically renews its tacit knowledge, it will maintain the strategic agility required by the knowledge era.

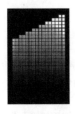

13

Generic Knowledge Strategies in the U.S. Pharmaceutical Industry

Paul Bierly and Alok Chakrabarti

The purpose of this study is to identify groups of firms with similar generic knowledge strategies, determine how these strategies change over time, and compare profit margins of the groups. Knowledge strategies of 21 U.S. pharmaceutical firms are analyzed from 1977 to 1991. Cluster analysis is used to group firms over different time periods based on: (a) balance between internal and external learning, (b) preference for radical or incremental learning, (c) learning speed, and (d) breadth of knowledge base. Our findings indicate that there are four generic knowledge strategy groups: 'Explorers', 'Exploiters', 'Loners', and 'Innovators'. Most firms remain in the same knowledge group over time. The firms in the 'Innovator' and 'Explorer' groups tend to be more profitable than the firms in the 'Exploiter' and 'Loner' groups.

The knowledge-based view of the firm identifies the primary rationale for the firm as the creation and application of knowledge (Demsetz, 1991; Nonaka, 1994; Spender, 1994; Grant, 1996). Performance differences between firms are a result of their different knowledge bases and differing capabilities in developing and deploying knowledge. The management of knowledge can be considered the preeminent dynamic capability of the firm and the principal driver of all other competencies and capabilities (Lei, Hitt, and Bettis, 1996).

Most of the research in this area has investigated the properties of different types of knowledge, in particular the distinction between tacit and explicit

From Strategic Management Journal, Vol. 17, Winter Special Issue, 1996, pp. 123–135. Reproduced by permission of John Wiley & Sons Limited.

Paul Bierly, School of Business Administration, Monmouth University, West Long Branch, New Jersey, USA; Alok Chakrabarti, School of Industrial Management, New Jersey Institute of Technology, Newark, New Jersey, USA.

knowledge, and the relationship between individual and social knowledge (Nonaka, 1994; Spender, 1994). These differences have critical strategic implications not only for innovation but also for barriers to imitation and the sustainability of competitive advantage (Winter, 1987; Kogut and Zander, 1992).

If knowledge and its management are so important a determinant of firm performance, then knowledge strategies are likely to be a critical area of strategic choice for the firm. In this paper we explore firms' choices of knowledge strategies within the U.S. pharmaceutical industry. We look for evidence of generic knowledge strategies within the industry, examining the characteristics of these strategies and their performance consequences.

KNOWLEDGE STRATEGIES

There are several strategic choices that managers make that shape and direct the organization's learning process and, subsequently, determine the firm's knowledge base. Specifically, our review of the organizational learning and related literatures identified four basic tradeoffs that require strategic decisions. These decisions can be either explicitly declared by top management or implicitly implied by their actions regarding the allocation of resources and the establishment of different customs, goals, procedures and incentive systems. (1) Firms need to find the proper balance between internal and external learning (Cohen and Levinthal, 1990. Grant, 1996; Chesbrough and Teece, 1996; Bierly and Hämäläinen, 1995). (2) They need to decide to focus more on either radical or incremental learning (March, 1991; Argyris and Schon, 1978; Lant and Mezias, 1992). (3) The optimal speed of learning needs to be decided (Levinthal and March, 1981; Lounamaa and March, 1987; March, 1991; Herriott, Levinthal, and March, 1985; Volberda, 1996). (4) Firms need to find the proper balance between the depth and breadth of their knowledge base (Leonard-Barton, 1995; Henderson and Cockburn, 1994; Hamel and Prahalad, 1994; Hedlund, 1994). The collective responses to these four strategic choices form what we refer to as the firm's knowledge strategy.

External vs. Internal Learning

A strategic choice for firms is to determine the balance of internal and external learning that best meets their needs and fits their resources. Internal learning occurs when members of the organization generate and distribute new knowledge within the boundaries of the firm. External learning occurs when boundary spanners bring in knowledge from an outside source via either acquisition or imitation and the knowledge is then transferred throughout the organization. An intermediate situation is when learning occurs via some type of strategic alliance where members of the partner organization assist in the transference of knowledge. Focusing more on internal learning will allow the firm to develop its own core competencies and appropriate more profits. For knowledge areas that are fundamentally systemic (complexly integrated with other knowledge areas), firms should focus more on internal learning than external learning so that they have more control over the development process and can better understand the tacit nature of the knowledge (Chesbrough and Teece, 1996). It is very difficult, if not impossible, to acquire knowledge that is mostly tacit from another company.

However, external learning is required for the firm to develop a broader knowledge base and to keep abreast of cutting-edge technologies. Access to a broader knowledge base through external learning increases the flexibility of the firm, which is critical to firms in a dynamic environment (Grant, 1996). Also, internal learning and external learning are mutually interdependent and complementary processes. Cohen and Levinthal (1990) described how firms must excel at internal learning and develop 'absorptive capacity' before they can learn from external sources. Absorptive capacity can be increased by internal R&D in the specific area, production experience, and advanced technical training (Cohen and Levinthal, 1990). On the other hand, the internal learning process can be substantially improved by effective external learning, since there will, obviously, be many new ideas generated outside of the firm. In addition, external learning will enable firms to view some issues from different perspectives, which may be difficult to do with only internal learning due to established organizational routines and biases. Thus, internal and external learning are both vital to the success of the firm and there exists a trade-off between the two. Each firm must determine what is the proper balance between internal and external learning for the firm to maximize its overall learning.

Radical vs. Incremental Learning

Part of a firm's knowledge strategy is to determine the radicalness of its learning. This concept is related to innovation radicalness, which has been discussed by others (e.g., Tushman and Anderson, 1986), but is different in the sense that we are more interested in the radicalness of the learning process than the end product. The issue is whether it is best for the firm to pursue radical learning that questions and changes the firm's basic assumptions (what Argyris and Schon, 1978, refer to as doubleloop learning) or to pursue incremental learning that gradually expands the firm's current knowledge base. Again, the firm faces a tradeoff in the sense that incremental learning, or exploitation of current knowledge, may be most effective in the short run, but radical learning, or exploration, is required to be successful in the long run (March, 1991). Firms that focus too much on exploration typically suffer the costs of experimentation without harvesting many of its benefits; but firms that focus too much on exploitation typically find themselves trapped in suboptimal stable equilibria (March, 1991). However, it is difficult to be successful at both because, besides the fact that there are limited resources, in general, a different type of organizational culture and structure is needed for each of these types of learning. (Volberda, 1996; Hedlund, 1994).

Learning Speed

Firms also need to determine how important it is for them to rapidly learn and apply new knowledge. Implicitly, this decision follows the decision concerning the degree of internal and external learning because, in general, the internal learning process is faster than the external learning process (Bierly and Chakrabarti, 1996). External learning is often slower because (a) there is no internal champion, (b) it may be difficult to interpret and understand the external knowledge, and (c) the 'not invented here' syndrome may be a substantial barrier. Related to determining the importance of learning speed is determining the amount of resources that will be allocated to speeding up both the internal and external learning processes. In general, firms want to maximize learning speed so they can utilize first-in advantages. However, learning too fast and committing oneself to a specific knowledge trajectory may be disastrous if one ends up on the 'wrong branch of the tree' (Levinthal and March, 1981). During a situation where environmental signals are ambiguous and complicate the learning process, it is often better to learn at a slower rate to ensure reliability (Lounamaa and March, 1987; Herriott, Levinthal, and March, 1985). Once a knowledge trajectory is established, it may be difficult to switch to a different trajectory because the firm may be too far behind competitors in the other area and it may be difficult to garner internal support to change, especially if the current learning path has experienced at least moderate success (March, 1991). In addition, slower learning may allow complementary knowledge streams to progress together, allowing for better integration and, in the end, superior collective knowledge.

Breadth of Knowledge Base

The final element of a firm's knowledge strategy is the decision of how broad or narrow the firm's knowledge base should be. With limited resources, it is usually best to focus on specific domains of knowledge (core competencies) so that you can become leaders in those areas. Hamel and Prahalad (1994) illustrated the strategic importance of developing core products and a depth in a few critical knowledge areas. However, with a broader knowledge base the firm will be in a better position to combine related technologies in a more complex manner. According to Reed and DeFillipi (1990), the combining of different technologies creates causal ambiguity, which increases the sustainability of competitive advantages. Also, as Leonard-Barton (1995) has pointed out, if a firm's knowledge base is too narrow, its core capabilities are likely to evolve into core rigidities since the firm lacks the ability to be adaptive to advances in different but related fields. A broader knowledge base results in increased strategic flexibility and adaptability to environmental changes (Volberda, 1996).

In two other studies of the pharmaceutical industry, Henderson and Cockburn (1994) and Pisano (1994) concluded that the ability to integrate different knowledge streams and competence in a discipline are linked to higher performance. Specifically, Henderson and Cockburn (1994) concluded that architectural competence—the skill of integrating a wide range of disciplines—and specific expertise in any of these disciplines provide a source of advantage in drug research productivity. They emphasized that the integration of different knowledge streams is critical both when two internal areas of expertise are combined and when an area of expertise is combined with an external source. Pisano (1994) illustrated the importance of integrating knowledge across different stages of the new drug manufacturing process. A broader knowledge base is integral to the successful integration of different knowledge areas in each of these different examples.

PURPOSE OF STUDY

Organizational configurations assist researchers in understanding the complexity associated with organizations by the identification of distinct sets of firms that demonstrate internal consistency across a variety of areas (Mintzberg, 1990; Miller and Friesen, 1984; Meyer, Tsui, and Hinings, 1993). In the strategic management field, the configurational approach has led to substantial advances by the introduction of generic strategy typologies (e.g., Miles and Snow, 1978; Porter, 1980) strategic archetypes (e.g., Miller and Friesen, 1978), and strategic groups (Caves and Porter, 1977; McGee and Thomas, 1986). Each of these typologies and taxonomies have enhanced the understanding of complex phenomena that would not have been uncovered if the entire industry was analyzed as a whole.

Traditionally, an assumption of the configurational approach is the concept of equifinality (Meyer, Tsui, and Hinings, 1993). However, many researchers have not accepted this notion and have attempted to identify a superior ideal configuration either for all industries or for a unique setting. But studies attempting to link financial performance with the Miles and Snow typology (e.g., Hambrick, 1983; Zajac and Shortell, 1989), the Porter typology (e.g., Miller and Friesen, 1986; White, 1986), and strategic groups (e.g., Cool and Schendel, 1987; Fiegenbaum and Thomas, 1990) have yielded inconclusive and contradictory results.

The purpose of this exploratory study is to empirically derive a generic knowledge strategy taxonomy that is theoretically grounded in the knowledge-based theory of the firm. After identifying distinct knowledge groups, the financial performance of the different groups will be compared to either support or reject the concept of equifinality. In a similar manner that Zajac and Shortell (1989) studied strategic change using the Miles and Snow typology, we will also analyze the stability of the knowledge groups. In general, since firms' organizational cultures and knowledge bases evolve through established learning routines (Bierly and Spender, 1995), firms establish momentum and their flexibility in the way they learn becomes limited by a number of organizational rigidities in many different parts of the organization (Bierly and Chakrabarti, 1997; Miller and Friesen, 1984). However, as Zajac and Shortell (1989) illustrated in their study, the conventional wisdom that strategies are mostly stable may be overstated.

Additional research questions are: Are firms starting in a specific knowledge group or firms changing to a specific knowledge group more able and willing to change than others? Are firms that are more flexible in changing their knowledge strategies more financially successful than firms that are more stable?

METHODS

The present study focussed on the U.S. pharmaceutical industry from 1977 to 1991. We separated the 15-year period into three 5-year periods to see how the clusters changed over time. Aggregate measures for each 5-year period were developed by averaging the measures for each year. This time period was used to ensure a long enough period to smooth out time-related fluctuations. The firms included in the study (a) primarily produce brand ethical drugs (no generic drug producers were included), (b) are U.S. publicly owned companies, and (c) have pharmaceutical sales-account for a substantial portion of company sales. Not all firms were included for the full time-frame due to mergers and acquisitions. Only U.S. companies were studied to control for differences across countries (e.g., different accounting methods).

The pharmaceutical industry was chosen for the following reasons. First, the industry is primarily a knowledge-driven industry. Technological learning is a key determinant of the competitiveness of each of the firms in the industry. External factors, such as changes in the economy or exchange rates, do not affect firm profitability as much as the internal capabilities of the individual firm. Second, most of the corporations in the pharmaceutical industry derive the majority of their revenues from the pharmaceutical industry. Thus, most firm characteristics reflect business level strategic orientations. Third, patent data provide more valid measures in this industry than other industries because of the enforceability of the patents and the lack of secrecy between firms.

Measurements

Financial performance is measured in two ways: return on sales (ROS) and return on assets (ROA), both of which are frequently used measures of financial performance in the strategy literature. The advantages and disadvantages of using ROS and ROA as measures of performance are discussed extensively elsewhere, but it should be noted that both of these financial measures of performance are a narrow conception of performance and do not take into consideration operational (i.e., nonfinancial) measures of performance (Kanter and Brinkerhoff, 1981). The following five independent variables are used to cluster the firms into knowledge groups:

R&D Intensity

The R&D intensity (RDS) of a firm is defined as the ratio of annual R&D dollars spent by the firm and the firm's total sales. R&D intensity is used as our primary input variable to internal learning. However, as Cohen and Levinthal (1990) pointed out, a measure of R&D is not only a satisfactory measure of internal learning, but also a prerequisite for effective external learning because firms must develop a certain degree of internal knowledge (absorptive capacity) so that they can understand, interpret, and apply external information.

Science Linkage

The level of external learning is measured by the average number of patent citations to the scientific literature, or scientific linkage (SCILINK). Patent citation information provides valuable data concerning the flow of information to a firm from external sources (Griliches, 1990). This is particularly true in the pharmaceutical industry, where technical journals have been cited as the most frequently used source for obtaining new information by research scientists in the industry (Sheen, 1992). The more inventions incorporate recent scientific discoveries from outside the organization and are linked to basic science, the more citations a firm will list on its patents (Narin, Noma, and Perry, 1987).

Knowledge Dispersion

The breadth of a firm's knowledge base is measured by using a dispersion index (DISP) that indicates the technological distribution of a company's patents. Specifically, the index is determined by the following equation:

$$\text{DISP} = -\ 1/\ln N \sum_{i=1}^{N} (f_i \times \ln f_i)$$

where f_1 = the fraction of patents in ith category. For example, a pharmaceutical company that is granted patents in several therapeutic areas will have a higher dispersion index than a firm focused primarily in one area. A firm with a higher R&D dispersion index is more flexible because (a) it will be better able to shift focus to different therapeutic areas, and (b) it will be able to better combine knowledge in different therapeutic areas (consistent with Kogut and Zander's, 1992, concept of combinative capabilities and Henderson and Cockburn's, 1994, concept of architectural competence).

Technology Cycle Time

A frequently used measure of learning speed, or technology cycle time (TCT), and a measure that is used in this study, is the median age of the patents cited by a given firm's patents (e.g., Narin, Carpenter, and Woolf, 1984; Bierly and Chakrabarti, 1996). If a firm takes a longer time to incorporate new technologies into its new products or processes, then the average age of its citations will be higher and it will have a higher technology cycle time. On the other hand, if a firm rapidly develops new technologies building on other state-of-the-art technologies, it will have a lower technology cycle time.

Learning Radicalness

Whether a firm preferred radical vs. incremental learning (RAD) is measured by the ratio of New Chemical Entities (NCEs) and approved New Drug Applications (NDAs). An NCE is a new product approved by the FDA that consists of an entirely new molecular formula.[1] NDA includes all new drugs that are approved by the FDA, except biologicals and medical devices. This includes all NCEs, new formulations, new combinations, and new indications (or uses). A firm with high learning radicalness is considered to follow a more highrisk knowledge strategy that attempts to hit more 'home runs' and fewer 'singles'.

Statistical Analysis and Data Sources

Cluster analyses, which were used to classify the firms into different groups based on their knowledge strategy, were carried out using the SPSS for Windows (1994) package. Specifically, we choose the Ward's hierarchical technique of clustering using squared Euclidean distances. All variables were standardized by using Z-scores so that variables with large units would not be overemphasized. The decision concerning how many clusters to use was guided by the agglomeration schedule, which displays the squared Euclidean distances between each case or group of cases combined to form a cluster for each step of the process. Cluster agglomeration is generally stopped when the increase between two adjacent steps becomes large. We stopped cluster agglomeration with four clusters for each of the 5-year time periods.

Measures of financial performance, R&D expenditures and sales for this study came from company annual reports and their 10K forms. Patent data were obtained from CHI Research Inc.'s data bases, which, for the years covered in this study, include all patents listed by the U.S. Patent Office. The data base is internationally recognized as one of the most reliable data bases of its type available. The two measures of new products used in this study, NCE and NDA, are primarily from FDA reports and were compared to the other industry sources to ensure the reliability of data.

RESULTS

Before discussing the differences among knowledge groups for each time period, it is important to identify industry changes that are occurring over the same time period. The most general change in the drug industry is the change

---

[1] New Chemical Entities, a term used by SCRIPT magazine, is a category similar to, but slightly different than the FDA's New Molecular Entity (NME) category. Specifically, NCEs are equal to the FDA's NMEs minus new biologicals and new medical devices. These two measures are almost identical because there are usually only one or two new biologicals or medical devices approved by the FDA each year.

from a trial-and-error method of drug discovery to a rational drug design approach (Office of Technology Assessment, 1993). In the past, a new drug was typically found by looking for chemicals that caused a particular clinical reaction, a process that did not require the researcher to necessarily understand how the drug worked. A rational drug design approach reverses the process in the sense that by studying the specific disease and having knowledge of how the process works, the researchers design drugs that will serve specific functions. This type of drug design requires more general knowledge about how the processes work and the integration of many different knowledge areas.

This general change within the industry, which is a change in the 'industry recipe' (Spender, 1989), has predictable changes on our data, as displayed by the summary data for each time period in Table 13.1. Internal and external learning steadily increase throughout our period of study. The average level of R&D intensity increases from 5 percent in Period 1 to 10 percent in Period 3. Likewise, our average measure of science linkage increases from 0.96 in Period 1 to 2.48 in Period 3, which is a clear indication that there is more transfer of knowledge within the scientific community. In addition, technology cycle time and learning radicalness steadily increase during our period of study, indicating that firms are focusing more on radical new drugs and less on 'me-too' drugs.

Existence of Different Knowledge Groups

The cluster analysis identified several distinct generic knowledge strategies among the pharmaceutical firms. Even though some of the firms shifted to different knowledge groups over time, the general characteristics of each of the groups remained stable. Table 13.1 displays the knowledge strategies for each of the knowledge groups based on our five independent variables for each of the three time periods studied and Table 13.2 displays each knowledge group membership. The Appendix displays the 'tightness' of each cluster (average squared Euclidean distance) and the 'nearness' of clusters (represented by the maximum squared Euclidean distances). The results of test comparisons between the group means of clustering variables found 54 out of a total of 90 group mean differences were significant at the 0.05 confidence level or higher, with each group significantly different than all other groups of the same period. The results of the t-test comparisons strongly support the existence of these different generic knowledge groups. For each of the three time periods, the different knowledge strategies can be summarized as follows.

Knowledge Group 4 can be viewed as the most aggressive learners in the sense that they most effectively combine internal and external learning. These firms have the highest level of internal learning (RDS), are strong in external learning (much higher than the other groups in Periods 2 and 3), focus on both radical and incremental learning, and are one of the fastest learners (lowest TCT). Thus, we label this group the 'Innovator' group, because besides following an aggressive strategy, they appear to have successfully balanced the trade-offs required to be successful, long-term innovators, as outlined in the above discussion.

TABLE 13.1 Variable Means for Cluster Groups and Sample for Each Time Period

	RDS	SCILINK	DISP	TCT	RAD
Period I: 1977–81					
KG1—Explorers	0.04	0.78	0.45	6.67	0.18
KG2—Exploiters	0.03	1.39	0.34	6.46	0.08
KG3—Loners	0.06	0.50	0.12	13.28	0.08
KG4—Innovators	0.08	1.22	0.41	5.34	0.34
All groups	0.05	0.96	0.37	7.26	0.19
Period II: 1982–86					
KG1—Explorers	0.09	1.52	0.45	7.72	0.46
KG2—Exploiters	0.06	1.56	0.50	8.61	0.14
KG3—Loners	0.09	0.37	0.15	11.23	0.21
KG4—Innovators	0.12	3.80	0.38	7.29	0.20
All groups	0.08	1.54	0.40	8.82	0.22
Period III: 1987–91					
KG1—Explorers	0.09	2.59	0.50	8.68	0.51
KG2—Exploiters	0.07	1.52	0.53	8.68	0.14
KG3—Loners	0.07	1.03	0.13	11.46	0.00
KG4—Innovators	0.13	3.80	0.41	8.69	0.29
All groups	0.10	2.48	0.42	9.11	0.23

Knowledge Group 3 can be viewed as mostly ineffective (or isolated) learners in the sense that even though they spend more than the industry average on R&D (except for Period 3), other knowledge indicators point to problem areas. Most importantly, their technology cycle time is much higher than each of the other groups, indicating that they are slow in applying new knowledge, and their science linkage is much lower than all of the others, indicating that these firms remain mostly isolated from the scientific community. In addition, their knowledge dispersion level is very low, indicating they may be too focused in certain areas and not able to integrate different streams of knowledge. We refer to this group as the 'Loners'.

Knowledge Group 2 can be viewed as the 'Exploiters'. The firms in this group spend the lowest amount on R&D, have a high level of science linkage, and have a broad (but shallow) knowledge base. Their priority is clearly on external learning more than on internal learning. Not surprisingly, they focus more on incremental learning, probably mostly improvements on competitors' ideas, and less on the development of radically new products. If they do have success with a breakthrough drug, it can be assumed that these companies would spend great effort in maximizing the benefit from the drug by finding new uses for the drug, combining the drug with other established drugs, and have many variations (e.g., different doses) of the drug. Even though marketing expertise was not analyzed as part of this study, one would expect that firms in this group would be excellent marketers to best exploit their line of drugs, which by looking at the firms in this group in Table 13.2 appears to be the case.

TABLE 13.2 Knowledge Group Membership

'Explorers' KG1	'Exploiters' KG2	'Loners' KG3	'Innovators' KG4
Period I: 1977–81			
Abbott	American Home Prod.	Carter Wallace	Lilly
American Cyanamid	Bristol Myers	Forest	Merck
Johnson & Johnson	ICN	Marion	SmithKline Beckman
Pfizer	Squibb		Syntex
AH Robins			Upjohn
Rorer			
Schering-Plough			
Sterling			
Warner Lambert			
Period II: 1982–86			
Abbott	American Cyanamid	Carter Wallace	Lilly
Merck	American Home Prod.	Forest	Upjohn
Pfizer	Bristol Myers	ICN	
Syntex	Johnson and Johnson	Marion	
	Rorer		
	Schering-Plough		
	SmithKline		
	Squibb		
	Sterling		
	Warner Lambert		
Period III: 1987–91			
Abbott	American Cyanamid	Carter Wallace	Lilly
Pfizer	American Home Prod.	Forest	Merck
	Johnson & Johnson		Schering-Plough
	Warner Lambert		Syntex
			Upjohn

Knowledge Group 1 can be viewed as the 'Explorer' group. The defining characteristic of this group is their very high levels of radicalness in Periods 2 and 3. They are roughly the same as the industry average in each of the other areas, indicating that they maintain a good balance between internal and external learning, just as the firms in Knowledge Group 4, but they are less aggressive learners than those other firms, as indicated by lower levels of R&D and science linkage for every period. However, their limited resources are spent attempting to 'hit the home run' with a new blockbuster drug. As the Appendix indicates, Knowledge Groups 1 and 2 are the most similar for each of the three time periods, and Knowledge Groups 3 and 4 are the most dissimilar.

Profit Differentials of Knowledge Groups

Table 13.3 displays the mean profit margins (ROS and ROA) for each cluster group for each time period. In general, the Innovator and Explorer knowledge groups maintained higher profit margins throughout the period of study and the Loner and Exploiter knowledge groups maintained lower profit margins. The results of t-test comparisons between group means found the following statistically significant differences at the 0.05 confidence level or higher: for Period 1, the Innovator group had significantly higher performance by at least one measure than all of the other three groups; higher performance by at least one measure than the Exploiter and Loner groups; for Period 3, the Innovator group had significantly higher ROS than the Exploiter group. These results, though they are not conclusive, tend to support the assertion that, in the pharmaceutical industry, firms that have a more aggressive knowledge strategy have higher financial performance. This finding emphasizes that, for this industry, a key success factor is the development of new blockbluster drugs, more so than the incremental improvements to current products.

Stability of Knowledge Groups

The analysis of the stability of the knowledge groups is difficult because there are several major industry changes, as noted above. Thus, unless a firm increases internal learning (R&D) and external learning (SCILINK) at a rate of at least as much as the industry average, its learning, relative to its competitors, will be decreasing. Thus, the critical characteristics of the knowledge groups changed over time as each of the groups evolved. Despite these changes, which make it difficult to have comparable knowledge groups in the different time periods, most of the firms remain in the same knowledge group over time. Specifically, 10 of the 20 firms in Period 2 were in the same knowledge group in Period 1 and 10 of the 13 firms in Period 3 were in the same group in Period 2. As expected, most of the movement to different groups is when a firm moves to another knowledge group that is 'close' to it (see the Appendix for squared Euclidean distances). For example, six of the 10 firms that moved between Periods 1 and 2 moved from the Explorer knowledge group to the Exploiter

TABLE 13.3 Group Financial Performance Means for Cluster Groups and Sample for Each Time Period

	ROS	ROA
Period I: 1977–81		
KG1—Explorers	0.09	0.09
KG2—Exploiters	0.06	0.08
KG3—Loners	0.06	0.06
KG4—Innovators	0.14	0.13
All groups	0.09	0.10
Period II: 1982–86		
KG1—Explorers	0.14	0.13
KG2—Exploiters	0.10	0.10
KG3—Loners	0.08	0.07
KG4—Innovators	0.12	0.10
All groups	0.10	0.10
Period III: 1987–91		
KG1—Explorers	0.14	0.13
KG2—Exploiters	0.11	0.13
KG3—Loners	0.15	0.10
KG4—Innovators	0.19	0.16
All groups	0.15	0.14

knowledge group, which are two groups that are 'close' together. This seems to indicate that during this time period these six firms shifted their primary focus from developing radical new drugs to maximizing their return by incrementally improving existing products. However, having this many firms move from one group to another may also be an indicator that the firms were clustered differently for the different time periods.

Despite the above precautions, looking at the stability and shift of firms' knowledge strategy is informative. Table 13.4 illustrates the strategically stable firms within each knowledge area and the firms that have changed their knowledge strategies. In addition, Table 13.4 displays the average adjusted ROS (AROS) for each group, which is defined as the return on sales above or below the industry average for the given time period. Even though this further segmentation has left us with groups with too low a number of firms in each group to analyze formally, several broad trends appear evident. First, firms that remain strategically stable throughout the study appear to be more profitable than firms that change their strategy, with the exception of the group that changes its strategy to become more aggressive learners. This group that has changed its knowledge strategy toward the Innovator category has the highest profit margin of all groups, even higher than the firms that have remained in the Innovator category throughout the study. Second, a large group of firms shifted their strategy from either the Innovator or Explorer group to the Exploiter group. On average, these firms had below average profit margins. Each of these firms have shifted from being one of the more aggressive learning organizations in the industry to a follower. These firms are no longer primarily seeking to create radically new ideas, but instead focus their resources on exploiting their past successes. Third, none of the firms in the Loner group changed their strategy to shift to another more profitable group. Only one firm changed its strategy to become a Loner, and its performance was very poor.

CONCLUSION

The purpose of this study was to initiate exploratory research in the area of knowledge strategies. By extending the knowledge-based theory of the firm and the literature on organizational learning, we outlined the core strategic decisions that comprise a firm's knowledge strategy. Focusing on one industry, the

TABLE 13.4 Knowledge Group Membership

	Strategically stable groups			
	1977–81	1982–86	1987–91	Average AROS[a]
KG1 'Explorers'	Abbott Pfizer	Abbott Pfizer	Abbott Pfizer	0.013
KG2 'Exploiters'	AHP Bristol Myers Squibb	AHP Bristol Myers Squibb	AHP	0.016
KG3 'Loners'	Carter Wallace Forest Marion	Carter Wallace Forest Marion	Carter Wallace Forest	−0.004
KG4 'Innovators'	Lilly Upjohn	Lilly Upjohn	Lilly Upjohn	0.032

	Strategic changes of groups		
Strategic change	Change path	Change path	Average AROS[a]
To 'Exploiter'	KG1 → KG2 → KG2 American Cyanamid Johnson & Johnson Warner Lambert Rorer Sterling	KG4 → KG2 SmithKline	−0.014
To 'Innovator'	KG1 → KG2 → KG4 Schering Plough	KG4 → KG1 → KG4 Merck Syntex	0.055
To 'Loner'	KG2 → KG3 ICN	–	−0.115

[a]Adjusted return on sales (AROS) is defined as the firm ROS minus the industry average ROS for that time period.

U.S. pharmaceutical industry, we quantitatively determined the existence of several different generic strategies in the way firms acquire and generate knowledge, which, for most firms, are stable over a long time period. We labeled these generic knowledge strategies: Innovators, Explorers, Exploiters, and Loners. Our study indicated that in the pharmaceutical industry certain strategies (Innovators and Explorers) are linked to higher profits, and other strategies (Loners and Exploiters) are linked to lower profits. However, the study also indicates that the firms in the less profitable knowledge groups either do not desire or are unable to change their strategies. Most likely, the explanation for this behavior is either that these firms' learning routines have become so ingrained that they have become rigidities and the firms can not change the way they learn, or that these firms lack the resources and capabilities to follow one of the other knowledge strategies.

Of course, the generalizability of these preliminary findings to other industries must be made cautiously until further research of other industries is completed. Logically, our results are most applicable to other knowledge-based industries in dynamic and complex environments (hypercompetitive conditions). We believe the four generic knowledge strategies derived in this study (Innovators, Explorers, Exploiters, Loners) exist in other industries. Examples of firms that follow each strategy readily come to mind: Intel, 3M, Chaparral Steel and WalMart are Innovators; Compaq, Toyota, Honda and many other Japanese firms are Exploiters; Netscape Communications, Ben and Jerry's, and many biotechnology companies are Explorers; Cray Computer Systems, Caterpillar, Kodak and Digital are Loners. There are certainly other possible configurations of our four basic strategic choices concerning knowledge management, but the four combinations which make up these generic knowledge strategies appear to display internal consistency. Each set of decisions appears to mutually reinforce a consistent organizational culture and provide fundamentally different approaches to managing internal and external learning. However, Henderson (1994) has described how in many respects the pharmaceutical industry is exceptional concerning how well the firms learn in a dynamic environment. Unlike many other large companies, they have avoided competency traps and have institutionalized a 'deeper' approach to learning. This is partially due to the unique industry structure and reward system influenced by the drug approval process, the health care system, and the patent system. Thus, firms in this industry may have more clearly defined knowledge strategies than firms in other industries, where some firms may have more haphazard strategies and some firms may follow no strategy at all.

On the other hand, we do not believe the same generic knowledge strategies of the firms in our study that are most highly associated with financial performance will also be the most successful in other industries. For each of our generic knowledge strategies there are examples of firms in other industries that have been successful, and firms that have been unsuccessful. More than one generic strategy may be successful in an industry. Industry characteristics such as the rate of change, the nature of the key technologies, the importance of economies of scale and scope, and the degree of competition will influence the appropriability of profits from an innovation. Also, in some industries the risk associated with failure may be very high, suggesting a more conservative knowledge strategy may be appropriate. Thus, whereas the generic strategies exist in other industries, the characteristics of the industry will determine which strategies are successful.

We believe the development of a dynamic knowledge strategy typology or taxonomy will offer more insight than the basic static strategy typologies developed to date. Other generic strategy typologies, such as Porter's (1980), rely on basic assumptions that are not valid for many industries today. Specifically, they assume that (a) the primary focus of strategy is about the positioning of an end-product within an identifiable industry structure and (b) the industry structure is relatively stable and changes to the environment are mostly incremental, linear changes that do not redefine the product or industry. However, other researchers have observed the preponderance of boundaryless industry structures, hyper-competition, increasing globalization, an increasing rate of technological change and diffusion, and a tremendous increase in access to information through the advances in computers and communications (Bettis and Hitt, 1995; D'Aveni, 1994; Hamel and Prahalad, 1994). The 'static' generic strategy typologies offer little practical value to top managers in determining how to develop a competitive advantage, which is the primary purpose of strategy. Alternatively, a knowledge strategy typology can provide a guide to action for managers and assist them in learning and building their core competencies into sustainable competitive advantages. It can be applied in a turbulent environment, is not constrained to business-unit level of analysis, and can provide guidance for action for firms competing in several related industries, including new emerging arenas. In addition, a generic knowledge strategy typology or taxonomy based on the knowledge-based theory of the firm will have a sound theoretical base, which has not necessarily been the case for other generic strategy typologies.

Acknowledgments

We gratefully acknowledge the helpful suggestions to improve this paper made by J.-C. Spender, Robert Grant, Eric Kessler, Ed Christensen, and Shanthi Gopolakrishnan.

REFERENCES

Argyris, C. and D. Schon (1978). *Organizational Learning: A Theory of Action Perspective*. Addison Wesley, Reading, MA.

Bettis, R. A. and M. A. Hitt (1995). 'The new competitive landscape', *Strategic Management Journal*, Summer Special Issue, 16, pp. 720.

Bierly, P. and A. Chakrabarti (1996). 'Determinants of technology cycle time in the U.S. pharmaceutical industry', *R&D Management,* 26(2), pp. 115126.

Bierly, P. and A. Chakrabarti (1997). 'Technological learning, strategic flexibility, and new product development in the pharmaceutical industry', *IEEE Transactions on Engineering Management,* in press.

Bierly, P. and T. Hämäläinen (1995). 'Organizational learning and strategy', *Scandinavian Journal of Management,* 11(3), pp. 209–224.

Bierly, P. and J.-C. Spender (1995). 'Culture and high reliability organizations: The case of the nuclear submarine', *Journal of Management,* 21(4), pp.639–656.

Caves, R. E. and M. E. Porter (1977). 'From entry barriers to mobility barriers: Conjectural decisions and contrived deterrence to new competition', *Quarterly Journal of Economics,* 91, pp. 241–262.

Chesbrough, H.W. and D. J. Teece (1996). 'When is virtual virtuous? Organizing for innovation', *Harvard Business Review,* 73(3), pp. 65–73.

Cohen, W. M. and D. A. Levinthal (1990). 'Absorptive capacity: A new perspective on learning and innovation', *Administrative Science Quarterly,* 35, pp.128–152.

Cool, K. and D. Schendel (1987). 'Strategic group formation and performance: The case of the U.S. pharmaceutical industry, 1963–1982', *Management Science,* 33, pp. 1102–1124.

D'Aveni, R. A. (1994). *Hypercompetition.* Free Press, New York.

Demsetz, H. (1991). 'The theory of the firm revisited'. In O. Williamson and S. Winter (eds.), *The Nature of the Finn.* Oxford University Press, New York, pp. 159–178.

Fiegenbaum, A. and H. Thomas (1990). 'Strategic groups and performance: The U.S. insurance industry, 1970–1984', *Strategic Management Journal,* 11, (3), pp. 197–215.

Grant, R. M. (1996). 'Prospering in dynamically-competitive environments: Organizational capability as knowledge integration', *Organization Science,* 7(4), pp. 375–387.

Griliches, Z. (1990). 'Patent statistics as economic indicators: A survey', Journal of Economic Literature, 28, pp. 1661–1707.

Hambrick, D. C. (1983). 'Some tests of the effectiveness and functional attributes of Miles & Snow's strategic types', *Academy of Management Journal,* 26, pp. 526.

Hamel, G. and C. K. Prahalad (1994). *Competing for the Future.* Harvard Business School Press, Boston, MA.

Hedlund, G. (1994). 'A model of knowledge management and N-form corporation', *Strategic Management Journal,* Summer Special Issue, 15, pp. 73–90.

Henderson, R. (1994). 'Managing innovation in the information age', *Harvard Business Review,* 72(3), pp.100–105.

Henderson, R. and I. Cockburn (1994). 'Measuring competence? Exploring firm effects in pharmaceutical research', *Strategic Management Journal,* Winter Special Issue, 15, pp. 63–84.

Herriot, S. R., D. Levinthal and J. G. March (1985). 'Learning from experience in organizations', *American Economic Review,* 75, pp. 298–302.

Kanter, R. M. and D. Brinkerhoff (1981). 'Organizational performance: Recent developments in measurement', *Annual Review of Sociology*, 7, pp.321–349.

Kogut, B. and U. Zander (1992). 'Knowledge of the firm, combinative capabilities, and the replication of technology', *Organization Science*, 3(3), pp. 383–397.

Lant, T. K. and S. J. Mezias (1992). 'An organizational learning model of convergence and reorientation', *Organization Science*, 3(1), pp. 47–71.

Lei, D., M. A. Hitt and R. Bettis (1996). 'Dynamic core competencies through meta-learning and strategic context', *Journal of Management*, forthcoming.

Leonard-Barton, D. (1995). *Wellsprings of Knowledge*, Harvard Business School Press, Boston, MA.

Levinthal, D. and J. G. March (1981). 'A model of adaptive organizational search', *Journal of Economic Behavior and Organization*, 2, pp. 307–333.

Lippman, S. A. and R. P. Rumelt (1982). 'Uncertain imitability: An analysis of interfirm differences in efficiency under competition', Bell Journal of Economics, 13, pp. 418–438.

Lounamaa, P. H. and J. G. March (1981). 'Adaptive coordination of a learning team', *Management Science*, 33(1), pp. 107–123.

March, J. G. (1991). 'Exploration and exploitation in organizational learning', *Organization Science*, 2(1), pp. 71–87.

McGee, J. and H. Thomas (1986). 'Strategic groups: Theory, research and taxonomy', *Strategic Management Journal*, 7(2), pp. 141–160.

Meyer, A. D., A. S. Tsui and C. R. Hinings (1993). 'Configurational approaches to organizational analysis', *Academy of Management Journal*, 36, pp. 1175–1195.

Miles, R. and C. Snow (1978). *Organizational Strategy, Structure and Process*. McGraw-Hill, New York.

Miller, D. and P. Friesen (1978). 'Archetypes of strategy formulation', *Management Science*, 24, pp. 921–933.

Miller, D. and P. Friesen (1984). *Organizations: A Quantum View*. Prentice–Hall, Englewood Cliffs, NJ.

Miller, D. and P. Friesen (1986). 'Porter's (1980) generic strategies and performance: An empirical examination with American data. Part 1: Testing Porter', *Organizational Studies*, 7, pp. 37–55.

Mintzberg, H. (1990). 'Strategy formation: Ten schools of thought'. In J. Frederickson (ed.), *Perspectives on Strategic Management*. Ballinger, Cambridge, MA, pp. 105–235.

Narin, F., M. P. Carpenter and P. Woolf (1984), 'Technological performance assessments based on patents and patent citations', *IEEE Transactions on Engineering Management*, EM-31(4), pp. 172–183.

Narin, F., E. Noma and R. Perry (1987). 'Patents as indicators of corporate technological strength', *Research Policy*, 6, pp. 143–155.

Nonaka, I. (1994). 'A dynamic theory of organizational knowledge creation', *Organization Science*, 5(1), pp. 14–37.

Office of Technology Assessment (1993). *Pharmaceutical R&D: Costs, Risks and Rewards*, OTA-H-522. U.S. Government Printing Office, Washington, DC.

Pisano, G. P. (1994). 'Knowledge, integration, and the locus of learning: An empirical analysis of process development', *Strategic Management Journal,* Winter Special Issue, 15, pp. 85–100.

Porter, M. (1980). *Competitive Strategy.* Free Press, New York.

Reed, R. and R. J. DeFillipi (1990). 'Causal ambiguity, barriers to imitation, and sustainable competitive advantage', *Academy of Management Review,* 15(1), pp. 88–102.

Sheen, M. R. (1992). 'Barriers to scientific and technical knowledge acquisition in industrial R&D', *R&D Management,* 22(2), pp. 135–143.

Spender, J.-C. (1989). *Industry Recipes: The Nature and Sources of Managerial Judgement.* Basil Blackwell, Oxford.

Spender, J.-C. (1994). 'Organizational knowledge, collective practice and Penrose rents', *International Business Review,* 3(4), pp. 353–367.

Tushman, M. and P. Anderson (1986). 'Technological discontinuities and organizational environments', *Administrative Science Quarterly,* 31, pp. 439–465.

Volberda, H. W. (1996). 'Toward the flexible form: How to remain vital in hypercompetitive environments', *Organization Science,* 7(4), pp. 359–374.

White, R. E. (1986), 'Generic business strategies, organizational context and performance: An empirical investigation', *Strategic Management Journal,* 7(3), pp. 217–231.

Winter, S. (1987). 'Skill and knowledge as strategic assets'. In D. Teece (ed.), *The Competitive Challenge.* Ballinger, Cambridge, MA, pp. 159–184.

Zajac, E. J. and S. M. Shortell (1989). 'Changing generic strategies: Likelihood, direction, and performance implications', *Strategic Management Journal,* 10(5), pp.413–430.

TABLE 13.5 Interdifference Matrices from Cluster Analysis[1]

Period I: 1977–81

	Explorers KG1	Exploiters KG2	Loners KG3	Innovators KG4
KG1-Explorers	2.3362	17.6635	25.0433	24.2713
KG2-Exploiters		4.6677	29.3569	28.1834
KG3-Loners			10.7503	41.6089
KG4-Innovators				5.0046

Period II: 1982–86

	KG1	KG2	KG3	KG4
KG1-Explorers	4.2392	13.9912	23.0740	15.5247
KG2-Exploiters		3.2192	31.1157	16.2437
KG3-Loners			11.1423	31.8465
KG4-Innovators				0.5592

Period III: 1987–91

	KG1	KG2	KG3	KG4
KG1-Explorers	3.4398	11.5958	19.8353	15.6317
KG2-Exploiters		1.8544	15.6620	16.4339
KG3-Loners			2.8264	26.2324
KG4-Innovators				4.7507

[1]The 'tightness' of a cluster (underlined diagonal) is represented by its average squared Euclidean distance. The 'nearness' of clusters is represented by the maximum squared Euclidean distances.

14

Is Your Firm a Creative Destroyer? Competitive Learning and Knowledge Flows in the Technological Strategies of Firms

Max H. Boisot

Abstract—A firm's technology strategy can be described either as war of position or a war of movement. The first kind of strategy leads the firm to hoard its technological assets in an attempt to defy the equilibrating action of market forces (neoclassical or N-learning), the second pushes for a selective diffusion of its technological assets that will move it beyond market equilibrium and towards new opportunities (Schumpeterian or S-learning). Using Boisot's (1986) culture space as an analytical tool the paper explores the difference between N- and S-learning and how they each affect a firm's technological prospects.

INTRODUCTION

A small Swiss pharmaceutical manufacturing firm employing 350 people has an explicit and long standing strategy of keeping its patenting down to a minimum. It feels that it lacks the financial clout to police its patents effectively, and to prevent competitors from inventing around them. It prefers, therefore, to keep its research knowledge more discretely stored in the heads of a few key researchers. When the chips are down, it is easier to hold on to these people through negotiations and the fostering of personal loyalty to the firm than to try to prevent the leakage of valuable technical knowledge that shines like a beacon from the pages of a patent application.

From *Research Policy,* Vol. 24, 1995, pp. 489–506. Reprinted with permission from Elsevier Science–NL, Sara Burgerhartstraat 25, 1055 KV Amsterdam, The Netherlands.

A large, established, French heavy engineering firm, a world leader in its sector, agonizes over whether it should sign a turn-key contract with a South Korean customer involving the transfer of potentially sensitive technologies. The French firm is keen to fill up its order book and the Korean firm is seeking to acquire state-of-the-art technology at a low cost. Could the latter one day turn competitor? Is current profitability being sought by the French firm at the expense of future technological leadership?

In hot pursuit of aircraft sales in Japan, Boeing enters into a partnership with Mitsubishi, Kawasaki, and Fuji to produce the 767. Japanese policy makers in the MITI have long targeted the aerospace industry as one that their country must enter if it is to achieve technological competitiveness in a broad range of leading-edge industries. Will Boeing be able to hold on to technologies that it considers strategic, or will its Japanese partners climb the technological gradient and eventually challenge the American firm in its key markets?

All the above cases deal with firms threatened with the erosion of a technology based competitive advantage. In each, the implicit assumption is that the firm's long-term interest are best served by retaining its strategic technologies as long as possible, and the challenge is to devise appropriate barriers to their diffusion. Of course, one day the barriers will fall—patents will expire, alternative technologies will emerge, etc.—but while they are available, it is believed that full use should be made of them. Many firms, both large and small, think of technology strategy in this way, i.e. as little more than piling up as many of their proprietary technologies as possible behind such barriers and then holding on to them for as long as possible. Only technologies not considered relevant to the firm's activities are subsequently either sold under license or traded for other more relevant ones.

Firms that adopt a retentive approach to their technology assets pursue what the military call a war of position. They build ramparts behind which they stack their technological treasures and hope that the fortifications are strong enough to withstand assaults by opponents. The orientation of such firms is essentially static: they hope to prolong a beneficial status quo for as long as possible. Such firms are today in the majority.

A growing number of firms, however, are coming to view their technology in more dynamic terms, and are actively diffusing selected strategic technologies to customers, subcontractors, and even to competitors (Rumelt, 1984; Garud and Kumaraswamy, 1983). Why do they do this? Because they seek to commit key players to the adoption of a given 'technological paradigm' (Freeman and Perez, 1988) within which they themselves plan to stay one step ahead as it evolves. These firms pursue a war of movement. The second kind of war often occurs around industry standards (Adams and Brock, 1982). By encouraging customers, suppliers and competitors to adopt one part of a firm's technology, it locks them in to other parts to which the first is linked but whose diffusion, this time, will be firmly controlled. Examples of battles over industry standards abound. To cite only one of the better known ones, Sony's struggle to get digital audio tape technology (DAT) accepted by recording companies is in many respects a replay of its battle in the early 1980s with Matsushita to get the

Betamax standard accepted for videocassette recorders instead of VHS. We can summarize the difference between these two approaches to technology management by saying that the first maximizes the current rents to be extracted from technology assets monopolistically held until the monopoly element has been competed away by market processes, whereas the second focuses on future rents that such assets could generate, rents that might best be secured by cannibalizing existing technologies and transferring their monopolistic potential in a selective fashion to emerging technologies, also under the same firm's control.

The two approaches are not mutually exclusive, and when combined we might use the language of an older strategic discourse and talk of harvesting and investment (Hedley, 1977). The first might be said to represent the weight of past technology choices in the firm's decision making whereas the second reflects future possibilities. In most cases, however, the dynamics of competition in an industry and the nature of the technological regime to which it is subjected is likely to favour one approach over the other, and therefore one approach predominates. Boisot uses the term neoclassical or N-learning to describe the first one and Schumpeterian or s-learning to describe the second (Boisot, 1992).

N-learning places emphasis on an objective external reality that can gradually be apprehended by all. Sooner or later we 'learn the model' (Lucas and Sargent, 1981), and this information sharing leads to a commonly perceived reality. It is an equilibrating process insofar as initial information advantages are gradually whittled away.

S-learning, by contrast, focuses on a more subjective apprehension of reality. We access the world through constructs that vary from person to person (Kelly, 1963). Thus, although data gets shared, interpretation does not get shared so fully. A random element enters into the learning process (noise) which has the potential to disequilibrate and destabilize. It lies at the origin of Schumpeter's 'creative destruction' (Schumpeter, 1934). It is in part cognitive: a differential perception by individuals of threats and opportunities in the environment as they construe it. The differences between the two kinds of learning will now be highlighted by comparing the way each handles the development and flow of new knowledge.

THE CODIFICATION-DIFFUSION CONCEPT (CD)

A firm's technology can be viewed as information assets embedded in objects, documents, and the minds of individuals, and capable of generating value (Boisot, 1994).

All artifacts carry information that is pressed into them: they are informed. They communicate to their users by their shape, what they are and how they are to be used and manipulated. No one today, except possibly a Papuan headhunter, for example, risks mistaking a telephone receiver for a shower head and attempting to wash his hair with it. In most societies, people have encountered telephones and have either used them or at least watched them being used. Yet objects by themselves can only convey a limited amount of information, even to those who are familiar with them. If my television set plays up, I may fiddle around with the controls for a while to try and retrieve the picture, but I will ultimately have to call the local repair person if I need to get inside the casing, which to me is pure black box. A repair person who is new to the job will bring a checklist (a document, sometimes now computerized) to guide his or her efforts at diagnosis. By far the greatest number of repairs to TV sets are, of course, carried out on the spot. Occasionally, however, the repair person encounters another black box nested inside the first. Neither the TV set as an object nor the diagnostic check list of themselves yield sufficient information to cover all repairing contingencies. In certain cases, the black box component, or sometimes the set itself, has to be shipped back to the manufacturer where the knowledge stored in the head of certain specialized technicians has to be drawn out and added to that of the other two sources to complete the repair.

If we now position on a diffusion scale the kind of knowledge of TV sets held by myself as a customer, by a repair person, and by the manufacturer's technical personnel, relating its position on the scale to where this knowledge is embedded—i.e. in objects, documents or heads (Fig. 14.1), it becomes clear that the kind of knowledge that is most widely diffused and hence available to customers is embedded in the object itself. The information available in documentary form to repair persons is much less diffused, and that carried around in the heads of specialist technicians does not diffuse much outside their own manufacturing organization.

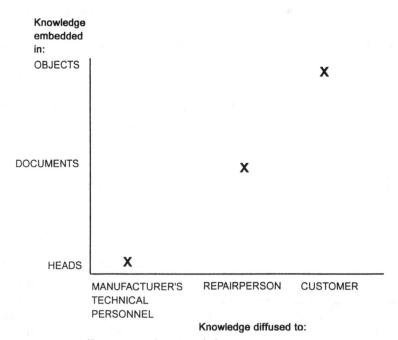

FIGURE 14.1 Diffusing Complex Knowledge

    What the diagram shows us is that as information gains in complexity so its diffusion becomes more limited (Polanyi, 1958). It is only as complexity is mastered and reduced—this often calls for a capacity to abstract—that the knowledge that one carries in one's head can be structured and either set down on paper or embedded in objects—i.e. it can be codified. Once information has been transposed from individual brains into documents or physical objects it acquires a life of its own and can diffuse quite rapidly and extensively, more so perhaps in the ease of physical objects—especially if these are portable—than of documents, since the latter typically presuppose some prior knowledge of the codes and conventions used. The use of everyday physical objects such as telephones may require some prior familiarity but in much smaller amounts than what is required, say, to interpret the instrument readings relating to a chemical experiment.

    Codification always involves a data sacrifice. A residual of uncodified data stays behind in the minds of the originators of the codes, generating a natural asymmetry that is often valuable to them. In many circumstances technology strategy is a game between those who want to maintain and renew such asymmetry, and those who want to eliminate it. In the real world the issue is one of choosing which items to make tacit and which ones to codify. The competition is not always one between firms, but often between a firm and its own employees. Publicly useful knowledge, however, whether it be the possession of firms or of the individual employees, always tends to move towards greater codification.

    The codification of knowledge and the speed at which it can be diffused are thus related, but in a way that turns out to be paradoxical for technology management. Consider Fig. 14.2, in which the curve indicates schematically the relationship that we have established between codification and diffusion. In the diagram, which describes what Boisot (1986) has labeled a culture space or C-space, the different possibilities for the structuring and sharing of knowledge within or between groups—the defining attributes of a cultural process—can be explored. Here we focus on technological knowledge.

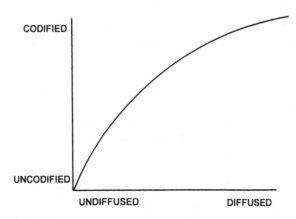

FIGURE 14.2 The C-Space

Science and technology both progress by eliminating complexity, by giving structure to what was hitherto ineffable, by simplifying what was intractable, in short, by solving problems (Laudan, 1977) and moving up the codification dimension. For this reason, knowledge located at the top of Fig. 14.2 is more useful than knowledge located at the bottom. For example, a laconic algebraic formula contains as much information as many tables of numbers expressing the same relationship and it may remain valid over a much wider range. In turn, tables of data, relating to the behaviour of a limited number of variables are more informative for many purposes than an exhaustive and fuzzy verbal description from which relevant relationships still have to be teased out.

More prosaically, and returning to the example of our TV set, the more the knowledge relevant to its proper functioning and repair can be codified and then either embedded in maintenance documents or, better still, in the design of the set itself, the less frequently will it have to be returned to the manufacturer thus incurring costs and delays. Codified knowledge is useful knowledge.

Yet as the diffusion curve of Fig. 14.2 tells us, codified knowledge is also inherently more diffusable than uncodified knowledge. That is to say, as it gains in utility it loses in scarcity. A little over a century ago, Leon Walras, one of the founding fathers of modern neoclassical economics, pointed out that economic value required the joining of utility and scarcity (Walras, 1984 (1926)), which is easy enough to achieve if you happen to own a purely physical asset like an oil-field, but apparently much harder to pull off if your value-creating assets are information-based. Information, especially when codified, is hard to domesticate; it likes to roam.

The paradox highlighted by the codification diffusion curve for the management of technology can be formulated thus:

> An effective technology strategy is one that maximizes the long-term value that can be extracted from technology assets. Maximum value however, is only achievable in the least stable region of the C-space—the northwest region—where, by dint of its degree of codification, knowledge is both at its most useful and at its most diffusable.

For this reason the generation of scarcity has to be made an explicit part of any effective technology strategy. Traditionally this has been done through the following ways.

- Patenting: Securing the right to control the diffusion of newly codified knowledge. Rents then become extractable from such knowledge during the patent's life.
- Developing esoteric codes: Creating barriers to diffusion by making the codes user unfriendly and hard to master by outsiders (encryption).
- Pursuing economies of scale: Embedding the codified knowledge in physical subjects that require a heavy and risky prior investment by outsiders.

Measures like these can either be thought of as barriers to diffusion of the technology or barriers to entry into the technology (Porter, 1985; Teece, 1987). Over the long term, however, the outcome will be strictly the same: competitors, customers and suppliers sooner or later will get hold of the firm's know-how and thus erode its technology-based competitive advantage, unless, that is, new technologies are being built up behind the barriers, in which case competitive advantage gradually shifts to these as the older technologies slip from the firm's grasp and lose their scarcity.

N-learners see little merit in introducing new technologies too fast while older ones are still yielding useful rents. To usher them in prematurely merely brings nearer the day when such rents will be exhausted. What N-learners are aiming for is to postpone that day into the distant future.

N-learners view the competition that follows the diffusion of proprietary technologies as contributing to the creation of efficient markets. Over time, knowledge that has been codified by an individual or a firm located on the left of the C-space moves to the right and, being now available as an input into the learning processes of an increasing number of players, eliminates the scope for rent-seeking and promotes instead neoclassical market equilibrium. N-learning, then, has occurred when codification and diffusion have run their course and have made well-structured technical knowledge available to a large population in the northeast region of the C-space. Since all players now possess the same knowledge, no rents are available and equilibrium is thus attained. The only effective strategy available to rent seeking firms for countering the effects of N-learning is to build bigger and better barriers to the diffusion of their technical knowledge, thus buying time for the development of new products incorporating new knowledge. Only in this way can rents continue to be extracted from value created.

S-learners, by contrast, do not believe that market equilibrium is the end of the line for them, and consequently are less concerned to erect barriers against it. They extend the strategic options available to them by moving beyond the codification and diffusion phases of N-learning and into new ones that complete a four phase social learning cycle (SLC) (see Fig. 14.3). The two new phases are:

Absorption

A move down the C-space in which the codified knowledge picked up in the northeast corner is tested and used in a wide variety of contexts and gradually internalized by learners. Over time, such learning-by-doing adds a great deal of 'tacit' knowledge to the codes themselves. It is the kind of knowledge that allows a chess master to 'see' a large number of patterns on a chess board, where the novice who has only just mastered the rules perceives only the movements of individual pieces (Simon, 1966). Tacit knowledge creates invisible 'fields' of forces between items of codified knowledge to produce gestalts (Miller, 1987). The more varied the repertoire of gestalts available to an individual for 'chunking' his knowledge in this way, the greater his expertise in applying it. Absorption, by embedding the codes of explicit knowledge in a cocoon of tacit uncodified knowledge, does not so much limit the diffusion of the former as reduce its relative utility. Without the know-how that allows one to make an effective use of the codes, their mere possession may offer little competitive advantage. Absorption provides this know-how.

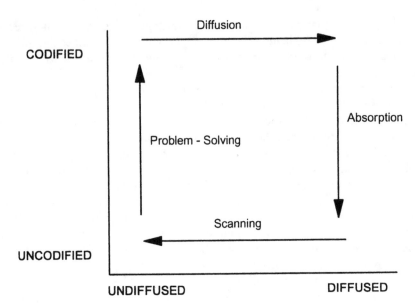

FIGURE 14.3 The Social Learning Cycle (SLC)

Knowledge is absorbed differently at different points along the diffusion scale. With absorption on the right, learning by doing is a shared experience. The tacit knowledge it creates, however, interacts with an existing stock of tacit knowledge that varies according to individual circumstances. This prior stock of tacit knowledge contains implicit models which the newly absorbed knowledge either fits or does not fit. When it does not, the opportunities for scanning arise.

Scanning

The integration of codified knowledge with uncodified tacit knowledge is something internal to the individual and hence highly personal. It is by no means automatic or trouble free, and individuals will vary in their ability to achieve it. On the right of the C-space, a large number of actors (i.e. individuals or firms) are absorbing the same codified knowledge and generating myriad gestalts, or patterns, with it. Most of these will be banal and quite common-place, and will merely serve to contribute to the creation of a shared language of implicit meanings among the users of the codes so absorbed.

When such sharing occurs inside a firm it helps to bring down its experience curve in an incremental fashion. Occasionally, however, something akin to a mutation takes place: one or two individuals absorb the codes in idiosyncratic ways and generate patterns that are not shared by others, and that may turn out to be anything but banal. When, for example, Alexander Fleming, returning to his laboratory after a holiday, casually glanced at the fungus spreading over a petri dish sitting at the bottom of a laboratory sink, he was making an observation that anyone passing by the sink in the laboratory could have made in the three weeks that the dish had actually been sitting there. The data which fed the observation was available to all comers, but only someone who had been working on the specific problems that Fleming had been wrestling with could have patterned the data and interpreted it in the way that he did. From such tacit scanning Fleming went on to develop penicillin (Macfarlane, 1984).

The extraction of novel and unique patterns from generally available data and experience constitutes a source of new knowledge. It reflects a reconfiguration of data from a diffused yet tacit state on the right of the C-space toward a tacit but undiffused state on the left of the C-space where, in its new form it now gets lodged in the heads of one or two insightful individuals. The new insights may be harbingers of problem areas, of possible threats or opportunities that remain latent in the data and that have to be teased out through a process of creative problem solving. If a given pattern appears promising enough to an individual scanning available data, it invites him to invest time and effort giving it structure and to codify it in some way, thus initiating another round of the SLC.

The difference between technology strategies based on N-learning and those based on S-learning is fundamental. The first view learning as an equilibrating rent-reducing process that comes to a halt in the northeast corner of the C-space, following the codification and diffusion of knowledge (Kirzner, 1979); the second view learning as alternately equilibrating and disequilibrating processes that operate continuously through the SLC in the C-space. If codification and diffusion eliminate rents, absorption and scanning, by contrast, might be considered the rent-creating entrepreneurial phases of the social learning cycle, those that generate opportunities, the perception of which becomes the personal, 'impacted' property of a few individuals (Williamson, 1975), and hence move social learning away from equilibrium.

In what circumstances is one kind of learning to be preferred to the other? In contrast to the retentive strategies suggested by N-learning (a war of position), S-learning advocates maximizing the speed of the social learning cycle (a war of movement). Value, to be sure, is extracted from knowledge assets as they pass through the northwest region of the C-space, but no great attempt is made to detain them there if the pressure is on to diffuse them. It is assumed that new knowledge is continuously moving up the C-space, and that sooner or later it will destroy the value of existing knowledge assets no matter how well these are thought to be protected by barriers to diffusion (MacMillan et al., 1985).

Such an assumption, however, is not always warranted. In some industries, the rate at which new knowledge moves up the C-space is sufficiently slow to justify investing in its barriers to its diffusion. Sometimes what is actually wanted is a partial barrier to diffusion, since the returns to the firm on sharing some of its technology and in this way 'locking in' customers and suppliers may be higher than the returns to total retention. In the telecommunications industry, for example, the scope for achieving network externalities (Katz and Shapiro, 1985; David, 1987) are set by the rate of adoption of a given technology by users themselves. They become a determinant of future demand and hence affect the possibility that the technology will be accepted as an industry standard. An established industry standard will not necessarily slow down the subsequent move of new knowledge up the C-space. It may, however, influence which types of new knowledge and technologies will be 'selected' by an industry as it evolves, and may therefore act to mitigate their destructive effects.

It becomes apparent, then, that a firm's choice of learning strategy must be a function of the speed at which the SLC operates in its external environment. Where the cycle is slow, retentive strategies will be appropriate; where it is fast, diffusion strategies will be preferred. It is in the latter case that the SLC is most appropriately thought of as an activator of what Joseph Schumpeter called 'creative destruction', i.e. the process through which fundamental innovations occur. Yet whereas Schumpeter assumed that the cycle always worked against the survival of existing firms, the current possessors of proprietary knowledge, and in favour of new ones, it has become apparent that a proper understanding of its dynamic can allow existing firms to internalize strategic parts of the cycle and to manage them, rather than to do battle against them in some kind of permanent rearguard action.

A rearguard action is in effect what IBM is struggling with today. Although the industry standards that it had established with the introduction of its personal computer in 1981 provided a valuable and stabilizing focus for product evolution—75% of PCs in operation today are IBM compatible—they had the effect of accelerating the industry's SLC rather than slowing it down. Entry barriers came down and software, rather than hardware, rapidly became the main source of profitability. The firm's internal SLC then failed to keep up with the industry SLC, the control of which subsequently passed to Intel and Microsoft, its suppliers of microprocessors and operating systems, respectively (Garud and Kumaraswamy, 1983). Whether these firms can successfully hold on to it, given the current pace of industry evolution, remains to be seen.

It is interesting to compare IBM's experience with that of Sun Microsystems, which entered the workstation market with off-the-shelf components to compete with Apollo, the industry pioneer of workstations. Apollo had discouraged multisystem compatibility by the in-house manufacture of several critical components and by limiting the access of outsiders to its proprietary technical knowledge (Bhide, 1989). In contrast to IBM, Sun's open system approach prevented system or component manufacturers to appropriate for themselves the standard setting process, which remains under the control of all the firms that had initially agreed upon the standard. In such circumstances, the only effective strategy is to ride the industry SLC rather than attempt to control it.

THE TECHNOLOGY PORTFOLIO

Control of an industry SLC is rendered problematic by the fact that a significant part of it is of necessity located outside any one firm. Product knowledge must be shared with customers, process knowledge with suppliers, and a good hit of both is shared with competitors through emerging industry norms, business associations, and the movement of skilled personnel from one firm to another.

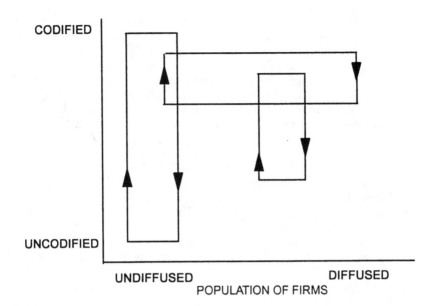

FIGURE 14.4 A Population of Firms

One way to visualize an industry SLC is to think of it as made up of a number of overlapping enterprise-level cycles that link together a population of firms. Such a population might then be distributed in the C-space as in Fig. 14.4. Clearly, any knowledge held by a firm that is located on the left of the space is less diffused than knowledge that is located on the right, and the greater the proportion of undiffused knowledge in a firm's knowledge assets, the more we can locate the firm as a whole, as described by its cycle, towards the left in the space.

Viewing the firm as operating an SLC allows us to reformulate what we mean by an effective technology strategy under an S-learning regime. *An effective technology strategy is one that maximizes the long-term value that can be extracted from a firm's technological assets as they move cyclically through the C-space. Since such assets, whether embedded in physical goods, in documents, or in the minds of employees, attain their highest value in the northwest corner of the space, a technology-based firm will strive firstly to locate part of its SLC in that region, and secondly to achieve an adequate fit between the speed of its own cycle and that of the industries that it competes in.*

Achieving such a fit may require the firm to think of its technology assets as an integrated system rather than as a portfolio of discreet technologies (Teece, 1988; Hughes, 1993).

The technologies that make up a product or a process are rarely independent of each other. Typically, they are linked in ways that establish close interdependencies.

- Reliable highspeed rail transport could only be achieved with changes in track technology, since sharp curves could not be negotiated at high speeds. Those who were willing to invest in an infrastructure of new tracks—i.e. the French national railways, SNCF—were able to avail themselves of traction systems and rolling stock which could operate within a broader set of technological limits. However, those who tried to achieve significantly higher speeds by focusing exclusively on rolling stock technology within the confines of an existing track system failed. The fate of British Rail's Advanced Passenger Train shows that an incremental approach to technology change based on 'muddling through' will not work where it is pursued without regard for the interdependencies involved. Where tilting trains have been introduced, they have operated at considerably lower speeds than the French TGV.

- The technology of highspeed lifts was 'induced' by the development of high strength steels which allowed the construction of tall buildings. Furthermore, such steels, by shifting the structural loadbearing function in tall buildings from masonry walls onto a frame, also generated a demand for light cladding, which in turn produced the modern curtain wall.

- The length of an airport runway is a function of the distance needed for an aircraft to get airborne, and hence of its aerodynamic properties, the thrust of its engines, etc. These, in turn, determine an aircraft's noise 'signature' on the ground, whether it will be allowed to fly at night, and thus the airport's overall capacity utilization.

Where strong linkages exist between the technologies used by a firm, it can rarely act upon one without affecting a good many of the others (Henderson and Clark, 1990; Tushman and Rosenkopf, 1992). For this reason, the elements of a technology portfolio cannot be handled in the same way as those of a product market portfolio. The difference between the two types of portfolio is illustrated in Fig. 14.5.

What the two portfolios have in common is that they both attempt to relate the attractiveness of an investment to a firm's competitive position. In the case of a product market portfolio, attractiveness might be measured by the growth of the market or of its profit potential, and the firm's competitive position is given either by its relative share of that market or by the barriers to entry that it can erect against competitors (Hedley, 1977). In a technology portfolio, on the other hand, the attractiveness of a technology is measured by the utility it has created through codification—i.e. uncertainty reduction—and a firm's competitive position with respect to that technology is given by its relative scarcity—i.e. by how little it has diffused either to competitors or to would-be competitors.

Now if technologies were discreet autonomous entities that could be added to, or removed from, the firm's stock at will, the approach to both portfolios would be quite similar: invest in elements that can in the future be harvested in the northwest corner of the space, gradually steer them into that region, and once there, keep them there as long as possible; the N-learning solution.

However, as we see from the arrows that link them in Fig. 14.5(b), the elements of the technology portfolio are in fact strongly interdependent. They make up technical systems. Invest in moving one of the elements in the space and you change the field of forces acting on the others, frequently leading to a reconfiguration of the system. Some illustrations are given below.

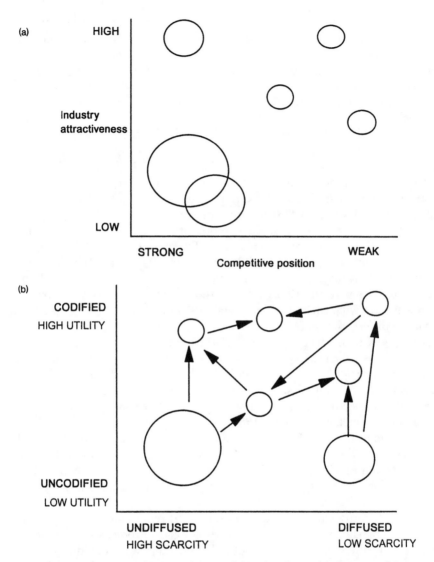

FIGURE 14.5 (a) The Product-Market Portfolio; (b) The Technology Portfolio.

- The diffusion of microelectronic technology has brought about the codification of user-friendly high-level languages as well as the disappearance of punched-card machines.
- The availability of expert systems is inducing a codification of tacit knowledge and reducing the value of that tacit knowledge, except in the case of pure connoisseurship.
- The advent of the quartz watch turned the watch into a convenience good, thus increasing the differentiation value of mechanical timepieces.

In some cases, technologies that were only loosely linked are brought closer together, as in the case of telecommunications and computation. In other cases, close links are loosened or severed altogether—unlike the high-speed train, where the interdependency between track technology and the rolling stock has increased, the amphibious hovercraft has almost declared its independence of tracking systems altogether and is free to roam about over a wide variety of terrains, including water.

It is clear, then, that in some circumstances a firm's technology assets will move towards greater integration and will come to constitute a system, and in others they may increase in differentiation and can then be handled as a portfolio of discreet, entities. Often external factors such as industry maturity and industry structure shape a firm's technological trajectory (Nelson and Winter, 1982; Dosi and Orsenigo, 1988) and thus influence its degree of integration and differentiation. Sometimes the modularization of a technology offers both integration and differentiation at the same time. The automated road guidance system Caminat, for example, on which Renault, TDF, Philips and The Sagem are currently collaborating, uses modularization to establish stable and well-integrated input-output relationships between the different elements of an evolving system while allowing each of these to retain its status as a black box, and hence its claim to differentiation.

Firms will hoard when they are led to treat their technologies as discreet. They will 'share' when they perceive them as a system. This will depend partly on the intrinsic properties of the technologies themselves, and partly on how the firm thinks of its technologies. A 'competence' view, for example, is more likely to highlight connectivities than a 'portfolio' view (Nelson and Winter, 1982; Prahalad and Hamel, 1990; Pavitt,1992).

Technological interdependencies call for an S-learning approach to the technology portfolio, one which exploits the system linkages between the different elements that make up the portfolio while pushing them through an SLC. As one element loses value, so another is brought into play. Such an approach can briefly be summarized as follows.

Step 1. Identify which technologies should be represented in the portfolio. In the case of product markets, the issue does not arise. Products sold by the firm in existing or emerging markets should all find their way into the portfolio. Technologies, though, are different, especially when they are defined broadly enough to cover almost any item in a firm's value chain. If you are manufacturing and selling widebodied aircraft, for example, do you include financial engineering in your technology portfolio or do you keep it out? If competitors design their aircraft and the different ways of manufacturing it, first and only then think of how they will assist customers in financing their purchase. Could not some competitive advantage be derived from thinking about customer financing, design and manufacturing simultaneously as an interlinked set of technologies in which financing techniques might modify design and manufacturing as much as it might be modified by them?

Step 2. Decide which of the technologies represented in the portfolio are, or are likely to become, basic, key or emergent. Base technologies are those the possession of which define the industry and without which one is not a player in that industry. They are usually well codified and diffused. Key technologies, by contrast, may be well codified but are much less diffused; they give a firm a specific competitive advantage within an industry. Emergent technologies are neither much codified nor as yet diffused, but they have the potential for becoming either basic or key technologies in the future. The three different types of technology can be located in the C-space, as shown in Fig. 14.6. What characterizes base and key technologies is the high degree of interconnectedness that they have achieved over their life and the extensive dependencies that they foster as a result of this. Emergent technologies are those capable of generating future dependencies. As shown in Fig.14.6, basic technologies, being highly diffused, are a common possession within an industry. Key technologies, by contrast, as well as emergent technologies, tend to be more firm specific.

Step 3. Reconfigure the technology portfolio so as to improve the value that can be extracted from the cyclical flow of its constituent elements in the C-space. This can be done either by modifying the linkages between a selected number of its elements, or by progressing a selected number of these through one or more phases of the social learning cycle. Much technological progress is a matter of stabilizing relationship between entities that were hitherto treated separately, or separating entities that were treated as one. Before the ball-point or felt-tip pen, ink and pen were sold separately, and in modern manufacturing important economies are achieved by designing parts in order to reduce their total number. On the other hand, modern construction technology was revolutionized when the load-bearing and weather-protecting function of the traditional wall were separated out from each other to create the structural frame and the curtain wall (see above). Like mutations, the elements that make up the technology portfolio can thus be combined or separated in ways that will modify the

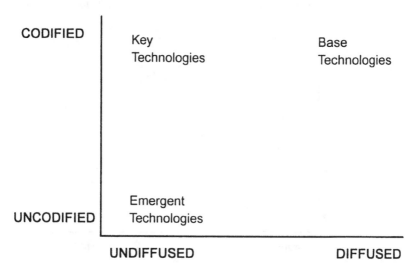

FIGURE 14.6 Base, Key and Emergent Technologies in the C-Space.

forces acting upon them in the C-space and that will, in consequence, affect their propensity to move in the space.

Which elements or linkages are good candidates for Step 3? An N-learning answer would be: those that move as many elements of the technology portfolio as possible closer to the northwest corner of the C-space where their value can be maximized provided that they can be kept in or close to that region. An S-learning answer would identify elements and linkages capable of enhancing the firms SLC, and this might involve the selective diffusion of elements already in that corner if their linkages to other technologies held by the firm has the effect of bringing the latter through that region (MacMillan, et al., 1985).

The basic difference between a technological strategy dependent on N-learning and one dependent on S-learning is that the first operates technology assets that have to be treated as discreet elements to be handled on a case-by-case

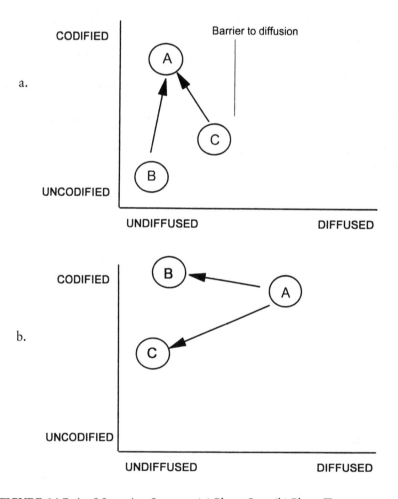

FIGURE 14.7 An S-Learning Strategy. (a) Phase One; (b) Phase Two.

basis, whereas the second can choose to handle them as a complex, highly connected system. For this reason, in order to induce movement in the rest of the technology portfolio, the second will be prepared to release technologies that the first might be tempted to hold on to. The process is illustrated in Figs.14.7(a) and (b), where a firm, by releasing a highly interconnected technology A, has stimulated demand for associated technologies B and C which are still in the firm's possession. The increased demand for these technologies has now made it worthwhile for the firm to incur risks and costs in further codifying them. Here, value is extracted not from individual technologies, but from the technological system treated as a dynamic whole in the C-space.

N- and S-learning will both go through Steps 1 and 2—the identification and classification of technologies—together, but only an S-learning orientation will allow the firm to exploit whatever systemic properties its technology portfolio might possess and therefore to treat it as an integrated whole. From an N-learning perspective it could amount in many cases to giving away the family jewels, since, for example, a downward movement on the right of the C-space is one in which outsiders come to master a firm's now diffused technology through a 'learning-by-doing' process that could turn them into competitors (Arrow, 1962), but the N-learning perspective only really applies where technologies remain discreet. If they are integrated, and if the 'absorption' by outsiders is carried out with the firm's active help, however, it can amount to a shrewd exploitation of the dynamics of technological evolution in which, through an intimate participation in joint learning with customers, suppliers or even competitors, the firm prepares itself for the entrepreneurial scanning phase that follows and hence positions itself favourably for a new run round the SLC. In effect, by selective diffusion, the firm is able to leverage its situation by exploiting for its own benefit the learning of others (Teece, 1987, Senge, 1990) a strategy used to great effect by a number of Japanese firms to deepen their core competencies (Prahalad and Hamel, 1990).

TECHNOLOGY STRATEGY AND TECHNOLOGY CULTURE

SLCs come in all shapes and sizes that reflect the nature of the population that one has chosen to place along the diffusion dimension as well as the various communication options it confronts: if, for example, the population is that of the firm's employees and the cycle is thus internal to the firm, one might be aiming to stimulate a much larger and freer flow of technological information than if one was dealing with a population of firms that were competitors. A careful specification of the target population to be positioned along the diffusion dimension is thus crucial to a proper use of the C-space.

The shapes of the different SLCs also condition and express the technology strategies pursued within a target population and the resources available for doing so. Each of the four phases of the cycle—codification, diffusion, absorption and scanning—consume scarce learning resources that might not always be readily available. Firms may be stronger in certain phases of the cycle than in others, so that the marginal costs to them of internalizing it in those regions will be lower. Witness the legendary ability of certain Japanese firms to 'absorb' well-codified and diffused Western knowledge and to internalize it through a systematic process of learning-by-doing (Irvine, 1988; Martin and Irvine, 1989); witness also the continued difficulties they face in dealing with the uncodified realm of pure research. To participate in a full learning cycle, therefore, such firms will either have to collaborate with outsiders or find other ways of securing the knowledge inputs that they need.

Small biotechnology firms, for example, are strong in moving scientific and technical knowledge from an uncodified state in basic research to a more codified development stage —i.e. they are competent in the problem-solving phase of the SLC. Also, as one might expect of research firms, they are skilled in picking up newly codified knowledge from specialized research journals and the patent literature and 'absorbing' and interpreting it (i.e. scanning it). They often lack the resources, however, to commercialize their products themselves whilst extracting full value from the diffusion of the knowledge embodied in them. Within a population of pharmaceutical firms and client organizations, they thus aim to operate with tall cycles on the left of the C-space, such as the one shown in Fig.14.8(a). Here the diffusion of their codified knowledge to outsiders is limited partly by the specialized codes which it uses, and partly by the fact that it is attached to a good deal of contextual 'tacit' knowledge further down the C-space which must also be mastered if the codified knowledge is to be of any use. Biotechnology firms build up this experiential tacit knowledge by investing in the downward absorption phase of the SLC before others do. Hence its location on the left in the space.

Larger chemical and pharmaceutical firms, by contrast, may have the distribution capacity to operate rapidly along the diffusion dimension and to reach client organizations before competitors do. An army of detail-men can systematically scan the client base of doctors, hospitals and patients for codified data on product use and feed it back rapidly into the product development and refinement process. Such firms, however, feel less comfortable in the lower regions of the C-space where the ambiguities and uncertainties of the information environment call for more risk taking and a greater entrepreneurial orientation. They will therefore tend to build their activities around flat cycles in the upper part of the C-space, as shown in Fig. 14.8(b), in which problem solving is incremental and is designed to respond to fast moving and well-codified market signals coming in from the left.

Firms with tall and flat cycles of the kind shown here can either compete or collaborate with each other (Fig. 14.8(c)). They all inhabit, at some moment or other, the northwest corner of the C-space with respect to products or technologies that they might share and invest in, and the strategic issue then becomes whether that corner is big enough for both of them. EMI, for example, lost control of its scanner technology to General Electric in the late 1970s because it had reached the northwest corner of the C-space and then promptly fell between two stools. The

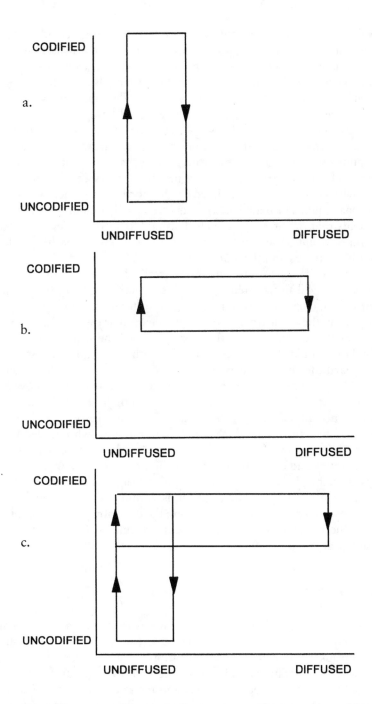

FIGURE 14.8 Alternative Technological Strategies. (a) The Research-Based Firm; (b) The Fast Mover; (c) Competition or Collaboration?

technology developed by the firm's chief scientist, Geoffrey Hounsefield, was essentially a systems integration of what was readily available off the shelf. It was therefore hard to patent, and what was patentable was easy to circumvent. Yet the absence of adequate barriers to diffusion would not have been so damaging had the firm been able to embed the technologies it had codified in a network of tacit technological dependencies (Bijker, 1993). These would have allowed the firm to pursue an S-learning strategy, diffusing its technology to users while remaining heavily invested in the northwest region on the basis on increased throughput— now codifications sedimented from the firms growing stock of tacit learning. EMI, however, was a classic N-learner: its attempt to erect barriers after the event to the diffusion of what it had already codified in the northwest corner of the space proved quite inadequate. General Electric was able to invent around the thin membrane of patents that the firm had stretched around its technologies and, with its own powerful distribution network, it managed to get hold of both the relevant technologies for scanners and the market for them.

In contrast to the zero-sum game just described, a number of large pharmaceutical or chemical firms often work in lose collaboration with biotechnology start-ups, financing their basic research and offering them general support because they see in them S-learners who complement their own cycles and whose continuously evolving competence, therefore, they will need in the future. The purchase by Hoffman la Roche of 60% of Genetech, for example, is structured so as to safeguard the latter's S-learning integrity. EMI was not an S-learner, nor was it perceived to be one: the scanner was a tentative diversification move based on a limited financial commitment and even less knowledge of the industry it was entering. Once an industry insider such as General Electric had got hold of EMI's newly codified and stand-alone scanning technology, who needed EMI?

To be an effective practitioner of S-learning in relation to a population of customers, suppliers and competitors, one has first to be able to apply it in one's own backyard, that is, inside the firm with respect to a population of employees. What we call a learning organization, in fact, is nothing other than an organization that has positioned all its employees along the diffusion dimension of the C-space and has successfully created an organizational culture that allows everyone to participate in an SLC.

CONCLUSION

The C-space creates a language that allows us to discuss a firm's technology strategy as an expression of its learning capacities in the ways that it processes and transmits information. Codification diffusion theory describes in a visualizable way the conditions under which new knowledge can be structured and shared both within and between firms, and integrates these into a dynamic model of learning. A genuine learning organization, however, turns out to be a very different animal from those which economists refer to when they talk about competitive firms. It is a Schumpeterian animal, a creative destroyer that is forever destabilizing markets. In the real world, in contrast to the abstract one inhabited by orthodox economic theory, the only equilibrium that really matters is that which results when innovating entrepreneurs gradually drive a market price to zero. While a non-zero price exists, it signals a continued scope for the further generation of utility and scarcity in the system, and hence invites the myriad improvements and changes that constitute Schumpeterian learning. In this sense, N-learning, whilst appropriate under certain circumstances and in certain technological environments, is best viewed as a constituent part of that wider process that we have called S-learning.

REFERENCES

Adams, W. and J.W. Brock, 1982, Integrated monopoly and market power: System selling, compatibility standards, and market control, *Quarterly Review of Economics and Business* 22 (4), 29–49.

Arrow, K.J., 1962, The economic implications of learning by doing, *Review of Economic Studies* 29, 155–173.

Bhide, A., 1989, Vinod Khosla and Sun Microsystems A, B and C, Harvard Business School Cases no. 9, 390, 049/050/051.

Bijker, W.E., 1993, The social construction of bakelite: Towards a theory of invention, in: W.E. Bijker, T.P. Hughes and T. Pinch (Editors), *The social construction of technological systems: New directions in the sociology and history of technology*, (MIT Press, Cambridge, MA).

Boisot, M., 1986, Markets and hierarchies in cultural perspective, *Organization Studies*, Spring 1986.

Boisot, M., 1992, Schumpeterian learning versus neoclassical learning: Development options for post-communist societies, in: S. Birley and I.C. MacMillan (Editors), *International perspectives on entrepreneurship research* (North Holland, Amsterdam).

Boisot, M., 1994, *Information and organization: The manager as anthropologist* (Harper and Collins, London).

David, P., 1987, Some new standards for the economics of standardization in the information age, in: P. Dasgupta and P. Stoneman (Editors), *Economic policy and technological performance* (Cambridge University Press, Cambridge).

Dosi, G. and L. Orsenigo, 1988, Coordination and transformation: An overview of structures, behaviours and change in evolutionary environments, in: Dosi et al. (Editors), *Technical change and economic theory* (Pinter, London).

Freeman, C. and C. Perez, 1988, Structural crises of adjustment: Business cycles and investment behaviour, in: G. Dosi et al. (Editors), *Technical change and economic theory* (Pinter, London).

Garud, R. and A. Kumaraswamy, 1983, Changing competitive dynamics in network industries: An exploration of Sun Microsystems' open systems strategy, *Strategic Management Journal* 14, 351–369.

Hamel, G., Y. Doz and C.K. Prahalad, 1989, Collaborate with your competitors — and win, *Harvard Business Review,* January-February.

Hedley, B., 1977, Strategy and the business portfolio, Long Range Planning 10 (2).

Henderson, R.M. and K.B. Cark, 1990, Architectural innovation: The reconfiguring of existing product technologies and the failure of established firms, *Administrative Science Quarterly* 35, 9–30.

Hughes, T.P., 1993, The evolution of large technological systems, in: W.E. Bijker, T.P. Hughes and T. Pinch (Editors), *The social construction of technological systems* (MIT Press, Cambridge, MA).

Irvine, J., 1988, *Evaluating applied research: Lessons from Japan* (Pinter, London).

Katz, M.L. and C. Shapiro, 1985, Technology adoption in the presence of network externalities, *Journal of Political Economy* 94, 822–841.

Kelly, G.A., 1963, *The theory of personality: The psychology of personal constructs* (W.W. Norton, New York).

Kirzner, I.M., 1979, *Perception, opportunity and profit: Studies in the theory of entrepreneurship* (University of Chicago Press, Chicago, IL).

Laudan, L., 1977, *Progress and its problems: Towards a theory of scientific growth* (University of California Press, Berkeley, CA).

Lucas, R.E. and T.J. Sargent (Editors), 1981, *Rational expectations and econometric practice* (University of Minnesota Press, Minneapolis, MN).

Macfarlane, G., 1984, *Alexander Fleming: the man and the myth* (Oxford University Press, Oxford).

MacMillan, I., M.L. McCaffery and G.V. Wijk, 1985, Competitors' responses to easily imitated new products: Exploring commercial banking product introductions, *Strategic Management Journal* 6, 75–86.

Martin, B. and J. Irvine, 1989, *Research foresight: Priority setting in science* (Pinter, London).

Miller, A., 1987, *Imagery in scientific thought* (MIT Press, Cambridge, MA).

Nelson, R. and S. Winter, 1982, *An evolutionary theory of economic change* (Belknap Press of Harvard University Press. Cambridge. MA).

Pavitt, K., 1992, Some foundations for a theory of the large innovating firm, in: G. Dosi, R. Giannetti and P.A. Toninelli (Editors), *Technology and enterprise in a historical perspective* (Clarendon Press, Oxford).

Polanyi, M., 1958, *Personal knowledge: Towards a post-critical philosophy* (Routledge and Kegan Paul, London).

Porter, M.E., 1985, *Competitive advantage: Creating and sustaining superior performance* (Free Press, New York).

Prahalad, C.K. and G. Hamel, 1990, The core competence of the corporation, *Harvard Business Review,* May-June.

Rumelt, R., 1984, Towards a strategic theory of a firm. in: R.B. Lamb (Editor), *Competitive strategic management* (Prentice Hall, Englewood Cliffs, NJ).

Schumpeter, J.A., 1934, *The theory of economic development* (Oxford University Press, London).

Senge, P., 1990, The fifth discipline: *The art and practice of the learning organization* (Doubleday, New York).

Simon, H.A., 1966, Thinking by computers, in: R. Colodny (Editor), *Mind and cosmos* (Pittsburgh University Press, Pittsburgh, PA).

Teece, D.J., 1987, Profiting from technological innovation: Implications for integration, collaboration, licensing and public policy, in: D.J. Teece (Editor), *The competitive challenge: strategies for industrial innovation and renewal* (Ballinger, Cambridge, MA).

Teece, D.J., 1988, Technological change and the nature of the firm, in: G. Dosi et al. (Editors), *Technical change and economic theory* (Pinter, London).

Tushman, M. and L. Rosenkopf, 1992, Organizational determinants of technological change. Towards a sociology of technological evolution, in: B. Staw and L. Cummings (Editors), *Research in organizational behaviour,* Vol. 14 (JAI Press, Greenwich, CT).

Walras, L., 1984 (1926), *Elements of pure economics or the theory of social wealth* (Orion Editions, Philadelphia, PA).

Williamson, O.E., 1975, *Markets and hierarchies: Analysis and antitrust implications* (Free Press, New York).

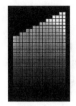

15

Leveraging Intellect

James Brian Quinn, Philip Anderson, and Sydney Finkelstein

Executive Overview—With rare exceptions, the productivity of a modern corporation or nation lies more in its intellectual and systems capabilities than in its hard assets—raw materials, land, plant, and equipment. Intellectual and information processes create most of the value-added for firms in the large service industries—like software, medical care, communications, and education—which provide 79 percent of all jobs and 76 percent of all U.S. GNP.₁ In manufacturing as well, AL intellectual activities—like R&D, process design, product design, logistics, marketing, marketing research systems management, or technological innovation— generate the preponderance of value-added. McKinsey & Co. estimates that by the year 2000, 85 percent of all jobs in America and 80 percent of those in Europe will be knowledge-based. Yet few managements have systematically attacked the issues of developing, leveraging, and measuring the intellectual capabilities of their organizations. What are the keys to these processes? What light do research and best practice shed on this subject?

WHAT IS INTELLECT?

Webster's defines intellect as "knowing or understanding; the capacity for knowledge, for rational or highly developed use of intelligence." The intellect of an organization, in order of increasing importance, includes: (1) cognitive knowledge (or know what), (2) advanced skills (know how), (3) system understanding and trained intuition (know why), and (4) self-motivated creativity (care why).² Intellect clearly resides inside the firm's human brains. Elements of knowledge, skill and understanding can also exist in the organization's systems, databases, or operating technologies. If properly nurtured, intellect in each form is both highly leverageable and protectable.

From *Academy of Management Executive*, Vol. 10, No. 3, 1996, pp. 7–27. Reprinted by permission.

The value of a firm's intellect increases markedly as one moves up the intellectual scale from cognitive knowledge toward motivated creativity. Yet, in a strange and costly anomaly, most enterprises reverse this priority in their training and systems development expenditures, focusing virtually all their attention on basic (rather than advanced) skills development and little or none on systems, motivational, or creative skills. (See Figure 15.1.) The result is a predictable mediocrity, and a failure to match training with value creation or profits.

CHARACTERISTICS OF INTELLECT

The best managed companies avoid this failure by exploiting certain critical characteristics of intellect at both the strategic and operational levels. These critical characteristics include the exponentiality of knowledge, the benefits of sharing, and the opportunities for expansion it offers.

Exponentiality of Knowledge

Properly stimulated, knowledge and intellect grow exponentially. All learning and experience curves have this characteristic.[3] As knowledge is captured or internalized, the available knowledge base itself becomes higher. Hence a constant percentage accretion to the base becomes exponential total growth. The strategy consequences are profound. Once a firm obtains a knowledge based competitive edge, it becomes ever harder for competitors to catch up.[4] Because the firm is a leader, it can attract better talent than competitors. The best want to work with the best. These people can then perceive and solve more complex and interesting customer problems, make more profits as a result, and attract even more talented people to work on the next round of complexity. Driving and capturing individuals' exponential learning has been the key to strategic success for most intellectual enterprises, from Bell Labs and Intel to Microsoft, McKinsey, and the Mayo Clinic. For example:

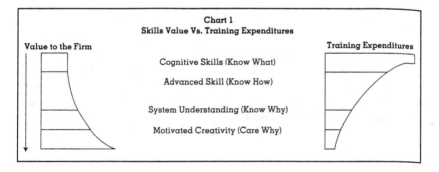

FIGURE 15.1 Skills Value Vs. Training Expenditure

- Microsoft, realizing that software design is a highly individualistic effort, interviews hundreds of candidates to find the few most suited to write its advanced operating systems. It then places its new members directly onto small (3–7 person) teams under experienced mentors to design complex new software systems at the frontier of user needs. Microsoft's culture drives everyone with the unstated expectation of 60–80 hour weeks on intensely competitive projects. The best commercial programmers seek out and stay with Microsoft largely because they believe that Microsoft will determine where the industry moves in the future and that they can share the excitement and rewards of being at that frontier. Each Microsoft success in turn builds the experience base and recruitment attractiveness for the next wave of challenges.

Benefits of Sharing

Knowledge is one of the few assets that grows most—also usually exponentially—when shared.[5] Communication theory states that a network's potential benefits grow exponentially as the nodes it can successfully interconnect expands numerically.[6] As one shares knowledge with other units, not only do those units gain information (linear growth) they share it with others and feed back questions, amplifications, and modifications that add further value for the original sender, creating exponential total growth. Proper leveraging through external knowledge bases—especially those of specialized firms, customers, and suppliers—can create even steeper exponentials. There are, however, some inherent risks and saturation potentials in this process. The choices about what knowledge is to be protected, what knowledge is to be shared, and how, are critical elements in intellectual strategies. For example:

- The core intellectual competency of many financial firms—like Fidelity, State Street Boston, and Aetna—lies in the human experts and the systems software that collect and analyze the data surrounding their investment specialties. Access to the internals of these centralized software systems is tightly limited to a few specialists working at headquarters. These HQ specialists leverage their own specialized analytical skills through close interactions with other financial specialists, "rocket scientist" modelers, and the unique access the firm has to massive transactions data. These companies then leverage their systems' outputs as broadly as possible through their extensive brokerage outlets, which in turn yield more information. Nevertheless, the structure of sharing must be carefully controlled. For security and competitive reasons, sales brokers cannot have access to their corporate system's analytics and corporate analysts must be kept out of brokers' individual customer files. Yet for maximum impact the system itself must capture and manipulate data aggregates from both sources. The managing of this sharing is a major source of competitive edge as is its integration into the software and support systems of the firm.

Opportunities for Expansion

Unlike physical assets, intellect (a) increases in value with use, (b) tends to have underutilized capacity, (c) can be self-organizing, and (d) is greatly expandable under pressure.[7] How can a company exploit these characteristics?

Arthur Andersen Worldwide (AAW) offers some interesting insights.

- Andersen attempts to electronically interlink more than 82,000 people in 360 offices in 76 countries. Its ANET, a T1 and frame relay network, connects 85 percent of Andersen's people through data, voice, and video interlinks. ANET allows AAW specialists—by posting problems on electronic bulletin boards and following up with visual and data contacts—to instantly self organize around a customer's problem anywhere in the world. It thus taps into otherwise dormant capabilities, and vastly expands the energies and successful solution sets available to customers. The capacity to share in AAW's enormous variety of problems and solutions is enhanced through centrally-collected and carefully-indexed subject, customer, and resource files accessible directly via ANET or from CD-ROMs, distributed to all offices. These in turn expand the intellectual capabilities AAW field personnel have available to add value for future customers.

Effective leveraging of intellectual processes requires attention to all opportunities for expansion. The techniques used for leveraging these resources closely resemble successful coaching.[8] The critical activities are: (1) recruiting and developing the right people; (2) stimulating these recruits to internalize the information knowledge, skills, and attitudes needed for success; (3) creating systematic technological and organizational structures that capture, focus, and leverage intellect to the greatest possible extent; and (4) demanding and rewarding top performance from all players. Much can be learned from how successful (and failing) practitioners have handled the leveraging of their intellectual resources. Our conclusions draw on an extensive literature search, hundreds of personal interviews, and numerous published case studies of the leading professional and innovative companies of the U.S., Europe, and Japan.[9]

PROFESSIONAL INTELLECT

There are important differences between professional and creative intellect. Professionals are an important source of intellect for most organizations, but little has been written about managing professionals.[10] What characterizes the management of such professionals?

Perfection, Not Creativity

While no precise delineation applies in all cases, most of a typical professional's activity is directed at perfection, not creativity. The true professional commands a complete body of knowledge—a discipline—and updates that knowledge constantly.[11] In most cases, the customer wants the knowledge delivered reliably with the most advanced skill available. Although there is an occasional call for creativity, the preponderance of work in actuarial units, dentistry, hospitals, accounting units, opera companies, universities, law firms, aircraft operations, or equipment maintenance requires the repeated use of highly developed skills on relatively similar, although complex, problems. People rarely want their surgeons, accountants, airline pilots, maintenance personnel, or nuclear plant operators to be very creative, except in emergencies. While managers clearly must prepare their professionals for these special emergency circumstances, the bulk of attention needs to be on delivering consistent, high quality intellectual output. What are the critical factors?

- Hyperselection. The leverage of intellect is so great that a few top flight professionals can create a successful organization or make a lesser one billow. Marvin Bower created McKinsey & Co.; Robert Noyce and Gordon Moore spawned Intel; William Gates and Robert Allen built Microsoft; Herb Boyer and Robert Swanson made Genentech; Einstein enhanced Princeton's Institute of Advanced Studies; and so on. The cultivation of extraordinary talent is thus the first critical prerequisite for building intellectual capital. McKinsey long focused on only the top one percent of graduates from of the top five business schools, and screened heavily from these. Microsoft typically interviews hundreds of highly recommended people for each key software designer hired, and tests not just their cognitive knowledge but their capacity to think under high pressure. Similarly, experienced venture capitalists spend as much time on relentlessly pursuing and selecting top people as on the quantitative aspects of projects.
- Intense training, mentoring, and peer pressure literally force professionals to the top of their knowledge ziggurat. The best students go to the most demanding schools. The top graduate schools—whether in law, business, engineering, science, or medicine—further reselect and drive these students with greater challenges and with 100 hour work weeks. Upon graduation the best of the graduates go back to even more intense boot camps in medical internships, law associate programs, or other demanding training situations. The result is that the best professionals drive themselves up a steep learning curve. People who go through these experiences quickly move beyond those in less demanding programs, becoming noticeably more capable—and valuable—than those facing lesser challenges. The best programs stimulate professional trainees' growth with constantly heightened (preferably customer induced) complexity, thoroughly planned mentoring, high rewards for performance, and strong stimuli to understand and advance their professional disciplines. The great intellectual organizations all seem to develop deeply ingrained cultures around these points.
- Constantly increasing challenges. Intellect grows most when challenged. Hence, heavy internal competition and constant performance appraisal are common in well run professional shops. Leaders tend to be demanding, visionary, and intolerant of half efforts.[12] At Bell Labs, 90 percent of carefully selected basic researchers moved on (voluntarily or through so called stimulated changes) within seven years. Microsoft tries to force out the lowest performing five percent of its highly screened talent each year. And at Andersen Consulting, only one in ten associates ever makes it to partnership. Leaders often set almost impossible stretch goals, as did HP's Bill Hewlett (improve performance by 50 percent), Intel's Gordon Moore (double the componentry per chip each year), or Motorola's Robert Galvin (six sigma quality). Top professionals, having survived the rigors of their training, relish competition and want to know that they have excelled against peers. The best organizations constantly challenge their young professionals to perform beyond the comfort of catalogued book knowledge,

learned models, and controlled laboratory environments. They relentlessly encourage associates to deal with the more complex intellectual realms of live customers, real operating systems, and highly differentiated external environments and cultural differences. They insist on mentoring by those nearest the top of their fields. And they reward associates for learned competencies. Mediocre organizations do not.

- Managing an elite. Each profession tends to regard itself as an elite. Members look to their profession and to their peers to determine codes for behavior and acceptable performance standards.[13] They often disdain the values and evaluations of those outside their discipline. This is a source of many problems since professionals tend to surround themselves with people having similar backgrounds and values. Unless consciously fractured, these discipline-based cocoons quickly become inward-looking bureaucracies, resistant to change, and detached from customers. Many professionals are reluctant to share knowledge without powerful inducements. Even then the different values of other groups become points of conflict. Hence, in manufacturing, researchers disdain product designers (who don't understand the physics), who disdain engineers (who aren't concerned with artistry and aesthetics), who disdain production personnel ("who just bang out stuff"), who disdain marketers ("who don't really understand the product's complexities"), who all disdain accountants ("who are only bean counters"). The same thing happens among the specialties of medicine, law, education, and so on.

These professional values—and the elitism they inculcate if not consciously ameliorated—cause contentiousness in professional organizations. Many professionals are reluctant to subordinate themselves to others, or to support organizational goals not completely congruent with their special viewpoint. This is why most professional firms operate as partnerships and not hierarchies, and why it is so hard for them to adopt a distinctive strategy. It is also why successful enterprises use multipoint cultivation—(1) by peers for unique experiments; a professionalism, (2) by customers for relevance, and (3) by enterprise norms for net value—to limit the bias induced by professional orientations. Later sections illustrate how successful organizations accomplish this.

Few Scale Economies?

Conventional wisdom has long held that there are few scale economies—other than obtaining a critical mass for interactions—in professional activities.[14] A pilot can handle only one aircraft; a great chef can cook only so many different dishes at once; a top researcher can conduct only so many unique experiments; a doctor can diagnose only one patient's illness at a time, and so on. In such situations, adding professionals simply multiplies costs at the same rate as outputs.

In fact, for years, growing an intellectual organization actually seemed to involve diseconomies of scale. Most often, increasing size brought even greater growth in the bureaucracies coordinating, monitoring, or supporting the professionals.[15] Universities, hospitals, personnel, accounting groups, and consultancies seemed to suffer alike. The only ways firms found to create leverage were to push their people through more intense training or work schedules than competitors or to increase the number of associates supporting each professional. This even became the accepted meaning of the term leverage in the legal, accounting, and consulting fields.

But new technologies and management approaches now enable firms to capture, develop, and leverage intellectual resources. The keys are: (1) Organizations and technology systems designed around intellectual flows rather than command and control concepts, (2) performance measurements and incentive systems that reward managers for developing intellectual assets and customer value—and not just for producing current profits and using physical assets more efficiently. Companies as diverse as Arthur Andersen, Sony, AT&T, Merck, Scandia, State Street Bank, and Microsoft have found ways to do this.

CORE INTELLECTUAL COMPETENCIES

The crux of leveraging intellect is to focus on what creates uniquely high value for customers. Conceptually, this means disaggregating corporate staff activities and the value chain into manageable intellectual clusters of intellectually based service activities. (See Figure 15.2.) Such activities can either be performed internally or outsourced. For maximum leverage, a company should concentrate its own resources and executive time on those few activities (most desired by customers) where it can perform at best-in-world levels.[16] Managers need to look behind their products to identify those intellectually-based skills, knowledge bases, or systems that enable the firm to produce higher value outputs per unit cost than its competitors. With rare exceptions, these resources (and not products or physical assets) are what create unique value for customers. By developing these unique core competencies in depth as a secure strategic block between its suppliers and its customers, the company can more aggressively outsource or enter alliances with the world's most effective external suppliers to leverage its fiscal and intellectual resources in other areas.[17]

External Leveraging

Through core competency with outsourcing strategies, managers can serve customers substantially better, simultaneously decreasing risk and size while increasing flexibility. Many entrepreneurial ventures like Apple Computer, Sony, Silicon Graphics, Nike, or Novellus have started in highly-concentrated and heavily-outsourced fashion, leveraging their fiscal capital by factors of three or more—and their intellectual capital by 10s to 100s—as compared with integrated companies. If a company is not best-in-world at an activity (including all external and internal transaction costs involved) it gives up competitive edge by performing that activity in-house. Today, most venture capitalists realize they can obtain bank returns only on fixed assets (unless these embody the company's core competencies). They seek to invest in and

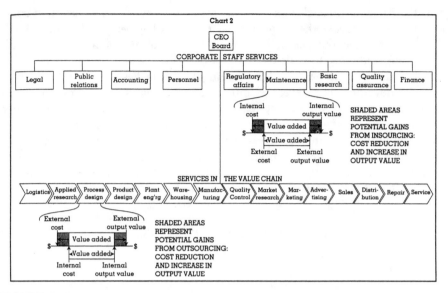

FIGURE 15.2

leverage the unique intellectual resources of a company, and not to undertake the investments and risks of activities others could perform better. Larger companies—from Continental Bank and WalMart to MCI, Honda, and Boeing—operate in this fashion too.

- When interviewed, MCI had only 1000 fulltime technical people internally, but had 20,000 professionals working for it full time on vendor promises. MCI did not have to invest in facilities, overhead, and benefits costs for these people on a permanent basis, and many outside professionals were said to be higher quality than those MCI could hire internally. These specialized suppliers could afford to invest in elaborate facilities to attract top talent to work with their firms on the frontiers of their particular specialties. Besides outsourcing software, construction, and system maintenance, MCI also actively sought out and exploited the innovations of thousands of small firms to attach to its core software and electronic hardware, thus leveraging its own innovative capabilities by hundreds of times.

Once strategists define each activity in their value chain or staff services as an intellectually-based service, managers often see many new opportunities to refocus the company's strategic commitments, restructure internal operations, or create external coalitions to leverage their fiscal and intellectual resources.[18] Generally, there are many external providers who, by specializing, can provide greater depth in a specific service and produce it with greater quality or lower cost than the company's internal department possibly could. No company can hope to be better than all outside specialists in all elements of its value chain. And new technologies and management systems have dramatically shifted the balance between what it pays to outsource and what the company can effectively produce internally. Strategic outsourcing of services has become a major means for leveraging intellect.

In today's hypercompetitive[19] climate, such core competency with outsourcing strategies let companies be simultaneously the lowest cost, broadest line, most flexible, and most highly differentiated producer in their markets. No other strategy supports: (a) efficiency (through focus), (b) innovative flexibility (multiple sourcing), and (c) stability (through market diversity) to the same extent. Many enterprises in financial services (State Street Bank or Continental Bank), retailing (L. L. Bean or Toys "R" Us), or communications, entertainment, and lodging services (Paramount, Turner, or Marriott) operate in this fashion. So do industrial giants like the oil majors, Boeing, Sony, or 3M. Integrated oil companies often outsource many intellectually-based service elements in their value chains to great advantage. (See Figure 15.3.) For example:

- Boeing outsources many parts of its commercial airliners to those who have greater skills in specialized areas. It produces internally mainly those portions of the craft that contain the critical flight control and power plant interfaces. It concentrates its own intellectual capabilities on understanding aircraft technologies and its customers' needs. Boeing focuses its operations on the design, logistics, and flexible assembly processes necessary to coordinate and control the quality and performance of the aircraft.
- 3M's extensive growth has rested on its R&D skills in four related historic technologies: abrasives, adhesives, coating-bondings, and nonwoven technologies. In each it has developed knowledge bases and skill depths exceeding those of its major competitors. When combined with two other core intellectual competencies—its remarkable entrepreneurial-innovation system and its strong, broad-based marketing distribution system—these historic technologies have allowed 3M to create and support over 50,000 products for a variety of markets, to maintain a flexible innovative culture, and to sustain continuous growth for six to seven decades.

ORGANIZING AROUND INTELLECT

The exploitation of intellectually-based strategies calls for new organization concepts. In the past, in order to enhance efficiencies, most companies formed their organizations around product clusters, process investments, geographical needs, or specialized management functions.[20] These clearly optimized the capacity of power holders to direct and control the organization. However, rapidly changing customer demands and increasingly independent professionals require entirely new structures. The extended capabilities of new technologies now enable design and management of much more highly disaggregated organizations, capable of responding to the needs of both customers and professionals. The term network organizations has been widely used to embrace a variety of these new forms, varying from flat, to horizontal matrix, to alliance, to cross-disciplinary team, to holding-company structures that merely finance a number

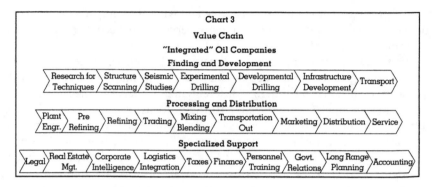

FIGURE 15.3 Value Chain

of unrelated divisions self-coordinating on an ad-hoc basis.[21] This categorization reveals little about how the various forms differ, when to use them, or how to manage them for maximum effect.

The main function of organization in today's hypercompetitive environment is to develop and deploy—i.e. attract, harness, leverage, and disseminate—intellect effectively. Each of the truly new organization forms does this in its own way, and should be used only for those particular purposes it handles best. Not only is no one form a panacea, many different forms can be used to advantage within the same company. Because they are useful for certain purposes, hierarchies will doubtless continue in many situations. But we expect much greater use of four other basic organizational forms that leverage professional intellect uniquely well. These are the infinitely flat, inverted, spider's web, and starburst forms. Table 15.1 summarizes the primary differences among these organization forms and their utility in leveraging intellect. The key variables in choosing among the new forms are:

(1) *Locus of intellect:* Where the deep knowledge of a firm's particular core competencies primarily lies.
(2) *Locus of customization:* Where intellect is converted to novel solutions.
(3) *Direction of intellectual flow:* The primary direction(s) in which value-added knowledge flows.
(4) *Method of Leverage:* How the organization leverages intellect.

All the forms tend to push responsibility outward to the point at which the company contacts the customer. All tend to flatten the organization and to remove layers of hierarchy. All seek faster, more responsive action to deal with the customization and personalization that an affluent and complex marketplace demands. All require breaking away from traditional thinking about lines of command, one-person-one-boss structures, the center as a directing force, and management of physical assets as keys to success. But each differs substantially in its purposes and management. And each requires very different nurturing, balancing, and support systems to achieve its performance goals.

TABLE 15.1 Outline of Four Forms of Organizing

	Infinitely Flat	Inverted	Spider's Web	Starburst
Definition of node	Individual	Individual	Individual	Business Units
Locus of intellect	Center	Nodes	Nodes	Center and Nodes
Locus of customization	Nodes	Nodes	Project	Center and Nodes
Direction of flow	Center to Nodes	Nodes to Center	Node to Node	Center to Nodes
Method of leverage	Multiplicative	Distributive	Exponential	Additive
Examples	Brokerage firms, aircraft operations	Hospitals, construction engineering	Internet, SABRE	Major movie studios, mutual fund groups

Infinitely Flat Organizations

In infinitely flat organizations—so called because there is no inherent limit to their span—the primary locus of intellect is at the center, e.g. the operations knowledge of a fast-food franchising organization or the data analysis capability at the center of a brokerage firm. The nodes of customer contact are the locus of customization. Intellect flows primarily one way, from the center to the nodes. The leverage is arithmetic: The amount of leverage equals the value of the knowledge times the number of nodes using it. Single centers in such organizations presently can coordinate anywhere from 20 to 18,000 individual nodes. (See Figure 15.4.) Common examples include highly dispersed fast-food, brokerage, shipping, mail order, or airline flight operations.

Several other characteristics are also important. The nodes themselves rarely communicate with each other, operating quite independently. The center rarely needs to give direct orders to the line organization. Instead, it is an information source, a communications coordinator, and a reference desk for unusual inquiries. Lower organizational levels generally connect into the center to obtain information to improve their performance, rather than to get instructions or specific guidance. Most operating rules are programmed into the system and changed automatically by software. Many operations may even be monitored electronically.

- For example, each of Merrill Lynch's more than 500 domestic brokerage offices connects directly into the parent's central information office to satisfy the bulk of its information and analytic needs. Although regional marketing structures exist, business is conducted as if each of Merrill Lynch's more than 18,000 branch-office contact people reported directly to headquarters, with their only personal oversight being at the local level. Technology permits the overall company to capture data with the full power and scale economies available only to a major enterprise. Yet local brokers manage their own small units and accounts as independently as if they alone provided the total service on a local basis.

Infinitely flat organizations operate best when the activity at the node can be broken down and measured to the level of its minimum repeatable transaction elements (as for example, the cooking and operating details in fast-food chains management or the basic components of financial transactions in brokerage operations). Control can be exercised at the most detailed level, yet, if desired, systems can eliminate most of the routine in jobs, free up employees for

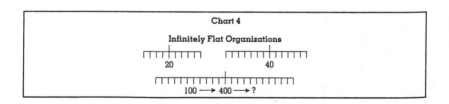

FIGURE 15.4 Infinitely Flat Organizations

more personalized or skilled work, and allow tasks to be very decentralized, individually challenging, and rewarding.[22] Under proper circumstances, the electronic systems of such organizations capture the experience curve of the entire enterprise, allowing less trained people quickly to achieve performance levels ordinarily associated with much more experienced personnel. Well designed systems simultaneously offer both highest responsiveness and maximum efficiency. Such has been their effect in firms like Fidelity Securities, Federal Express, WalMart, or Domino's Pizza.

Infinitely flat organizations present certain inherent management problems. Without hierarchy, lower level personnel wonder how to advance in a career path.[23] Traditional job evaluation ("Hay Point") systems break down, and new compensation systems based upon individual performance become imperative.

Reward systems need to include a great variety of titles, intangible performance measurements and rewards, and constant training and updating by advisory teams from the central office.[24] There is a tendency for systems to rigidify with time if companies continue use of the same measurement and control systems. Consequently, external scanning systems, customer sampling, or personal observation systems must supplement the structured hard information linkages of these very flat organizations. Note that this form of organizing is neither horizontal nor a network in the true sense. It is hierarchical, but with only one level of hierarchy.

The Inverted Organization

In the inverted form, the major locus of both corporate intellect and customization is at the nodes contacting customers, not at the center. Hospitals or medical clinics, therapeutic caregiving units, or consulting-engineering firms provide typical examples. The nodes tend to be highly professional and self sufficient. Accordingly, there is no need for direct linkage between the nodes. When critical know-how diffuses, it usually does so informally from node to node or formally from node to center—the opposite of the infinitely flat organization. The leverage of this form is distributive, i.e. the organization efficiently distributes logistics, analysis, or administrative support to the nodes. But it does not give orders to the nodes.

In inverted organizations, the line hierarchy becomes a support structure, not intervening except in extreme emergencies—as might the CEO of a hospital or the chief pilot of an airline in crisis situations. (See Figure 15.5.) The function of line managers becomes bottleneck breaking, culture development, consulting upon request, expediting resource movements, and providing service economies of scale. Hierarchy may exist within some groups because members of this support structure must ensure consistency in the application of specialized knowledge (like government regulations or accounting rules) that the organization needs. Generally, however, what was line management now performs essentially staff activities.

TABLE 15.2 How Different Organizing Forms Develop Intellect

Type of Intellect	Infinitely Flat	Inverted	Starburst	Spider's Web
Cognitive (Know-what)	Deep knowledge and information at center	Primary intellect at nodes, support services from center	Depth at center (technical) and (markets) at the nodes	Dispersed, brought together for projects
Advanced Skill (Know-how)	Programmed into systems	Professionalized skills informally transferred node to node	Transferred from center to node, then node to node via the core	Latent until a project assembles a skill collection
Systems Knowledge (Know-why)	Systems experts at the center. Customer knowledge at the nodes	Systems and customer expertise at the nodes	Split: between central technical competency at the core, systematic market knowledge at nodes	Discovered in interaction or created via search enabled by the network
Motivated Creativity (Care-why)	Frees employees from routine for more skilled work	Great professional autonomy	Entrepreneurial incentives	Personal interest, leveraged through active interdependence stimulation

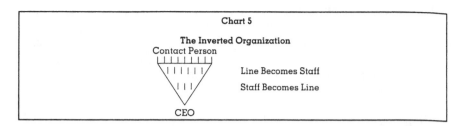

FIGURE 15.5 The Inverted Organization

- A well known example of an inverted organization was SAS after Jan Carlzon became CEO. He utilized the concept of inverting to empower SAS's contact people and to bypass heavily entrenched bureaucracies. Another example is NovaCare, the largest provider of rehabilitation care in the U.S. With its central resource—well trained physical, occupational, and speech therapists—in short supply, NovaCare, through the NovaNet, provides the business infrastructure for over 5,000 therapists, arranging and managing contracts with over 2,000 nursing homes and care giving facilities in 40 states, handling accounting and credit activities, providing training updates, and stabilizing and enhancing therapists' earnings. However, the key to performance is the therapists' knowledge and their capacity to deliver this individually to patients.

The inverted organization works well (1) when servicing the customer at the point of contact is the most important activity in the enterprise, and (2) when the person at the point of contact has more information about the individual customer's problem and its potential solutions than anyone else. Experience suggests that because they present unique problems, inverted organizations should be used sparingly, and not as gimmicks to improve empowerment. While seeming to diminish line authority, intermediate line members' roles often increase in importance as they are freed from their traditional information passing routines and perform more influential activities—such as strategic analysis, resource building, or public policy participation.

The inverted organization poses certain unique challenges. The apparent loss of formal authority can be very traumatic for former line managers.[25] Given acknowledged formal power, contact people may tend to act ever more like specialists with strictly professional outlooks, and to resist any set of organization rules or business norms.[26] Given their predilections, contact people often don't stay current with details about the firm's own complex internal systems. And their empowerment without adequate controls can be extremely dangerous. A classic example is the rapid decline of People Express, which enjoyed highly empowered and motivated point people, but lacked the systems or computer infrastructures to let them self-coordinate as the organization grew.

A frequent cause of failure in both the inverted and the infinitely flat modes is inadequate segmentation and dissemination of information into detailed elements that monitor and support individuals' actions at the nodes.[27] Many such organizations fail because they attempt to make a transition from their more traditional hierarchies to the new forms without thoroughly overhauling their measurement and support systems. In our recent study of over 100 such situations in major service organizations, less than 20 percent had changed their performance measurement systems significantly; and only about five percent had yet changed their reward systems.[28] The complications were predictable. People continued to perform against traditional norms, and at a bureaucratic pace.

The Starburst

Another highly leverageable form, the starburst, serves well when there is very specialized and valuable intellect at both the nodes and the center. Starbursts are common in creative organizations that constantly peel off more permanent, but separate, units from their core competencies. (See Figure 15.6.) These spinoffs remain partially or wholly owned by the parent, usually can raise external resources independently, and are controlled primarily by market mechanisms. Examples of different forms and ownership relationships include: movie studios, mutual fund groups or venture capitalists, among service firms, and Thermoelectron, TCG, or Nypro, among industrials.

In operation, the center retains deep knowledge of some common knowledge base (e.g. specialized plastic molding technology for Nypro, managing no-load funds for Vanguard, or risk-taking and resource-assembly skills for movie studios). Unlike holding companies, starbursts are built around some central core of intellectual competency. They are not merely banks that collect and disseminate funds. The nodes—essentially separate permanent business units, not individuals or temporary clusters—have continuing relationships with given marketplaces and are the locus of important, specialized market or production knowledge. The nodes may in time spin out further enterprises from their core. The flow of intellect is typically from the center toward the outer nodes. The organization rarely transfers knowledge from one node laterally to another, but feeds back to the core specialized information that other nodes may find useful (without direct competition among their marketplaces). The nodes both multiply the number of outlets using the firm's core competency and leverage it (a) through their access to specialized market expertise, and (b) through the independent relationships and external financing they can generate as separated entities.

Starburst organizations work well when the core embodies an expensive or complex set of competencies and houses a few knowledgeable risk-takers who realize they cannot micro-manage the diverse entities at the nodes. They work well in very ambiguous environments where it is difficult to estimate outcomes without undertaking a specific market test. Usually they occur in environments where entrepreneurship—not merely flexible response—is critical. To be effective, the nodes require the economies of scale and new opportunity spinoffs that only a large, specialized, knowledge base can provide. The center usually maintains and renews its capacities to develop these opportunities by charging the market units a fee or taking a share of their equity. In addition to maintaining the core competency, the corporate center generally manages the culture, sets broad priorities, selects key people, and raises resources more efficiently than

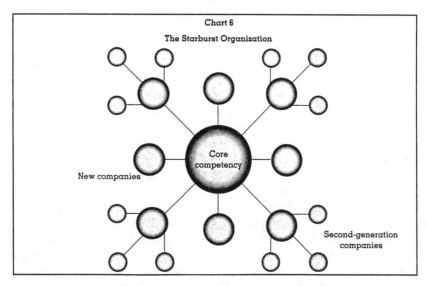

FIGURE 15.6 The Starburst Organization

could the nodes. Unlike conglomerates, starbursts maintain some cohesive, constantly renewed, and critical intellectual competencies at their center.

The classic problem of this organizational form is that managements often lose faith in their freestanding spinoffs. After some time, they try to consolidate-functions in the name of efficiency or economies of scale—as some movie studios, HP, TI, and 3M did to their regret—and recover only by reversing such policies. Starbursts also encounter problems if their divisions move into heavy investment industries, or into capital-intensive mass production activities where one unit's needs can overwhelm the capacity of the core—as HP's computer division overwhelmed its test equipment groups. In most starburst environments, the nodes are so different that even sophisticated computer systems cannot provide or coordinate all the information needed to run these firms from the center. Rather than try, managers must either live with quasi-market control or spin-off the subsidiary entirely. Starbursts tend to work extremely well for growth by innovating smaller scale, discrete product or service lines positioned in diverse marketplaces.

The Spider's Web

The spider's web form is a true network. The term spider's web avoids confusion undertaking a specific with other more network-like forms, particularly those that are more akin to holding companies or matrix organizations. In the spider's web there is often no intervening hierarchy or order-giving center among the nodes. In fact, it may be hard to define where the center is. The locus of intellect is highly dispersed, residing largely at the contact nodes (as in the inverted organization). However, the point of customization is a project or problem that requires the nodes to interact intimately or to seek others who happen to have the knowledge or special capabilities that a particular problem requires.

The purest example of a spider's web is the Internet, which is managed by no one. Common operating examples include most open markets, securities exchanges, library consortia, diagnostic teams, research, or political action groups.

The organization's intellect is essentially latent and under-utilized until a project forces it to materialize through connections people make with one another. Information linkages are quite complex; intellect flows from many nodes to many others. Nodes typically collaborate only temporarily in delivering a specific service or solution in project form to a particular customer. The intellectual leverage is exponential. Even with a modest number of collaborating nodes (eight to 10), the number of interconnections and the leverage of knowledge capabilities multiplies by hundreds of times. (See Figure 15.7.)

Individual nodes may operate quite independently, when it is not essential to tap the knowledge of other sources to solve a problem efficiently. On a given project, there may or may not be a single authority center. Often decisions will merely occur through informal processes if the parties agree. Occasionally, however, the various nodes may need to operate in such a highly coordinated fashion that they delegate temporary authority to a project leader—as when widely dispersed researchers present a contract proposal or an investment banking consortium services a multinational client.

The spider's web form has existed for centuries (among universities and scientists, or within trading groups), but was overlooked in the mass production era, which sought the greater stability, predictability, and control that military or clerical hierarchies seemed to offer. In today's highly competitive environments it offers unique advantages because it can simultaneously support high specialization, multiple geographic locations, and a disciplined focus on a single problem or customer set.[29] It is particularly useful in situations where problem sites are very dispersed and radically different specialties need to be tapped. Often no one person in a given organization knows exactly what the problem's dimensions are, where issues may be located, or who may have potential solutions. The spider's web form releases the imaginations of many different searchers in diverse locations, multiplies the numbers of possible opportunity encounters, and encourages the formation of entirely new solutions from a variety of disciplines.[30]

While it is usually effective for problem finding and analysis, a spider's web presents important challenges when used for decision making. Dawdling is common, as nodes refine their specialist solutions instead of solving the complete problem together. Assigning credit for intellectual contributions is difficult, and cross-competition among nodes can inhibit the sharing necessary in such networks. Extreme overload can emerge as networks become jammed with trivia. Significant changes at both the network and local levels are usually essential to make a spider's web effective in professional situations. The first change is to create a culture for communication and willing sharing. How groups communicate and what they are willing to communicate are as important as the knowledge

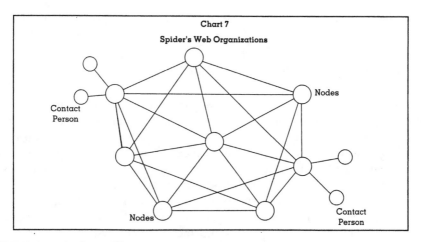

FIGURE 15.7 Spider's Web Organizations

they have. Overcoming the natural reluctance of professionals to share their most precious asset, knowledge, usually presents some common, and difficult, challenges. One enterprise exemplifies many patterns:

- Arthur Andersen Worldwide (AAW) found that effective use of its ANET required major practice shifts. Despite the large sums it initially spent on hardware, travel, and professional training to encourage utilization of the network, results were disappointing. Major changes in incentives and culture were required. To stimulate wider use of the system, senior partners deliberately posed questions into employees' e-mail files each morning "to be answered by 10 o'clock" and followed up on queries in their own units. Most importantly, participation on ANET began to be considered in all compensation and promotion reviews. Until these and other supporting structural changes achieved cultural modifications, ANET—despite its technological elegance—was less than successful.

Because a spider's web is so dependent on individual goals and behavior, there is no best way to manage one except to stimulate a sense of interdependency and identity with the problem at hand. Shared interest of participants, shared value systems, and mutual personal gains for members are, of course, the essential starting points for any network relationship. However, research suggests that effective network managers generally: (1) force team overlaps in order to increase learning and shared information, (2) purposely keep hierarchical relations ill-defined, (3) constantly update and reinforce project goals, (4) avoid over-elaborate rules for allocating profits to individual nodes, (5) develop continuous mechanisms for updating information about the external environment (e.g. tax code changes, customer needs, or scientific results), (6) involve both clients and peers in performance evaluations, and (7) provide node members with personal and team rewards for participation.[31] These active management interactions are usually needed to avoid the most common failures and frustrations. The other key leverage factor, technology, requires special attention.

INTEGRATING DIVERSE FORMS

Special technology structures are required to support each organizational form. If they are properly designed, they will also enable integration of forms across the entire company. We expect most enterprises to require a mixture, not just a single form, of these basic building blocks, combined with more traditional hierarchical structures. Integrating and leveraging diverse forms within the same firm is very complex.[32] The critical non-organizational element in the process is software. The key is to develop a software framework that can capture, mix, match, and manipulate the smallest replicable units of tasks, customized data, and transactions. When information and measurement systems are developed around these microunits, a properly designed technology structure can enable both maximum flexibility and lowest cost for the firm and its customers. In today's hypercompetitive environment these are essentials for success.

The Smallest Replicable Level

In earlier years, the smallest manageable unit of measurement for organizations and data seemed to be an individual store, office, or franchise location. Later, as volume increased, it often became possible for a parent corporation to manage and measure critical performance variables at individual departmental, sales counter, activity, or stock-keeping-unit (SKU) levels. Then the successful formula approaches of McDonald's, Pizza Hut, H & R Block, and insurance companies pushed the repeatability unit to even smaller micro management levels, such as cooking processes, detailed work schedules, maintenance cycles, accounting transactions, and document phrases. Proper management around these units permits franchisees, agents, and headquarters to continuously guarantee quality and desired service levels and to make corrections within minutes when something goes wrong.

In banking, publishing, communications, structural design, entertainment, or medical research, it has become possible to disaggregate the critical units of service production into digitized sequences, electronic packets, data blocks, or bytes of information that can be endlessly combined or manipulated for new effects and to satisfy individual customer and operating needs. These micro units permit the highest possible degrees of segmentation, strategic fine-tuning, value-added, and customer satisfaction at the lowest cost.[33] The larger the organization, the more refined are these replicability units, and the greater their leverage for creating value-added.

Systems that capture and leverage such data from the outset can build up an information base that provides an insurmountable edge. By constantly updating and analyzing data patterns from these detailed sources, successful IT systems automatically capture the highest level of experience available within the enterprise.[34] Effective dissemination of data throughout the firm allows inexperienced people to vault over normal learning curve delays and enables customer contact people to provide greater quality, customization, personalization, and value-added. Wages can be higher and managers and workers can concentrate on the more conceptual, personalized, and human tasks that provide greater satisfaction for both employers and customers. Properly collecting and distributing such information also provides the basis for integrated lateral coordination among highly diverse organization forms. For example:

- American Airlines' well-known SABRE and its associated operating systems are interlinked to provide consistent data for the airline's very different reservation service (spider's web), flight operations (infinitely flat), financial controls (conservative bureaucratic), ground operations and maintenance (decentralized bureaucratic), personnel training (specialized functional), and other operating modes. The organization structure, operating style, and culture within each unit can remain unique and appropriate to its tasks. Yet the software system ensures coordination among the units, minimizes costs, and ensures that desired service levels and consistency are delivered to customers.
- Similarly, NovaCare (described above) keeps track of the activities of its 5,000 therapists in 15 minute units of detail. These units provide the basis for scheduling, compensation, billing, and follow-up on all therapies. They enable NovaCare to ensure that all its customers (patients, nursing homes, hospitals, hospital directors, doctors, nursing directors, payers, and regulating bodies) are properly served, charged, or compensated. The system serves a variety of centralized functional (accounting), geographical hierarchical (hospital), inverted (therapy), and spider's web (professional knowledge exchange) structures. Although it collects information in immense detail, the system has unburdened caregivers (who hated detailed paperwork), and freed up regional coordinators (who earlier spent enormous amounts of time in collecting, analyzing, and relaying activity reports) for more personalized and higher value-added activities. The same detailed information about individual operations and transactions also helped to coordinate the purchasing, logistics, financial, and regulatory compliance groups that support these operations.

Far from depersonalizing operations, software provides a framework that allows professionals to behave independently, responsibly, and consistently even though they do not understand major portions of the system outside their realm. It leverages their individual capacities to perform to the point where specialists—like scientific researchers, lawyers, accountants, designers, doctors, market researchers, reporters, authors, or logistics experts—are totally noncompetitive without such systems. Such software systems are also the glue that welds together the highly dispersed service delivery nodes that characterize large-scale intellectual organizations. Leading companies invest heavily in their software to attract, retain, and leverage their very best talent. Software is a key element in managing intellect for competitiveness. Properly developed, it becomes the major proprietary repository of the firm's intellect.

MEASURING OUTPUTS

Recognizing that the fundamental building blocks of such systems are objects—integrated packets of data with built-in instructions for manipulation, many information technology producers and users are moving toward object-oriented systems as the preferred solution.[35] Whether these (or their packet surrogates in more conventional systems) are used to implement the minimum replicable units concepts suggested above, many important quantitative aspects of intellectual and service output can now be measured in real-time, and new sensing devices will capture more in the future.[36] Such sensing, of course, is the basis for the direct output measures now used in most communications, airlines, retailing, wholesaling, banking, health care, fast foods, and electric power systems. Monitored in this way are many aspects of quality—e.g., signal quality, signal strength, power variations, fluid flows, service cycle times, error rates, delays, downtimes, credit-worthiness, variability costs, inventory levels, environmental and operating conditions, and vital systems performance in health care. New technologies, particularly software systems, for capturing such detailed data about customers, operations, and the environment are becoming the most valuable competitive tools of intellectual management.

However, effective management systems typically must go well beyond just software. They must encompass four critical dimensions of (a) peer review of professional performance, (b) customer appraisal of outputs received, (c) business evaluation of efficiency and effectiveness, and (d) measurement of the intellectual assets created. While such measurements would appear critical to professional success, surprisingly few firms perform all four. Merck's and AT&T's approaches to measuring intellectual outputs have been widely publicized, but incompletely explained. Although we cannot provide a detailed treatment here, a few examples will suggest how certain leading enterprises attack individual aspects of this problem.

- After each project, a major investment banking concern asks each team member, its customer group, and a team head to rank all important participants on the project in terms of their demonstrated professional knowledge, specific project contributions, and team support. Customers rate their overall satisfaction with the project and with the firm as a service supplier. Annual surveys, which rank the company against the performance of all competing firms on 28 critical dimensions, supplement this. The firm collects costs and profits for each project and allocates the latter among participating groups on a simple formula basis. Annually, for each division, it calculates the net differential between the market value of each division (if sold) and its fixed asset base. This net intellectual value of the unit is tracked over time as a macro measure of how well management is growing its intellectual assets.

- McKesson Drugs, at the strategic level, emphasizes five major themes for competitiveness: customer-supplier satisfaction, people development, market positioning, relative net delivered cost, and innovation. For each factor it uses internal and external metrics to track its position relative to competitors. It has 42 so-called customer satisfactors that it measures on a routine basis with, among other things, a seven-page questionnaire that goes to more than 1000 customers each year, and with quarterly updates on a smaller set of factors it considers most important. Through its ECONOMOST system, which links its warehouses directly to PCs on druggists' desktops, it can track all costs and such measurable quality features as fulfillment accuracy, delivery times, or stockouts at both customer and warehouse levels. The same system tracks detailed costs and profits by SKU, and uses market feedback data to advise customers on how they can improve their own productivity. The profits from such services and measures of McKesson's probable costs and profits without its various ECONOMOST software packages give the company a measure of this system's enormous value as intellectual property.

We observed similar systems in our studies of over 100 of the most effective U.S. service companies. Not only must a company design its recruiting, organizing, outsourcing and software support systems to focus and leverage its intellectual capabilities, it must also develop its measurement and reward infrastructures to reinforce its strategic intentions in four critical dimensions. These are professional skill development, customer value creation, internal productivity, and intellectual asset appraisal.

SUMMARY

While managing professional intellect is clearly the key to value creation and profitability for most companies, few have arrived at systematic structures for developing, focusing, leveraging, and measuring their intellectual capabilities. Based on careful research, we have tried to provide some practical guidelines suggesting how successful enterprises have designed their strategies, organizations, training, and measurement systems to maximize the value of their most critical asset, intellect. Technology has created new opportunity and rules for organization design. Customers quickly discover and reward those organizations that understand these new rules.

ENDNOTES

1. "The National Income and Product Accounts of the United States," Series in *Survey of Current Business*. 1995. (Tables 6.3B and 6.4C).
2. This structure was first published in an interview article, J.B. Quinn with A. Kantrow, *McKinsey Review,* Spring edition, 1995.
3. For a thorough discussion of the learning curve literature, see J.M. Dutton, J.E. Butler, "The History of Progress Functions as a Managerial Technology," *Business History Review,* Vol. 58 No. 2 (1984) pp. 204–233.
4. J.B. Quinn, *The Intelligent Enterprise* (New York, NY: The Free Press, 1992) develops the arguments for this in detail.

5. An excellent discussion of group and organization-level learning as opposed to individual learning is contained in L. Argote, "Group and Organizational Learning Curves: Individual, System and Environmental Components," *British Journal of Social Psychology,* Vol. 32 (1993) pp. 31–51.

6. E.M. Rogers, R. Agarwala-Rogers, *Communication in Organizations* (New York, NY: Free Press, 1976).

7. J.B. Quinn. *Intelligent Enterprise* (New York, NY: Free Press, 1992).

8. Our discussion draws heavily from the literature on managing professionals. See for example D.H. Maister, *Managing the Professional Service Firm* (New York, NY: Maxwell Macmillan International, 1993) or J.A. Raelin, *The Clash of Cultures: Managers Managing Professionals* (Boston, MA: Harvard Business School Press, 1991). The best book of readings covering a broad range of issues in managing professionals is R. Katz (ed.), *Managing Professionals in Innovative Organizations: A Collection of Readings* (Cambridge, MA: Ballinger, 1988).

9. Made in connection with National Academy of Engineering, *Technology in Services: Policies for Growth, Trade and Employment* (Washington, D.C.: National Academy Press, 1988); and Computer Science and Telecommunications Board, National Research Council, *Information Technology in the Service Society,* (Washington, DC: National Academy Press, 1994).

10. H. Mintzberg, "The Professional Bureaucracy," in *Mintzberg on Management: Inside Our Strange World of Organizations* (New York, NY: The Free Press, 1984).

11. D. Schon, *The Reflective Practitioner: How Professionals Think in Action* (New York, NY: Basic Books, 1983).

12. See, for example, J.M. Kouzes and B.Z. Posner, *The Leadership Challenge* (San Francisco, CA: Jossey-Bass, 1995).

13. D. Schon, *op. cit.,* 1983.

14. G. Loveman, "An Assessment of the Productivity Impact of Information Technologies," *Management in the 1990s Program,* 88–054, (Cambridge, MA: MIT, July 1988): W. Baumol, S. Blackman, E. Wolff, *Productivity and American Leadership: the Long View* (Cambridge, MA: MIT Press, 1989).

15. S. Roach, "Services Under Siege: The Restructuring Imperative?," *Harvard Business Review,* Sept.-Oct. 1991.

16. J. Quinn, T. Doorley, P. Paquette, "Technology in Services: Rethinking Strategic Focus," *Sloan Management Review,* Winter 1990, was the first published expression of this theme.

17. J. Quinn, R. Hilmer, "Strategic Outsourcing, *Sloan Management Review,* Summer 1994, develops this argument in depth.

18. J. Quinn, T. Doorley, P. Paquette, "Beyond Products; Services Based Strategies," Harvard Business Review, developed this concept in depth, as did J. Quinn, *Intelligent Enterprise, op. cit.,* 1992.

19. R. D.'Aveni, *Hypercompetition,* (New York, NY: Free Press, 1994).

20. One of the best discussions of organizational design is by J.R. Galbraith, *Designing Complex Organizations* (Reading, MA: AddisonWesley, 1973). A more recent analysis, J.R. Galbraith, *Designing Organizations: An Executive Briefing on Strategy, Structure, and Process* (San Francisco, CA: JosseyBass, 1995) extends this earlier work by focusing on new organizational forms.

21. For a cogent discussion of the different ways the term network is used, see the introduction to N. Nohria, R.G. Eccles, *Networks and Organizations* (Boston, MA: Harvard Business School Press, 1992).

22. For an extended discussion of the relationship between work and information technology, see Zuboff, S. *In the Age of the Smart Machine: The Future of Work and Power* (New York, NY: Basic Books, 1988).

23. In fact, this is one of the classic defenses of bureaucracy. See for example C. Perrow, *Complex Organizations: A Critical Essay* (Glenview, IL: Scott Foresman, 1979).

24. For a thorough discussion of human resource management issues in innovative firms, see M. Badawy, "What We've Learned About Managing Human Resources," *Research Technology Management*, September-October 1988, pp. 19–35.

25. For example, see W.G. Bennis, *Why Leaders Can't Lead: The Unconscious Conspiracy Continues* (San Francisco, CA: Jossey-Bass Publishers, 1989).

26. For a managerial discussion of coping with such problems, see H. Donovan, "Managing Your Intellectuals," *Fortune*, October 23, 1989 pp. 177–180.

27. Quinn, *Intelligent Enterprise, op. cit.*

28. National Research Council, *Information Technology in the Services Society, op. cit*, 1994.

29. H. Mintzberg, A. McHugh, "Strategy Formulation in Adhocracy," *Administrative Science Quarterly*, June 1985.

30. An interesting discussion of cross-functional synergy is contained in M. Jelinek, C.B. Schoonhoven, *The Innovation Marathon: Lessons from High Technology Firms* (Oxford, U.K.: Basil Blackwell, 1990).

31. E. Giesler, A. Rubenstein, "How Do Banks Evaluate their Information Technology," *Bank Administration*, November, 1988; S. Harris and J. Katz, "Organization Performance and Information Technology Investment in the Insurance Industry," Organization Science, 2:263–296, 1991.

32. P.R. Lawrence, J.W. Lorsch. *Organization and Environment; Managing Differentiation and Integration* (Homewood, IL: Richard D. Irwin, 1969).

33. For example, see G. Gilder, *Microcosm: The Quantum Revolution in Economics and Technology* (New York, NY: Simon and Schuster, 1989).

34. For an extended discussion of how IT systems capture experience, see T.J. Allen, M.S. Scott Morton, *Information Technology and the Corporation of the 1990s: Research Studies* (New York, NY: Oxford University Press, 1994).

35. A good, managerially-oriented overview appears in D.A. Taylor, *Object-Oriented Technology, A Manager's Guide* (Reading, MA: Addison Wesley, 1990).

36. For a fairly technical discussion of sensors and real-time data processing, see P. LaPlante, *Real-time Systems Design and Analysis: An Engineer's Handbook* (New York, NY: Institute of Electrical and Electronics Engineers, 1993).

ABOUT THE AUTHORS

James Brian Quinn is emeritus professor of management at the Amos Tuck School, Dartmouth College and Leo Block Visiting Professor at the University of Denver. He has published extensively on corporate and national policy issues involving strategic planning, research and development management, the management of entrepreneurial organizations, and the impact of technology in services. His book, *Intelligent Enterprise,* was named Book of the Year in Business and Scholarship by the American Publishers Association and Book of the Year for Outstanding Contribution to Advancing Management Knowledge by the American Academy of Management.

Philip Anderson is an associate professor of business administration at the Amos Tuck School, Dartmouth College. His scholarly interests include organizational evolution, strategic management of technology, and the dynamics of the venture capital industry. His research has been published in the *Academy of Management Journal, Administrative Science Quarterly,* and other journals.

Sydney Finkelstein is an associate professor of business administration at the Amos Tuck School, Dartmouth College. He has conducted extensive research on strategic leadership, in particular on executive compensation and corporate governance. He has published in the *Academy of Management Journal, Administrative Science Quarterly, Harvard Business Review,* and *Strategic Management Journal.* He is coauthor with Donald C. Hambrick of *Strategic Leadership: Top Executives and Their Effects on Organizations.*

Index